THE HUNDRED YEARS WAR

THE
HUNDRED YEARS WAR
A PEOPLE'S HISTORY

DAVID GREEN

YALE UNIVERSITY PRESS
NEW HAVEN AND LONDON

For information about this and other Yale University Press publications, please contact:
U.S. Office: sales.press@yale.edu   www.yalebooks.com
Europe Office:sales@yaleup.co.uk   www.yalebooks.co.uk

Set in Adobe Caslon Pro by IDSUK (DataConnection) Ltd
Printed in Great Britain by TJ International Ltd, Padstow, Cornwall

Library of Congress Cataloging-in-Publication Data

Green, David, 1969-
   The Hundred Years War : a people's history / David Green.
      pages cm
   ISBN 978-0-300-13451-3 (cl : alk. paper)
   1. Hundred Years' War, 1339-1453. 2. France—History, Military—1328–1589.
   3. Great Britain—History, Military—1066–1485. 4. France—Foreign relations—Great
   Britain. 5. Great Britain—Foreign relations—France. I. Title. II. Title: 100 Years War.
   DC96.G74 2014
   944'.025—dc23
                                                                        2014014233

A catalogue record for this book is available from the British Library.

10 9 8 7 6 5 4 3 2 1

Contents

Chronology

1378	Great Schism begins (papacy)
1380	accession of Charles VI (r. to 1422); Olivier IV de Clisson appointed constable of France (dismissed 1392)
1381	Peasants' Revolt (England)
1383	Henry Despenser, bishop of Norwich, launches 'crusade' to Flanders
1385	battle of Aljubarrota (14 August)
1386	Merciless Parliament (February–June)
1390	accession of Robert III of Scotland (r. to 1424)
1392	first signs of Charles VI's madness
1396	28-year-truce agreed (9 March); Richard II marries Isabella of France; battle of Nicopolis (25 September)
1399	accession of Henry IV (Lancastrian dynasty) (r. to 1413)
1404	death of Philippe the Bold, duke of Burgundy (27 April)
1405	French troops sent to support Owain Glyn Dŵr's revolt in Wales
1407	assassination of Louis, duke of Orléans (23 November)
1409	Council of Pisa
1411	Orléanists/Armagnac and Burgundian factions both seek aid from Henry IV
1413	accession of Henry V (r. to 1422); *cabochienne* uprisings in Paris (April–May)
1414–18	Council of Constance
1415	siege of Harfleur; battle of Agincourt (25 October)
1416	Anglo-Imperial alliance secures the neutrality of Emperor Sigismund in the Anglo-French war
1417	Henry V invades Normandy
1418	Jean 'the Fearless', duke of Burgundy, secures control of Paris; Henry V besieges Rouen (July)
1419	surrender of Rouen (January); assassination of Jean the Fearless (10 September)
1420	battle of Fresnay (3 March); treaty of Troyes (21 May)
1421	battle of Baugé (22 March); death of Thomas, duke of Clarence
1422	accession of Henry VI of England (r. to 1461; 1470–71); accession of Charles VII of France (r. to 1461)
1423	battle of Cravant (31 July)
1424	accession of James I of Scotland (r. to 1437); battle of Verneuil (17 August)
1425	Artur de Richemont appointed constable of France (7 March)
1428	siege of Orléans begins (12 February)
1429	'battle of the Herrings' (12 February); battle of Patay (18 June); coronation of Charles VII (17 July)
1430	siege of Compiègne; capture of Joan of Arc (23 May)
1431	execution of Joan of Arc (30 May); Council of Basel begins (ends 1449)
1435	Congress of Arras; death of John, duke of Bedford (14 September); treaty of Arras (10 December) establishes peace between Philippe the Good of Burgundy and Charles VII
1436	French retake Paris (13 April)
1437	accession of James II of Scotland (r. to 1460); Charles VII enters Paris (12 November)
1438	Jacques Coeur appointed *argentier* (personal treasurer) to Charles VII; Pragmatic Sanction of Bourges (7 July)
1440	Charles d'Orléans is released from English captivity; *Praguerie* revolt (15 February–17 July)
1442	Yolande of Aragon (Charles VII's mother-in-law) dies (14 November)
1444	truce of Tours (22 May); Agnès Sorel (Charles VII's mistress) enters the French court
1445	Charles VII issues military *ordonnances* (January–March) that create a 'standing army'; marriage of Henry VI and Margaret of Anjou (23 April)
1448	formation of the *francs-archers* (April); Henry VI surrenders Maine
1449	English attack Breton fortress of Fougères (March); Charles VII invades Normandy (31 July); Rouen surrenders (10 November)
1450	death of Agnès Sorel (9 February); battle of Formigny (15 April); French capture Caen (24 June) and Cherbourg (12 August); Cade's Rebellion (May–July)
1451	French capture Bordeaux (12 August)
1452	John Talbot recaptures Bordeaux
1453	battle of Castillon (17 July); French capture Bordeaux (19 October)

Illustrations

Glossary

Affinity/Retinue – a characteristic feature of 'bastard feudalism' in England, comprising a network of servants and supporters who assisted a magnate in local affairs, in his household and on military campaign. Such men might be contracted to serve in a variety of ways including the payment of annuities, the grant of household privileges and indentures (both for life service and more limited durations).

Aides – taxation on retail and wholesale consumption introduced in 1360 in France to pay royal ransoms incurred after the battle of Poitiers (1356). This developed from an earlier system of 'feudal aids' payable on designated occasions.

Allod/*allodium* – inherited family land held absolutely rather than of a lord or monarch. The Plantagenets often claimed the duchy of Gascony was an allod rather than a fief held of the French king.

Appanage – arrangement for the support of children of a royal person, usually property set aside to be held by a younger son. The Capetian and Valois kings adopted an '*appanage* policy' by which the French royal domain was divided into a number of semi-independent territorial units. Of these Burgundy became the most powerful.

Appatis – protection money paid following an agreement made between a community (often a town or village) and a military force (soldiers or mercenaries).

Appellants – group of English nobles who opposed Richard II and his ministers in 1387. They included: Thomas of Woodstock, duke of Gloucester (1355–97); Henry Bolingbroke, earl of Derby, later Henry IV (1366–1413); Richard FitzAlan, earl of Arundel (1346–97); Thomas Beauchamp, earl of Warwick (c.1339–1401); Thomas Mowbray, earl of Nottingham (1366–99).

Bailli – French royal administrative officer operating north of the River Loire, with judicial, military and financial responsibilities.

Ban/arrière-ban – summons to the nobility for military service. The troops serving in this capacity are usually referred to as comprising the *arrière-ban*.

Bastides – fortified towns constructed in Languedoc during the thirteenth and fourteenth centuries.

Bouche de/en court – the right to eat at a lord's table; a household privilege often granted in return for service or as part of a contract with a member of a retinue/affinity, possibly in addition to wages or an annuity.

Chambre des comptes – French royal financial institution founded in 1303 with the power to raise and spend revenue. It served as the chief audit court of the monarchy. Many princes also had their own *chambres des comptes*.

Chevauchées – military expeditions conducted by English armies in France with the intention of destroying revenue and resources. These raids may have been deliberately provocative, launched with the aim of forcing the French into a pitched battle.

Condottiere – leader of a mercenary company, so called because he contracted (*condotta*) soldiers to serve under him.

Écorcheurs – (literally 'skinners' or 'flayers', because they often stripped peasants of everything, even their clothes), these unemployed soldiers/mercenaries terrorised large parts of northern France in the aftermath of the treaty of Arras (1435) (see also *Routiers*).

États (estates) – assemblies of regional political elites (nobles, churchmen and burghers) summoned and consulted by royal officers to facilitate and legitimise the collection of taxes.

États généraux (estates general) – representatives of local political society gathered to consult with the French king/ruler or his regent/deputy.

Fletcher – a maker of or dealer in bows and arrows.

Gabelle – export duty/taxation on salt imposed in France.

Guet et garde – system of urban defence in France (literally, 'watch and ward'). *Guet* involved mounting watch on a town's ramparts, usually at night; *garde* meant sentry duty at the town gates in daytime.

Inquisition – an ecclesiastical commission of inquiry staffed by trained theologians, entrusted with detecting those guilty of heresy and of taking depositions from them under oath.

Langues d'oc – group of broadly related languages spoken in southern and central France.

Langues d'oïl – group of broadly related languages spoken in northern France.

Liege homage – a form of elevated homage that clearly established a lord's superiority/sovereignty. Service could involve the provision of military assistance, and a vassal could not act in concert with his lord's enemies or assist them in other ways.

Lit de justice – special session of the *parlement* which the French king could call in order to enforce his power against another legal authority.

Lollards – insulting name applied, sometimes wrongly, to the followers of the heresiarch John Wyclif (c.1330–84). Wyclif attacked the papacy, the secular authority of the Church, the doctrine of transubstantiation, masses for the dead, pilgrimages and the veneration of images. The beliefs of the later Lollards were strongly influenced by unorthodox interpretations and translations of the New Testament.

Marmousets – royal favourites of King Charles VI of France (r.1380–1422) who replaced the king's uncles on the council prior to the first manifestation of his madness in 1392.

Mercer – merchant or trader, usually in textiles.

Napery – office in a medieval household responsible for table and other linens.

Ordonnance/Compagnies d'ordonnance – established in 1445 by King Charles VII of France (r.1422–61), these permanent military units formed the core of a standing army. The *compagnies* consisted of men-at-arms (*gens d'armes*) and archers.

Parlement – French legal body that dispensed royal justice. The *parlement* of Paris claimed jurisdiction over the whole of the French kingdom for most of the late Middle Ages. Some of its powers were delegated to Poitiers, Toulouse, Grenoble and Bordeaux in the fifteenth century.

Prévôt (provost) – local judicial officer of the French Crown.

Prince of the Blood – a legitimate descendant in the male line of the monarch of a country.

Purveyance – compulsory purchase of foodstuffs for the English king's army during a period of war. The imposition was extremely unpopular because purveyors set the price to be paid for the requisitioned goods, which was often lower than the market value. Payment was frequently slow and sometimes not made at all.

Routiers – bands of mercenary soldiers (deriving from the word *route*, meaning troop or band).

Sénéchal – French royal administrative officer operating south of the Loire, with judicial, military, and financial powers.

Staple – place designated by English royal ordinance as a special centre of commerce.

Tail male – limitation of the succession of property or title to male descendants.

Taille – French system of municipal/household taxation.

Villeins – peasants occupying land subject to a lord. They were effectively tied to the land/manor and not allowed to leave without permission.

A Note on Money

During the Hundred Years War financial transactions might be conducted in money of account (a conventional measure of value) or money of payment (i.e. the coins in which payment was actually made).

In England the mark was a unit of account worth two-thirds of a pound (13s. 4d.). The main coins in circulation were made of gold silver or billon (silver-copper alloy). They included the silver penny ('d.'), the shilling ('s.', worth 12d.), and the pound ('£', worth 20s. or 240d.). In 1344 the gold noble was introduced, valued at 6s. 8d.

The French unit of account, the *livre* (*l*), was worth 20 *sous* (*s*), each with the value of 12 *deniers* (*d*). The value of the *livre* depended on its place of origin (Tours, Bordeaux or Paris) and on levels of devaluation. The sum of £1 sterling was usually valued as: 5–6 *livres tournois* (*l.t.*); 5–6 *livres bordelais* (*l.b.*); 4–5 *livres parisis* (*l.p.*).

The main coins in circulation in France were the silver *gros* (worth 1 *sou parisis*) and the gold franc (*franc d'or*) (worth 1 *l.t.*), which was gradually replaced by the *écu d'or* (there were approximately 9 *écus d'or* to the £). The English administration in northern France in the fifteenth century also minted the *salut d'or*, which had a similar value. The French *mouton*, worth 4s. 10d., was first produced in 1355.

The Castilian unit of account was the *maravedi* (comprising 10 pennies/ *dineros*). The sum of £1 sterling was worth about 230 *maravedis*. The main Castilian coins in circulation were the *real* and the gold *doblas* (worth about 4s.).

The other major coin in circulation in Europe was the gold florin of Florence (worth about 4s. sterling).

A Note on Names

The French spelling of personal names has been retained unless they are particularly familiar in their English form, for example, Joan of Arc and Margaret of Anjou.

Plantagenets, Capetians and Valois, c.1220–c.1420 (regnal dates)

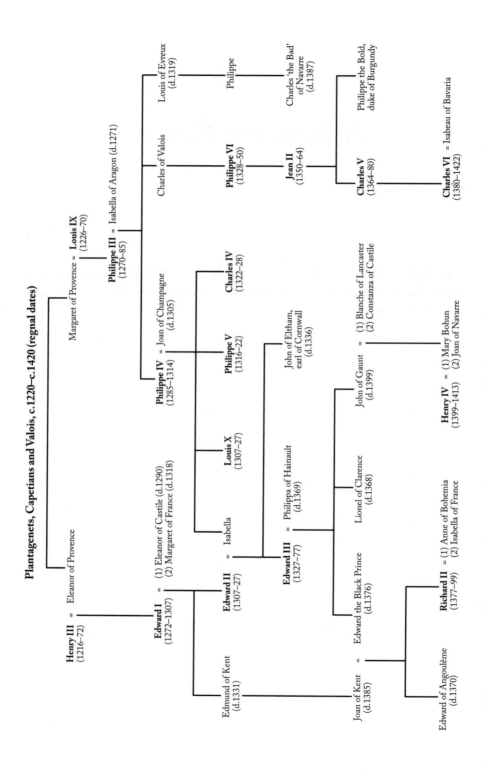

Lancastrians and Valois, c.1350–c.1470 (regnal dates)

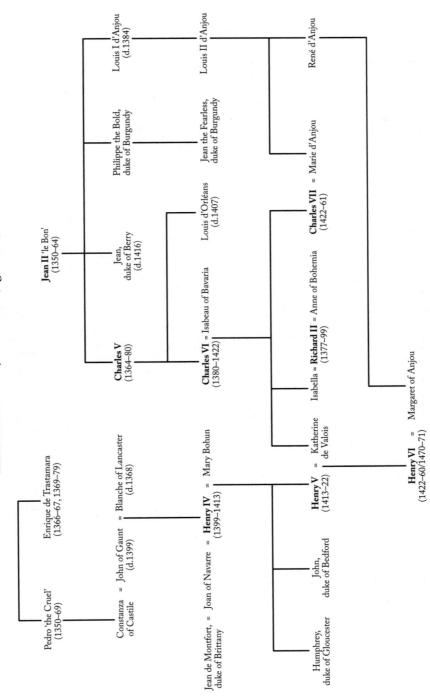

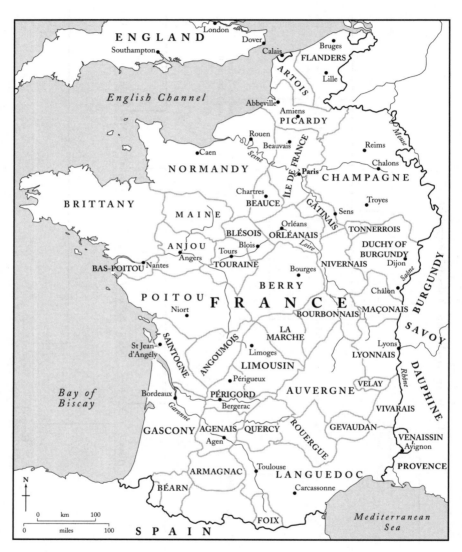

ENGLAND
London
Southampton
Dover
Calais
Bruges
FLANDERS
Lille
ARTOIS

English Channel

Abbeville
Amiens
PICARDY
Rouen
Beauvais
Reims
Chalons
Seine
Caen
NORMANDY
ÎLE DE FRANCE
Paris
CHAMPAGNE
Chartres
BEAUCE
Troyes
BRITTANY
MAINE
Sens
GÂTINAIS
Orléans
TONNERROIS
ANJOU
BLÉSOIS
ORLÉANAIS
Blois
Loire
DUCHY OF
BURGUNDY
Angers
Tours
TOURAINE
Bourges
NIVERNAIS
Dijon
Nantes
BAS-POITOU
BERRY
FRANCE
Saône
Châlon
POITOU
Niort
BOURBONNAIS
MAÇONAIS
BURGUNDY
St Jean-
d'Angély
SAINTONGE
LA
MARCHE
Lyons
SAVOY
Limoges
LYONNAIS
ANGOUMOIS
LIMOUSIN
Bay of
Biscay
Périgueux
Rhône
DAUPHINE
Bordeaux
PÉRIGORD
AUVERGNE
VELAY
Garonne
Bergerac
VIVARAIS
GASCONY
AGENAIS
QUERCY
ROUERGUE
GEVAUDAN
Agen
VENAISSIN
Avignon
ARMAGNAC
Toulouse
LANGUEDOC
PROVENCE
BÉARN
Carcassonne
N
0   km   100
0   miles   100
FOIX
Mediterranean
Sea
SPAIN

1 France in the later Middle Ages.

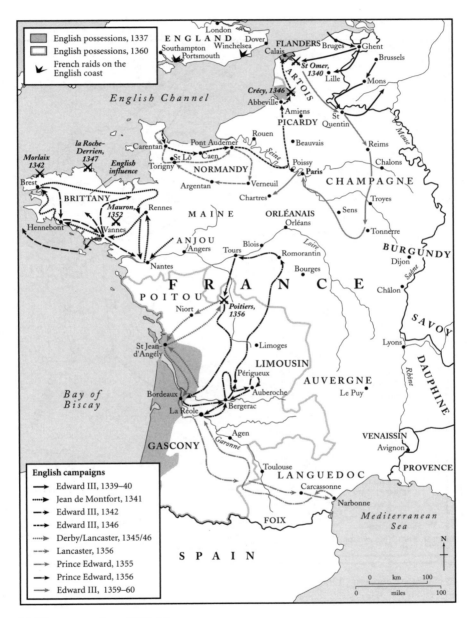

2 Military campaigns, 1337–60.

The following labels appear on the map:

Legend:
- English possessions, 1337
- English possessions, 1360
- French raids on the English coast

ENGLAND — London, Dover, Winchelsea, Southampton, Portsmouth

English Channel

FLANDERS — Bruges, Ghent, Brussels, Mons, Lille
St Omer, 1340
Calais
ARTOIS
Crécy, 1346 — Abbeville
Amiens
PICARDY
St Quentin
Reims
Chalons
Meuse

Morlaix 1342 — Brest
la Roche-Derrien, 1347
English influence
Carentan, Pont Audemer, St Lô, Caen, Torigny
Rouen
Beauvais
Seine
Poissy
Paris
NORMANDY
Argentan — Verneuil
Chartres
CHAMPAGNE — Troyes, Sens, Tonnerre

BRITTANY — Rennes
Mauron, 1352 — Vannes
Hennebont
ANJOU — Angers
MAINE
ORLÉANAIS — Orléans
Blois, Tours, Romorantin
Loire
Bourges
BURGUNDY — Dijon, Châlon
Saône

Nantes

F R A N C E

POITOU — Niort
Poitiers, 1356
Limoges
LIMOUSIN
St Jean-d'Angély
AUVERGNE — Le Puy
Périgueux, Auberoche
Bordeaux
Bergerac
La Réole
GASCONY
Agen
Garonne
Bay of Biscay

SAVOY
Lyons
DAUPHINÉ
Rhône
VENAISSIN — Avignon
PROVENCE

Toulouse
LANGUEDOC
Carcassonne
Narbonne
FOIX
Mediterranean Sea

SPAIN

N

English campaigns
- Edward III, 1339–40
- Jean de Montfort, 1341
- Edward III, 1342
- Edward III, 1346
- Derby/Lancaster, 1345/46
- Lancaster, 1356
- Prince Edward, 1355
- Prince Edward, 1356
- Edward III, 1359–60

0 km 100
0 miles 100

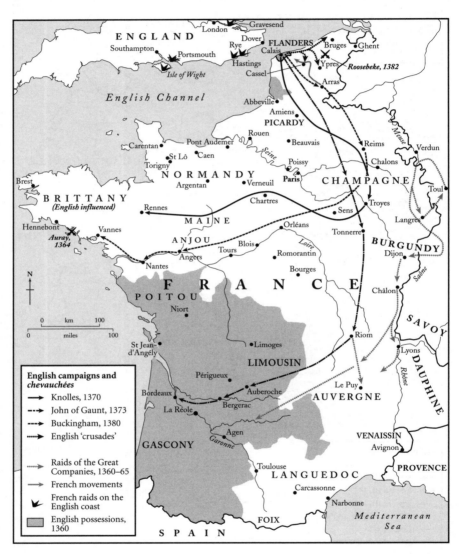

ENGLAND

London Gravesend
Southampton Portsmouth Rye Dover FLANDERS Bruges Ghent
Hastings Calais Ypres *Roosebeke, 1382*
Isle of Wight Cassel Arras

English Channel

Abbeville
Amiens PICARDY
Carentan Pont Audemer Rouen Beauvais Reims Verdun
St Lô Caen Chalons
Torigny Poissy
Brest Argentan Verneuil **Paris** CHAMPAGNE Toul
BRITTANY Chartres
(English influenced) Rennes Sens Troyes
Hennebont MAINE Orléans Tonnerre Langres
Auray, Vannes ANJOU Blois BURGUNDY
1364 Tours Dijon
Nantes Angers Romorantin Châlon
Bourges

F   R   A   N   C   E

POITOU SAVOY
Niort Riom
Lyons DAUPHINE

St Jean Limoges
d'Angély
Périgueux LIMOUSIN
Bordeaux Auberoche Le Puy
Bergerac AUVERGNE
La Réole VENAISSIN
Agen Avignon
GASCONY PROVENCE
Toulouse LANGUEDOC
Carcassonne
Narbonne *Mediterranean*
Sea
FOIX
SPAIN

N

0   km   100
0   miles   100

English campaigns and
chevauchées

→ Knolles, 1370
--→ John of Gaunt, 1373
-·-→ Buckingham, 1380
····→ English 'crusades'

·····→ Raids of the Great
       Companies, 1360–65
→ French movements
↘ French raids on the
   English coast
▨ English possessions,
   1360

3 Military campaigns, 1360–80.

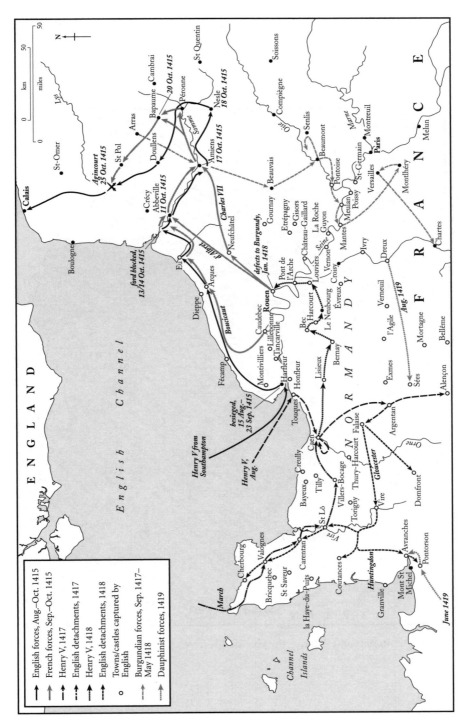

ENGLAND

English Channel

English Channel

FRANCE

NORMANDY

Channel Islands

Calais

St-Omer

St Pol

Arras

Bapaume   Cambrai   St Quentin   Soissons

20 Oct. 1415

Péronne   Compiègne

Nesle
18 Oct. 1415

Doullens   Senlis   Montreuil

*Agincourt
25 Oct. 1415*   Amiens
17 Oct. 1415   Beaumont   Montreuil

Crécy   *Charles VII*   Beauvais   St-Germain   Paris   Melun

Abbeville   Gournay   Pontoise   Versailles   Monthéry
11 Oct. 1415
*ford blocked,   Neufchâtel   Erépagny   Gisors   La Roche   Meulan   Poissy
13/14 Oct. 1415*   Chateau-Gaillard   Guyon
Eu   *defects to Burgundy,*   Pont de   La Roche   Mantes   Chartres
Arques   *Jan. 1418*   l'Arche   Louviers   Vernon   Croisy
Bouciaut   Rouen   Harcourt   Le Neubourg   Évreux   Ivry   Dreux
Dieppe   Caudebec   Bec   Vernon   *Aug. 1419*
Lillebonne   Bernay   l'Agile   Verneuil
Fécamp   Montvilliers   Tancarville   Lisieux   Mortagne   Bellême
Harfleur   Honfleur   Exmes   Sées   Alençon
besieged,   Touques
*15 Aug.–
23 Sep. 1415*   Caen   Argentan
Boulogne   Creully   Villers-Bocage   Falaise
Bayeux   Tilly   Thury-Harcourt   *Gloucester*   Domfront
*Henry V from
Southampton*   St Lô   Torigny   Vire   Orne
*Henry V,
Aug.–*   Villedieu
Cherbourg   Valognes   *Vire*   Avranches
St Saveur   Carentan   *Huntingdon*   Pontorson
Bricquebec   Coutances   Mont St
la Haye-du-Puits   Michel   *June 1419*
Granville
March

4 Military campaigns, 1415–20.

5 France: territorial control during the Hundred Years War.

Introduction
1337

*There were these two powers, the one before the other . . . always injuring
and harassing each other in all the ways they could. But at the last the English
and Gascons . . . asked for favourable terms and [the Gascons] took an oath to
never rise or rebel against the crown of France, and to recognise and affirm
that the king of France was their sovereign lord and to remain his true and
obedient subjects . . . This agreement was made . . . in the year fourteen
hundred and fifty-three.*[1]

Jean Chartier, *Chronique de Charles VII*

The world did not shift on its axis when the Hundred Years War ended in
1453. When Bordeaux fell to the forces of King Charles VII on 19 October,
no one knew that the Hundred Years War was over. Indeed, no one knew
that England and France had been fighting the Hundred Years War – the
struggle was first described as such in 1855. But the 116 years between
1337, when Philippe VI, the first Valois king, confiscated Gascony from
Edward III, and the duchy's final capitulation, brought fundamental
changes both to the kingdoms of England and France and to the lives of
their people. The reach of government, the role of the monarch, the place
of the Church, the relationships between rich and poor, noble and ignoble,
and the very identities of both nations were refashioned by more than a
century of war with the 'ancient enemy'.[2]

This book offers a fresh perspective on a period of vital, vibrant,
brutal change. The crucible of war forged and reforged the English and
French nations into something new; it redefined the loyalties and links of
individuals to one another, their internal organisation, and their place in a
widening world. The Hundred Years War brought about a revolution that

fundamentally changed the character of military conduct and organisation. It led to the professionalisation of warfare, resulted in the decline of (chivalric) cavalry and the rise of infantry and artillery. The war forced the peasantry into a new role: as both victims and perpetrators of violence peasants were battered and brutalised by the conflict, but they also emerged stronger despite their terrible experience. The Church and clergy, too, were compelled to adapt to new circumstances, shaped as they were by political conflict and riven by disputes among the ecclesiastical hierarchy, but also galvanised by a period of intense spirituality. The war reshaped political and personal priorities, driving some individuals to remarkable lengths in search of a resolution to the struggle, whereas others fanned the flames of the conflict, drawn to it, lured by the promise of riches, booty and ransoms. The diverse experiences of occupation and the conditions endured by prisoners of war and women reflect many of these changes both in the wider population and in distinct groups brought into being by the grinding pressure of endemic warfare. Many were assaulted and abused, others treated with care and consideration.

This is not a narrative history of the Hundred Years War; rather it explores the impact of the conflict on those groups and individuals who fought in a struggle that redefined the peoples of England and France, and the nations in which they lived. The war has been a natural subject for writers and scholars since it began; indeed, historians, lawyers and chroniclers battled for supremacy on the page even while the armies of England and France fought bloodier battles at Crécy and Agincourt, before the walls of Orléans and amid the gun smoke of Castillon. The propaganda of the later Middle Ages would first give way to new origin myths centred on individuals such as Edward III, Charles V, the Black Prince, Bertrand du Guesclin, Henry V and Joan of Arc, and later to new historical 'realities' coloured by the experience of revolution and world war. In recent years the Hundred Years War has lost some of its political resonance but it has, instead, emerged at the centre of a wealth of scholarship. This book draws that scholarship together in a new way. It seeks to show the human cost of war within a framework of institutional change, and in the context of a struggle that propelled France and England into a new phase of development, perhaps into a new age.

It is usually said that the Hundred Years War finally came to a halt at the battle of Castillon (17 July 1453), although the surrender of Bordeaux three months later (on 19 October) offers a more pleasing symmetry. (The duchy of Gascony had been at the centre of Anglo-French hostilities since it first came under English control in 1152.) It is usually said that, in many ways, little changed thereafter. Edward IV would lead an army to France in 1475, and Henry VIII followed his example across the Channel to win his spurs in 1513. Calais, the last English bastion in France, did not fall until 1558. And even then England and France remained at each other's throats in wars throughout Europe and across the globe until at least the *Entente Cordiale* of 1904. As Charles de Gaulle would say in 1962, 'Our greatest hereditary enemy was not Germany, it was England. From the Hundred Years War to Fashoda, she hardly ceased to struggle against us . . . she is not naturally inclined to wish us well.'[3]

However, the wars that followed the fall of English Bordeaux differed in character and, until the Napoleonic era, in intensity from those that went before. Different, too, were the aspirations and objectives of the main protagonists. English (and British) monarchs may have continued to claim they were also rightful kings of France until 1801, by which time the Revolution had seen to it that there was no throne left for them to claim, but this was not a serious or realistic objective. More importantly, the political ambitions of both sides took on very different dimensions in the immediate aftermath of the Hundred Years War. In France, Valois power was finally free to extend throughout the 'natural' geographical area of the country. In England, by contrast, the humiliation in France led, after civil war, to a complete re-evaluation of the nation's role and place in Europe and a widening world.[4]

The Hundred Years War, then, ended in 1453. Where it began is a rather more vexed question. The roots of this 'Tree of Battles' were many, varied and complex. They can be traced to Gascony, Normandy and elsewhere in France; to England and Scotland. Once the conflict gathered momentum it drew energy from crises and struggles in the Iberian Peninsula and the empire, from the papacy, the Low Countries and Wales. As for *when* the war began the answer is even more uncertain. Should we date the beginning of the war perhaps in 1066, with the battle of Hastings and the unification of England and Normandy? Is 1152 a better date, when Eleanor of Aquitaine married Henry Plantagenet, soon to be King Henry II of England, helping create the so-called Angevin Empire? In 1200, when King John agreed the treaty of Le Goulet with Philippe II (Philip Augustus), the political dynamic between England and France shifted markedly – the king of England acknowledged that his French lands were held as fiefs of the Capetians. In 1204 the French regained Normandy and Anjou – this, too, was deeply significant. Many have seen the origins of the war in 1259, when Henry III sealed the treaty of Paris with (St) Louis IX, became a peer of France and renounced his claim to much of his Angevin birthright. Perhaps the war truly began in 1294, when Philippe IV (r.1285–1314), 'the Fair', confiscated the duchy of Gascony from his recalcitrant vassal, Edward I, or in 1323 with the War of Saint-Sardos. It was in 1328, however, that matters altered radically. The death of Charles IV, the last Capetian king of France, gave the young Edward III a claim to the French throne, and it was this claim and the hostilities it generated that led Philippe VI, the first of the Valois line, to pronounce Gascony confiscate in 1337 when the Hundred Years War truly began.

Anglo-French relations, then, were acrimonious long before 1337 and they remained so long after 1453. The years between 1337 and 1453 were, however, highly distinctive and they marked an intense phase on that continuum. War dominated political agendas to an unprecedented degree and brought radical change to nations, governments, social and military institutions. Indeed, it left few if any aspects of life in England and France unchanged. War affected everyone, from kings to serfs, clergy and laity, men and women. The Hundred Years War refashioned whole nations, breaking and remaking them and their peoples.

Although the war did not begin until 1337, its origins can be found in the turbulent, shared histories of England and France reaching back to the eleventh century. When William the Bastard became William the Conqueror following the battle of Hastings, he established a new political paradigm in western Europe. The ramifications were not immediately apparent at his coronation in Westminster Abbey on Christmas Day 1066, but William had created what would prove a fundamentally unstable and ultimately untenable relationship between France and England. The duke of Normandy was now also king of England, and hence both a sovereign lord and a vassal at one and the same time. His political identity had become inherently contradictory. But for the best part of a century this incongruity seemed not to matter; the authority of the French royal dynasty – the Capetians – rarely extended far beyond Paris and the Ile de France, and Normandy remained all but autonomous, as it had been since first granted to the Viking leader Rollo in 911.[5] In the middle years of the twelfth century, however, tension began to grow. Through marriage, conquest, diplomacy and good fortune, the Anglo-Norman state swelled to become the Angevin Empire, with Anjou, Brittany and the vast duchy of Aquitaine appended to the cross-Channel realm, and with English power extending throughout the islands of Britain and Ireland. As a consequence,

William's descendant, Henry II (r.1154–89), wielded greater influence in France than his French overlord.

But the power of the French Crown was also growing at this time, and for all its size – indeed, because of its size – the Anglo-Norman Empire was unwieldy. Soon wracked by rebellion, instigated mainly by Henry's wife Eleanor and their mutinous children, then undermined by Richard I's absence on crusade and his later imprisonment, the empire was fractured – as it proved, terminally so – during the disastrous reign of King John (1199–1216). John should not be held wholly culpable for the loss of Normandy in 1204, nor for the failure of his international coalition to regain it at the battle of Bouvines (1214), but he should certainly shoulder a good deal of the blame for the collapse of the Angevin Empire. It had become clear that the tide was turning in 1200 when John agreed to the terms of the treaty of Le Goulet. By this John paid Philippe II 'Augustus' (r.1180–1223) homage and 20,000 marks in return for his lands in France. Although previous Capetian kings had claimed overlordship of those Norman and Angevin territories held by the English king, they had not dared ask Henry II or King Richard to pay homage (or pay such an enormous sum) for their French lordships. The treaty reflected a new balance of power between England and France: it was a clear statement of Philippe's superiority and of his right to involve himself in the government of John's continental territories.[6]

Once that involvement began, it led swiftly to the French conquest of Normandy.[7] The loss of the family patrimony was politically devastating to the English Crown and the impulse to regain the duchy as well as other territories in France would shape English royal policy for at least the next half-century. This urge to restore the Angevin Empire remained evident throughout the Hundred Years War. However, when it became clear to Henry III (r.1216–72) that he could not reclaim his ancestral lands by force and that what remained of his grandfather's inheritance might soon be lost, he agreed the treaty of Paris (1259) with Louis IX (r.1226–70). This accord restored the tie of vassalage that had been broken when Philippe II had confiscated John's fiefs. Henry offered to pay homage for Gascony in return for an acknowledgement of his rights to the duchy and he renounced English claims to various other 'Angevin' territories including Normandy, Anjou, Touraine, Maine and Poitou. By this agreement, Henry formally became a peer of France and in so doing he accepted his position as a vassal of her king.

The treaty ensured a period of peace but it gave a new legal structure to the already contentious feudal relationship. This only fuelled Anglo-French hostilities in the long term: for one sovereign ruler to be the vassal of another flew in the face both of political realities and developing theories of kingship. The inherent incongruity of the relationship created in 1066 and refashioned in 1200 had now been placed within strict legal confines, which allowed little room for diplomatic manoeuvre. The demand that the king of England pay liege homage for Gascony proved extremely problematic. This created a more binding relationship than simple homage and it forced the English king to perform a humiliating ceremony. He was required to kneel before his 'lord', offer him his hands and promise allegiance for his lands. It was deeply problematic from an English perspective not only because it was a public declaration of personal inferiority but also because it placed major restrictions on a king's military, political and diplomatic activities. By swearing liege homage he promised to provide military service to the French king as needed, to make no alliances with his lord's enemies, and it meant that the judgments of the duke of Aquitaine's courts remained subject to the whim of the Capetians. The treaty of Paris set England and France on paths that would collide in 1337.[8]

As the overlord of the duke of Gascony, the king of France had a solemn responsibility and numerous advantageous political opportunities to involve himself in the affairs of the duchy. The role that he took most often was a judicial one, and because of the stipulations of the treaty of Paris the final arbiter of Gascon justice was no longer Plantagenet but Capetian. Appeals against the legal judgments of the king of England and his officials were now made with irritating regularity to the king of France. This consistent emphasis on French royal authority became increasingly irksome to Henry's successor, Edward I (r.1272–1307). Appeals to Paris slowed down the business of government, clogged up administrative processes and generally interfered with fiscal activities. Such interference impinged directly on the authority of the English monarch even in his capacity as duke. The competence to oversee, guide and direct the legal process was a central component of medieval kingship, therefore to have this circumscribed and decisions overturned (even when they concerned a duchy overseas) struck a blow to the heart of royal power.

If this suggests that French kings precipitated the Hundred Years War by a niggling, gratuitous and entirely unnecessary show of strength, then it must also be recognised that the Plantagenets were just as willing to flex their muscles. Their actions, particularly those of Edward I in Scotland, were intensely provocative, and perhaps intentionally so. Having been asked to judge the respective merits of various claimants to the Scottish throne following the untimely death of Alexander III in 1286, Edward ruthlessly exploited the authority that this gave him. Indeed, Edward may have hoped his interference in Scottish affairs would goad a reaction so furious that it would give him an excuse to invade. This was deeply significant because the Auld Alliance, which Scotland and France contracted in 1295, tied the issue of Anglo-Scottish relations to the growing problem of Franco-Gascon (and by implication Anglo-French) hostilities. Edward does not seem to have understood the irony involved in 'extending his overlordship into Scotland using the same techniques employed by Philip IV of France to strengthen his position in Edward's duchy of Gascony'.[9] Furthermore, just as Gascony had been a thorn in the flesh of the French monarchy because it gave England a bridgehead across the Channel, so Scotland proved equally irritating to England since she provided France with a foothold on the northern border.

Edward's first Scottish campaign began soon after, in 1296, and it formed part of an intense phase of military activity that laid some of the foundations for the Hundred Years War. War with France had already broken out, in 1294, with Philippe IV's confiscation of the duchy of Gascony; there was a Welsh rising in 1294–95, and in 1297 Edward led an army to Flanders. These expeditions proved unproductive and ruinously expensive; military costs in the period from 1294 to 1298 may have reached £750,000.[10] As a result late medieval government became shaped by and subject to the demands of war; Edward's reign laid the foundations for the English 'war state'.[11]

If, however, the scale of warfare was new, its cause was very familiar. The war with France centred on questions of sovereignty – in Gascony and also in the county of Ponthieu, which Eleanor of Castile (d.1290), Edward's first wife, had inherited in 1279. On 27 October 1293 Philippe IV summoned Edward to his court to answer complaints that had been made against his officials in Gascony. The English king refused to answer the summons and Philippe took the opportunity, with some relish, to begin action formally to confiscate the duchy. Anglo-Gascon resources were spread thinly and French troops faced little opposition as they marched into Gascony and Ponthieu. The complete expulsion of the English from France seemed a distinct possibility – the Hundred Years War could have been over before it began. French attention, however, was soon distracted by a revolt in Flanders and a violent argument with the papacy. Consequently, a truce was agreed in 1297 and a full peace in May 1303. This re-established the status quo by restoring the confiscated territories to Edward in return for the payment of liege homage.[12]

It was common practice to seal such agreements with marriages. The agreement of 1297 had been marked by the betrothal of Edward to his second wife, Margaret of France, Philippe's sister, and the full peace would be secured with the union of Philippe's daughter, Isabella, and Edward's eldest son, the future Edward II. As it proved, far from easing tensions, this arrangement would only fuel Anglo-French aggression and make any long-term solution increasingly unlikely. After his accession and following his marriage to Isabella, Edward II (r.1307–27) paid homage, but not liege homage, to Philippe IV. The question of the precise relationship between the two monarchs arose repeatedly in the period between 1316 and 1322 when three French kings were crowned in quick succession. The ceremony should have been performed with each new ruler, but homage was only paid in 1320 and, again, it was not explicitly liege homage. A further development took place in 1312 when Isabella gave birth to the future Edward III. This did not cause any immediate concern across the Channel; nonetheless, it proved to be a deeply significant moment – if the Capetian line should fail, the next king of England now had a claim to the French throne.[13]

Given the increasingly febrile atmosphere it is not surprising that war erupted again in the 1320s. The War of Saint-Sardos began in October 1323 following the foundation of a French *bastide* (a fortified town) in the Agenais on the borders of Gascony. A provocative act, certainly, if not an immediately hostile one, it led to a Gascon assault in which the town's sergeant was executed. In response Charles IV (r.1322–28) declared the duchy confiscate and despatched an army. A truce, however, was arranged and in September 1325 Prince Edward (later Edward III) paid homage and a fine, which secured the return of much of the land that had been overrun. Nonetheless, it would take further military action in 1326–27 before all the captured territories were returned.[14]

By this stage Edward II's tenuous grip on political realities was reflected in his grip on political power, and he was soon to lose his throne and his life. Edward's deposition in 1327, which Queen Isabella orchestrated, was not only significant in England but had considerable implications for the Hundred Years War.[15] Edward III acceded to the throne and soon began to fashion a new template for English monarchy, one distinguished by its chivalric and martial characteristics. It was distinctive from that evolving over the Channel and eventually it would be expressed in a claim to the French throne. One year later Charles IV, the last Capetian king, died, and to all the other issues that set France and England at each other's throats was added a fundamental question regarding the French royal succession.

Although hostilities did not begin again for nearly ten years, 1 February 1328 marked a crucial point in the degeneration of Anglo-French relations; thereafter it became increasingly difficult to keep tensions in check. With the death of the last Capetian monarch there were three main contenders for the French throne (see Family Tree: Plantagenets, Capetions, and Valois). Edward III was the nearest male heir but his claim descended through his mother. Philippe de Valois and Philippe d'Evreux (Navarre) were related more distantly but in the male line. It is hardly surprising that an assembly of French nobles, secular and ecclesiastic, determined that the throne should pass to Philippe de Valois. The new king had served as regent since Charles IV's death and enjoyed considerable support in the court and country. He was an experienced leader by comparison with the teenage Edward, who in 1328 governed England under his mother's close supervision and that of her lover, Roger Mortimer. Unable to contest the decision, Edward III was forced to accept the situation; on 6 June 1329 he paid homage to Philippe at Amiens.[16]

Conditions in England changed in the following year when the young Edward III staged a coup at Nottingham Castle and seized power from his mother and Mortimer. The new king's priorities were clear: he wished to re-establish the power and prestige of the Crown. He determined to do so through war and found his first target north of the border. In 1332, in a manner foreshadowing policies adopted by both sides elsewhere in the Hundred Years War, King Edward helped revive the Scottish succession dispute and gave his support to a series of expeditions designed to unseat the young Scottish king, David II (r.1329–71), and replace him with the Anglophile Edward Balliol.

Edward's intervention in Scotland had two main aims. The king sought to reverse the political humiliation of 1328 when Robert I (Robert Bruce) had compelled him to agree to the treaty of Edinburgh-Northampton, the terms of which were so one-sided it became known as the 'Shameful Peace'. In addition Edward wished to use a war with Scotland to strengthen his own fragile kingship by uniting the aristocracy in a national cause. Following the English victory at Halidon Hill (19 July 1333), the infant King David II was taken into exile in France. His presence there served only to inflame Anglo-French tensions. Thereafter, Philippe VI insisted that negotiations over Gascony would have to take the status of Scotland into consideration.[17] Later, the chronicler Henry Knighton would argue that when the war began, Philippe VI vowed to 'destroy the king of England whether in so doing he made himself the richest or the poorest king in Christendom. And all that because King Edward had been at such pains to humiliate the Scots.'[18]

Royal status and the status of dependent territories (or what the kings of France and England wished to consider dependent territories, Gascony and Scotland respectively) therefore lay at the heart of the struggle that broke out in 1337. But these were not the only causes. There was also an economic dimension to the Hundred Years War. Gascony was not only of symbolic and political value, but it also generated huge amounts of money through the wine trade. Furthermore, it was home to a number of Atlantic ports which the French monarchy coveted. The wine trade in the south balanced the wool trade in the north where relations with Flanders, the main processing region for English wool, added a further, complicating dimension to Anglo-French relations. Flanders, like Brittany and Castile, provided another theatre in which to fight the Hundred Years War. French relations with the region were rarely easy and had been especially problematic since the defeat at Courtrai in July 1302.[19] This was a stain on French military honour not unlike that which the English suffered at the hands of the Scots at Bannockburn (1314).

As Anglo-French antagonism intensified, the papacy made a determined effort to prevent all-out war – the incentive of a joint crusade was used to keep Philippe VI and Edward III from each other's throats. Then, in 1337, the duchy of Gascony was declared confiscate on Philippe's orders because Edward was harbouring a renegade French nobleman, Robert d'Artois (1287–1342), in direct contravention of his vows of homage and duty to his overlord. Robert was seen throughout Europe as the man directly responsible for the war, although this was, in part, the result of an effective French propaganda campaign.[20] As the French king's cousin and brother-in-law he had been favoured at court, but relations soured when his aunt's claim to the county of Artois was preferred to his own. He came to England in 1334 where he lived quietly for two years. Edward III provided him with a number of castles and a pension in return for his agreement to fight in Scotland. However, in December 1336 the king refused to hand him over to French justice. Edward undoubtedly realised the implications of harbouring a man Philippe VI described as 'our mortal enemy'. It was a provocative act, perhaps deliberately so – its consequences lasted more than a century.[21]

Hostilities began in Gascony and the Channel Islands before the formal confiscation of the duchy and Ponthieu in May 1337. In general, however, the early years of the war saw few advances on either side. Edward III's strategy centred on the construction of a major European alliance against the French, but this proved unwieldy and ineffective. It achieved very little and its exorbitant cost caused a political crisis in England. The only substantial military encounter took place at sea – a naval battle at Sluys, off the coast of Flanders. However, a deeply significant political development did take place in 1340 when Edward made a formal declaration of his claim to the French throne. In token of this he quartered the *fleur-de-lys* with the English leopards on the royal coat of arms. This was a major statement – the claim to the throne of France had become an integral part of the king's own identity. Despite this, campaigning ended in late September 1340 when a nine-month truce was agreed at Esplechin.[22]

In 1342 the struggle took on a new dimension when both sides intervened in the duchy of Brittany, seeking to influence the succession dispute between the houses of Montfort and Blois. Meanwhile the papacy continued to make what turned out to be futile efforts to negotiate a settlement. Consequently, in 1345 a new phase of the war began which marked the start of several decades of English military success. After the limited gains and almost unlimited expense of Edward III's grand continental alliance, the king now adopted a very different approach. Three expeditionary forces, recruited mainly from within the king's dominions, departed England and sailed for Gascony, Brittany and Flanders. All three saw some success and the raid led by Henry, earl (later duke) of Lancaster (c.1310–61), from Gascony was remarkably effective.[23] Then, in the following year, the king led perhaps 14,000 soldiers across the Channel. He launched a *chevauchée* (a wide-scale raid of deliberate devastation) through Normandy, then on towards Paris. However, faced with a numerically superior French army near the capital, the English retreated towards Calais. On 26 August 1346 the king came across a defensible site between the villages of Wadicourt and Crécy where he made his stand. What followed was a resounding English victory – Crécy was a savage battle, a devastating loss for Philippe VI, and the scene of thousands of French casualties.

The weary English army then made its way towards Calais, where a long siege began. Meanwhile with English attention elsewhere, David II of Scotland, who had regained his throne in 1341, took the opportunity to cross the border. However, in battle at Neville's Cross near Durham in October 1346 he also was defeated and captured. The litany of English victories continued in May 1347: at La Roche-Derrien, Sir Thomas Dagworth overcame and captured Charles de Blois (1319–64), France's preferred candidate for the duchy of Brittany.[24]

Edward III celebrated this remarkable series of military successes by founding the Order of the Garter in 1348. However, the ghastly intervention of the Black Death put the celebrations on hold and prevented another major expedition to France until 1355. In France conditions changed in August 1350 with the death of Philippe VI and the accession of his son, Jean II 'the Good' (r. 1350–64). From the outset his reign proved to be anything but good; rather it was scarred by plague, war and revolt. He sought to unite the aristocracy, much as Edward had done, with the formation of a new chivalric order, the Company of the Star. Despite this, Jean faced considerable opposition from within the kingdom as well as from across the Channel. Charles 'the Bad' (1332–87), son of Philippe of Navarre, proved a particular problem. He tried to exploit Anglo-French divisions and his own claim to the throne to carve out an independent principality. Charles's political chicanery eventually led to his imprisonment. Domestic problems such as this explain Jean's apparent inactivity when the war resumed in earnest in 1355. The English launched two expeditions, the more prominent of which was the so-called *grande chevauchée*. This extraordinary campaign of calculated destruction progressed from Bordeaux, on the Atlantic coast of France, to Narbonne on the Mediterranean. Led by Edward III's eldest son, Edward the Black Prince (1330–76), it cut a ruinous swathe through the country. No major battles were fought but hundreds of villages, small towns, fortifications and other settlements were destroyed. It was the example par excellence of the *chevauchée* strategy.[25]

In the following year the prince led a further expedition, penetrating the Valois heartlands, raiding and riding northwards: it was an insult to the authority of Jean II which he could not ignore. The French and Anglo-Gascon armies met in battle at Maupertuis near Poitiers on 19 September 1356. Although a closer-run affair than the encounter at Crécy ten years before, the outcome was the same and the implications far greater because Jean himself was taken captive. The profound political resonance of this French defeat greatly changed the character of the Hundred Years War. King Jean was not the only important captive taken that day; his young son, Philippe, later Philippe the Bold, duke of Burgundy (1342–1404), and 15 other key members of the French nobility were also taken prisoner.[26]

The governmental vacuum this created threw France into confusion. The dauphin Charles, duke of Normandy (the future Charles V), aged only eighteen and politically inexperienced, sought to gain a vestige of control over a country wracked by defeat and increasingly divided both politically and socially. He summoned a meeting of the Estates General, which did nothing to help matters as its first act was to call into question the administration's competence. Etienne Marcel, the *prévôt des marchands*, led the opposition which followers of the imprisoned Charles de Navarre soon joined. They demanded a complete reform of the government and a major reorganisation of the king's council. The dauphin tried to defuse the situation but to no avail and King Jean, from his imprisonment, refused to countenance many of the demands. Tension between the parties rose. Then, in November 1357, Charles de Navarre escaped from captivity. If conditions in Paris had been feverish before, they were now explosive, and that tension erupted alongside a peasant revolt, the Jacquerie, which broke out on 28 May 1358. Taxation, increasing feudal dues, a stagnant grain market, casual violence perpetrated by soldiers and mercenaries and the indignity of the defeat at Poitiers all added to the political ferment – a torrent of hatred was unleashed against the nobility.[27]

Although crushed swiftly and savagely, the revolt was an indication of the political dislocation the war had caused and the void that Jean II's absence had left. Edward III sought to capitalise on this. With the kings of France and Scotland his captives, he was, seemingly, at the height of his power, and he exulted in this, revelling in a series of luxurious ceremonies and pageants. Direct political benefit, however, was more difficult to accrue. Edward made extortionate financial and territorial demands in the First and Second Treaties of London (January 1358, March 1359). When the French council refused these terms the king set sail with perhaps the largest English army ever deployed in the Hundred Years War – more troops had been used over the course of the siege of Calais but not concurrently. However, the campaign that marched on Reims ended in military failure. Poor weather, lack of provisions for men and animals alike and stalwart French defence forced the English to abandon attacks on both the coronation city and, later, the capital; terms for a truce were reached at Brétigny in May 1360. This provided Edward with a ransom of 3,000,000 écus for King Jean, major territorial concessions and the renunciation of Valois sovereignty over English lands in France. In return Edward offered to abandon his claim to the French throne. However, these 'renunciation clauses' were later transferred to a separate document to be ratified after the transfer of various lands and hostages. The ratification never took place.[28]

Thus, for the time being, the war came to a halt. Edward III granted the duchy of Gascony and those newly acquired lands appended to it to his son the Black Prince, which the latter ruled from 1362. A cessation of Anglo-French hostilities did not, however, mean peace for France. The treaty of Brétigny left large numbers of mercenaries (the Free Companies) without gainful employment. In the absence of a paymaster they continued to 'earn' a profitable living by plundering the French countryside. Far more than a mere disruption, they constituted a truly formidable military force that defeated a French royal army at Brignais on 6 April 1362. Dealing with this mercenary threat became a priority for the new king of France, Charles V (r.1364–80), called 'the Wise'.[29]

Soon after Charles V's accession, an English spy reported the new king's objectives to Edward III. Charles intended to bide his time, negotiate the release of those hostages still in captivity following the treaty of Brétigny, build up his army and deal with the ongoing threat posed by Charles de Navarre. Only then would he seek to reconquer those lands surrendered in 1360.[30] First, however, Charles V had to put a stop to the ravages the mercenary companies were inflicting. The opportunity to do so came with the outbreak of a civil war in Castile between King Pedro, known as 'the Cruel' (r.1350–69), and his half-brother Enrique, 'the Bastard', of Trastamara (r.1369–79). Charles hoped that a change of ruler in Castile would put paid to the alliance Pedro had made with Edward III in 1362. Consequently, the mercenary commander and future constable of France, Bertrand du Guesclin (c.1320–80), was despatched to recruit an army from among the Free Companies and lead it to Castile in support of Enrique. This proved partially successful. Pedro was deposed but not eliminated. He fled to the sanctuary of the Black Prince's court in Aquitaine. Negotiations followed as Pedro offered anything and everything in return for the support he needed to regain his throne.

The terms were finalised in the treaty of Libourne (23 September 1366). This placed the huge financial burden for a military expedition on the Black Prince's shoulders. Pedro agreed to repay the colossal sum (more than £250,000) with interest and further territorial inducements. The army the prince and Sir John Chandos (d.1369) recruited consisted, in part, of some of those very soldiers who had recently fought under the Franco-Trastamaran colours to depose Pedro. Now they battled to reinstate him, defeating Enrique and du Guesclin at Nájera on 3 April 1367. Pedro was restored to the Castilian throne, albeit briefly. The victory, however, came at great cost to the Black Prince. The financial implications of the expedition were very considerable and Pedro was unable even to begin to repay his allies. It also cost the prince his health – it was in Spain that he contracted the illness, usually although uncertainly diagnosed as amoebic dysentery, which would eventually cut short his life.[31]

It was, therefore, in very changed circumstances that Charles V and Bertrand du Guesclin engineered the reconquest of the principality of

Aquitaine from 1369 onwards. The war took on new characteristics in this period, shaped as it was by the defensive impossibility of the English (Anglo-Gascon) position. The combination of a vastly extended border with Valois France and revolt from within meant that the principality could not be held. The war reopened in 1369 after Charles V summoned Prince Edward to Paris to answer certain charges brought by a coalition of Aquitainian nobles led by Jean, count of Armagnac (1311–73). Edward offered to appear before the French king but with the small proviso that he would come sword in hand and with an army at his back. It was a proud but empty boast. Its consequences were the swift and shameful loss of nearly all that the English had acquired since the war began. The Black Prince's illness and incapacity and Edward III's declining years left the command of English forces in less capable hands. The French refused to be brought to battle, and the *chevauchées* launched by commanders such as Sir Robert Knolles and John of Gaunt, duke of Lancaster (1340–99), achieved little. The French and their allies were victorious at sea, notably in 1372 when a chiefly Castilian force (following Pedro's final deposition and death in 1369) defeated an English flotilla commanded by the earl of Pembroke off the coast of La Rochelle. Thereafter, for much of the 1370s, the horrors of war were brought home to the English people in a series of devastating raids on the south coast. The English position seemed to be in (literally) terminal decline when in 1376 the Black Prince predeceased his father by a year. It was said that at this point 'the hopes of the English utterly perished'.[32] From 1377 the defence of the English realm and its overseas dominions was left in the hands of Edward III's grandson, Richard II (r.1377–99) – then only ten years old.[33]

But the momentum of the French advance faltered in 1380 when both Charles the Wise and du Guesclin died – both were laid to rest in Saint-Denis, the one-time Breton mercenary not far from his 'most Christian king'. As a result the minority government of Richard II faced a rather less potent regime across the Channel. Charles VI (r.1380–1422) was aged only eleven when he succeeded his great father. Seeking to fill the political space and gain control of the treasury, senior members of the royal family struggled for control until the king proclaimed himself of age in 1388. For three and a half years Charles then ruled effectively with the assistance of a group known as the *Marmousets*, which included the constable of France, Olivier V de Clisson (1336–1407), and the extraordinary Philippe de Mézières (c.1327–1405). Then, catastrophically, in August 1392, the king suffered the first manifestation of madness that would plague the remainder of his long reign and throw France into chaos. For some time it had appeared that the dangerous divisions within the French nobility, which the English had been able to exploit in the early stages of the war, had been healed. Navarre and Brittany no longer posed a threat to the Valois monarchy, and Flanders had been incorporated into the growing Burgundian patrimony. But as Charles VI struggled for control of his wits, so a new struggle began for control of the Crown (or, rather, its resources) between Louis d'Orléans (1372–1407), Philippe of Burgundy, and the queen, Isabeau of Bavaria (c.1370–1435). The feuds and vendettas that grew out of this struggle would escalate into civil war.[34]

Matters were no more settled in England. The country had been wracked by the Peasants' Revolt in 1381, in which the young king had distinguished himself, and by the Appellant Crisis in 1386, in which he had not. These incidents marked a period of considerable turmoil and it was one in which political disputes were played out to a new extent in Parliament. The Good Parliament of 1376, which involved a sustained attack on perceived corruption at court, saw the introduction of the system of impeachment as well as the appointment of the first Speaker of the Commons. During the crises of the later 1380s the so-called Wonderful and Merciless Parliaments (1386, 1388) saw further attacks on the royal administration. By the 1390s, however, Richard II had regained much of his power and he used this to punish his enemies and pursue a peace policy, one that Charles VI's government supported. This resulted in a truce sealed in 1396 and seemingly confirmed by a marriage between Richard and Isabella, Charles's young daughter – she was six. (Richard's first wife, Anne of Bohemia, had died in 1394.)[35]

In France, Charles's madness led to growing political friction, while in England Richard's actions against the former Lords Appellant (nobles so-called because they made an appeal of treason against a number of the king's ministers) brought about his own downfall – he was deposed in 1399 by Henry Bolingbroke, son of the recently deceased John of Gaunt, who took the throne as Henry IV (r.1399–1413). The new Lancastrian dynasty in its turn faced successive revolts in England, mostly orchestrated by the Percy earls of Northumberland, and in Wales, conducted by Owain Glyn Dŵr. The Welsh revolt might have been even more serious given that it received some French support. However, by the time of Henry's death a modicum of royal control had been re-established. This was not so in France. There the assassination in 1407 of Louis d'Orléans on the order of Jean the Fearless of Burgundy led to the outbreak of civil war.

In 1410, fearing Burgundian ambitions and their consequences, the dukes of Berry, Brittany, and Orléans, and the counts of Alençon, Clermont, and Armagnac, formed a league against Jean the Fearless. Charles d'Orléans (1394–1465), the son of the murdered Louis, married Bonne d'Armagnac, and Charles's father-in-law, Bernard VII d'Armagnac, became the nominal head of the family; for this reason the Orléanist allies were commonly called Armagnacs.[36]

Both sides sought support from England – the Armagnacs even offered Henry IV full sovereignty in Gascony in return for an army of 4,000 men (the treaty of Bourges, 18 May 1412). As part of this agreement, Thomas of Lancaster, duke of Clarence (1387–1421), led an army that devastated much of western France south of the Loire. Soon after, Thomas was bought off following a brief reconciliation in the civil war, but peace did not last long. During this period Paris experienced a great deal of violence as both sides struggled for control of the capital. Much of this was recorded by an anonymous resident commonly called the Parisian Bourgeois, although he may have been a clergyman. Henry V (r.1413–22) succeeded his father and took full advantage of these chronic political divisions by launching a campaign in 1415. Like Edward III he sought to bolster a shaky regime in England by taking war to France. After capturing the port of Harfleur on 22 September he marched towards Calais, determined to demonstrate his enemy's impotence by ransacking the northern coast. His army, however, wracked by disease and dysentery, was intercepted by a substantially greater French force on St Crispin's Day near Agincourt on 25 October. What followed was a remarkable, almost miraculous victory for the English. For Henry, personally, it provided seemingly divine confirmation of the legitimacy of the Lancastrian claim to the thrones of both England and France. For the French, the chaos of Charles VI's mind was reflected in confusion on the battlefield and division throughout his realm. Henry soon returned to begin the systematic conquest of Normandy, which he finally achieved in 1419. In the meantime the French civil war continued; Burgundy gained control of Paris, purging the capital of Armagnac adherents in the process.[37]

It should have been clear to both sides in the civil war that England presented by far the greatest danger to France. Advances in Normandy and the threat Henry posed to Paris brought about another attempt at reconciliation between Armagnacs and Burgundians. This, however, proved utterly disastrous. In a meeting on the bridge at Montereau on 10 September 1419, in revenge for the killing of Louis d'Orléans more than a decade earlier, the dauphin's entourage assassinated Jean the Fearless of Burgundy. This changed the political dynamic in France fundamentally. There would be no resolution to the civil war – it simply could not be contemplated. Henry V advanced, virtually unopposed, on Paris. For the sake of family honour and out of political necessity Burgundy, now led by Philippe the Good (1396–1467), made an alliance with England. Given the extent of combined Anglo-Burgundian power, Charles VI and Queen Isabeau had no option but to acquiesce to their terms: they sealed the most important treaty of the Hundred Years War on 21 May 1420. The treaty of Troyes did not seek to divide France: it did not partition the country as the agreement made at Brétigny had done sixty years before. Rather it aimed for a more complete resolution. Henry V became heir to the French throne; Charles VI would remain king with Henry as his regent, but when the occasionally lucid king finally died his successor would be the king of England. The dauphin Charles (later Charles VII) was disinherited, and to add a soupçon of legitimacy to the proceedings Henry married Charles's daughter, Katherine. The treaty did not, however, seek to unite England and France: it created a Dual Monarchy; the countries would be governed separately and according to their own laws and customs, but by the same man.[38] This, at least, was the arrangement agreed in 1420. In practice France did, again, become partitioned because the dauphin and the Armagnac faction refused to comply and established a separate jurisdiction in central and southern France, what became known as the kingdom of Bourges; while the north, including Paris, came under Anglo-Burgundian control.[39]

Charles VI of France, known, kindly, as the Well-Beloved, died in October 1422, but his son-in-law did not succeed him. Two months earlier Henry had succumbed to an illness contracted while besieging Meaux. And so Henry VI, not yet a year old, became king of England and France. His regent across the Channel was his uncle, the very capable John, duke of Bedford (1389–1435), who maintained the English position extremely effectively for several years. The English, under Thomas, duke of Clarence, did suffer a reverse at Baugé in 1421, but this was overturned in a major Anglo-Burgundian victory against the dauphinist (Franco-Scottish) forces at Cravant on 31 July 1423. Bedford, in person, defeated another 'French' army at Verneuil (17 August 1424). Consequently, despite the loss of Henry V, the English position did not wither; indeed, it strengthened. By 1427 much of Maine and Anjou had been taken and the line of Anglo-Burgundian control driven south to the River Loire. There it halted. The English did not wish to cross the river, which would leave major French outposts behind them that could harbour troops capable of harassing them from the rear.

The most significant of these outposts was Orléans. In the autumn of 1428 Thomas, earl of Salisbury, laid siege to the town. Salisbury was killed in the early exchanges but the siege held and matters seemed extremely bleak for the Orléanais. On the point of capitulation the town was, however, relieved, in a manner that seemed almost wonderous. On 8 May 1429 the English abandoned the siege following the intervention of a peasant girl at the head of a French army. Joan of Arc's arrival marked a major reversal for the English. Under her leadership English forces were defeated at Jargeau, Patay, and elsewhere. Joan then led the dauphin to Reims, deep in Burgundian territory, to have him crowned king as Charles VII on 17 July.[40]

However, Joan's actions did not begin an unstoppable tide of Valois success. Some of those territories she gained in 1429 were soon recovered by the Lancastrians, such as Maine in 1433–34, and, of course, despite an undoubted change of fortunes, Charles still did not control Paris. Henry VI was himself crowned there, albeit in a rather unsatisfactory ceremony, on 16 December 1431. Furthermore, Joan became a somewhat awkward ally soon after Charles's coronation. Certainly, Charles made no great effort to ransom or rescue her after she fell into Burgundian hands at Compiègne in 1430. Sold first to the English and then handed over to the Church, Joan's conviction of heresy posed a number of 'presentational' problems for Charles VII as a king crowned through the efforts of a condemned heretic. Nonetheless, her actions stemmed the English advance and gave huge momentum to the French response. The major barrier to a Valois advance northwards, however, still remained, in the form of England's alliance with Burgundy. Despite disagreements over policy in the Low Countries, Philippe the Good remained unwilling to withdraw from the alliance. Indeed, he would not do so until the death of his close friend the duke of Bedford. It was only then and following the Congress of Arras in 1435 that Philippe ended the civil war by reneging (with papal dispensation) on his agreement with the English. In return he gained a number of strategically important towns along the Somme and was, somewhat scandalously, personally exempted from having to pay homage to the king. This was a clear indication of his political significance as well as his ambitions for an independent Burgundy.[41]

Without Burgundian support the English position was hugely weakened. Dieppe and Harfleur fell almost immediately, in the winter of 1435–36, although the latter was recovered in 1440, and, most seriously, Paris capitulated in the following April. However, important towns such as Meaux, Creil, Pontoise and Mantes remained in English hands, and

Philippe the Good's attack on Calais failed. Although Burgundy had been a vital element in the construction of the English Dual Monarchy in France, the end of the alliance did not immediately result in disaster. Nonetheless, the position in Normandy became increasingly precarious, and French assaults began on Gascony. Perhaps the chief reason that the English were able to maintain a tenuous grip in France was that Charles VII's own position was not entirely secure. In 1440 he faced the Praguerie, a major rebellion by elements of the French nobility, including the dauphin, Louis (later Louis XI). Named after recent civil unrest in Bohemia, the revolt aimed to place effective power in the hands of Jean d'Alençon, Charles de Bourbon and Jean IV d'Armagnac, the dauphin's allies. Following some serious military action, the duke of Burgundy took a comfortable seat near the summit of the moral high ground from where he mediated a reconciliation. Charles VII emerged from the crisis relatively unscathed, but it was an indication that his position was far from impregnable.[42]

Henry VI's situation was far weaker, however. Hampered by a succession of poor harvests which resulted in severely reduced taxation, the king, increasingly desperate, sought a diplomatic resolution to the war. He finally managed to broker a truce at Tours in 1444 – the first real cessation to hostilities since 1417. By the terms of the agreement Henry VI was to marry Margaret of Anjou, Charles VII's niece. Henry then suggested that as part of a permanent settlement he might renounce his claim to the French Crown in return for sovereign rule in Normandy. As evidence of his goodwill, in December 1445 he surrendered the county of Maine. It proved a disastrous decision – deeply divisive in England and, as far as the French were concerned, merely evidence that Henry would yield to pressure. That pressure was applied in earnest in 1449 when Charles VII launched the final attack on Normandy. By this point Charles had instituted the major military reforms that would secure his ultimate victory. In May 1445 he had created the royal *ordonnance*. This laid the foundations for a permanent standing army. As part of this process the royal artillery was put on a professional footing under the command of the Bureau brothers, Jean and Gaspard. These reforms, instituted after the truce, may have been more concerned with addressing the mercenary problem in France than with defeating the enfeebled English. There was also the associated problem of unchecked military power wielded by the French nobility, which Charles needed to address.[43]

Charles invaded Normandy in August 1449, following an ill-advised English raid on the Breton *bastide* of Fougères. The English defences swiftly crumbled in Normandy before Charles's army in those places where they were maintained at all. Henry V had conquered the duchy in two years; Charles recovered it in barely half that time. His forces attacked on three fronts; Rouen surrendered on 4 November. Charles pushed on despite the winter, capturing Harfleur and Honfleur. English reinforcements were then crushed in battle at Formigny in 1450. Caen and Cherbourg fell in the summer of the same year. Soon after, attention returned to Gascony. It too fell, although after much more serious resistance. Support for England remained strong in the duchy, and although Bordeaux capitulated on 23 June it was soon retaken by the Gascons with the support of John Talbot, earl of Shrewsbury (1384×87–1453), who had been despatched from England. Old Talbot, 'the English Achilles', could not, however, hold out long. He died before the French guns at Castillon on 17 July 1453, and Bordeaux fell, once again, on 19 October. It marked the end of what we have agreed to call the Hundred Years War.[44]

The war's relative impact on England and France differed markedly. The expulsion of the English from France, with the exception of Calais, allowed for the expansion of Valois power within the 'natural' geographical area of France. Certain areas, notably Burgundy and Gascony, retained a clear regional identity. These would take some time to erase and for those areas to become wholly 'French' and brought entirely under royal control. The slow and uneven process by which victory had been achieved over England, and the mechanisms put in place in order to achieve that victory, however, established a new governmental system in France which provided the foundations for the *Ancien Régime* and a form of absolutist kingship that endured until the Revolution of 1789. In England, by contrast, the attempt to reforge the Angevin Empire (the Angevin chimera?), which had been at the heart of the Hundred Years War, failed utterly. After 1453 the geopolitical focus of the nation shifted first to expansion within the British Isles and then to a new imperial mission in the New World. Before this could be contemplated, however, the humiliation of the Hundred Years War had to be assuaged – it was a bloody process and took the form of civil war. Although the Wars of the Roses did not begin in 1455 only because of the expulsion of England from the heartlands of Normandy and Gascony, there is no doubt that this was a major factor. The defeat at Castillon did not lead directly to the bloodbath at Towton in March 1461, but a meandering path certainly connected the two.

It is also the case that English society, like French, had become accustomed to war. Political and economic structures had been refashioned with the aim of protecting oneself and harming the enemy. Cultural mores had altered. Social structures had changed on account of war as well as that other ghastly manifestation of the 'apocalyptic' later Middle Ages – the Black Death. There is no doubt that the Hundred Years War, especially when accompanied by plague and famine, was an abominable time for many. The peasantry, particularly in France, suffered intolerably in this period. Yet the war, because of its all-consuming nature, served as a crucible in which many if not all groups were affected – their roles and situations substantially reforged through and by endemic warfare.

The following chapters will explore the impact of the war on the people of England and France. They will consider the changing roles of representative groups within the Three Orders that had comprised earlier medieval society – those who fought, prayed and worked. This book will also explore the impact of the war on those individuals drawn from a range of social backgrounds, who comprised distinct groups within the context of the struggle – such as prisoners of war, or who were influenced by the war in distinctive ways – such as women. Given the centrality of kingship to the Anglo-French war, the position and status of monarchs will also be questioned. Finally, the impact of the conflict on the peoples of England and France as a whole will be considered through a discussion of the ways in which the war fashioned new senses of national identity on both sides of the Channel.

In 1346 it started to become clear that this war would be different from those that had preceded it. The battle of Crécy marked a new high point in Anglo-French hostilities and revealed that the war would be fought according to a new and changing set of rules. Those who had previously comprised the core of French and English armies, the military aristocracy, would be changed fundamentally by the experience.

CHAPTER ONE

Knights and Nobles

FLOWERS OF CHIVALRY

1346

*I will cross the sea, my subjects with me, and I will pass through the Cambresis
... I will set the country ablaze and there I will await my mortal enemy,
Philip of Valois, who wears the fleur-de-lys ... I will fight him ... even if I
have only one man to his ten. Does he believe he can take my land from me?
I once paid him homage, which confounds me now, I was young; that is not
worth two ears of corn. I swear to him as king, by St George, and St Denis
that ... neither youth nor noble ever exacted such tribute in France as
I intend to do.*[1]

Anon., *Vow of the Heron* (c.1340)

According to the anonymous author of the *Vow of the Heron*, King Edward III
began the Hundred Years War with these words. The poem tells how the
French nobleman Robert d'Artois sought sanctuary in England and goaded
the young king into taking up arms against Philippe VI. Robert is said to have
publicly taunted Edward, accusing him of nothing short of cowardice, and to
emphasise his point he presented him with a heron pie – the heron being
the most craven of birds. The ladies of the court, echoing the jeers of the
renegade Frenchman, demanded Edward lead an expedition into France to
defend his honour and theirs. Indeed, the queen, Philippa of Hainault, swore
she would take her own life and that of her unborn child (the future Lionel of
Antwerp) if the king did not attempt to take what was rightfully his – the
French throne.[2]

The *Vow of the Heron* was a political fiction but one that reveals a number
of truths. It emphasises the importance of chivalry and shame in late medieval culture; indeed, it shows chivalry at the core of medieval aristocratic
identity. Although subject to a variety of definitions, chivalry had dominated

the thinking of the secular elite for three hundred years and it remained central to the self-image of the aristocracy in the Hundred Years War. Chivalry had become a cult, an ideology, little less than a 'secular religion', and as such it influenced conduct during the conflict; the struggle was shaped by demands of honour, demonstrations of prowess and exigencies of loyalty. As the ethic associated with the knight – the *chevalier* – chivalric strictures chiefly dictated the behaviour of and relations between knights and nobles, and so in accounts of the war written for aristocratic readers and audiences matters of politics, the fate of the peasantry, prosaic issues of finance and diplomacy, were often lost. Such works focused on the rivalries and (great) deeds of (great) men because this was the image of warfare in which the chivalric caste revelled and that it wished to project.

But chivalry was much more than a game, fantasy or a self-delusion: it exercised enormous influence over military and diplomatic conduct.[3] The knights and nobles who constituted the 'chivalry of England and France' (the word 'chivalry' was used most commonly as a collective noun) determined strategy and policy, and the chivalric ethic conditioned their behaviour, tailoring it to certain (loose) specifications. These qualities were not, however, 'gentle', except in so far as they applied to gentlemen and gentlewomen, and so they do not always conform to a modern conception of chivalry. It is sometimes assumed that chivalry died as the Middle Ages waned, but chivalry was far from dead in the Hundred Years War. The conflict, however, did exert new and weighty pressures on knights and nobles – social, military and political.

Among the many influences that coloured the character of chivalry and the role of the knightly aristocracy during the Hundred Years War, one of the most important was the nature of warfare itself. As the struggle progressed, soldiering became an increasingly professional business, with innovations in strategy, tactics, weapons and recruitment. As the nature of combat changed, so did the nature of the hardships and perils faced by all the chivalrous and all 'those who fought' – the *bellatores*.[4] These developments threw into sharp relief some apparent contradictions between the theory and practice of chivalry. Was true chivalry exemplified by the mercenary leader Bertrand du Guesclin or the *prud'homme* (literally 'worthy man') Geoffrey de Charny, author of the *Livre de chevalerie*, one of the key chivalric treatises of the fourteenth century? This was not a simple question, for du Guesclin was laid to rest alongside the Valois kings in the abbey of Saint-Denis in northern Paris and became the subject of a chivalric biography,[5] while Charny was not above stooping to bribery in his attempt to take Calais in 1350, an act for which he was reproached by no less a chivalric icon than Edward III – who himself had broken a central tenet of chivalry when he ordered the execution of prisoners after the battle of Halidon Hill in July 1333. Was chivalry exemplified by the glorious deeds of arms that Jean Froissart (c.1337–c.1405) recounted in his chronicles or by those pitiless actions condemned by Honoré Bonet (c.1340–c.1410) in his hugely influential treatise L'arbre des batailles (the Tree of Battles)?[6] Was this a chivalry that mitigated the worst of war or encouraged it, feeding it with delusions of honour and promises of loot and booty?

Such questions were of as much interest and importance to contemporaries as they had been to their predecessors. From its inception chivalry had comprised many elements – religious, courtly and militaristic. As a result contending definitions of the ethic had been evident from at least the early twelfth century. Many groups and individuals had an interest in chivalry and a wish to influence the behaviour of those who comprised the order of knighthood. Such diverse views made the chivalric ethic highly adaptable, which explains its enduring potency, but it also gave rise to its apparent incongruities. Chivalry comprised an amalgam of qualities, and the priority one gave to those qualities reflected one's interests. Chivalric romances, for example, often projected an ideal of knightly behaviour dominated by courtesy, and their authors prioritised the relationship between knights and ladies. Others had little time for courtoisie and placed much greater emphasis on the knight's skill-at-arms, reflecting the code's martial antecedents. Religious authorities, meanwhile, viewed knighthood as a divine order, albeit one that often fell far from grace, and believed that the latent violence of knighthoodto needed to be channelled into ecclesiastical service. According to church authorities it was service to God that made knights into something more than mere soldiers. Such differences in interpretation became even more apparent in the later Middle Ages because of new stresses placed on the various conceptions of chivalry and on the members of the chivalric orders.[7]

As the author of the Vow of the Heron suggested he should, Edward III did invade France, and in July–August 1346 he burned and laid waste to the Cambresis region in the north. Then, following a chevauchée – a raid of calculated and widespread devastation – he met his 'mortal enemy, Philip of Valois' (Philippe VI), his liege lord, in battle at Crécy on 26 August of that year. What followed was a comprehensive English victory and a French catastrophe, the impact of which was not only deeply symbolic but also had colossal military and political resonance. God, it was believed, expressed His will through such tests of strength; victory in battle confirmed divine favour for the nation and those who represented it on the field. Military success represented heavenly benediction. The Crécy campaign, however, also reveals those new strains to which knighthood was subjected in this professional age, in addition to the apparent dichotomies intrinsic to the chivalric ethic.

The campaign was the most important element in a number of military expeditions which the English launched in the mid-1340s. The aim of the strategy, involving multiple incursions, was to disrupt French defensive preparations and to keep English plans covert. The scale of the expedition was such that it could not be kept secret, but the French were not aware of the true target until very late in the day. Nor, frankly, were many of Edward's commanders, since the king's intentions appear to have changed several times. Initially, it seems, he intended to lead an expedition from Gascony. Later he decided to land in Normandy and establish a bridgehead there. Only at the last moment did he choose to launch a *chevauchée*.[8]

The army landed at La Hougue on the Cotentin peninsula on 12 July 1346. It split into three divisions to cause maximum damage over a wide area and rode south, then east. The strategic purpose of the initial phase of the campaign was to inflict financial damage on the French government, psychological damage on the French people and to humiliate the Valois regime. In a series of such *chevauchées* the chivalry of England (the military aristocracy) attacked those least able to defend themselves in order to undermine the legitimacy of the French monarchy economically and symbolically. And yet this was considered chivalrous behaviour. At its heart chivalry was a military code concerned with war, and '[w]ar as conducted by the chivalrous meant raiding and ravaging'.[9] So, in 1346, in a display of often pitiless chivalry, the English laid waste to Cherbourg, Harfleur and much of the Normandy coast. Caen fell, and there, in proper chivalric fashion, a number of eminent (and valuable) French noblemen were taken captive and held for ransom; then the army turned towards Paris. On 12 August it came within 20 miles of the capital. Edward, however, chose not to engage the superior enemy forces arrayed before him there, and retreated to the Somme. After struggling for some time to ford the river, he eventually forced a passage at Blanchetaque and drew up his troops in battle formation at Crécy. Philippe VI, who had been at his heels from Paris, attacked almost immediately.[10]

The English deployed at the end of an expanse of gently rising ground, their backs to the forest of Crécy-Grange and the sun. Edward the Black Prince, then sixteen years old, took nominal command of the vanguard alongside a number of highly experienced soldiers, including the earls of Warwick (Thomas Beauchamp), Northampton (William Bohun) and Kent (Edmund of Woodstock), as well as Godfrey d'Harcourt (a Norman noble who had rebelled against King Philippe) and Sir John Chandos. The king commanded the centre and the bishop of Durham, with the earls of Arundel (Richard FitzAlan) and Suffolk (Robert Ufford), took charge of the rearguard. Facing them were the French king, Philippe VI, and several princes of the blood royal, including Charles, count of Alençon (the king's brother), Louis, count of Blois (Philippe's nephew), and Louis of Nevers, count of Flanders (the king's cousin). In addition, there were Philippe's relatives by marriage: John of Luxembourg, the blind king of Bohemia (stationed on the left wing), and his son Charles, king of Germany, later Emperor Charles IV (on the right wing). A number of the great officers of state were also present, including the marshals of France (stationed with the rearguard) – Charles of Montmorency and Robert of Wavrin, lord of Saint-Venant.[11]

The battle that followed shocked Christendom. Crécy was an encounter that redefined chivalric presumptions and reputations throughout Europe. Victory in 1346 transformed the image of English chivalry that had been so tarnished in the defeat at Bannockburn more than thirty years previously. In truth it was an image that in the British Isles had recovered much of its sheen in the early years of Edward III's reign through battles in Scotland such as Dupplin Moor (1332) and Halidon Hill. Indeed, many of those who fought in France in 1346 had been blooded in the Scottish wars of the 1330s and it was those experiences that tempered them, forging a redoubtable fighting force. However, to the rest of Europe this was an unwelcome revelation. As the poet Petrarch (1304–74) noted, in his youth the *Angli* had been considered the most timid of barbarians but now they were regarded as 'a fiercely warmongering people'.[12] This new military reputation would last until Shakespeare's time and beyond. As the archbishop of Canterbury advised Henry V:

Look back into your mighty ancestors:
Go, my dread lord, to your great-grandsire's tomb,
From whom you claim; invoke his warlike spirit,
And your great-uncle's, Edward the Black Prince,
Who on the French ground play'd a tragedy,
Making defeat on the full power of France,
Whiles his most mighty father on a hill
Stood smiling to behold his lion's whelp

Forage in blood of French nobility.
O noble English, that could entertain
With half their forces the full Pride of France.[13]

By 1346 the English had certainly become militarily formidable. The army that fought at Crécy consisted of mixed retinues of archers and men-at-arms, many of whom were knights who usually fought on foot. These units worked most successfully when positioned defensively, using the terrain to their advantage, having prepared the front and flanks with pits, traps and other means of disrupting an enemy charge. It was a tactical model employed to good effect for much of the Hundred Years War, but one that had serious implications for the chivalric elite. The knight had acquired his august position, his social kudos and cultural cachet, because of his skills as a mounted warrior, and chivalry developed as a code for and a means of defining those who demonstrated these skills.[14] However, the tactics the English adopted in the Hundred Years War did not rely on heavy cavalry; indeed, they were developed to counter its use. The cavalry charge, which had proved a highly effective weapon for much of the Middle Ages, could no longer be relied upon. The crushing defeat which the Scots inflicted at Bannockburn had deeply influenced English strategic thinking. With absolute and brutal clarity Robert Bruce's army had shown that cavalry, with all its chivalric connotations, could be terribly vulnerable to infantry, and its weaknesses exposed not by individual prowess but by collective action and discipline.

The French had received a similarly chastening lesson in July 1302 at the hands of the Flemish militia, at Courtrai, the battle of the Golden Spurs. It was so called because of the number of gilded spurs collected from the bodies of fallen French knights. It was not a lesson, however, that the French took to heart. This was, in part, because Philippe VI had reversed the defeat at the battle of Cassel in August 1328 using the traditional might of French cavalry. At Crécy he persisted in using these same older tactics, but with disastrous consequences. It was shocking evidence of a changing of the guard; cavalry was no longer pre-eminent on the battlefield.[15]

The battle of Crécy began with a French attack, but not with cavalry: Philippe VI did not only command horsemen. A substantial body of infantry and a large contingent of Genoese crossbowmen led the assault. The crossbow would develop into a highly formidable weapon over the course of the Hundred Years War, but at this stage of its evolution it proved no match for the English longbow.[16] (Nor did it help that the Italian mercenaries who comprised the majority of the crossbowmen had been commanded to attack without their *pavises*, large shields behind which they could reload, which were still en route to the battlefield with the rest of the French baggage.) Faced with English archers who could shoot further and more quickly, the Genoese soon retreated. This incensed the French cavalry. Furious with the crossbowmen's 'cowardice', the count of Alençon led a charge against the English vanguard, but one that was poorly organised. They rode into the arrow storm 'in a jumbled mass, with no order whatever', and soon they were 'tumbling over each other like a vast litter of pigs'. Some, however, made it through to the English lines where the hand-to-hand fighting began.[17] At one point the English standard fell, only to be raised again by Thomas Daniel, one of the Black Prince's retainers; indeed, the prince himself was struck down and had to be rescued by his standard-bearer, Richard FitzSimon.[18] The French cavalry repeatedly wheeled, rallied and charged. During one of these attacks King Edward was entreated to send reinforcements to bolster his son's position. The king, however, after being assured that the prince was, as yet, unharmed, proclaimed 'let the boy win his spurs, for if God has so ordained it, I wish the day to be his'.[19]

As the French attacks faltered then failed, horses were brought up from behind the English lines; the men-at-arms remounted and charged the surviving French troops. A small bank or escarpment at the foot of the slope facing the English, perhaps six feet in height, had disrupted the French assault and now impeded their retreat, turning the valley into a killing ground. Seeing this, the bulk of the army fled, leaving King Philippe with only a handful of companions, his personal bodyguard and some infantry levies from Orléans. After being injured, he was led away, forced to abandon the Oriflamme (the sacred banner French kings carried to war) and the royal standard.[20]

After the battle, heralds began the grisly task of identifying the fallen. They counted 1,542 French knights and squires who fell near the front line alone, one of whom was John, the blind king of Bohemia.[21] Although defeated and slain in battle, John of Bohemia's conduct at Crécy reveals a good deal about the values of the chivalric community at this time. When he heard that the tide had turned against his French allies, the king asked his household knights to lead him into the fray so that he might strike a blow:

> [And] because they cherished his *honour* and their own *prowess* [my emphasis], his knights consented . . . In order to acquit themselves well

and not lose the king in the press, they tied all their horses together by the bridles, set their king in front so that he might fulfil his wish, and rode towards the enemy ... They were found the next day lying around their leader, with their horses still fastened together.[22]

Together, the experiences of the Black Prince and John of Bohemia at Crécy and in the wider campaign reveal a great deal about the role of chivalry in the early stages of the Hundred Years War. They show that in spite of major changes in military organisation, the chivalric ethos continued to shape the mindset of the aristocracy and the image that its members wished to project of themselves. Indeed, it may have been because of John's bravery, witnessed at first hand, that the Black Prince adopted the king's emblem, the ostrich feathers, as his device as Prince of Wales.[23] At Crécy, John of Bohemia and the Black Prince demonstrated many of the key chivalric virtues – prowess, honour and loyalty. Among these qualities prowess was valued most highly. As Froissart noted, 'as firewood cannot burn without flame, neither can a gentleman [*gentilz homs*] achieve perfect honour nor worldly renown without prowess'.[24] This was vital since, first and foremost, the late medieval aristocracy was responsible for the defence of the kingdom, and to shirk that responsibility meant 'their nobility [was] nothing but a mockery'.[25]

Because of this responsibility there was always a certain pragmatism intrinsic to chivalry. For Geoffrey de Charny, military achievement determined chivalric worth. One achieved 'worth' through deeds of arms, be they in tournaments, at war or on crusade.[26] Hence, he counselled knights and nobles to love deeds of arms, to be bold and give heart to one another, to be truthful and fulfil their oaths, and to love and desire honour. Charny, however, also recognised the changing nature of the military landscape and that success in war depended on a high level of practicality. Hence, he argued, to defeat their enemies his readers should be wise and crafty, as well as brave. Tricks and stratagems were not necessarily contrary to the strictures of chivalry. Prowess was valued, primarily because it brought victory, and victory might also be achieved through subterfuge. Being caught while engaged in such acts, however, might still be problematic. There was a fine line between shrewd strategies and low cunning. If one employed some of the more underhand ruses which Charny and other authors such as Christine de Pizan advocated (noblemen, she wrote, should 'be wise and crafty against their enemies'), it was as well not to get caught, as happened to Charny, to his shame, at Calais in 1350.[27]

Charny had become obsessed with recovering Calais, which had been lost to the English in 1347 after the defeat at Crécy. He plotted to regain the port by bribing the captain of the town, a Lombard named Aimery de Pavia. Despite being offered the princely sum of 20,000 *écus* to let Charny and his men inside the city walls, Aimery warned Edward III of the forthcoming attack and they set a trap. The king secretly reinforced the garrison and he, the Black Prince and some trusted companions travelled to Calais determined to defend it and to capture the plotters. They did so with some ease and, later, Edward publicly reproved Charny at a feast he held to celebrate the victory, saying 'Sir Geoffroi, I've little cause to love you when you try to steal by night what I bought at such expense and effort! [The siege of Calais had lasted eleven months.] It gives me great satisfaction that I caught you in the act!' However, despite Charny's somewhat tarnished chivalric reputation, the new king of France, Jean II (r.1350–64), considered him well worth ransoming and soon did so.[28]

Charny's actions at Calais, as well as those of the Black Prince and John of Bohemia at Crécy and in the preceding *chevauchée*, reveal the broad scope of chivalrous activity. Much of this behaviour does not fall within the compass of chivalry as it is typically understood and it also raised questions for contemporaries. The potency of the chivalric cult was such that it imbued military service of all sorts with an allure and a certain glamour. Concerned with the 'deeds of great men', certain writers rarely noticed or cared about the depredations the peasantry suffered. As a consequence some found it difficult to separate the actions of knights serving a king from soldiers (*milites* in the older sense of the word) serving their own interests. In this way chivalry became associated with and also tainted by the actions of the various mercenary companies that flourished in the Hundred Years War. Criticism could become particularly acute during peacetime when, now unemployed, the Free Companies continued to fight for their own profit, offering the French population no respite. The companies' military potency was considerable: at the battle of Brignais (1362) they defeated a French royal army. Chivalry had previously been a concept linked to military service for one's lord, engaged in a just cause. This association was compromised when much of the fighting in the Hundred Years War came to be seen as unjust and self-serving.[29] This weakened the link between chivalry and 'righteous' violence that had been established in the crusades and other 'just wars'.

It is not surprising that the actions of the Free Companies, alongside the English *chevauchée* strategy, the pitiless character of siege warfare and the casual brutality of occupation, have little in common with popular views of chivalry today. There is little in such actions that suggests the chivalrous should disdain conflict with their social inferiors or protect women and clergymen. But the disparity with modern conceptions of chivalry does not mean that the ethic was simply a fantasy in the late Middle Ages. It was not merely a literary construct – an ideal perhaps, but one that few took truly seriously during wartime. Chivalry did exert a real influence over the military elite and it remained potent during the 'autumn of the middle ages'. What has changed in the intervening years is the dominant conception of chivalry. During the Hundred Years War it offered more than a cynical and hypocritical facade, and it provided something greater than a simple justification for looting, pillage and rape. It is not correct to assume that by the time of Crécy all that remained of this once idealistic military and social system was its bastard child.[30]

Nonetheless, chivalry did provide a justification for the actions of the ruling elite, and it served as a mechanism to protect the international, aristocratic, military caste on the battlefield. During the Hundred Years War chivalry remained the military code it had always been, one that shaped behaviour for and between members of a warrior caste, despite having become bound up with concepts of courtesy and imbued with a certain spirituality. Throughout the war it continued to celebrate prowess and the defence of honour. Although chivalry encouraged restraint in some circumstances, without violence there was no chivalry.[31]

A *chevauchée*, therefore, such as that which led to Crécy, was not intrinsically unchivalric; many contradictions become evident only from the vantage point of hindsight, by which time definitions of chivalry had changed substantially. There was no incongruity in the fact that the anonymous author of the highly laudatory *Vie du Prince Noir* should record in the course of the same 1346 expedition that

> the fair and noble Prince, made a right goodly beginning [as a knight]. All the Cotentin he overrode and wholly burnt and laid waste, La Hogue, Barfleur, Carentan, Saint-Lô, Bayeux, and up to Caen, where they conquered the bridge; and there they fought mightily; by force they took the town, and the Count of Tancarville and the Count of Eu were taken there. There the noble Prince gained renown, for he was eager to acquit himself well.[32]

The Black Prince, therefore, built himself a chivalric reputation on the ashes of peasant houses; he gained renown by burning the property of those least able to defend themselves and by taking valuable prisoners. This military strategy, which destroyed livelihoods and tax revenues, and that sought to undermine the authority of the French king, was in no way unknightly, ignoble or ungentle. Henry V knew this as well and would be glorified for it. He was celebrated for campaigns that sought to destabilise France and destroy the political legitimacy of the Valois monarch by razing his lands and demolishing his source of income; hence Henry's oft-repeated comment that war without fire had little to recommend it – like sausages without mustard.[33]

Burning and looting, then, were not contrary to the dictates of chivalry. It is more difficult, though, to determine whether victories such as Crécy or Agincourt – victories shaped by new, perhaps revolutionary military approaches – were equally chivalrous.[34] A tactical approach based on discipline and defence ran counter to certain chivalric principles; it did not rely on a number of traditional knightly virtues.[35] Qualities such as skill-at-arms, prowess and bravery of course remained essential. However, the battlefields of the Hundred Years War were dominated not by the mounted aristocracy but by infantrymen, many of them commoners, and not by the lance but the longbow, and later by artillery. As a result, in England, as the war progressed, knighthood lost some of its cachet; fewer men sought to become knights, fewer knights fought in English armies, and those who did so fought mainly on foot. Such changes reflected a fundamental re-evaluation of military strategy and tactics, a military revolution that also involved a major shift in the social composition of armies. These changes also resulted in a challenge to another central tenet of chivalry – the ransom system. The need for discipline in the ranks, the greater use of long-range weapons and the increasing proportion of lower-class soldiers in armies limited the protection that chivalry had once offered the chivalrous, namely the opportunity to surrender to a fellow member of the international chivalric brotherhood. The military model that developed over the course of the Hundred Years War increased casualty rates and limited the opportunities to take prisoners. However, because chivalry remained a practical ethic, its practitioners recognised the changing nature of military strategy. Consequently, while mercy remained a chivalric ideal and ransoming very valuable (financially and politically), Henry V could slaughter a number of his prisoners at Agincourt and receive remarkably little censure because he did so for sound military reasons.[36]

The battlefields of fourteenth- and fifteenth-century Europe, therefore, marked the graveyards of chivalry, literally but not figuratively, although there is no doubt that the role of chivalry on the battlefield altered over the course of the Hundred Years War. Nonetheless chivalry remained central to military thinking. Ransoming, too, continued to offer practical advantages to both sides. Prisoners of war retained great political and financial value, and many continued to be treated according to traditional conventions. Unless taken by a vindictive captor – the Spanish and Germans were often stereotyped as such – the aristocratic captive could expect conditions to be none too onerous. Periods of captivity were not supposed to be unreasonably extended either, although this might be because a hostage took the place of the captured man-at-arms. Ransom demands, similarly, should not be financially crippling. Reality and theory might be very different but chivalry thrived throughout the war nonetheless. Although exceptions in practice were numerous, this is not to say that contemporaries completely ignored chivalric proprieties or that they considered them worthless. Consequently, in March 1416, when Bernard d'Albret, duke of Alençon, called on the duke of Dorset, Thomas Beaufort, to surrender near Harfleur, he said:

> Look, you are caught between us and the sea; there is no place for you to escape. Surrender to me therefore, so to not perish by the sword, but to be treated most honourably as the nobility of your birth demands, and to be ransomed not for an excessive sum, but for a reasonable one.[37]

As it was, Dorset chose not to accept the offer and, indeed, drove off the French attack. The duke was very valuable, politically and financially, but his experience does show that while the ransom system was a little bruised it remained in good health.

The ransom system also allowed for the production of a key text concerned with attitudes to war and chivalry during the Hundred Years War, Sir Thomas Gray's *Scalacronica*. Gray (d.1369) was captured while leading a retaliatory attack on a Scottish raiding party in 1355. He spent the next year in comfortable captivity in Edinburgh Castle, where he had leisure to write his chronicle – the musings of a conventional knight on the military deeds of his family from the beginning of Edward I's reign until his own times. Prior to his capture Gray had been active in the Hundred Years War. He fought in Flanders in 1339, against the Scots at Neville's Cross in October 1346, and after his release he served with the Black Prince on the Reims campaign (1359–60). He was also constable of Norham Castle in Northumberland. Gray's attitudes, revealed in the *Scalacronica*, show how a knight managed to blend the practical with the more flamboyant aspects of chivalry.

For Gray, honour was the focus of a chivalric life. Like the author of the *Vow of the Heron*, he believed Edward III had a duty to wage war; indeed, he argued it would have been dishonourable had Edward not taken up arms against the French. The nation's honour depended on the king fighting for his rights. Second, Gray recognised the importance of prowess. He delighted in traditional knightly skills but understood that a new military environment had developed in which the shock and awe of cavalry had diminished. 'Chivalric deeds,' he argued, 'should be done on horseback rather than on foot,' yet he added the caveat '*whenever this can suitably be done*.'[38] Gray was a pragmatist and this is particularly apparent when he discussed the subjects of raiding and 'collateral damage'. He spent no time whatsoever in his chronicle remarking on the depredations the Scots inflicted south of the border, because such events were so commonplace as to be entirely unremarkable. Consequently, the *Scalacronica* reveals Gray's recognition of the changing character of warfare, while at the same time acknowledging the continuing importance of chivalric convention and showing its author's deep respect for deeds of arms and those who performed them.[39]

Chivalry, therefore, remained alive and well in the Hundred Years War. It remained more than just a literary ideal and it continued to dictate 'proper' behaviour between the chivalrous. That sense of 'propriety' altered over the course of the conflict, but the war continued to be fought in a chivalrous manner – and not only because it remained, chiefly, the business of the chivalric classes. Those who commanded armies in the Hundred Years War may have been more or less chivalrous than their ancestors but, for the most part, they were cut from the same cloth and they were of the same order (*ordo*), members of the chivalry of France and England. Some of them were also drawn together into even tighter associations through chivalric bonds created in a wholly new way during and because of the Hundred Years War.

The importance of chivalry is clear in the manner by which English and French kings sought to employ the ethic to defend their political ambitions and unite the military aristocracy. Edward III founded the Order of the Garter in 1348 to commemorate his own 'honourable' struggle in France, which had, surely, received divine approval in the God-given victory at Crécy. This was a scheme Edward had been toying with for some time. Plans had been well under way in 1344 for the development of a more grandiose foundation, the Round Table. This, however, gave way to an Order dedicated to St George after the *annus mirabilis* of 1346 with the victories against the 'auld enemies' at Neville's Cross and Crécy. The Garter motto, *Honi soit qui mal y pense* ('dishonour on he who thinks ill of it'), referred, most likely, to Edward's French campaigns and his claims to French lordship. The founder knights of the Order were the king's comrades in arms; many served in his household or as chamber knights, and almost all were closely associated with his campaigns, most especially the victory at Crécy.[40]

In this way the Order of the Garter linked the aristocratic community together in common cause against France. The Garter served as a perpetual chivalric memorial to Edward III's continental ambitions and as a means to harness the chivalric ethic, tying it to his political goals. It established a military elite at the apex of English society, a fraternity bound to the king and each other by ties of loyalty and a shared mission to make good the king's and the nation's claim in France. The Order was also at the heart of a wider project – the redefinition of English kingship; it imbued the monarchy with a new, strongly chivalric character.[41]

Meetings of the Garter Knights on St George's Day (23 April) emphasised the continuing importance of chivalry and the military qualities of the aristocracy. These gatherings, usually at Windsor, often included tournaments as well as religious festivals, both of which were designed to strengthen the bonds between the king and key members of the politico-military elite. Even though the lance and the cavalry charge had proved somewhat ineffectual at Crécy, traditional military skills and those who employed them were still valued and seen to be valued. Valour and skill-at-arms were displayed in the company of fellow members of the elite and presented before the public, who served to ensure the continuing validity of the chivalric order.

The Garter soon gained an international reputation, and as it did so successive monarchs used membership of the Order to further their political ambitions at home and abroad. Consequently, men such as Jean IV, duke of Brittany (d.1399), Duke William I of Guelders (d.1402), Emperor Sigismund (d.1437) and King Juan I of Portugal (d.1433) were granted membership and the places in St George's Chapel, Windsor, which accompanied the honour. In a similar fashion Henry V knighted his captive King James I of Scotland at Windsor on St George's Day in 1421. Although James was not made a knight of the Garter, this was a clear attempt to use chivalry to secure the young king's loyalty.[42] Influenced by this, James adopted a similar policy on his return to Scotland in 1424, as King David II had done some seventy years earlier. Both were encouraged by their time in English captivity to use chivalry as a means of promoting loyalty to the Crown.[43]

Such relationships were not to be entered into lightly. Membership of chivalric orders such as the Garter had serious implications because of the emphasis placed on loyalty to the master of the Order. In certain circumstances, because of conflicting political priorities, membership might be refused. In 1424, despite his alliance with England, Philippe the Good of Burgundy turned down Garter membership for fear it might compromise his political independence. For similar reasons Enguerrand de Coucy, Edward III's son-in-law, surrendered his membership of the Order in August 1377, as did the Aragonese mercenary captain François de Surienne after the sack of Fougères in March 1449.[44]

In France, Jean II imitated Edward III's attempt to meld chivalry with royal policy by establishing the Company of Our Lady of the Noble House, more commonly known as the Company of the Star, in 1350. Spurred by the disaster of Crécy and the defections of noblemen such as Robert d'Artois and Geoffrey de Harcourt, the new king saw the potential of using the chivalric ethic to draw together the military aristocracy in common cause despite the apparent poverty of traditional cavalry tactics. The Company's headquarters were sited just north of Paris at the royal manor of Saint-Ouen-lès-Saint-Denis, later renamed the Noble Maison. This was located between the capital and the Abbey of Saint-Denis, both symbolic sites of French royal power. Jean II spent lavishly expanding the manor's facilities – a great deal of space was required for the 500 knights who he intended would comprise the Company.[45] Improvements centred on the hall and chapel: like the Garter and other orders such as the duke of Burgundy's Golden Fleece (founded in 1430), the Star used religious ceremonies to promote a sense of fraternity. Jean le Bel recorded that the Company of the Star also had clear Arthurian connotations:

> And at least once a year the king would hold a plenary court which all the companions [of the Star] would attend and where each would recount all his adventures – the shameful as well as the glorious – that had befallen him since he had last been at the noble court; and the king would appoint two or three clerks to listen to these adventures and record them all in a book so that they should be reported each year in front of all the companions, so that the most valiant should be known and those honoured who most deserve it.[46]

The Companions of the Star were directed in their conduct by the *Livre de chevalerie*, a guide written by a man still considered a shining exemplar of chivalry despite his shaming at Calais in 1350. Geoffrey de Charny's *Book of Chivalry*, although aspirational and exhortatory, is no Arthurian romance; nor is it an entirely pragmatic military guide such as Vegetius's *De re militari*. Rather, it is something between the two, which reveals the attitudes and priorities of an aristocratic soldier, albeit an exceptional one.[47] The foundation of such orders shows the continuing appeal of chivalry, although there is no doubt that conceptions of the chivalric ethic altered and were twisted in the war.

One reason for changing conceptions can be found in the composition of armies. Peasants had become *bellatores*, which had major implications for the links between chivalry, nobility and deeds of arms. For much of the first three centuries after the millennium a simple correlation existed: chivalry was the code of the nobility and the noble classes were chivalrous. The origins of this association and the caste distinction that lay behind it can be found in the tripartite division of society, the Three Orders, which first emerged in an organised form in the ninth century. According to this construct, those who fought (*bellatores*) were distinguished in their divinely ordained function from those who prayed (*oratores*) and from those who worked (*laboratores*). Within these orders there were various ranks, sometimes ill defined, but a common function bound their members together. When an association developed between military function and noble status, *miles* and *nobilis* became almost interchangeable terms; knights became noble and nobles joined the knightly Order. As the twin poles of the aristocracy – nobles and knights – were brought together by various military, political and social influences, chivalry (the knightly ethic) became ennobling.[48]

In the later Middle Ages this simple correlation became uncertain, major differences within the aristocracy re-emerged, and an exclusive Order of knighthood was divided, defined and increasingly gradated. In England, beneath the nobility, a lesser group developed – the gentry – while at the same time the chivalric ethic began to be applied to the actions of men-at-arms of all sorts. In France, while the *petite noblesse* had always been a group divided from the greater nobility, the gap between the two widened and the distinctiveness of the lesser aristocracy declined. This took place for two main reasons: changes in military strategy, and the socio-economic ramifications of the Black Death. As a consequence of these factors the impact and value of the mounted knight declined on the battlefield, while at home the distinctions – economic, social and political – between the lowest ranks of the (military) aristocracy and the upper echelons of the peasantry became blurred. This, however, was no simple transition.[49]

In France in the early fifteenth century Christine de Pizan maintained that a clear link remained between knights and nobles by writing of 'the rank of knighthood – that is, the worthy nobles who carry arms'. These men should not be merely *milites in armis strenuis* (militarily active knights/ soldiers), they should be men of integrity, experienced in arms, noble in manners and condition, loyal in deed and in courage, and wise in government as well as diligent in chivalrous pursuits.[50] They should be men fit to serve the king and protect and govern his people. During the turmoil of the reign of the mad Charles VI and the ferment of the Armagnac-Burgundian civil war, France was sorely in need of such men. It was, in part, to address this need that Christine also composed a military treatise, *The Book of Deeds of Arms and of Chivalry* for the dauphin. Much of her writing was undertaken in the midst of great political upheaval, and Christine's vision of society as well as her extremely practical military approach were shaped by these conditions.[51] In her work we see a clear realisation that the chivalry of France needed to unite to face the English threat, but also a recognition that tactical changes had to be made in order to defeat it. Acts of stupendous, independent bravery and sacrifice may have been wonderful but they were not (often) effective and (usually) no match for disciplined infantrymen and troops armed and well trained in the use of longbows, crossbows and artillery.

Such a realisation reflected a wider question being posed about the correlation between and respective purposes of knighthood and nobility (*noblesse*). In the late thirteenth century the link between the two certainly did remain strong. The earliest royal ennoblements made by Philippe III and Philippe IV gave commoners permission to become knights. As *lettres d'anoblissement* became more elaborate in the fourteenth century, they reveal significant differences between nobles and non-nobles. A noble might arm himself as a knight if he wished; he would enjoy tax exemptions and a range of judicial and other privileges; in particular he could hold fiefs without the penalties that applied to commoners. As a nobleman he would join the community of the *noblesse*. This final element was of considerable importance – to be noble was, foremost, to be judged noble by other nobles.

This definition was central to a remarkable incident that took place in 1408 in the Dauphiné province of southeastern France. Twenty-one persons, including 2 ecclesiastics, 11 nobles, and 8 commoners, were asked what it was to be noble. The case involved a trial concerning the claim to exemption from tax by an innkeeper on the grounds that he was a noble. The majority decided that to be noble was 'to live from one's revenues and property without doing manual labour, which is to say, not ploughing, reaping, digging, or doing other peasant work'.[52] Sixteen witnesses, with representatives from all groups, asserted this – all the ecclesiastics and commoners and 6 of the 11 nobles. Nobility was therefore, for most, a way of life. Remarkably, of the Dauphiné witnesses, only two believed nobility to be dependent on birth and, equally significantly, only 11 saw it as being tied to a career in arms, including 5 of the 11 nobles. Strangely, nine of the witnesses, two fewer, stated that a noble was supposed to go to war on behalf of his lord. Others suggested a nobleman had a duty to defend the Church, perhaps going on crusade, and 5 of the 21 said a noble should not engage in usury or trade. Another aspect emphasised by some of the deponents was the importance of dining and entertaining in a suitable fashion, as well as being clothed elegantly. In this sense, to be noble was to appear noble, so keeping company with others of similar standing and participating in 'noble' activities such as tournaments were also mentioned. Those who were or who considered themselves noble viewed the 'courtly' virtues of probity, goodness, mildness and good manners as significant.[53] Nobility had to be acknowledged publicly for it to be valid.

The public acknowledgement of nobility might also be achieved through service to the Crown. This might, increasingly, be in administrative or even legal service. It was not easy in this new world of infantry and weapons that killed at a distance to make a chivalric name for oneself on the battlefield. It may have been for this reason that other forms of service, in law and administration, became more acceptable. By serving in these areas members of the aristocracy still contributed to the war effort and the fulfilment of a national cause. The bureaucracy of government and the developing 'State' machine needed the services in the treasury and the courts of those who previously had ridden out to defend their country's borders and mete out justice to her enemies.

As the nature of the military aristocracy changed in this period, nobility and knighthood, once almost synonymous, became disentangled from one another. Both faced financial threats in the post-plague economic world, and also military threats from commoners on foot or wielding long-range weapons. In England the aristocracy became increasingly stratified, leading to the development of a sub-knightly aristocracy, or gentry, who adopted the ranks of esquire and gentleman. One could be chivalrous, one could bear arms (militarily and heraldically), yet not be a knight. Just as knighthood and nobility were no longer synonymous, nor were knighthood and chivalry. In France the distinctions between the lower levels of the *petite noblesse* and the peasantry also became increasingly uncertain, and chivalry started to be spread thinly, as it was extended to a wider social group and as heavy cavalry lost some of its potency on the battlefield.

Chivalry, therefore, did not die in the Hundred Years War; it was not battered into submission like the English in 1453 at Castillon, the concluding battle in the conflict. The war was intrinsically chivalric; it could not be otherwise. It defined and dominated the identities of the chivalrous in England and France. But the conflict placed chivalry under new stresses, and these increased as it drew to a close. The implementation of Charles VII's military *ordonnances* led to the creation of a standing army, and professionalisation cost chivalry some of its purpose. At the heart of the reforms was the royal artillery, coordinated and administered by Jean Bureau, which would destroy the remnants of the Anglo-Gascon army in 1453. But this was not only an infantry and artillery force, and the enduring appeal of cavalry is reflected in the composition of the new national army. Despite the thousand natural shocks the chivalry of France had suffered over the course of the struggle, aristocratic cavalry remained central to French military thinking.[54] Over a decade after the end of the Hundred Years War, Jean de Bueil, who fought at Verneuil in 1424, alongside Joan of Arc in the reconquest of Normandy, and at Castillon, wrote *Le Jouvencel*, a didactic romance for young noblemen. In it he exulted in warfare and the living values of chivalry. 'The most dangerous arms in the world,' he wrote, 'are those of horse and lance, because there is no means of stopping them.'[55] He was, of course, wrong. However, the author was not alone in expressing this opinion; the conclusion of the war saw a flourishing of chivalric literature in England. Such works reveal the enduring appeal and influence of chivalry, albeit a conception reshaped by the Hundred Years War. Alongside the changes in military strategy and tactics, chivalric individuality had been transformed by the war into an ideal of collective service in defence of the nation.[56]

The production of such works may show a touch of nostalgia but also the continuing significance of the chivalric ethic. So, too, somewhat perversely, does the criticism poured on knights and nobles when they were seen to be failing to fulfil their responsibilities. Despite major military developments that compromised the traditional skills of the chivalric elite, individual commentators and the population at large in both England and France expected the aristocracy to defend the nation and its honour through deeds of arms. Unsurprisingly, criticism was most vociferous after a defeat. In England venom dripped from the pen of the monk and chronicler Thomas Walsingham following the military reversals of the last quarter of the fourteenth century. 'It is so awful,' he said, in an entry for 1383:

> The land that once bore and gave birth to men who were respected by all who dwelt nearby and feared by those who lived far off, now spews forth weaklings who are laughed at by our enemies and a subject for gossip among our people. For seldom or never is one of our knights found to be a man who devotes himself to his country, or labours for the good of its citizens.[57]

In a similar fashion the chivalry of France was condemned after Crécy, Agincourt, and Poitiers most especially – for there its members 'abandoned' their king to captivity and dishonour.[58] The consequences were not restricted to literary attacks. The social and political upheaval caused by the defeat at Poitiers in 1356, the disruption caused by soldiers of all sorts and the humiliating failure of the military aristocracy to fulfil their responsibilities to the king and nation resulted in a major revolt – the Jacquerie.

CHAPTER 2

The Peasantry
VOX POPULI
1358

In these days all wars are directed against the poor labouring people and against their goods and chattels.[1]

Honoré Bonet, *The Tree of Battles*

Although it lasted just two weeks, the Jacquerie of 1358 is the best-known uprising in French history before the Revolution of 1789. It was not only the defeat and capture of Jean II at Poitiers in September 1356 that caused his subjects to rebel in such numbers and so violently, but the revolt of the Jacquerie certainly exploded out of the tumult of the Hundred Years War. The failure of the French nobility in battle, the inability of the government to restrain the depredations of the mercenary companies and increasing demands for taxation all played their part in bringing about the rising. So too did the increasing price of grain, which had been a continual concern since the Great Famine (1317–22) had devastated much of Europe. The final straw was the behaviour of the royal troops tasked with blockading Paris and commandeering food and supplies in and around the city. Requisitioning without payment had been declared illegal in a royal ordinance of the previous year, and these sorts of exactions were resented even more than taxation. The revolt was also characterised by a growing sense of class consciousness. Jean de Venette tells us:

In the summer of ... 1358, the peasants living near Saint-Leu-d'Essérent and Clermont in the diocese of Beauvais, seeing the wrongs and oppression inflicted on them on every side and seeing the nobles gave them no protection but rather oppressed them as heavily as the enemy, rose and took up arms against the nobles of France.[2]

If the chronicler was correct, it is not surprising that the peasants rose in anger on 28 May 1358 in the Beauvaisis, Île de France, Picardy, Brie and Champagne. Although primarily a rural phenomenon, the actions of the *Jacques* also galvanised revolts in such cities as Amiens, Caen, Rouen, Montdidier and Meaux. While the peasants' demands were not clearly articulated, the rising was, undoubtedly, a social as well as a political protest. Carefully planned, with elected village leaders, and shaped by anti-clerical as well as anti-aristocratic feeling, it reflected the distrust and disgust of many of the peasantry with the nobility that could not or would not protect them from the miseries of warfare, and, indeed, perpetrated some of its horrors.[3] In this regard the Jacquerie has much in common with the English revolts of 1381 (the Peasants' Revolt) and 1450 (Cade's Rebellion).[4]

Following the success of the Crécy–Calais expeditions, the terrible intervention of the Black Death (1347–50) had prevented the English from taking further action. Campaigning only recommenced in earnest in 1355 when Edward the Black Prince led a raid from Bordeaux to Narbonne and back, devastating a great swathe of southern France. In the following year he marched north into the Valois heartlands. The political and personal affront to the French monarch had to be answered and Jean II needed to put an end to the disruption and destruction that threatened his authority and compromised his tax revenues. On 19 September 1356 he led an army against the Anglo-Gascons in battle outside Poitiers. There, once again, English military tactics triumphed. Ten years before, Philippe VI had been humbled at Crécy, but the political capital of this new victory was far greater for the English since Jean himself was captured.

The dauphin Charles (later Charles V) struggled to maintain even a vestige of control as mercenary companies pillaged the countryside, and the political tide even ran against him in the capital. There, in the Estates General, Etienne Marcel, the provost of Paris, sought to limit the powers of the monarchy and to reform the regency council. When King Jean forbade the resulting Great Ordinance of 1357, Marcel took up arms against the dauphin and allied with Charles 'the Bad' of Navarre, who took the opportunity to exploit the chaos in France to further his own political ambitions. What developed was little short of anarchy, and the breakdown of central authority seemed complete when a peasant revolt known as the Jacquerie (named after Jacques Bonhomme, the supposed leader of the peasant rebels) broke out in May 1358.

The two-week revolt was, by all accounts, appallingly violent. Jean Froissart provides an especially vivid description of the uprising, one that suggests the peasantry had become so brutal they were barely human:

> They [the peasants] said that the nobility of France, knights and squires, were disgracing and betraying the realm . . . They had no leaders [and] pillaged and burned everything and violated and killed all the ladies and girls without mercy like mad dogs. Their barbarous acts were worse than anything that ever took place between Christians and Saracens . . . They killed a knight, put him on a spit, and turned him at the fire before the lady and her children. After about a dozen of them had violated the lady, they tried to force her and the children to eat the knight's flesh before putting them cruelly to death.[5]

Such extreme accounts – and there were others – may well have been distorted for aristocratic and clerical audiences aghast at the implications of social upheaval. This is something common to many if not all of the revolts that wracked Europe in the later fourteenth century. As a consequence, it is difficult to find an authentic 'voice of the people' in these periods of acute social and political tension.[6] The peasants themselves left few written records and almost all the accounts of revolts such as the Jacquerie were written by those virulently opposed to the rebels' objectives. The picture is complicated further because the lot of the peasantry has been used by successive historians as a cipher for the political concerns of their own times. This is particularly the case in France. For Jules Michelet, one of the most celebrated of nineteenth-century French historians, the leaders of the Jacquerie, like Joan of Arc subsequently, embodied the innate character of the French people who would eventually seize political power in the Revolution of 1789 and so give birth to a new nation. Then, in more recent times, a number of the *Annalistes* (members of the Annales School of historians), and others writing during and in the aftermath of the Second World War, described the raiding and occupation of Mother France in the Hundred Years War in terms scarred by and deeply reminiscent of more recent attacks.[7] Descriptions of the peasantry, therefore, during the war and subsequently, tend to be shaped by distinctive agendas. Nonetheless, there is much that can be learned about their experience during the Hundred Years War. The conflict saw this lowliest section of society undergoing enormous change. While, undoubtedly, a horrific time for peasants who were deliberately targeted for attack, the war gave the group a new sense of identity and political awareness, and their position in the hierarchies of both France and England altered radically.

Even if the accounts of Froissart and his fellow chroniclers were exaggerated, there is little doubt that the various peasant revolts that took place during the Hundred Years War were often terrible (and terribly violent) episodes, and it is tempting to imagine the French peasantry as completely brutalised by the experience of such a long conflict. There is no doubt whatsoever that the French peasant and his fellows suffered greatly after 1337. As the target of deliberate English raiding tactics (the *chevauchée* – the English *blitzkrieg*), and subject to ever-higher levels of taxation, the war heaped great privations on a group that had barely recovered from the Great Famine when war began, and its members were soon subjected to the inexplicable terrors and unprecedented mortality of the Black Death (1347–50, 1360–61, with further outbreaks thereafter). Unlike accounts of peasant revolts, a number of authors recorded the impact of these events sympathetically. Writers as diverse as Jean de Venette, Honoré Bonet, Alain Chartier and Jean Gerson also lamented the depredations that troops on both sides inflicted in the Hundred Years War. Christine de Pizan declared furiously:

> The soldiers should not pillage and despoil the country like they do in France nowadays [c.1406] when in other countries they dare not do so. It is a great mischief and perversion of law when those who are intended for the defence of the people, pillage, rob, and so cruelly, that truly short of killing them or setting their houses on fire, their enemies could do no worse.[8]

Their enemies, of course, *could* and did do worse; killing and burning became terrifyingly mundane. Fear, devastation, raiding, looting and perhaps rape had been and remained commonplace weapons of war, despite spiritual and chivalric injunctions and those ordinances successive English kings promulgated to restrain their armies' excesses. Military decrees of this sort were issued throughout the Hundred Years War, beginning in Edward III's reign, and they took on a detailed form in 1385. They aimed, primarily, to safeguard church property and stop acts of sacrilege, but some also afforded at least theoretical protection to certain non-combatants such as clergymen (unless they had weapons), women, children, and sometimes unarmed male labourers. Some attempts were also made to regulate the theft of foodstuffs from the native population and to ban the burning and wasting of an area.[9] In some (rare) circumstances such efforts did reduce levels of brutality – after all it might be considered impolitic to devastate the land and property of those whose loyalty one courted. More often, however, the peasantry suffered, and their suffering was a matter of policy and planning. The Black Prince, Henry V and others among the most celebrated examples of English chivalry made their reputations through just such acts of calculated devastation. The Black Prince, blooded in the devastation of the raid before Crécy, orchestrated the hugely effective and calamitous *grande chevauchée* of 1355. And while Henry V tried to restrict looting from churches – famously, he had an English soldier executed for stealing a pyx (a container for the consecrated host) – he clearly recognised the military value of burning, looting, and the widespread destruction of property.[10]

Given such circumstances it is not surprising that a French peasant might feel aggrieved when his lord, to whom he offered service in return for land, security and justice, could not or would not protect him. The series of revolts that shook Europe in the fourteenth century show the peasantry's growing willingness to take direct action against those they believed to have failed in their duties. In both France and England, on several occasions throughout the war, the wrath of the peasantry was directed against those they believed had failed militarily. The Jacquerie was one such response, while the Peasants' Revolt was directed at those seen as mismanaging the English war effort in 1381; and Cade's Rebellion reflected the disgust of some of the peasantry with the humiliating debacle of the loss of Normandy (1450). Together such revolts indicate the changing complexion, attitudes and expectations of the peasantry shaped by more than a century of near constant warfare.

The impact of the Hundred Years War on the peasantry was direct and often shattering. The consequences of war, however, were far from uniform. Inevitably, the peasantry did not all experience the war alike: its members were so numerous and lived in such diverse circumstances. The French peasantry bore the brunt of the struggle – sieges, burning, raiding, etc. – although those in England who lived on the south coast, the Scottish border and, for a brief time, along the Welsh Marches also suffered. The peasantry's experience of war also varied as the struggle unfolded: military pressures increased in some areas and waned in others, differing widely between regions and nations.

Peasants comprised the vast majority of the populations of France and England – about 90 per cent in both cases. Accurate population figures are in short supply and difficult to interpret when available; however, it appears that on the eve of the Black Death, France was home to about 16–20 million people spread among some forty thousand rural communities. This is a particularly high total considering that the number had only returned to a comparable level by the early nineteenth century (26.5 million souls lived in rural France in 1846), and it was more than three times the total population of England and Wales in about 1347 (approximately 4 million people).[11]

Within France, the experience of war was determined chiefly by one's location. Geographically and topographically the country divided into four main zones. The first and most populous of these (containing approximately 30 per cent of the population) lay in northern France, between the River Loire and Flanders (south to north), and upper Normandy and Burgundy (west to east). It was open country (the *Plat Pays*), dominated economically by Paris and agriculturally by wheat production with some viticulture. The second zone, in the west, consisted of lower Normandy, Brittany, Anjou and Maine – accounting for about 25 per cent of the population. This was hillier country, less fertile and dotted with isolated hamlets and small villages. Mediterranean France (Languedoc, Provence and Gascony) formed the third zone, which was nearly as heavily populated as the Parisian Basin. The climate with its hot, dry summers meant grapes, olives and fruit could be grown, but little wheat. The fourth zone consisted of large areas ill-suited to permanent cultivation and occupation, including mountainous regions such as the Pyrenees and the Alps, but which could be used, in some parts, for pasture or forestry. These regions were populated only temporarily and subject to regular cycles of migration.[12]

France did not only have clear regional distinctions, it was also a country of astonishing social, cultural and political diversity. Indeed, the striking lack of uniformity in later medieval France determined Valois policy. The French monarchy fought the Hundred Years War, in part, to enforce a greater measure of consistency, governmental and cultural, over its disparate territories. Internal divisions as well as English territorial interests led to inherent tensions and conflicting loyalties. Cultural diversity was particularly apparent with regard to language: there were wide variations in regional dialects and also a broad distinction between the *langue d'oc*, spoken in the south, and the northern *langue d'oïl*.[13] Legal traditions also varied widely throughout the country, as did seigneurial rights and demands. Rents differed considerably, as did the conditions by which land was held and leased. These conditions shifted over the period of the war, as did the status of the peasants themselves, many of whom gradually freed themselves from traditional manorial restrictions.

In England there were similar disparities: the country was divided between urban and rural areas, and upland and lowland zones. Upland zones, typically, were characterised by rough pasture and woodland with dispersed and isolated settlements. Lowland England was home to nucleated villages surrounded by open fields. There was also considerable disparity between the people who lived and farmed in late medieval England: unfree villein tenants who owed labour services to their lord of two to four days a week worked alongside hired freemen. In the late thirteenth century unfree villeins constituted about three-fifths of the rural population. At that time, as in France, when the population was at its height the most important distinction was not between free and unfree but simply between those who had sufficient land for subsistence and those who did not. In England serfdom became increasingly rare after the Black Death. Endemic plague encouraged its decline, although relations between lords and peasants remained strained. For much of the period of the Hundred Years War both sides were locked in a cold and not-so-cold war over working conditions and tenurial obligations.[14]

In France, serfdom also remained predominantly a rural phenomenon characterised by the requirement to perform various labour services for a lord who exercised a high degree of social and legal authority over his peasants. He could, for example, control his serfs' marriages, and he had the right to dispose of their property as he saw fit if no heir existed. To be a serf in France also meant that one bore a heavy burden of taxation. However, by the time the Hundred Years War began serfdom had already disappeared from many parts of the country. Increasingly lords sold charters of freedom to their serfs in an effort to deal with changing economic conditions and maintain their own diminishing incomes.[15]

The Black Death encouraged this process: alongside the Hundred Years War, plague caused something of a social and economic revolution that bettered the lot of many of those peasants who survived it. The structure, economic prospects and social status of the peasantry were reshaped, improving conditions over the long term, broadly speaking. In addition, a much keener political awareness developed among the group, brought about by a closer engagement with national issues of which war was the most important. Such developments meant that those who survived war and plague usually found themselves in a somewhat easier situation than their predecessors. During the war, however, there were more immediate priorities – military depredations, the breakdown of law and order, the depopulation of towns and villages, the desecration and desertion of religious communities. The descriptions of such events fill the pages of French and English chronicles. Jean de Venette felt deeply for the plight of the peasantry and was clearly appalled by the horrific impact of the war. In 1358 he described conditions in the following terms:

> Losses and injuries were inflicted by friend and foe alike upon the rural population and upon monasteries standing in the open country. Everyone robbed them of their goods and there was no one to defend them. For this reason many men and women, both secular and religious were compelled on all sides to leave their abode and seek out the city . . . there was not a monastery in the neighbourhood of Paris, however near, that was not driven by fear of freebooters to enter the city or some other fortification, abandoning their buildings and, 'Woe is me!' leaving the divine offices unsung. This tribulation increased in volume, not only around Paris but also in the neighbourhood of Orléans, Tours, Nantes in Brittany, Chartres, and Le Mans, in an amazing way. Villages were burned and their population plundered. Men hastened to the cities with their carts and their goods, their wives and their children, in lamentable fashion.[16]

This litany of devastation was not mere hyperbole on the author's part. Petrarch, Honoré Bonet, Thomas Basin and many others wrote sometimes in anger, sometimes in despair, about the terrible effects of the war. Letters of remission and taxation accounts provide stark evidence of a country ravaged by English *chevauchées*, mercenary attacks and destroyed by a predatory aristocracy. But the impact of the war was far from uniform. While *chevauchées* could be very wide-ranging, other forms of military action tended to be regional and restricted. Some parts of France suffered repeated assault, others were attacked only rarely, and there might be considerable variation within a small area. Consequently, while the impact of war was felt keenly, for example in the plains of northern and northwestern France and in the Agenais and Quercy, Béarn in the Pyrenees and Alsace in the east were virtually unharmed.[17] Nonetheless, because of the political complexity of the period, which saw disputes not only between France and England, but also between the houses of Valois, Navarre and Brittany, Armagnac and Foix, Orléans and Burgundy, few areas were completely untouched and the results were often horrendous. About eight years after the war ended, Thomas Basin noted:

From the Loire to the Seine, and from there to the River Somme, nearly all the fields were left for a long time, for many years, not merely untended but without people to cultivate them, except for rare patches of land, because the peasants had been killed or fled.[18]

Such comprehensive destruction threatened not only the peasantry directly but the institutional support systems that Church and State traditionally provided and on which the people relied. At times almsgiving, trade, and the economy almost completely collapsed and they were often severely compromised. Refugees became a common sight, seeking protection in towns and cities; others took to brigandage, preying on their neighbours as they themselves had been preyed upon.[19] This social and economic dislocation was a chief aim of English military policy in the years leading to the Jacquerie. A succession of English *chevauchées* during Edward III's reign was designed to undermine the legitimacy of the Valois monarchy by proving Philippe VI and Jean II could not protect their people, while at the same time preventing them from doing so by reducing their ability to raise troops and taxes.

As this suggests, the peasantry played a direct role in sustaining the war effort, which was another reason its members were targeted specifically. Because of the connection between taxation (paid chiefly by the peasantry in France) and military defence, the status of 'non-combatants' became very uncertain. By attacking taxpayers the English attacked French military resources. In the same way attacks on the French clergy struck at the spiritual and sometimes material support they provided for the war effort. Furthermore, as the war became a consciously 'national' struggle there were fewer reasons why non-combatants should be immune from its effects.[20]

This policy and its brutally sophisticated implementation are clear from a letter written in 1355 by Sir John Wingfield, who held the office of 'governor of the prince's business' – he was responsible for the finances of Edward the Black Prince:

It seems certain that since the war against the French king began, there has never been such destruction in a region as in this raid. For the countryside and towns which have been destroyed . . . produced more revenue for the king of France in aid of his war than half his kingdom . . . as I could prove from authentic documents found in various towns in the tax-collectors' houses.[21]

Wingfield wrote in the aftermath of the so-called *grande chevauchée*. In the course of a single raid, an army of around 6,000 soldiers destroyed 500 settlements of various sorts – villages, castles, towns, hamlets – and devastated up to 18,000 square kilometres of territory.[22] The Black Prince was not content, however, merely to witness the destruction; he wished to assess the extent of the financial damage precisely, and so he brought officials such as Wingfield with him to calculate the exact cost to the French Treasury.

The psychological cost of this sort of raiding, the fear and insecurity it surely engendered, is (and was) more difficult to measure. In France as the war drew on, the ringing of church bells might as easily mean an impending attack as a call to prayer. The conflict affected daily lives and working practices almost constantly in some areas. According to Thomas Basin, during the 1430s, when the mercenaries known as *écorcheurs* (literally skinners or flayers) were at their most pernicious, farm labourers had to work in an area within earshot of a trumpeter placed on a lookout point so they could run to safety if necessary.[23] Such a measure was one of many responses to a potential assault. When soldiers of whatever sort approached a settlement, some communities would flee almost in their entirety. They might seek refuge in woods or caves, perhaps where a site had been prepared. These might just involve makeshift huts and were only a short-term solution. Others were much more substantial dwellings. Some were subterranean, some extended into quarries; others were tunnelled beneath villages. Many of these were constructed in the chaotic period after the battle of Poitiers in 1356. Some were extremely extensive and highly defensible. The typical *souterrains-refuge* consisted of a long central corridor, approximately two and a half metres high and wide with chambers radiating from it. The refuge beneath the village of Naours (Somme) was remarkable and consisted of 2,000 metres of corridor with 300 chambers and six ventilation shafts running to the surface.[24] Alternatively one might flee to a royal or seigneurial castle, perhaps bringing along goods and livestock. This, however, was rarely a viable option for an extended period of time as refugees placed great pressure on space and supplies. Such actions also meant abandoning one's crops, which could prove fatal in the longer term or when winter arrived.

In order to stay close to home many communities fortified their villages: some built walls, others used a monastery, mill or, most commonly, the parish church as a centre of defence. A church offered various advantages as a defensive structure. It was, typically, a stout building, and it benefited from protection by canon law: to attack it was an act of sacrilege, although this rarely served as an effective deterrent. A church might also have a bell-tower, which allowed the villagers to keep a look-out and warn of approaching soldiers. Sometimes churches were fortified with a lord's assistance, sometimes villagers acted independently.

The situation at Vitry is representative of many communities. In August 1354 the town's parishioners petitioned the captain-general of Auxerre for the right to fortify their church. They had, they said, been reduced to 'wretched poverty by the wars of the king of England and by the enemies who daily come and go through [their] village robbing, injuring and laying waste'.[25] They had also been forced to pay *patis* (protection money) to one William Starkey, the captain of Ligny-le-Châtel, and they had been plundered by French garrisons, including those from Auxerre. When granted permission they fortified the church with four towers, a curtain-wall and two moats, which allowed them to beat off a mercenary attack in 1369.

This sort of community action did, however, acquire dangerous connotations after the revolt of the Jacquerie in 1358, and it might be opposed, for other reasons, by ecclesiastical authorities, the local aristocracy and the French Crown, which sought to maintain a monopoly on the right to construct fortresses. Objections were raised about the 'profane' role churches were required to play as well as to the diversion of manpower from the protection of seigneurial castles. Few fortifications were demolished, however, even though fines were often demanded when they had been constructed without licence.[26]

In some cases the peasantry were given an alternative to flight or assault. Communities might choose, if given the opportunity, to pay *patis* to mercenary forces or regular troops (French, English and Armagnac and Burgundian during the civil war). This, in theory, allowed daily life and farming to continue without too much disruption. During the Agincourt campaign, Henry V demanded ransoms from small villages as he rode from Harfleur to what proved to be the battlefield: if payment was not forthcoming they were 'to be set on fire and utterly destroyed'.[27] The scale of *appatisation* in France was very considerable at certain times, especially in those areas, often near political frontiers, where villages and communities could be paying *patis* to several different 'protectors' simultaneously. In Brittany in the 1340s and 1350s it has been estimated that revenue from *patis* paid 85 per cent of the costs of the principal English garrisons.[28] Even large communities were not safe. The city of Reims was compelled to pay 300 *livres tournois* to a mercenary company in 1437, 'so as to be spared the pillaging and robbery which [Captain Guillaume de Flavy and] his men from Nesles might have carried out upon this city and the surrounding countryside during the months of July, August and September 1437'.[29]

Those who did not or could not find shelter or buy off their assailants were particularly vulnerable to attack and their plight was recounted in various works. The *pastourelle*, for example, was a literary form often used in this period to rail against war by showing its terrible impact on rural people. Some of these, known as *bergerie*, focus specifically on shepherds and shepherdesses often because of their biblical and classical connotations. One such work, the *Pastoralet*, written soon after 1422 by an author known only as Bucarius, describes the devastation inflicted during the Armagnac-Burgundian civil war. In this allegorical and rabidly anti-Burgundian work, France, which should have been a bucolic paradise, becomes, instead, reminiscent of Hell – shepherdesses are raped, the countryside is desecrated and shepherds are slaughtered. 'There in the dung, without a bed, were the dead sleeping, one on top of the other, in piles . . . Many noble shepherdesses were left alone without their lovers . . . So many heads cut off, so many feet, fists, so many arms without hands. I think there never was so much shedding of human blood nor a slaughter more cruel.'[30]

When English strategy changed in the fifteenth century and raiding was replaced, in part at least, by a programme of direct conquest, the French people had to face different challenges. Sieges, of course, had been far from unknown in earlier stages of the war; in many ways they serve as a leitmotif of the struggle: Calais (1346–7), Reims (1359) and Limoges (1370) were particularly noteworthy for political reasons. The Black Prince's siege (sack) of Limoges has also become, in some circles, a byword for violence disproportionate even by the lax standards of the fourteenth century. The event took place after the resumption of the war in 1369 when the city renounced its allegiance to England and Edward III. His response is said to have been excessively brutal, although such a conclusion depends, almost exclusively, on Froissart's account of the event. He wrote that after mining the town walls the Prince's Anglo-Gascon army entered the city

> in a mood to wreak havoc and do murder, killing indiscriminately, for those were their orders. There were pitiful scenes. Men, women and children flung themselves on their knees before the Prince, crying: 'Have mercy on us gentle sir!' But he was so inflamed with anger [at their 'treachery'] that he would not listen. Neither man nor woman was heeded, but all who could be found were put to the sword.[31]

Froissart suggested that three thousand were killed in the ensuing massacre, but the lack of comment from local chroniclers implies the sack was not unusually savage.[32]

Whatever really took place at Limoges, the increasing frequency of sieges, brought about by changes in military strategy and advances in gunpowder artillery, had terrible implications for non-combatants, both those in a besieged town and those who lived in its vicinity. During a siege the line differentiating combatants from non-combatants became even more blurred than usual. If one assisted by dowsing fires, or bringing food, water or supplies to the garrison, and so helped to defend a town, was one really a non-combatant? Furthermore, the 'laws of war', based in part on biblical authorities, decreed that if a town or city resisted attack but eventually fell to a besieging army, then the defenders had no rights to mercy.[33] Deuteronomy 20:10–154 was unequivocal in its instructions to military commanders:

When you march up to attack a city, make its people an offer of peace. If they accept and open their gates, all the people in it shall be subject to forced labour and shall work for you. If they refuse to make peace and they engage you in battle, lay siege to that city. When the Lord your God delivers it into your hand, put to the sword all the men in it. As for the women, the children, the livestock and everything else in the city, you may take these as plunder for yourselves.

Given this, when Harfleur was captured in September 1415 after a month's siege, Henry V could be said to have acted with considerable restraint. As at Caen later, he merely expelled the inhabitants. Because he claimed to be king of France he could not treat the French people as if they were his enemy; however, from his perspective, in resisting their true lord the people of Harfleur were rebels who had to be punished with the confiscation of property and expulsion from the city.[34] As one would expect, English accounts of the event focus on the king's mercy:

The king of England entered Harfleur on 21 September [1415] and emptied it of all women, children and priests of the town, and had each of them given 10 sous parisis, and had it cried by sound of the trumpet that at the king's command no one should do anything to women or to the others under pain of death. But as soon as the women were some way from the town the French pillaged them and violated them to a great degree.[35]

French accounts, by contrast, dwell on the humanitarian tragedy:

> Also driven out of the town were a large number of women with their
> children. They were left with only five sous and some of their clothing.
> It was such a piteous thing to see the sorrow and lamentations ... All
> the priests and men of the church were also dismissed.[36]

If the situation at Harfleur was piteous, then what unfolded at Rouen
during the siege of 1418–19 was horrific and a clear demonstration of the
vile possibilities of siege warfare. By the time King Henry reached the city it
was filled with refugees who had fled before the advancing English army.
Many of these then tried to escape when it became clear the city would be
besieged. Henry, however, sealed Rouen completely. Partly to keep people in
and partly to protect his army from attack the king had a bank, ditch and
other defences constructed. He barricaded the River Seine to prevent supplies
reaching the city while using it himself to bring in provisions and reinforcements. Within Rouen the blockade soon began to bite: food became scarce,
many died, disease spread. Then, as supplies became ever more limited, the
town's authorities took the painful decision to expel the old, infirm and others
who could not contribute to the defence. They were driven out of the city,
into the no-man's-land between the walls and the English defences. Henry
would not let them pass, the townsfolk would not let them return. The events
were described in verse by an English soldier, John Page:

> Thenn with yn a lytylle space,
> The poore pepylle of that place,
> At every gate they were put oute
> Many a hundryd in a route;
> That hyt was pytte hem to see
> Wemme[n] come knelyng on hyr kne,
> With hyr chyldryn in hyr armys,
> To socoure them from harmys;
> Olde men knelynge them by
> And made a dolfulle cry.
> And alle they sayden at onys thenne,
> 'Have marcy uppon us, ye Englysche men.'

The people of Rouen could not feed them; nor would the English. Most
starved, slowly.

As the siege entered the new year, conditions within Rouen deteriorated still further. Prices had long been exorbitant; now there was hardly anything left to buy and the people were forced to eat vermin. Page reported: 'They ate up dogs, they ate up cats, they ate up mice, horses and rats.' A cat cost two nobles, a mouse sixpence, a rat 30 pennies. There was talk of cannibalism:

They etete doggys, they ete cattys;
They ete mysse, horse and rattys.
For an hors quarter, lenc or fatte,
At C s. hyt was atte.
A horsse hedde for halfe a pound;
A dogge for [th]e same mony round;
For xxxd. went a ratte.
For ij noblys went a catte.
For vj d. went a mous.

Henry V offered the people of Rouen a stark choice – death or surrender. When it became clear that they could expect no help from outside, the citizens of the town chose to live; they agreed to pay a fine of £50,000 and handed over 80 hostages. Henry entered the Norman capital on 19 January 1419; when the news reached England there was singing and dancing in the streets of London.[37]

The atrocities of war were, therefore, brought home to urban and rural communities in France with horrible regularity. The English peasantry was subjected to far less frequent assault, but even so, attacks, real or merely threatened, sometimes engendered almost palpable tension. In 1336, before the war even began formally, a naval raid on the Isle of Wight raised fears of invasion and led to the widespread implementation of defensive measures. Coastal attacks by French vessels then began in earnest: in March 1338 Portsmouth was plundered and burned – only the parish church remained standing; the Channel Islands were raided in the same year; then in October, French, Genoese and Castilian galleys attacked Southampton in a raid that destroyed between 40 and 50 per cent of the town's buildings. French and French-allied assaults on English coastal towns continued throughout much of the fourteenth century: in 1340 the Isle of Wight and the Dorset coast came under attack; Portsmouth was raided once more in 1342, and again in 1351 and 1370; in 1360 the French turned on Winchelsea; and in 1377 they besieged Carisbrooke Castle on the Isle of Wight. Then in 1385–86 terror gripped the country as the French admiral Jean de Vienne mustered an invasion force: 'rumours spread . . . greatly alarming the inhabitants . . . All over the country . . . religious processions were instituted . . . and observed in a spirit of deep devotion and contrition. Prayers were offered to God to deliver them from this peril.'[38] It appeared that 'there was no hope of safety, all began to be afraid, not only the common people but also the knights themselves who had been brave, trained soldiers full of spirit but were now timid, womanly and spiritless. And they began to talk not about resistance and fighting but about escape and surrender.'[39]

As it proved, on this occasion the main threat to the peasantry came not from the French but from their own soldiers. Troops, mustered to protect against the invasion, plundered the countryside when their pay ran out. Henry Knighton recounted an event in Leicestershire when a farmer beat a soldier who had tried to steal one of his horses. The soldier returned, Knighton said, with 140 of his companions – Cheshire archers – who intended to kill the farmer and burn the village. The inhabitants were forced to pay them £10 to make them leave. It was, essentially, a demand for *patis* made by English soldiers, exploiting the English peasantry.[40]

The Hundred Years War was, therefore, generally a dreadful time for the peasantry, however, the period also witnessed a transformation in the legal and social status of peasants that was far from negative. War was not the only factor that brought about this change: natural disasters – climatic, agricultural and biological – contributed to and compounded earlier and ongoing developments in social, tenurial, political and seigneurial structures. Somewhat perversely, misery was the catalyst for an improvement in the peasantry's way of life. A series of agricultural crises in the early years of the fourteenth century, which led to the Great Famine, accelerated the process. Climatic pressures returned in England in the 1330s and 1340s when flooding seems to have been a constant problem, and a hugely destructive tidal surge of the Wash took place in 1338. Marginal land was abandoned, and cereal production declined significantly, although the reduction in population size meant the price of many agricultural products fell. After 1337 endemic warfare added new burdens in the form of assault and taxation. Agricultural decline and the limited success of Edward III's first campaign meant that tax collectors in 1340–41 faced a deluge of complaints.[41] Then, in an event that seemed to foreshadow the Apocalypse, the Black Death struck, first in 1347–50 and again at irregular intervals, albeit less virulently for the rest of the century and beyond.

It is likely that the populations of England and France fell by about 50 per cent in the years between 1300 and 1400. However, the consequences of this series of natural and man-made disasters were not entirely negative. Depopulation meant that the coercive powers of landlords diminished, villeinage declined further and the demand for labour services reduced. As traditional seigneurial powers decayed, wage rates escalated and prices fell. Landlords undertook less direct management of their land and rented out larger areas to the peasantry.[42] This led to a redistribution of wealth and what was for some an uncomfortable blurring of social boundaries. In 1422 Alain Chartier blustered, but with real concern, that the wealth of the common people

is as a cistern which hath gathered and still gathers the waters of all the riches of this realm [France], for the coffers of the nobles and of the clergy are greatly diminished through the continuing of the war ... [Daily] they [the peasantry] heap up riches and now they have in their possession our chattels and goods. And yet they cry against us and blame us that we do not fight at any time, they would not fear to put into hazard without reason and order all the nobility of the realm. For they would have noble blood given up cheaply, and when all is lost, then will they weep later.[43]

Similarly, towards the end of the war, in 1445, Jean Juvénal des Ursins (1388–1473) wrote: 'No one is poor nowadays except the clergy and the gentlemen.'[44] This, of course, was a great exaggeration, but those who survived famine, plague and war did gain something: their scarcity in a new world made them valuable. Legislation introduced in England in an almost immediate response to the Black Death is indicative of the ruling class's fear of the implications of the great mortality. The Ordinance (1349) and statute (1351) of Labourers were desperate attempts to buttress the socio-economic status quo, because as early as 1348 peasants were leaving their manors and offering their services to the highest bidder. The 1351 statute was designed to prevent this wilful disruption of the proper order and what the Crown described as the 'malice of servants'.[45] However, at the same time as the 'life chances' of these malicious peasants were being restricted, they were also being called upon to support king and country perhaps in battle and certainly with taxation. As the targets of propaganda they became, in a sense, investors in national policy and, as a result, increasingly 'politicised'.

Consequently, as the war evolved so too did the political awareness of the English peasantry. Peasants became acutely aware of the government's political failings, especially its failures in the war, and they demanded redress for these. Similarly in France, the failure of the nobility in battle caused outrage and there was considerable opposition to demands for taxation. This continued even when the political tide had clearly turned in the Valois' favour: the obligation to provide money, let alone food and lodging, for soldiers, caused a great deal of resentment and often violence. Resistance was particularly virulent in the 1440s to the taxes demanded to support Charles VII's *compagnies d'ordonnance*.[46]

The combination of growing political awareness, dissatisfaction with the limitations placed on social mobility, governmental and aristocratic corruption (or perceived corruption), and, in particular, the growing tax burden, often led to violence and in some notable cases to outright revolt. In both France and England the economic pressures brought by military action, especially when it was unsuccessful, were deeply unpopular. The requisitioning of goods was particularly loathed. In England purveyance, particularly for the royal household, had long been a cause of disaffection and it grew to new heights when the Hundred Years War began. Although peasants could expect to be compensated for their goods, payment was rarely swift and it tended to be set at an arbitrarily low level.[47]

As in France, the Hundred Years War caused the most significant and dangerous peasant revolt of the Middle Ages in England. When the treaty of Brétigny (1360) failed and the war reopened in 1369, the English position collapsed and a series of poll taxes was demanded to raise the revenue needed to defend Gascony and the English coast. The combination of military humiliation, factionalism at court, socio-economic disruption – a legacy of endemic plague – the fear of Franco-Castilian raiding and the political vacuum created by Richard II's minority formed a lethal cocktail. The poll tax demands were deeply provocative but also entirely understandable. Population movement and decline after 1348 meant that few communities could pay the traditional lay subsidy that had last been assessed in 1334. Consequently, in an attempt to raise money the chancellor, Lord Scrope instigated the first poll tax in 1377. Initially this was charged on everyone over the age of 14 at a rate of 4d. Then, in 1379, the age was raised to 16 and the tax applied on a sliding scale. The tax levied in 1380 (but collected in 1381) demanded 12d. from everyone over 15, but within each village the rich were encouraged to help the poor. The tax is a clear indication that the labour legislation had failed to control wage rises and that it was felt that everyone should contribute to the national war effort: the tax was bitterly resented, especially by those who had to pay for the first time.[48]

In addition to the (perceived) iniquity of the poll taxes, the collectors were less than gentle in carrying out their duties. The peasants' response was a remarkably well coordinated campaign centred on the counties of Kent and Essex. The rebels marched on London in June 1381, many fewer than the sixty thousand the *Anonimalle* chronicler suggested but still in very considerable numbers. The citizens of the capital who shared their griev- ances opened the city gates, and for a few days in 1381 it appeared that the rebels would take control of the city and the government. The revolt is an indication not only of the increasing politicisation of the peasantry and their hatred of certain socio-economic burdens, but also of their greater aware- ness of whom to blame for those burdens and for the military and political failures that had engendered them. The propaganda machine of the English state had, in some ways, done its job too well. From the beginning of the war, the English Crown had stressed the threat to the nation's political and eccle- siastical hierarchy: in 1381 that threat was genuine and it came from within the nation. The rebels' demands, articulated by their leader, Wat Tyler, were truly revolutionary: there were, as one would expect, demands concerning wages, rents and land ownership, but much more remarkable was a call for the disendowment of the Church – all ecclesiastical property was to be handed over to the people; there was to be an end to serfdom; and, most extraordinarily, an end to all lordship save that of the king.[49]

The revolt failed, mainly because of the actions of the young Richard II who defused the potentially disastrous tension in a series of famous meet- ings with the rebels, and then reneged on his agreements with them. But the rebels did execute, gruesomely, a number of eminent figures, including Simon Sudbury, the archbishop of Canterbury. John of Gaunt's palace, the Savoy, was burned. The rebels also broke into the Tower of London and, according to Thomas Walsingham, into the bedchamber of the king's mother, Joan of Kent. There they were said to have jumped up and down on her bed and waved what the chronicler coyly described as 'their filthy sticks' at her. Although a minor incident, it shows the complete breakdown of central authority and of the barriers between social classes.[50]

There were similarly egalitarian impulses behind various revolts in France that followed the Jacquerie. The Tuchinerie, a revolt that began in the late 1360s in the upper Auvergne, spread throughout the Midi in the early 1380s. (The term derived from *tue-chiens* or 'killers of dogs', the revolt being comprised of men brought so low they would kill and eat dogs.) In this instance 'class' hatred combined with political instability, brigandage, military oppression from garrisons and, again, increasing taxation. Groups of peasants, soldiers and townsmen sought to exploit the situation to their best advantage, until they were crushed by forces under the command of Jean 'the Magnificent', duke of Berry, in 1384.[51]

The political awareness of the peasantry is also evident in the Cabochien revolt, which began in Paris on 28 April 1413. Named after one of the leaders, Simon Caboche, it started with a mass demonstration outside the Bastille and the capture and imprisonment of several leading government figures. Although primarily a rising of the urban peasantry, it was also gently encouraged by Jean the Fearless of Burgundy as part of his campaign to capture the capital from the Armagnac faction during the civil war. In Normandy the peasantry took similar action in 1434–36 when the English regime faced an outbreak of popular brigandage. And even when the fortunes of war had clearly shifted in Charles VII's favour, revolt remained a possibility. The Lyons *Rebeyne* of 1436 was caused, like so many similar events, by taxation and what was seen as government corruption and heavy-handedness. Lyons had suffered considerably in recent years, having experienced rationing, food scarcity, unemployment and a sharp rise in the cost of living. The Peace of Arras (21 September 1435) had resulted in renewed mercenary activity (roaming bands of *écorcheurs*) and an increasing tax burden, both *taille* and *aides* – the latter was levied on commodities and so affected everyone.[52]

The final English revolt of the war broke out in May 1450. Cade's Rebellion took the form of a protest against Henry VI's government, unfair taxes and national and local corruption which, the rebels said, had led to territorial losses in France. Since the summer of 1449 the French had retaken English-held lands in northern France with humiliating ease, and by the end of 1450 all Normandy had capitulated.[53] The rebellion initially took the form of a mass petition in June called the 'Proclamation of Jack Cade' or 'The Complaint of the Poor Commons of Kent'. It declared:

We believe the king our sovereign lord, by the insatiable, covetous, malicious persons that daily and nightly are about his highness, and daily inform him that good is evil and evil is good. They say that at his pleasure our sovereign is above his laws, and he may make them or break them as he pleases ... The contrary is true ... The king's false council has lost his law, his merchandise is lost, his common people are destroyed, *the sea is lost, France is lost* [my emphasis], the king himself is so placed that he may not pay for his meat and drink, and he owes more than ever any King of England ought . . . We desire that all extortions be laid low; [the Statute of Labourers, be outlawed as well as the] taking of wheat and other grains, beef, mutton and other victuals, which is an intolerable burden on the commons . . .[54]

The rebels were mostly peasants but their numbers were swelled by members of the lesser gentry, yeomen and husbandmen, and hundreds if not thousands of defeated and disillusioned soldiers recently returned from France. These were men who felt they had lost their livelihoods and property because of corruption or who feared the possibility of a French attack.[55]

There was widespread violence in Kent, and demands for the arrest of certain 'public traitors'. Henry VI complied – James Fiennes, Lord Saye (c.1390–1450), who had recently been appointed Lord Treasurer, was placed in the Tower of London. In early July, Cade crossed London Bridge and in a desperate attempt at appeasement the king had Saye and another hated figure, William Crowmer, sheriff of Kent, executed. Negotiations between the rebels and a delegation of churchmen, the archbishops of Canterbury (John Stafford) and York (John Kempe), and William Waynflete, bishop of Winchester, took place in St Margaret's Church, Southwark. They were presented with the rebels' petitions and offered free royal charters of pardon in return. As in 1381 this proved sufficient to mollify the rebels. A week after the forces disbanded, however, Cade learned that the government still regarded him as a traitor and had issued a reward for him dead or alive. Soon after he was mortally wounded in a skirmish near Heathfield, East Sussex (12 July 1450); his body was taken to London and quartered to be displayed in different cities, his preserved head set up on a pike on London Bridge (along with those of the other leaders of the rebellion).

Cade's Rebellion is a further indication of the increasing politicisation of the peasantry which the Hundred Years War brought about. The peasant rebel became an icon of late medieval life, reviled by some, adored by others. It is no coincidence that this period saw the first written evidence of the Robin Hood legend. Robin emerged over the course of the Hundred Years War 'not only as a new sort of hero but as a hero for a new and large social group, the yeomanry of England'.[56] Robin, the yeoman forester, reflected one aspect of a new social order that arose out of the confusion of war and plague; he stood on the border between the common folk and the gentry.

The changing balance of economic power had narrowed the boundaries between classes, especially between the upper echelons of the peasantry and the lowest ranks of the aristocracy.[57] This period of extraordinary social unrest is reflected in the fact that the years between 1350 and 1500 were the only time before the modern era in English culture that a commoner, not a nobleman, was a major literary hero.[58] Robin rejected the traditional hierarchy; he stood outside the law and so represented the aspirations of many of the 1381 and 1450 rebels. And, of course, he was armed with a longbow, the weapon that was overturning military hierarchies on the battlefield.

Cade's Rebellion also reflected the fragility of English power in France as well as the extent to which the nation as a whole had become invested in the Hundred Years War. Nearly a century earlier, the revolt of the Jacquerie had revealed similar forces at work across the Channel. That uprising had marked a particularly low point in Valois fortunes, one on which Edward III sought to capitalise, but his campaign of 1359–60 failed in its objective to capture Reims, the French coronation city. Instead, he brokered a truce at Brétigny that held, in some form, until 1369. But conditions changed in the intervening years. Charles V acceded to the French throne and proved to be an immensely shrewd leader. When hostilities resumed, he swiftly oversaw the reconquest of the lands surrendered in 1360. Pressure began to mount on English Gascony and raiding resumed on the south coast of England, building towards a proposed invasion in 1385. But the deaths of Charles the Wise and his constable, Bertrand du Guesclin, in 1380 slowed then stalled the French advance. A change of policy followed and the pressure declined. By this time, however, the Hundred Years War was being fought on yet another battleground.

CHAPTER 3

The Church and the Clergy
VOICES FROM THE PULPIT
1378

On 26 March [1378] came the death of Pope Gregory [XI]. He was a particularly good and just man, who had been greatly troubled by the losses suffered by the kingdoms of both England and France and had worked hard to bring about peace between them . . . He was succeeded by Bartholomew, archbishop of Bari, who suffered many tribulations.[1]

Thomas Walsingham, *Chronica Maiora*

In his description of the pontificate of Urban VI (the former archbishop of Bari), Thomas Walsingham was, for once, rather restrained. The 'tribulations' he described were to do with nothing less than the Great Schism (1378–1417), a disastrous rift that divided the Western Church, caused by a struggle for the papal throne. With one claimant resident in Rome and his rival at Avignon the secular European powers – France and England chief among them – sought to gain advantage in their own conflicts by securing the papacy for their respective candidates. Consequently, like the Hundred Years War with which it became linked, the Schism polarised Western Christendom and, because of it, churches throughout Europe became bound increasingly tightly to their respective nations and to issues of national politics. War and the Schism acted together to place great pressure on the institutional fabric of the Church and on relations within Christendom. Churchmen found themselves in an invidious position, torn between the demands of the 'universal' Church and those of their royal masters.

Churchmen had, of course, always been closely involved in national and local government, but during the Hundred Years War members of the monastic and secular clergy played increasingly important roles in diplomacy, tax collection, military planning, local defence and the distribution of information. This growing involvement had a considerable impact on those men and women, on ecclesiastical institutions and on attitudes towards the Church, much of it negative. The reputation of many of the clergy suffered and its members faced escalating criticism of their involvement in and failure to heal both the Schism and the Anglo-French conflict. Consequently, the Hundred Years War and the ecclesiastical disruption that accompanied it increased scrutiny of the Church and its members, and some were found wanting; others, however, saw their reputations enhanced. Communities still looked to their parish priest for guidance – spiritual and temporal; people continued to go on pilgrimage, and the fifteenth century saw a huge resurgence in church-building. So, whereas some monastic and mendicant orders were subjected to biting criticism, others were praised for their religious commitment.[2]

The Hundred Years War also had much more direct consequences for clergymen and members of religious communities: many suffered terribly during the conflict and faced brutal assaults with fire and sword. This shaped not only the clergy's wartime experience but also the impressions of the war which they left to posterity, because despite the disruption to daily life they continued to write accounts that coloured contemporary and later attitudes to the conflict. Their involvement in the distribution of propaganda helped form popular opinion, and the records they left – administrative, legal, literary and historiographical – continue to inform modern views of the war. Hence, although an increasing number of laymen and some very notable women began writing their accounts in the fourteenth and fifteenth centuries, ecclesiastical authors offer some of the most telling perspectives on the Hundred Years War. Through their works they immersed themselves directly in the war effort. Clerical writings and sermons provided a mouthpiece for royal policy and a vehicle for propaganda, and they also armed each side with a range of additional intellectual and spiritual weapons. In this fashion the clergy played a central role in the prosecution of the Hundred Years War. The academic exchange between the French and English clergy mirrored the physical exchange between the French and English armies – it is entirely appropriate that a *débat* (an intellectual debate) can also be translated as a battle.

The war began with a flurry of bulletins, broadsides and manifestos: both sides placed great value on winning the propaganda war at home and abroad, and the Church provided the main conduit for that propaganda. In England, as Edward I had done, Edward III mobilised the Church. Every parish and monastic church gave the Crown a direct link to the population – from the centre to the periphery – and a means of accessing local communities. 'It was through prayers and other liturgical practices on behalf of the war effort that the king's ambition was presented to the English people.'[3] Prayers for king and kingdom were supplemented with bell-ringing, processions and other ceremonial events. Sermon collections were distributed containing model prayers so that priests might exhort their congregations to beseech God to aid their king in his just cause. Sermons, of course, were delivered in the vernacular and so they provided an ideal way of transmitting information about the political, military and economic issues confronting the kingdom – or at least those about which the Crown wished the people to be informed. Such actions were considered vital in guaranteeing tax revenue and encouraging general support for the war. They were not, however, merely propagandist; they were believed to have real spiritual value. In the religious climate of the fourteenth and fifteenth centuries it was thought they might even tip the balance in a battle.[4]

Edward III issued writs *de orando pro rege* (prayers for the realm and its good government) almost annually from the late 1330s to the mid-1350s. He also called on the preaching talents of the English clergy to explain his reasons for going to war, the legitimacy of his claim to the French Crown and to emphasise the remarkable patience he had shown before he had been compelled to take up arms. The friars were particularly important in delivering these messages. The Dominicans were required to present the king's claim in 'public and private sermons' and to emphasise his restraint, his desperate attempts to keep the peace in the face of the duplicity of 'Sir Philip de Valois' (Philippe VI), who 'calls himself king of France' and who 'by force and against justice' had usurped the French throne, seized Gascony, stirred up the Scots and conspired even to 'subvert the English language'.[5]

The use of the Church for these purposes continued throughout the war. Richard II ordered the clergy to stage masses and processions for Bishop Henry Despenser's 'crusade' against the Flemings in 1383, to pray on behalf of the earl of Arundel's expedition to the continent in 1386 and to support his own Irish campaign of 1394. During Henry V's reign lavish processions and ceremonies were organised to thank God for the remarkable triumph of Agincourt. When the king returned to London in 1415 he was greeted en route to St Paul's Cathedral by 12 bishops wearing mitres, who led him to the high altar before he rode through the city to Westminster, where the monks and abbot escorted him into the abbey church so the king could make his devotions to St Edward. In 1419 a writ announced the discovery of a 'magicians' plot' against Henry V, which, it was said, could be countered only by prayers offered for the success of his French expedition. In 1436 prayers and processions were requested for the campaign that Humphrey, duke of Gloucester (1390–1447), led to relieve the siege of Calais. This work and the administrative tasks the clergy undertook ensured the Church played a vital role in prosecuting and promoting the Hundred Years War, and in sharpening a sense of national identity and patriotic feeling in both countries.[6]

The clergy also furnished successive kings with more formal legal foundations for their respective claims to France and to territories within France. Like their English counterparts, French ecclesiastics were involved with popular propaganda, especially pamphleteering, but they made a more distinctive contribution in the composition and distribution of major treatises and legal documents that emphasised the rights and legitimacy of the Valois claim to the French throne and exalted French royal power. They also wrote histories, some of which the Crown commissioned, in order to present an official perspective on recent events and to shape a powerful image of royal authority and legitimacy. Some of these works were designed to win over public opinion and were disseminated to a wide audience; others were for diplomatic use and reflect the unique intellectual character of the Valois court.[7] The Parisian abbey of Saint-Denis was at the heart of this work. There, successive generations of Benedictine monks from the time of Abbot Suger (d.1151) onwards chronicled the history of France from a consciously royalist perspective. From the beginning of the thirteenth century some of these works, such as the *Grandes Chroniques*, were composed in or translated into the vernacular.

By the time the Hundred Years War began, monks at Saint-Denis were appointed to the position of royal historiographer. Richard Lescot (d.1358) styled himself 'historiographer royal', and as such publicised a Carolingian redaction of Salic law that he 'discovered' in the archives of Saint-Denis; this played a vital role in discounting any claim to the French throne transmitted through a female. Michel Pintoin (c.1349–1421) was another who composed his chronicle 'by the authority of the king', and Jean Chartier received the title *chroniqueur du roi* in 1437. Clearly a great deal of importance was placed on this role and on the 'fabrication' of an official account of the Hundred Years War. Following this example, Philippe the Good, duke of Burgundy, appointed Georges Chastellain his official chronicler in 1455. It is striking that, by contrast, after the *Anglo-Saxon Chronicle* ceased to be compiled in the twelfth century no English royal historical writing centre existed, and although monarchs did try to influence the contents of individual chronicles there appears to have been no comparable production line of official historiography during the war.[8]

There was, however, no shortage of English chronicles in the later Middle Ages composed by monastic authors, clerks and, increasingly, laymen. A number of those clerical authors were closely associated with the royal court. Adam Usk (c.1350–1430), for example, was a Crown lawyer, while the anonymous author of the *Gesta Henrici Quinti* (written 1416–17) was almost certainly a chaplain in Henry V's household. Other monastic writers had fewer direct connections to the centre of power but were still well informed. Henry Knighton (d. c.1396), an Augustinian canon from St Mary of the Meadows, Leicester, wrote extensively on the prosecution of the war and fearfully of John Wyclif (c.1320–84) and the threat posed by England's first heresy. Knighton had close links to the Lancastrian households of Henry of Grosmont, John of Gaunt and Henry Bolingbroke. Thomas Walsingham (c.1340–c.1422), a monk from St Albans, also had links to the court – although he was far from favourably disposed to Gaunt. Walsingham continued the monastic chronicle tradition championed by Matthew Paris and produced a series of remarkably detailed and extraordinarily vitupera-tive works on a wide variety of subjects during Richard II's reign and those of the early Lancastrians. His comments on the poverty of the English war effort after 1369 are particularly scathing. For Walsingham '[t]he land that once bore and gave birth to men who were respected by all who dwelt nearby and feared by those who lived far off, now spews forth weaklings who are laughed at by our enemies and a subject for gossip among our people'.[9]

In France, in addition to those writing the *Grandes Chroniques* and other official records, there were a number of other important ecclesiastical authors. The Carmelite friar Jean de Venette (c.1307–c.1370) expressed his deep concern for the lot of the French peasantry and blamed a vain, avaricious and venal knighthood for many of the early disasters in the war. Jean Gerson (1363–1429), chancellor of the University of Paris, provided fascinating insights regarding the conciliar movement (the series of church councils which sought a resolution to the Great Schism), and on the career and reputation of Joan of Arc. He argued that the French were a chosen people, and that because their king's power was divine everyone should offer him obedience.[10] The royal notary and secretary Jean de Montreuil (1354–1418), a writer deeply influenced by Italian humanism, was another

who promoted Salic law, especially in his *Traité contre les Anglais*, in order
to repudiate English pretensions to the French throne.[11] Jean Juvénal des
Ursins (1388–1473) drew heavily on Montreuil's work and discussed
similar themes in *Audite celi* (1435) and *Tres crestien, tres hault, tres puissant
roy* (1446).[12] Alain Chartier (c.1385–1430) wrote of *Mère France* (Mother
France) in *Le quadrilogue invectif* (c.1422), a work designed to unite the
people of France in the service of the dauphin (Charles VII).[13] Noël de
Fribois (fl.1423–67/8), *sécrétaire du roi*, who presented Charles VII with his
Abrégé des Croniques in 1459, considered the changing political landscape of
France at the end of the Hundred Years War and the growth of royal
power.[14] By no means do all these accounts, French or English, provide
first-hand experiences of war and many are exaggerated, formulaic and
driven by personal and political impulses. Some clerical authors wrote to
encourage moral reform and saw conflict as evidence of social and spiritual
decay; they are, nonetheless, vital for an understanding of English and
French *mentalités* during the Hundred Years War.

Churchmen and clerics were not, however, the unthinking tools of kings
– many criticised royal policy and personnel. In a number of sermons
Thomas Brinton, bishop of Rochester from 1373 to 1389, censured both
Edward III and Richard II: 'Armies go to war,' he said, 'not with the prayers
of the people behind them but with the curses of many; for they march not
at the king's expense or their own, but at the expense of churches and the
poor, whom they spoil in their path.'[15] Jacques Legrand, an Augustinian
preacher, is well known for condemning the vices of Charles VI's court and
particularly what he saw as Queen Isabeau's excesses.[16] Thomas Basin,
bishop of Lisieux (1447–75), chronicled the reign of Charles VII and
detailed the misery of the French people. He was certainly no royal apolo-
gist: Charles, he argued, 'allow[ed] his English enemies to bleed and
dismember his people like fierce beasts, [and] he even in a certain fashion
participated himself, since he had to know that these cruelties were perpetrated not only by the enemy but also by his own men'.[17]

Despite these exceptions, both sides were generally able to use the
Church to justify the war and their respective aims. The English also
employed clergymen to legitimise territorial conquests. Once he had recaptured Normandy (1417–19), Henry V took steps to ensure the French
clergy were well treated. This was not only for the good of his soul; Henry
was keen that he should be accepted as *de jure*, not just *de facto*, ruler of the
duchy. The Church could help with this since it played a key role in determining political and social attitudes; it served as a stabilising force in local

communities where priests tended to be influential. Additionally, the new regime made extensive use of the clergy as administrators. Henry encouraged churchmen to cooperate with the new government by offering patronage and/or threatening to remove it. In the initial phase of the reconquest of Normandy many clergymen fled before the invaders; Henry urged them to return and while they could easily be replaced if they did not, their absence could result in considerable upheaval just at the time when the fledgling administration required stability. There was also some outright resistance: a number of clergymen were deeply involved in plots against the English administration. For example, the canons of Sées in Normandy contacted the Armagnacs in 1421 offering them access to the fortress through the cathedral treasury. The plot was discovered while workmen were digging a hole through the treasury wall, but the Armagnacs were able to capture the town nonetheless and it remained under their control for eight weeks. Elsewhere defiance often did not extend beyond a refusal to offer prayers for the new regime, and many clergymen decided that the English, although not entirely welcome, did at least offer the possibility of political and economic security.[18]

In Paris, the Church also played an important role in shaping political attitudes in the 1420s and 1430s. There was considerable support for the Burgundians in the capital: in 1418, 227 priests, ranging from important figures in the hierarchy of Notre Dame to (some impoverished) men without benefices, swore an oath of allegiance. This level of support would prove vital in sustaining the English and their allies in the French capital after the treaty of Troyes in May 1420. During that period of occupation oaths of allegiance and spiritual sanctions were used extensively to try to control political behaviour. Indeed, this was the case throughout the French civil war: both sides deployed a variety of weapons from the religious arsenal. Images of saints were decorated with 'party' symbols, and Armagnacs and Burgundians excommunicated each other with vehement frequency, bringing the spiritual power of the Church to bear on their own struggle.[19]

Churchmen were also involved in a variety of other aspects of the war effort. Although clerics no longer held a monopoly on governmental office, they represented a significant proportion in both administrations. A number were, of course, hugely significant in the Hundred Years War, such as Cardinal Henry Beaufort (1375–1447) who served the Lancastrian kings in numerous offices and often bankrolled their military efforts. Pierre de la Forêt, chancellor of France from 1349, rose through the ecclesiastical ranks to become archbishop of Rouen in 1352 and then cardinal. He was closely involved in diplomatic activities within France and in negotiations with England.[20] Men such as these, at the apex of the ecclesiastical hierarchy, were supported in great numbers by less eminent clergymen who paid taxes and sometimes collected them;[21] some of them had duties in local defence, and others, like the extraordinarily martial Bishop Henry Despenser (c.1341–1406), even led campaigns. Indeed, ecclesiastical influences meant that the Hundred Years War gained some crusading characteristics in both England and France. Such attitudes were not difficult to inculcate when the enemy, often described as all but heathen, attacked churches, abbeys and monasteries, some of which had been converted to defend parishioners against assault. As the Parisian Bourgeois (the anonymous author of a chronicle composed in the French capital) wrote in an entry for 1419: 'Alas, never, I think, since the days of Clovis the first Christian king, has France been as desolate and divided as it is today. The Dauphin and his people do nothing day and night but lay waste all his father's land with fire and sword and the English on the other side do as much harm as Saracens.'[22]

Such attacks, perpetrated by both sides on ecclesiastical property and non-combatants alike, were very frequent in France and not unknown in England despite the prohibitions of military ordinances and spiritual dictat. They imply that although the Church remained wealthy and highly influential, certain aspects of its authority declined in this period, and there is a good deal of evidence to suggest this was the case. If so it happened for several reasons. Of these the most important were the relocation of the papacy in 1309 to Avignon (soon denigrated as a 'Babylonish Captivity') and the Great Schism of 1378–1417. These events brought the Church into disrepute and firmly within the grubby orbit of Anglo-French politics. The Church had never been apolitical but, as a result of these events and because of the Hundred Years War, its 'universal' character was diminished. It was symptomatic of this decline that soldiers on both sides could raid churches and monasteries with impunity and impiety, and ecclesiastics were often looked on with suspicion.

As a consequence, slowly and partially over the period of the Hundred Years War, the English Church became divided from the rest of the Continent. This influenced the character of worship and the political and spiritual orientation of the clergy in England: churchmen were forced to decide where their priorities and loyalties lay – with the king or the pope.[23] In France, too, national loyalties began to influence attitudes to the Church and papacy detrimentally. Throughout the period of the war increasing French royal control over the Church, a process known as 'Gallicanism', saw the Crown gain greater influence over ecclesiastical resources, appointments and policies. This began in the years leading up to the relocation to Avignon when the vicious dispute between King Philippe IV (r.1285–1314) and Pope Boniface VIII (1294–1303) placed Franco-papal relations under enormous strain. However, once the papacy had taken up residence near the southern border of the French kingdom the Capetians and their Valois successors sought to take advantage of its proximity. The association also improved on account of the nationality of the Avignon popes – all were French. Valois influence waned, however, when Gregory XI (1370–78) returned to Rome in 1378, at which point French cardinals, at the instigation of Charles V, helped engineer the Great Schism.

As Philippe de Mézières noted in 1395, the political division between England and France became mirrored in the division of the papacy. This intensified an ongoing process of ecclesiastical politicisation and ensured that the Church itself became a subject of contention. De Mézières wrote: 'This accursed wound . . . is the mortal schism in Holy Church, the mother of these two sons of St Louis. And, what is worse, each of our two kings has taken to himself one half of his said mother, claiming to heal her sickness, while abandoning the other to be devoured by dogs and birds of prey.'[24]

Prior to 1378 churches, monasteries and clerics were attacked, churchmen raised money for the war effort, preaching on behalf of their respective king's campaigns, and successive popes made determined but forlorn efforts to resolve the struggle. But in 1378, with the election of Antipope Clement VII (1378–94) as a rival to the recently installed Urban VI (1378–89), the institutional Church itself also became a battleground for the Anglo-French conflict; and because of the Hundred Years War the ramifications of the Schism would be felt deep into the fifteenth century and perhaps until the Reformation.

The Schism divided Europe as it divided the Church and further compromised the authority of the papacy. This had been in decline for some time. Over the course of the thirteenth century, conflicts with European rulers, first the German emperors and later the French and to a lesser extent English kings, had seen the Papal Monarchy fall from the position of apparent political and spiritual impregnability it had acquired during the pontificate of Innocent III (1198–1216). The clearest indicator of this decline was the relocation of the papal curia from Rome to Avignon in 1309. There were good reasons for doing this, not least Rome's disruptive political climate and uncomfortable (and often unhealthy) summer weather. Indeed, because of such considerations it had not been uncommon for the papal curia to reside outside the Eternal City for extended periods, although it tended to remain in the Papal States. Pope Clement V (1305–14), however, never even managed to get to Rome after his election. Poor health, a fondness for his home in southern France and the political chaos of northern Italy were among the reasons that led to the papal curia taking on a somewhat peripatetic existence until 1309 when it became fixed, more or less, in Avignon.

Located in the Comtat Venaissin, Avignon was a possession of the Church on the borders of, but not technically within, the Capetian kingdom. However, especially in those countries that opposed France, this soon came to be seen as a 'Babylonish Captivity', which did nothing to strengthen the papacy's increasingly fragile spiritual authority. Even before 1305, when the papacy left Rome, Anglo-papal relations had been strained, but thereafter many in England believed, not without some justification, that the Holy Father was little better than a French pawn. Clement V, the first of the Avignon popes, had been archbishop of Bordeaux (as Bertrand de Got) and as such he tended to be well disposed to England, but there is little doubt that for much of the fourteenth century the Avignon papacy favoured – and was seen to favour – the French monarchy. As a consequence it came to be widely felt in England, certainly by the time of the pontificate of Clement VI (1342–52), that whereas Christ Jesus was, unquestionably, English, his vicar was unapologetically French.[25] Clement, perhaps the most overtly Francophile of the Avignon popes, was a product of the French court and former keeper of the seals in Paris, whose pontificate has been characterised by its 'subservience to French interests'.[26] Because of this the papacy could not play its traditional role as an arbiter in European affairs effectively, and certainly not in those disputes involving England and France. The English became increasingly and instinctively wary of any measures originating from Avignon that sought to bring a peaceful resolution to the war.

Although its spiritual authority was compromised, in other spheres the papacy gained a great deal from the 'Babylonish Captivity'. The seven Avignon popes sought and, in the early fourteenth century, gained ever greater control over patronage and appointments to benefices throughout Europe. This provided the papacy with political leverage but did nothing to improve its popularity. In addition, the machinery of papal government improved very considerably during the Avignon period, and the Holy See used that administrative efficiency to raise the very considerable sums of money needed to build and expand the extraordinary papal palace at Avignon and to wage a number of military campaigns in Italy to re-establish its authority. Although this was a tribute to the organisational ability of various members of the papal curia and perhaps financially necessary, because the papacy had been cut off from many of its traditional Italian revenues, it too proved deeply unpopular.[27]

In part because of the papacy's attempts to increase its income and influence over ecclesiastical appointments, by the middle years of the fourteenth century relations between Avignon and England had deteriorated markedly. Then, in the 1360s, matters became even worse when, under pressure from Charles V, Pope Urban V (1362–70) refused a dispensation for a marriage between Edmund of Langley (Edward III's fourth surviving son) and Margaret of Flanders – this was needed because they were related within the prohibited degree. It proved to be a decision of enormous significance because, as one of the richest heiresses in Christendom, Margaret's eventual marriage to Philippe of Burgundy provided the foundations for the development of the Burgundian state. Edward III, furious at being thwarted in his attempt to extend English influence in the Low Countries, stymied a programme of ecclesiastical reform which Urban wished to implement in England.[28] Widespread anti-papal feeling coupled with a substantial dose of political expediency had already led to the Statutes of Provisors (1351, 1365) and Praemunire (1353, 1365), which Richard II reissued in 1390 and 1393 respectively. This legislation replaced papal with royal provision to many ecclesiastical benefices in England and, as a result, the Crown began to exercise increasing authority over ecclesiastical affairs. It became common to promote king's clerks into the ranks of the episcopacy. Simon Islip, for example, became archbishop of Canterbury (1349–66) having served as keeper of the seal (1347–50). In this period, when the state sought to maximise and exploit all the resources at its disposal, it is no surprise that attempts were also made to extend secular administrative control over the Church.

It was this desire that also explains royal support for the heresiarch John Wyclif in the 1370s: his call for royal supremacy over the *ecclesia Anglicana* and the disendowment of church property proved very popular in this febrile climate. For Wyclif the king of England held the same political and spiritual authority as the kings of the Old Testament – he was *rex et sacerdos* – with the power to appoint, depose and dispossess priests. It was only with the Peasants' Revolt of 1381, when any threat to the social or political status quo became tainted with suspicion, that Wyclif truly fell from favour with the royal family. The proposal to take church land into secular control did not disappear, however; it resurfaced in the early years of Henry IV's reign when the October Parliament of 1404 suggested the confiscation of church property would alleviate a financial crisis.[29]

The situation was different in France but not completely reversed. The Avignon Papacy was popular, broadly speaking. But the violent disputes between Philippe IV and Boniface VIII had soured Franco-papal relations at the beginning of the 1300s and Gallicanism became an ever more potent force, as the French monarchy, like the English, sought greater authority over the Church. Over the course of the Hundred Years War Gallicanism developed into a movement that promoted the concept of an independent French Church, free from papal interference while acknowledging it should remain 'Roman' and Catholic. The movement gathered pace during the Avignon period and subsequently when various French theorists such as Nicole Oresme (1320×25–82) and Jean Gerson argued that the French king as *rex Christianissimus* (the Most Christian King) had the authority to stamp out religious abuses and a duty to restore the Church to spiritual health.[30]

The Hundred Years War directly contributed to the process by which secular rulers gained greater authority over their 'national' Churches. Numerous attempts were made to establish control over ecclesiastical lands, properties, resources and revenues, and to make the Church subject to secular authority and a part of the state machine. The Great Schism galvanised this. In January 1377, after nearly eighty years in Avignon, Gregory XI returned the papal court to Rome. He died, however, in the following year, and in a reaction against what was widely seen as the extravagance and licentiousness of the papal curia his successor, Urban VI (elected on 8 April 1378 partly because of pressure brought to bear by the Roman mob), instituted major reforms, beginning with the college of cardinals itself. This proved deeply unpopular and Urban was far from diplomatic in his dealings with the cardinals – he is even reported to have punched one of them. Consequently, and with the support of Charles V, on 20 September thirteen disgruntled cardinals, led by Jean de la Grange, the cardinal-bishop of Amiens, elected a new pope, Robert of Geneva (the French king's cousin), who took the title Clement VII and established a rival curia back in Avignon. Each pope immediately excommunicated the other and created his own bureaucracy and college of cardinals. Clement received support from the French Crown and those countries allied to it, including Scotland, Naples, Castile and Aragon. The anti-French powers – England, Scandinavia, Germany, much of Italy, and the eastern European states – supported Urban. The Great Schism was, therefore, shaped by the European political situation which the Hundred Years War had created.[31]

This led to the most dramatic manifestation of clerical military activity during the Hundred Years War – the Flemish 'crusade' of Henry Despenser, bishop of Norwich. The targets of the campaign were the supporters of the Avignonese pope, Clement VII. The Roman pope, Urban VI, was naturally supportive of the venture as were the English Parliament and aristocracy, since it had clear political and economic advantages which the Church would fund. Plans began to be put in motion in 1381, not long before the Peasants' Revolt, which Despenser brutally suppressed in Norfolk. With his reputation subsequently enhanced (and probably exaggerated), he began a major preaching campaign in 1382 that laid the foundations for a crusade against the schismatics. His message was warmly received. On 17 May 1383 Despenser crossed to Calais with an army of 8,000 soldiers. After some initial success against a Flemish and French force near Dunkirk he besieged Ypres. This proved disastrous and soon had to be abandoned. The bishop then proposed to invade Picardy but was opposed by his lieutenants, including the highly experienced mercenary captain Sir Hugh Calveley (d.1394). Despenser continued in spite of this, but the appearance of a French army led by Charles VI himself forced him to submit to a humiliating settlement at Gravelines. Despenser returned to England to face bitter recriminations and impeachment in Parliament, although he was not imprisoned nor did he lose his episcopacy.[32]

The political climate that emerged in the following years soon brought changes to Anglo-French diplomacy and their respective relationships with the papacy/papacies. Albeit with opposition from the more hawkish elements at their respective courts, the efforts of Charles VI and Richard II to resolve the Hundred Years War became mirrored in attempts to heal the Schism. Following the deliberations of the First National Council of the French clergy (February 1395) – a meeting that itself indicated the increasingly national focus of the French Church – it became Valois policy to try and end the Schism by securing the abdication of both popes, an approach known as *via cessionis*. This marked a major change in strategy – from creating the Schism to ending it – and it involved a significant reorganisation of ecclesiastical life throughout France. This intensified in 1398 when, in order to try to compel papal compliance, ecclesiastical obedience was 'subtracted' from the papacy – a process given teeth since it involved withholding taxes due to the pope. The French Church instead found itself paying its dues into royal coffers. This policy, drawn up by various members of the University of Paris, amplified wider calls for a General Council of the Church and further encouraged 'Gallican' ideas that were again expressed in a National Council in 1406.[33] The policy did not, however, succeed.

More than twenty years of failure to heal the rift in the Church was accompanied by the outbreak of heresies in England (Lollardy) and Bohemia (Hussitism), and, in response, demands for a General Council of the Church grew louder. Neither pope, however, would call one. Finally, in 1408, a sufficient number of cardinals from both colleges agreed to summon a council under their own collective authority – this met in Pisa in the following year. There the council deposed both the Avignonese pope (Benedict XIII, 1394–1417) and the Roman pope (Gregory XII, 1406–15), and replaced them with Alexander V (1409–10). However, neither Benedict nor Gregory accepted the legality of the proceedings and each maintained just enough support to cling to office. The first council, therefore, merely compounded the problem – there were now three popes.

The second council met with more success. Primarily the work of Emperor Sigismund, who was eager to heal the Schism so that the Church could turn its attention to the problem of the Hussites in Bohemia, the Council of Constance (1414–18) made much better progress. Gregory XII resigned voluntarily in 1415, and the new Pisan pope who had succeeded Alexander V, John XXIII (1410–15), was deposed and imprisoned. Benedict XIII was able to retain a vestige of power until his death in 1424, but the council's preferred candidate, Martin V (1417–31), became broadly accepted as the Holy Father, with his income, rights and powers much reduced.

In essence the process that led to the resolution of the Great Schism established the principle that the authority of a General Council super-seded that of the pope. In token of this, from 1417 onwards the pope was required to summon a council at regular intervals (in five years, again seven years later, and then every ten years thereafter). The first of these meetings had to be postponed because of plague, but in 1431 a council met at Basel that saw a pope, Eugenius IV (1431–47), again in conflict with his cardi-nals. Once more the papacy found itself dependent on the support of secular rulers to secure its position. It was in this context that Charles VII was able to extend royal control further over the French Church through the Pragmatic Sanction of Bourges (1438), which placed still more restric-tions on papal rights. Hence, as a consequence of developments during the Hundred Years War, by the start of the sixteenth century at the latest, effec-tive royal control over the Church in France had been achieved.[34]

The struggle within the Church and the battle to establish control over the Church were, therefore, in large part, a consequence of the Hundred

Years War. The war itself also had a deeply significant and much more direct impact on churchmen in England and France. As Honoré Bonet said, witheringly, 'the man who does not know how to set places on fire, to rob churches and usurp their right and to imprison the priests is not fit to carry on war'.[35] The Church had tried to provide its members with protection from physical attack for many generations prior to the outbreak of the conflict – those who attacked churchmen and their property had long been subject to dire spiritual sanctions. This tradition stretched back at least as far as the Peace and Truce of God movements in the tenth century and the practice continued in the later Middle Ages. For example, the archbishop of Canterbury threatened excommunication to anyone who plundered church property – a sanction proclaimed twice-yearly, on All Saints' Day and Palm Sunday. English military ordinances also sought to protect churchmen and church property.[36] However, in spite of the dangers to soul and salvation, there was in reality little regard for the belongings and persons of the Church, particularly in France. Attacks on churchmen and ecclesiastical property fill the pages of chronicles and administrative documents. In 1357 Jean de Venette wrote that 'enemies' – he did not distinguish between English soldiers and European mercenaries of various nationalities, some French – 'seized castles and fortresses and captured the men who dwelt around them. Some they held for ransom; some they slaughtered miserably. Nor did they spare the religious. Monks and nuns abandoned their monasteries and took refuge as best they could.'[37] Froissart, similarly, tells of an English squire who entered a church during mass and stole a chalice from a priest at the very moment of consecration.[38] Such items were clearly valuable and highly prized: Sir John Harleston, captain of Cherbourg and one of Richard II's chamber knights, was witnessed sitting with some companions drinking from the silver chalices they had recently looted from churches.[39]

Such attacks were an implicit if not explicit part of English *chevauchée* policy in the fourteenth century. As raiders in the past had recognised, churches and monasteries were often storehouses of valuable goods. So, despite military ordinances and spiritual prohibitions designed to protect churchmen and their property, both suffered a great deal. Chronicles and government documents are littered with examples such as that of the *curé* of Comblisy who, during the turmoil that followed the battle of Poitiers in September 1356, was set such an excessive ransom by the Navarese forces who captured him that he was forced to repay them by singing masses in their fortress.[40] The depredations of mercenary troops meant that even

during so-called periods of truce there was little relief for the clergy. Because
of this there was barely a church, monastery or hospital in France which the
Hundred Years War did not affect adversely, for if not subjected to direct
attack then its revenues and goods, even its ability to give alms, were
damaged. Of course, as the conflict wore on the demands on churches
mounted because of the trauma suffered by members of their congregations and those others who depended upon them. Ecclesiastical revenues
plummeted because of the war. When combined with the effects of depopulation brought on by plague and famine, many religious institutions faced
a financial crisis.

The Hundred Years War, therefore, tested, and in some places tore the
institutional fabric of the French Church. By the 1370s problems had become
acute: in Brittany and Normandy parishes were deserted in the dioceses of
Dol and Bayeux; successive English raids devastated Artois and Picardy, and
the situation in the Île de France was not much better. Conditions in
Champagne – in Troyes, Reims and Chalons-sur-Marne – were also very
difficult. In Burgundy a great deal of land and property was laid waste and
many villages were deserted. A quarter of the population of Beaune had been
lost by 1366 and numbers continued to fall thereafter. Auvergne suffered too,
from depopulation brought on by disease, and emigration encouraged by
heavy taxation. In Languedoc the three *sénéchaussées* of Toulouse, Carcassonne
and Beaucaire all experienced major population decline. In Quercy that
decline is very evident from the time of the first outbreak of the Black Death
and it continued after the treaty of Brétigny in 1360 which brought the area
under English control. Numerous towns and villages were abandoned. In
Figeac more than five hundred wealthy inhabitants felt so impoverished on
account of the new administration that they left the town. Cahors may have
lost half its population; the outskirts of the town were deserted and so silent,
it was said, that not even a cock crowed there. Some of the surrounding areas
remained desolate for thirty years afterwards. War, mercenary activity, heavy
taxation, plague and famine each devastated whole areas in their turn, and
the consequent depopulation impacted heavily on ecclesiastical incomes and
on the role the Church could play in people's everyday lives. Parishes were
left without priests.

Because of its economic, political, social and physical consequences, the
war also adversely affected religious discipline and reduced the pastoral
activities of both monastic and secular clergy.[41] In 1360 the 'infestation' of
the diocese of Lyon with mercenary companies forced many communities
to abandon their monasteries. In 1375 the Augustinian priory of

Sainte-Gulles at Montpellier had its cloister destroyed by the Free Companies and the brethren were forced to beg for food. The Benedictine abbey of Montolieu in the diocese of Carcassonne suffered regular attacks by mercenary forces until, finally, they invaded the property, and stabled their horses in the church, cloisters and even the sanctuary. The divine office ceased to be sung and many monks renounced their vows. Mont-Saint-Michel in Normandy was besieged in the winter of 1423. Even Paris suffered: there were regular embargos, and the Benedictine monastery of Saint-Denis-en-France had to pay for protection for its property outside the city and its income was severely reduced. Mercenary activity also affected academic life in the capital: in 1387 the General Chapter of the Cistercian Order deplored the attacks that led to the college of Saint-Bernard in Paris being abandoned by students. Parochial life was also affected even when parishes were defended. The fortification of many parish churches protected congregations from raiding parties but often invited attack from French royal and aristocratic authorities concerned about the unlicensed construction of fortifications. There were also serious consequences for ecclesiastical activities: by compromising the sanctity of the buildings one might compromise the rigour, rhythm and routine of religious life.[42]

It was not only French churches that were devastated. In 1364 Urban V had to borrow 30,000 florins to improve the defences of Avignon against potential mercenary attack. Anglo-Scottish warfare, meanwhile, put ecclesiastical possessions on both sides of the border in jeopardy. For example, in 1385, partly because of Scottish support for the Avignon pope, Clement VII, English forces burned the abbeys of Melrose, Dryburgh, Holyrood and Newbattle. Nor were ecclesiastics in southern England safe. Monastic properties on the coast suffered sporadic assault. Thomas Walsingham described, perhaps in exaggerated terms, a particularly brutal episode in 1379. An English raiding force under the command of Sir John Arundel sought lodging at a nunnery near Southampton, probably Cornworthy, while awaiting a favourable wind to take it across to France. Despite the objections of the mother superior, the soldiers entered the house where they proceeded to assault and rape the sisters. The surrounding countryside was pillaged for food and other supplies. Walsingham even suggests that Arundel and his men kidnapped many of the nuns to take them to France, and then when the weather turned the women were thrown from the ships to lighten them.[43]

Attacks on ecclesiastics in England also took on a more institutional form. Alien monks, like other foreigners in England, became objects of suspicion from the outbreak of hostilities. From 1337 until 1360, and then from 1369 onwards, dependent houses of French monasteries, the so-called alien priories, were taken into royal control and exploited financially. The practice of seizing alien priories and ecclesiastical resources was not new; it had a history stretching back to 1208 when Pope Innocent III had placed the realm under Interdict and King John had responded by taking possession of church property. Edward I (in 1295) and Edward II (in 1324–27) had followed suit, although in response to war with France. These alien priories were said to be havens for enemy spies and serve as channels through which money, goods and resources poured in aid of the French war effort. Of these concerns the most serious was money, and the confiscation of the alien priories, which were defined very loosely and inconsistently, proved extremely profitable to the Crown in terms of hard cash as well as ecclesiastical patronage. The Crown granted seized properties to individuals, some as rewards, some in return for an annual payment. The beneficiaries often had little interest in maintaining the fabric of the priories and many caused considerable financial damage through exploitation and lack of care. Many priories were 'farmed' (rented) at too high a rate, and so when faced with the Exchequer's demands, the keepers had two choices, to sell off financial assets and neglect repairs or go into debt to the Crown. From 1375 a stream of commissioners was sent to investigate claims of damage perpetrated by keepers and former keepers.[44]

While action was taken to prevent excessive exploitation, some priories became so impoverished that they could not continue to exist as religious foundations and were sold as secular manors. Some tried to save themselves by seeking denization and hence 'becoming English', whereas others took on a new identity and were used to endow a different house or Order. The Carthusians became particular beneficiaries of this process: Henry V was a keen supporter of the Order, like a number of soldiers before him. Sir Walter Mauny (c.1310–72), for example, founded the London charterhouse in 1371; William, third Lord Zouche (c.1340–96), that at Coventry in 1381–2. Henry V founded a house at Sheen for forty Carthusian monks in 1415, partly to fulfil the penance Gregory XII imposed on his father in 1408 for the execution of Richard Scrope, archbishop of York, who had been implicated in the Percy family rebellions against Henry IV. The charterhouse was to be simple and austere – clothing, bedding and diet were all plain, silence was to be maintained, and individuals lived separately except in choir and chapter. The house was, however, richly endowed with properties confiscated from alien priories.[45] Carthusian austerity explains the patronage and support the Order enjoyed in the later Middle Ages. By comparison with the criticism suffered by some of the larger and wealthier Orders, they were praised and flourished during the Hundred Years War.[46]

Despite action taken against the alien priories, concern about the activities of foreign ecclesiastics continued to be voiced regularly in Parliament. For example, in 1373 the Commons called for legislation to prevent daughter-houses of French monasteries sending resources and intelligence across the Channel.[47] In reality, members of alien priories often supported the English war effort. They included the French-born prior of Lewes in Sussex, who in 1377 defended the town against a raid by his former countrymen.[48] This is an indication of the new role demanded of the clergy in this period. For the first and only time, between 1369 and 1418 the English clergy were arrayed for military service as part of royal policy and were compelled to take up arms to defend against threatened invasion. Stipulations were made regarding the arms and armour with which a clergyman should be equipped. A clerk with a benefice worth between £40 and 100 marks should be armed with chain-mail gloves, plates of armour covering his back and chest, a helmet with visor, and with protection for the stomach, arms, thighs and lower legs. Alternatively he could substitute this expensive plate armour with a leather tunic and shirt of chain mail. He was also to provide a lance, shield, sword, knife and three horses. Those clergymen with a larger income were to bring armed retainers with them; those with fewer resources did not have to bring horses; and the poorest merely had to bring a longbow or send an archer in their place. Those unable to serve because of age or infirmity were to contribute towards a replacement.[49] These responsibilities were defensive, but clergymen were often called on to fulfil them. Haimo of Offington, abbot of Battle in Sussex (1364–84), spent a good deal of the later years of his abbacy defending the south coast against French assault. In response to an attack on Rye in 1377, he prepared a defence plan and fended off an attack on Winchelsea. He was less successful in 1380 when the town was captured and one of the monks captured.[50]

Hence, despite the fact that clerics were forbidden to shed blood, clergymen of all ranks participated in the war and many served on campaign. Guillaume de Melun, archbishop of Sens, and the bishop of Châlons were in the French ranks at the battle of Poitiers in 1356, and Richard Courtenay, bishop of Norwich, died of dysentery while serving at the siege of Harfleur in 1415.[51] English priests regularly accompanied expeditions to France:

those who did so needed special episcopal licences permitting them to be absent from their parishes. Soldiers, it seems, could find plenty of foreign priests to rob while on campaign, but they did not always trust or understand them sufficiently to look to them for confession or to receive the Eucharist. And perhaps French priests were less than amenable to the idea of caring for the spiritual welfare of soldiers who plundered their churches.[52]

Campaigning, undoubtedly, was harsh and a difficult experience for those unused to long periods in the saddle, out of doors and under threat of attack. The author of the *Gesta Henrici Quinti* described the discomfort of the priestly contingent on the 1415 campaign: how they were 'made faint by great weariness', their 'dire need of food', and their fear that caused them to look 'up in bitterness to Heaven, seeking the clemency of Providence'. He and his fellows accompanied the army to celebrate the divine office, hear confessions and pray for success. He described how, during the battle of Agincourt in 1415, he remained with the baggage train, sitting on a horse and praying for the destruction of the enemy, calling on God to 'Destroy their strength and scatter them'. And when the French finally engaged the English and drove them back, having fought through successive volleys of arrows, the anonymous chaplain and his fellows feared the worst: 'And then we who had been assigned to the clerical militia and were watching fell upon our faces in prayer . . . crying out aloud in bitterness of spirit that God might even yet remember us and the crown of England and, by the grace of His supreme bounty, deliver us from this iron furnace and the terrible death which menaced us.'[53] Henry V and his men may well have believed that their prayers secured the miraculous victory.

The Hundred Years War placed ecclesiastical life under enormous strain. Forms of observance and the character of worship were changed by the experience of war, but spiritual life was not completely stifled. Rather, the struggle helped stimulate a process of reorganisation and revival. Clergymen were not only victims of war; they shaped and directed the conflict. In their literary and diplomatic efforts, they promoted the war and sought resolutions to it. They were victims and instigators of violence, propagandists and peacemakers. The war divided the European Church and the Great Schism made that theoretical division a practical reality. Such divisions were, in part, the product of the Hundred Years War and they ensured that the Church could not play an effective role in resolving the conflict. This was a great pity when the calls for peace resounded in the 1390s.

CHAPTER 4

Making Peace
BLESSED ARE THE PEACEMAKERS
1396

Those who want war and follow the camps and are eager for spoils and thirsting for loot are like the vulture who eats men and follows the camps of war.[1]

John Gower, *Vox Clamantis*

After Charles V's formal confiscation of the principality of Aquitaine in 1369, the reversal of English military and political fortunes was dramatic. Almost everything gained as a consequence of the great victories at Crécy (1346) and Poitiers (1356), which the treaty of Brétigny (1360) had, seemingly, confirmed, was lost by about 1372. But the English hold on southwest France, though weakened, was not entirely broken, and in 1380 Charles V and his principal military commander and constable of France, Bertrand du Guesclin, both died – the successors to these architects of the French revival were not men of the same calibre. The English, however, could not take advantage of this to strike back. The turmoil of the Peasants' Revolt in 1381 rocked Richard II's minority government and the king himself soon had to face a personal threat from a group of magnates known as the Appellants (1386–87). In such difficult circumstances significant elements at the French and English courts began to seek a peaceful resolution to the Anglo-French war. In particular, although militant voices remained strident in some quarters, both kings wished for peace (at least when Charles VI was sufficiently lucid to express an opinion). But the development of a peace policy was not solely the result of royal initiatives; by the later fourteenth century a social climate had developed in which calls for a diplomatic solution to the Hundred Years War resounded. The conflict had taken a heavy toll in lives and taxation; trade had been disrupted and crops destroyed. The military aristocracy – those 'flowers of chivalry' – had begun to be viewed by some as little better than warmongers who revelled in killing, pillage and brutality. In short, around the end of the century an almost palpable sense of war-weariness pervaded England and France.

The negotiations of the 1390s, which Richard II and Charles VI sponsored and which led to the truce of 1396, were far from the first of their kind. The Hundred Years War was framed and, somewhat perversely, caused by a series of peace treaties. These agreements often did more harm than good: in the long term they perpetuated hostilities rather than resolving them. In the thirteenth century diplomatic 'solutions' to Anglo-French antagonism had tended to exacerbate rather than reduce tension. The treaties of Le Goulet (1200) and of Paris (1259) shaped the political contours of Anglo-French relations until the outbreak of war in 1337 and they created an untenable relationship that made war almost inevitable. Similarly, the major treaties that punctuated the conflict, particularly that of Brétigny and then Troyes (1420), solved little and soon gave new momentum to the conflict. As this pattern suggests, finding a resolution was far from easy; the divisions between England and France were ever-more difficult to bridge as the war progressed and mutual hostility became a way of life. The arguments at the heart of the struggle began to reflect fundamental political differences and these became increasingly entrenched as the war went on.

In addition, the Hundred Years War involved powers other than France and England, and they each had their own agendas and antipathies that required resolution. Scotland's entangling alliance with France from 1295 (the Auld Alliance) heightened Anglo-French tensions, while Edward III's support in the 1330s for the Disinherited (those nobles who fought against Robert the Bruce and had been deprived of their lands) and Edward Balliol, the rival claimant to the Scottish throne, drove David II into French exile and ensured that the central area of Anglo-French contention – the issue of sovereignty in the duchy of Gascony – could not be addressed without reference to similar problems in Scotland.[2] The Franco-Scottish accord, therefore, fuelled the war from its outset, and continued to influence policy and attitudes on both sides of the border and both sides of the Channel long after 1337.[3]

A similar situation developed in the Iberian Peninsula. Castile took on particular significance after the English treaty with King Pedro 'the Cruel' in 1362, which the subsequent Franco-Trastamaran alliance (1368) contracted with Pedro's half-brother sought to counter.[4] In Brittany and Flanders, too, succession disputes offered the English and French potential political advantage should the side they supported win out. A number of smaller national and regional disputes, therefore, became subsumed under the chaos of the Hundred Years War and these entanglements made the struggle yet more intractable. As it unfolded the war acquired new dimensions and intricacies: it became multinational, of increasing political complexity, and fought in an ever greater number of theatres, not only geographical but also legal and theoretical. Any effective resolution would have to take account of all these variables.

Although the Hundred Years War began in 1337, England and France had been at war on numerous occasions in the recent and more distant past. Hostilities had been common since the Norman Conquest and they gathered intensity when English continental expansion conflicted with the growing power of the Capetian monarchy towards the end of the twelfth century. The subsequent fragmentation of the 'English' Angevin Empire laid the groundwork for many of the disputes fought over during the Hundred Years War. Those disputes were reshaped and given diplomatic form first in the treaty of Le Goulet and later the treaty of Paris. Soon after his accession in 1272, Edward I began to look for ways to redefine his relationship with his French overlords, Philippe III (r.1270–85) and Philippe IV (r.1285–1314). Edward questioned the precise nature of the agreement his father Henry III had reached in 1259. He was concerned, in particular, with the form of homage that his father had paid for the duchy of Gascony. The English claimed that the duchy was an *allod*: that it was not held by liege homage of the French Crown, and hence that Edward had all but sovereign rights to Gascony. Meanwhile Louis IX's successors were stressing their own sovereignty throughout the entirety of France (including Gascony). In such circumstances the political status quo was placed under extreme pressure. Resolutions were explored and occasionally found to specific disputes, but the underlying issues were not, indeed could not, be addressed without recourse to arms. When the succession dispute was added to the explosive mix already created by French ambitions in Flanders, England's claim to sovereignty in Scotland, and finally by the case of Robert d'Artois, the firebreak could not hold.

The outbreak of war in 1337 might not, however, have been any different from those conflicts that followed earlier confiscations of Gascony by Philippe IV (r.1294–99) and Charles IV (r.1324–25), and it could, in theory, have ended equally swiftly. Certainly there was far from universal support for the war in either country. Demands began to be made for a resolution in both England and France while the struggle was still in its infancy. The nature, though, of these demands differed significantly between the two countries and they would change further as the war progressed.

Despite a welter of propaganda designed to garner support for Edward III's campaigns, criticism of the war started early in England. It focused chiefly on the weight of the new economic burdens and was expressed in various works of popular literature such as the 'Song against the King's Taxes' from the late 1330s ('Now runs in England year after year, the fifteenth, and thus brings harm to all'), the 'Song of Husbandman' c. 1340 ('the bailiff summons up misery for us and thinks he does well'), and *Wynnere and Wastoure* from the late 1340s ('You destroy all my goods with your strife and violence/With feasting and wassailing on winter nights/ With extravagant spending and arrogant pride'). Then, in 1381, criticism of taxation exploded into the Peasants' Revolt. Around this time, however, condemnation of warfare was acquiring a new dimension; it began to extend from complaints about the financial costs of the war to grievances over its social implications.[5] Writers in the late fourteenth and early fifteenth centuries became deeply troubled by the behaviour of those who made war, with soldiers and their motivations for fighting and, in England, perhaps even with war itself.

In France, since the war was waged on home soil, such considerations were muted – the struggle with England was almost always considered just. Consequently, the calls for peace made by French men and women tended to take a different form. In the early stages of the conflict writers such as Jean de Venette stressed the pity of war, and the suffering it caused, especially for the peasantry. As he showed, conditions in 1356, following Jean II's defeat and capture at the battle of Poitiers, were particularly difficult:

> From that time on all went ill with the kingdom and the state was undone. Thieves and robbers rose up everywhere in the land. The nobles despised and hated all others and took no thought for the mutual usefulness and profit of lord and men. They subjected and despoiled the peasantry and the men of the villages. In no way did they defend their country from its enemies. Rather they did trample it under foot, robbing and pillaging the peasants' goods. [As a consequence] the country and the whole land of France began to put on confusion and mourning like a garment.[6]

Venette's was not a lone voice; the poet Petrarch provides an Italian perspective on events in France and the harm the nation and its people were forced to endure. He described a country ravaged by war: deserted, broken and barely recognisable. In 1359, he recorded, 'Everywhere was grief, destruction and desolation, uncultivated fields filled with weeds, ruined and abandoned houses . . . In short wherever I looked were the scars of defeat.'[7]

The Reims campaign of 1359–60 brought the first phase of the Hundred Years War to a conclusion – a somewhat pallid hiatus – and it was marked with the treaty of Brétigny–Calais. In addition to Jean II's kingly ransom the treaty provided Edward III with an enlarged Gascony in return for his renunciation of both the French throne and his claim to Normandy and other Angevin territories. The king of France, meanwhile, offered to abandon his claims to sovereignty and *ressort* (the right to hear appeals over judicial decisions) in all Edward III's lands. However, both parties agreed to postpone signing these 'renunciation clauses' (the *cest assavoir* clauses) until various lands and castles had changed hands. In the event those clauses were never sealed. For the next few years, certainly until Jean II's death in 1364, relations remained remarkably amicable. Edward III created the principality of Aquitaine out of the enlarged Gascony and granted it to his eldest son, Edward the Black Prince. Although technically illegal, the English exercised sovereign rights in the new lordship and Jean II made no move to interfere. In return Edward ceased to style himself king of France in official documents although he continued to use the fleur-de-lys on the English royal arms.

The political tide, however, soon began to turn against the English following Charles V's accession in 1364 and because of the deteriorating situation in Aquitaine. The new Valois regime exploited the widespread disgruntlement with the Black Prince's regime, caused in part by the enormous expense of the Castilian venture (1367–68). The Brétigny settlement of 1360 had suited few of the French nobility forced to bow to English authority in the new principality, and in 1368 Charles took the opportunity to test his authority and to hear appeals against the Black Prince's administration.[8] The war resumed almost immediately and the territories ceded in 1360 were, nearly as quickly, back in Valois hands. For the remainder of the 1370s the English position in France continued to deteriorate, albeit more slowly, and the French were able to strike back, raiding the southern English coastal towns. In the 1380s, however, following the deaths of Charles V and du Guesclin, the French advance stalled. Like the English *chevauchées*, French naval attacks brought disruption and fear but few major political gains. When plans for a major invasion of England in the middle years of the decade failed, a stalemate set in.

It was in this context that Charles VI and Richard II began to negotiate and it was at this time that some of the most resonant calls for peace were made by some of the most significant English writers of the age – William Langland, Geoffrey Chaucer and John Gower among them. All these men questioned the war's purpose and its conduct to varying degrees and some became increasingly disenchanted with the conflict as it progressed. Langland's opinions, for example, grew more condemnatory as he revised the three texts of *Piers Plowman* (c.1370–1377/9) and he declared that 'peace was the most precious of virtues'.[9] Chaucer's writings also show a growing disillusionment with the war, its conduct and particularly with the role of the military aristocracy. 'The Tale of Melibee', the chivalric parody 'Sir Thopas' and the 'Parson's Tale' reflect his belief that although war might be necessary to redress certain material wrongs, it inevitably caused a disproportionate level of spiritual and physical destruction. As a result, in the world about him Chaucer saw only 'treason and envy, poison, manslaughter and murder'.[10]

Of all those Englishmen writing in opposition to the war at this time John Gower was the most passionate. In the decade between writing his long poems *Mirour de l'omme* (*The Mirror of Man*, c.1376–78) and *Confessio Amantis* (*The Lover's Confession*, c.1386–93), Gower shifted from a grudging acceptance of the case for the war with France to a position that might be described, awkwardly, as one of militant pacifism. In *Confessio Amantis* he wrote:

> If charity be held in awe,
> Then deadly wars offend its law:
> Such wars make war on Nature too;
> Peace is the end her laws pursue –
> Peace, the chief gem of Adam's wealth;
> Peace which is all his life and health.
> But in the gangs of war there go
> Poverty, pestilence and woe,
> And famine, and all other pain
> Whereof we mortal men complain ...
> For it is war that brings to naught,
> On Earth, all good that God has wrought:
> The church is burnt, the priest is slain;
> Virgin and wife, vile rapes constrain ...[11]

In a society that, traditionally, viewed struggle as both endemic and natural, perhaps even necessary, Gower condemned all bloodshed between Christians. He took this position for a variety of reasons but chief among them, as he also argued in his third major poem, *Vox Clamantis* (*The Voice of One Crying*, c.1377–81), was his belief that by this stage the war was being fought solely for the benefit of the knightly aristocracy: any national interest had been lost to their individual and collective greed. Those who should have maintained law, order and justice now sowed only discord and destruction.[12] A number of the clergy shared this view, including Thomas Brinton, Richard FitzRalph and John Bromyard, who wrote in *Summa Predicantium*:

> For victory in battle is not achieved by the size of one's army but by the help of God. Yet now, alas, princes and knights and soldiers go to war in a different spirit; with their cruel actions and desire for gain, they incline themselves more to the ways of the devil than to those of God . . . nor do they fight at the expense of the king or of themselves, but at that of the Church and of the poor, despoiling both.[13]

It was not only orthodox clerics who opposed the war. John Wyclif expressed his increasing fury in a series of works. Wyclif first became concerned with the subject in 1375 when seeking to reconcile the reality of warfare with the fifth of the Ten Commandments, 'Thou shalt not kill' (*De Mandatis Divinis* – 'On the Divine Commandments'). Soon after, he became convinced that such conflicts were pointless (*De Civili Dominio* – 'On Civil Lordship', c.1375), and by 1378 he saw those who perpetrated war needlessly, particularly the mercenary Free Companies, as 'hateful to God'. By this stage England's war in France had become 'the sin of the kingdom'. Wyclif grew even more indignant when planning was underway for Bishop Despenser's 1383 crusade to Flanders. He argued in *De Cruciata* ('On Crusade', 1382) that the offer of indulgences, remission from sins and the chance of martyrdom made the papacy culpable of promoting an inherently corrupt endeavour.[14]

In France, as the fourteenth century drew to a close, calls for peace were also resounding. By this time the devastation of the nation and the failure of the nobility to defend the realm had become familiar refrains. The brutality inflicted by soldiers on all sides was recognised and lamented. Honoré Bonet pleaded with his readers, arguing that 'Valiant men and wise . . . who follow arms should take pains, so far as they can, not to bear hard on the simple and innocent folk but only on those who make and continue war and flee peace.'[15] Christine de Pizan, driven by similar concerns, advocated the need for Roman-style military discipline among French troops and argued that no 'honour can accrue to a prince in killing, overrunning, or seizing people who have never borne arms nor could make use of them, or poor innocent people who do nothing but till the land and watch over animals'.[16]

But in the main, although the devastation of war was deplored, the calls for peace made by French writers took on a different character from those in England. This was perhaps an inevitable consequence of the war being conducted, for the most part, on French soil, and the threat it posed to French social and political structures. For Christine de Pizan, as for Jean Gerson, peace was vital but conditional – it should be accepted only on honourable terms. As a result there seems to be comparatively little criticism of war per se in France – at least not of war with England – and to use Christine's words, although 'many great wrongs, extortions and grievous deeds are committed [which] may well seem to some detestable and improper . . . the evils committed are the result . . . of the evil will of people who misuse war'.[17] For many French writers, therefore, war was a necessary prelude to peace, and peace would only be secured once the English withdrew voluntarily or after they had been driven out of France. As Jean Juvénal des Ursins noted in 1435, 'For war is only made in order to have peace; make strong war and you will have peace by subjugating your enemies.'[18]

It is hardly surprising that European intellectuals wrote extensively on the conjoined subjects of war and violence – the conditions demanded it. A persistent conflict waged in the heart of Christendom, atrocities perpetrated by both sides with depressing regularity and changes to the basic fabric of the state wrought by taxation and bureaucratic innovations led to philosophical, moral and religious debate, posturing, confusion and indignation. The Church tried to lead this debate and it was closely involved in a number of schemes that sought a resolution to the conflict. The Avignon popes inundated European courts and individual power brokers with letters seeking such a resolution. In addition, prior to 1378, successive popes and their agents called numerous peace conferences – there were meetings at Avignon (1344–45), Calais (1347, 1372), Guines (1354), Bruges (1373, 1375–76) and elsewhere. The first of these was presided over by Clement VI and six cardinals (although there were only two cardinals for the latter stages of the discussion). The discussions took the form of informal and brief bilateral meetings between the papacy and the English and French delegations. Only on two occasions did all sides come together for a plenary meeting.[19]

In seeking to fulfil its spiritual responsibility to promote peace throughout Christendom the Church also tried to prevent specific battles. In 1356 Cardinal Talleyrand de Périgord made a series of rather pitiful efforts, riding frantically between the forces of Jean II and the Black Prince in a forlorn attempt to avert the battle of Poitiers.[20] That these efforts did not succeed may be attributed in part to the English belief, held with some justification, that the Avignon papacy was little more than a puppet of the Valois monarchy.[21] The Church also used the spiritual weapons in its armoury to try and prevent hostilities in a more direct fashion, especially when those hostilities came close to Avignon – a case in point being the excommunication of du Guesclin and various other members of the Free Companies in 1368.[22]

Regardless of its partiality, real or perceived, the Church as a whole and its members in England and France in particular became deeply concerned with the war and its conduct. Many churchmen came to believe – and expressed those beliefs in writings and sermons – that the war had degenerated from a just conflict into a killing spree motivated less by right and honour than by bloodlust and the chance to plunder. Such derogatory feelings about the conduct of the war soon fed into a wider debate concerning social order and the social responsibilities which nobles and, indeed, kings neglected when they took up arms. This was an unfair criticism of Richard II and Charles VI. Both were more than amenable to the idea of an Anglo-French truce. In Richard's case this was not a policy he pursued because of any inherent pacifism but because it allowed him to explore political and military opportunities elsewhere. In this sense the brief truce secured in 1396 proved disastrous for Richard since it allowed him to lead an expedition to Ireland, and so he was absent from the kingdom when Henry Bolingbroke launched his campaign in July 1399. This led to the king's deposition in September of that year, the beginning of the Lancastrian dynasty under Bolingbroke as Henry IV and a massive renewal of the war effort by Henry V. This was not what either England or France had had in mind when negotiations opened in the 1390s.

England's initial bargaining position in these discussions was extreme. Richard's ambassadors demanded Aquitaine in full sovereignty, as defined in the treaty of Brétigny, along with Calais and Ponthieu, and the arrears of

Jean II's ransom plus further reparation payments. The agreement would be secured by a marriage between King Richard and Charles VI's daughter, Isabella; their eldest son would, in time, receive Normandy, Anjou and Maine as an independent *apanage*. Unsurprisingly, the French did not agree. What emerged from the discussions was a settlement that reflected contemporary political realities. A truce of twenty-eight years was concluded, secured by Richard's marriage to the six-year-old Isabella of France in 1396 along with a substantial dowry.[23]

Although Richard chanced his arm, in the 1390s there was considerable support for a longer-lasting settlement. That it could not be secured was due to three major problems: Charles VI's madness, Richard's deposition, and the refusal of the Gascons to accept John of Gaunt as lord of Aquitaine. This last element had formed a major part in the negotiations after the English realised their initial terms would not be accepted. The scheme's failure indicates the problems of securing a negotiated settlement in a politically and culturally divided France. A proposal was explored to resolve the perennial problem of the duchy of Aquitaine by granting it to a senior member of the English royal house who would hold it on behalf of the French Crown. However, in response to the suggestion that Gaunt might govern Aquitaine as a Valois vassal, representatives from the duchy visited Richard II and 'claimed that they never had been nor never would be governed by any man other than the king of England or his heir'.[24]

The failure of the 1396 truce can also be attributed to the changing complexion of French domestic politics. Tensions were building between the houses of Orléans/Armagnac and Burgundy as each sought to gain power in the political vacuum that Charles VI's madness had created. In the early fifteenth century this would lead to a fully fledged civil war. When it erupted the Armagnac-Burgundian struggle altered the nature of the peace discourse in France radically. Christine de Pizan argued passionately for the need to resolve the conflict, stating that 'Every kingdom divided in itself will be destroyed, and every city or house divided against its own good cannot endure.'[25] She wrote extensively on the subject; both the *Lamentation on the Evils of the Civil War* (1410) and the *Book of Peace* (1413), composed during the tumult following Louis d'Orléans's assassination in November 1407, were pleas for peace in a period of disastrous political upheaval. According to her, Louis of Guienne, the dauphin, was charged by God with the task of staunching this wound from which France was dying.[26]

Louis of Guienne was the third son of Charles VI to hold the title of dauphin, and he too predeceased his father, dying in December 1415. Continuing uncertainty over the succession did little to calm the political ferment, and Henry V took full advantage of this by renewing the war in 1415, capturing Harfleur and orchestrating the extraordinary victory at Agincourt. The continuing vicissitudes of the French civil war, which lasted from Louis d'Orléans's assassination in 1407 until the Congress of Arras in 1435, emphasise the political complexities of this period and hence the problems that had to be overcome before a resolution to the wider Anglo-French conflict could be achieved. Indeed, for those caught up in the struggle it might be difficult to determine who the enemy truly was. Certainly, the anonymous writer known as the Parisian Bourgeois was often unsure whether Englishmen or dauphinists posed the greater threat to his security and to that of his city. In 1430 he wrote, 'Not a man of all those now under arms, whichever side he belongs to, French or English, Armagnac or Burgundian ... will let anything escape him that is not too hot or too heavy ... if God does not take pity on France she is in great danger of being entirely destroyed.'[27]

Depending on where he or she happened to live, a French peasant could be threatened by English soldiers, French noblemen, Navarese, Burgundians, Bretons, Castilians or any number of mercenaries and écorcheurs. In such circumstances making peace was extremely difficult. Individuals and communities were often required to negotiate their own peace agreements with different parties independently of central concerns and policies. Negotiations might be compelled in extremis: mercenary and official forces on both sides offered communities 'peace' in return for patis. French lordships and principalities negotiated with England without the agreement of the French Crown. So, for example, during the late 1350s communities in the Nièvre in central France paid local troops 'fat, cheeses, eggs and other victuals and necessities in order to be able to live peacefully in their homes and go about their work without constant threat and fear'. Local agreements were made by all and sundry during the Armagnac-Burgundian war.[28]

The presence of the Free Companies was another complicating factor that made a long-term peace settlement particularly difficult to secure. One reason the major treaties failed to resolve the war was that peace with England did not always bring peace to the French people: indeed, mercenary forces tended to be brutally disruptive in France during periods of truce. The end to official hostilities left the Free Companies out of work and they maintained themselves by exploiting local populations. If soldiers were not paid they 'had nothing but what they could get by murder and by kidnapping men of all conditions, and women too and children'.[29] After the treaty of Brétigny, Charles V and du Guesclin sought to solve this problem and use the Free Companies for French advantage in the Castilian civil war – an action that served only to complicate further the political dynamics of the Hundred Years War. Later Charles VII took a different approach to the same problem by co-opting mercenary troops and incorporating them into his permanent army. Even in the service of the state, however, they remained a threat to national stability.[30]

The Free Companies also caused more theoretical problems. Certain authors, such as Jean Froissart, described the exercise of arms as intrinsically ennobling. For them, those who were *bellatores* were by their very nature noble. Froissart's account of the deeds of the mercenary captain the Bascot de Mauléon ('a good soldier and a great captain') shows this clearly. Froissart could not always distinguish between independent mercenary activity and legitimate warfare waged on princely authority. He could not help but view the depredations of the Free Companies as part of the cultural orbit of chivalry.[31] For others, however, mercenary activity reflected a widespread degeneracy that brought the conduct of all those fighting in the Anglo-French war into question. For Philippe de Mézières, by the 1390s, the English had gone too far:

It may be said, sadly enough, that the valiant chivalry of England, while obeying the divine order to punish sin for about sixty years, has been changed and made into an iron needle or goad, so sharp that it has forced souls without number to burn in hell; and the Black Boars, pitiless towards their Christian brothers, under pretence of prowess and worldly valour ... have sharpened their tusks against the chief cities of Spain, France and elsewhere.[32]

Philippe de Mézières was the best known of those in France calling for a resolution to the war. A scholar, soldier, mystic, royal adviser, incessant traveller, prolific author and a champion of the crusade, Philippe made a desperate plea for peace in the Anglo-French struggle. In his 1395 'Letter' to Richard II, he described the war as one of the wounds of Christendom that had to be healed; another was the Great Schism, and he saw the two as closely connected.[33] This was certainly true: the papacy should have taken a leading role in efforts to resolve the Anglo-French war as the

Avignon popes had sought to do, although without success. The Schism prevented such attempts as both sides recognised the authority of a different pope. De Mézières used the image of the Black Boars regularly throughout the 'Letter' to indicate the most war-mongering aspects of the English military aristocracy – those who had perpetrated the most violence and damage in France, those who stood most resolutely in the way of peace.[34]

De Mézières, of course, did not seek peace for its own sake but to clear the way for a crusade. He was not the first. Crusading was a consistent theme, underpinning many formal peace negotiations, and it lay at the heart of numerous peace overtures made during the war and in negotiations prior to 1337. Peace between England and France, it was argued, would allow a joint operation to take place against the enemies of Christendom. The discussions that led to the treaty of Paris in 1259 had considered just such a possibility.[35] Then, in the 1290s, Edmund of Lancaster, Edward I's lieutenant in Aquitaine, recorded that the king sought a settlement in the Anglo-French war 'for the peace of Christendom and the furtherance of the crusade'.[36] The fall of Acre, the last crusader state, in 1291 had increased the need for such an expedition. Similarly, the prospect of a crusade to Spain or the Holy Land had forestalled the outbreak of the Hundred Years War. When that possibility evaporated, and with the transference of the Valois crusade fleet from Marseilles to the Norman ports in the summer of 1336, war with England soon followed.[37]

Crusading remained a potent ideal in the later Middle Ages, and for at least the first half of the Hundred Years War a number of efforts were made to launch a major European campaign.[38] The efforts of the papacy and those of Peter of Cyprus (1360s) and de Mézières (1390s) were particularly notable.[39] However, the failure of these projects, particularly the disaster at Nicopolis in 1396, when the Ottomans crushed a Franco-Burgundian and German army, and the longevity of the Anglo-French war, saw a redirection of some of that crusading zeal. The war channelled the crusading impulses of many among the English and French chivalric classes away from the infidel and towards their neighbours: a form of 'sanctified patriotism' emerged on both sides of the Channel.[40] The crusades had previously formed a potential area for negotiation; in the fifteenth century crusading ideology served as a catalyst for the fighting. It is also the case that the expedition to Hungary in 1396 (the Nicopolis crusade), although it ended calamitously, played an important part in the emergence of Burgundy as a European power. In this expedition Philippe the Bold acted independently of France as ruler of a new semi-autonomous political power. The expansion of Burgundian authority, which the Nicopolis expedition demonstrated, further complicated Anglo-French relations not only because of Burgundy's role in the civil war but because of Burgundian ambitions for statehood and independence within France.[41]

The Great Schism and the defeat at Nicopolis, therefore, added hugely to the difficulties in achieving a resolution to the conflict: international cooperation became increasingly problematic thereafter, and, to complicate matters still further, the Hundred Years War started to take on a new character. The war began to be viewed as a struggle between chosen peoples.[42] Aspects of this were already evident; they can be seen, for example, in Louis I d'Anjou's commission of the 'Apocalypse' tapestries at Angers around 1373, which reflect the unprecedented catastrophes of the English *chevauchées* and recurring plague. The English were portrayed as monstrous and demonic but, like the forces of the Apocalypse, the tapestries suggest they would be defeated with God's help.[43] By contrast, the author of the *Gesta Henrici Quinti* compared the English army at Agincourt to the Israelites, and Henry V to both King David and Judas Maccabeus.[44] In France the extraordinary intervention of Joan of Arc exacerbated such attitudes. She seems to have viewed her own campaign as a crusade and one that might continue after the English had been defeated or withdrawn. In her 'Letter to the English' (22 March 1429) Joan claimed she had come 'from God to reclaim the blood royal'. She was 'very ready to make peace' if the English would make suitable reparations, but if they did not retreat she would 'have them all killed [since she had] been sent here by God the King of Heaven to drive [them] out of France'. If, however, the English did 'not bring destruction upon [themselves then they might] still join her company, in which the French will do the fairest deed that has ever been done for Christianity'[45] – they would recapture the Holy Land.

Joan's intervention certainly gave Christine de Pizan hope that peace really could be achieved on honourable terms. In 1417, when Christine wrote her *Prison de la vie humaine* for Marie de Berry after the disaster of Agincourt, she had given up all hope that peace could ever be brought to France under the Valois monarchy. But there were grounds for optimism once again by the time she wrote the *Ditié de Jehanne d'Arc* (completed 31 July 1429).[46]

In England, for contrasting reasons, the deteriorating situation after Joan's intervention also renewed interest in a settlement. Henry V's triumphs had galvanised the war effort in Parliament and the country at large: the lavish celebrations after Agincourt in 1415 are testament to this.

Fabulous and outlandish entertainments and decorations were prepared when the king returned in triumph from France. The citizens of London constructed giant figures on London Bridge: one, a man who

> ... held like a champion, a great axe in his right hand and, like a warder, the keys of the city hanging from a baton in his left. At his side stood a figure of a woman ... wearing a scarlet mantle ... and they were like a man and his wife who ... were bent upon seeing the eagerly awaited face of their lord ... And all around them, projecting from the ramparts, staffs bearing the royal arms and trumpets, clarions, and horns ringing out in multiple harmony embellished the tower [on the bridge], and the face of it bore this choice and appropriate legend inscribed on the war: Civitas Regis Iustice.

There were turrets bearing heraldic emblems and insignias, statues of St George, tapestries, choirboys dressed as angels, a company of older men dressed as the Apostles and others as prophets; flocks of small birds were released as the king passed by. Maidens sang to the returning king as if he were David returning from the slaying of Goliath.[47] Later, in 1419, there was dancing in the streets of London when news arrived of the capture of Rouen. Henry V's victories and the Burgundian alliance led to the treaty of Troyes in 1420 and the chance of a permanent resolution. However, like previous agreements, the treaty only led to further conflict. Indeed, it did not result in any period of peace at all. The treaty of Troyes was far more ambitious than the Brétigny settlement of 1360. It did not seek merely to transfer various French territories to English sovereign control. Rather King Henry sought to gain sovereignty over all France and seize the French throne. Through his marriage to Charles VI's daughter Katherine he would change the line of succession, thereby avoiding a conflict with Salic law. Henry became Charles's son and heir: the aging, deluded king retained his title but with Henry serving as regent: on Charles's death he would take the Crown.

This scheme depended on the disinheritance (and political disappearance) of the dauphin, who proved not to be amenable to such an idea. As a consequence, rather than bringing peace to France the treaty led to the nation's partition between the Anglo-Burgundian north and the dauphinist south (the so-called kingdom of Bourges). Henry V, therefore, had only a little while to enjoy his triumph. He found time to return to England to witness his new bride's coronation but returned to campaign in France almost immediately. Then, while besieging Meaux near Paris in 1422, he contracted dysentery – he died three months later.

This, also, did little to encourage peace. Thomas Montague, earl of Salisbury (1388–1428), triumphed at Cravant in Burgundy in July 1423, and John, duke of Bedford (1389–1435), was victorious at Verneuil ('a second Agincourt') in Normandy in August 1424. England was determined not to squander the late king's military inheritance. Nonetheless, while Henry himself had been lauded to the skies, the cost of his military ventures had started to become unpopular. Almost immediately after the reconquest Parliament indicated its reluctance to subsidise the defence of Normandy. Concerns over royal expenditure in France encouraged the decision to ensure a clear governmental division between the nations (the Dual Monarchy), which had been expressed in the treaty of Troyes. As king of France, Henry could, it was argued, find the money to pay for French expenditure out of French resources.[48] Thus, even before the setbacks of 1429 the war effort was pursued in some quarters in England with diminishing enthusiasm. As Adam Usk stated in an entry in his chronicle for 1421:

> Yet I fear, alas, that both the great men and the money of the kingdom will be miserably wasted on this enterprise. No wonder then, that the unbearable impositions being demanded from the people to this end are accompanied by dark – though private – mutterings and curses, and by hatred of such extortions.[49]

As always, taxation remained unpopular. Despite this, although many did not wish to pay for the war they did not necessarily want peace with France. With the exception of a brief period in the 1390s an official peace policy rarely proved popular in England, and even then there had been strident voices of protest among the nobility. The situation in the 1440s was not dissimilar, except that the English, in a political sense, now had much more to lose. Henry VI became convinced of the need for peace, and he was willing to accept terms that fell far short of those agreed in the treaty of Troyes. The English position had deteriorated sharply following the appearance of Joan of Arc in 1428 and still further with the Congress of Arras in 1435. Worsening economic conditions exacerbated by the costs of the king's religious and educational projects made Parliament increasingly unwilling to fund military operations.[50] Some, indeed, argued that an end to the Anglo-French war offered a number of political and economic advantages. Richard II had hoped to use peace with France as a means to extend English authority in Britain and Ireland. In a similar fashion the author of the *Libelle of Englyshe Polycye* (1436) argued that an end to French hostilities (while retaining Calais) would permit the redirection of English resources in order to exercise control of the sea, and so maintain trade and national security: 'Cherish merchandise,' he wrote, 'keep the Admiralty, that we be masters of the Narrow Sea.'[51]

Following this diplomatic change of heart in London, William de la Pole, earl of Suffolk (1396–1450), a key member of the king's council and steward of the household, brokered the truce of Tours in May 1444. The agreement secured nothing more than two years of peace sealed by a marriage between Henry VI and Margaret, a younger daughter of René, duke of Anjou and count of Provence (1409–80). Henry's government employed John Lydgate (c.1370–c.1450), the poet and prior of Hatfield Regis, as a spokesman to justify the truce.[52] Lydgate, who had often discovered patrons among the Lancastrian regime, probably did not find this a difficult commission; his 'A Praise of Peace', written prior to 1443, stated:

> All war is dreadful, virtuous peace is good,
> Strife is hateful, peace the daughter of pleasure,
> In Charlemagne's time there was shed much blood,
> God send us peace between England and France;
> War causes poverty, peace causes abundance,
> And between both might it the more increase,
> Without feigning, fraud, or variance,
> Between all Christians, Christ Jesus, send us peace.[53]

Charles VII chose Margaret carefully: she was not a direct blood relation of the royal house, which could have strengthened the Lancastrian claim to the French throne, although the marriage did provide Henry with a useful link to a powerful family at the Valois court. The union, however, was of greater benefit to the king of France. He faced considerable opposition at home from various dissident noble houses, and England's alliance with Anjou meant Henry could not forge ties with one of those families. For Charles, the marriage was a means to control domestic threats to his power, which now appeared more serious than those posed by England. Meanwhile Henry and the earl of Suffolk believed, wrongly, that the marriage would provide the means for future negotiations and a permanent resolution of the war.[54]

The truce of Tours was welcomed in some circles in England and
Normandy; however, a powerful faction led by the king's uncle, Humphrey,
duke of Gloucester (1390–1447), opposed it vigorously and remained
determined to continue the struggle. Henry VI ploughed on regardless.
Without consulting key figures in the nobility the king tried to extend the
duration of the settlement by offering, in 1445, to surrender the county of
Maine to Charles VII. Again, Henry hoped to extend the truce and so gain
time to negotiate a permanent resolution. It may be that in earlier negotiations the earl of Suffolk had suggested the possibility that Maine could be
sacrificed, but Henry's actions provoked fury.[55] Maine was a buffer to
Normandy and several captains refused, initially, to hand their castles over
to the French. It took until 1448 for the surrender to take place. Soon
afterwards the captains' fears were realised. Henry and Suffolk had gambled
that the truce and the surrender of Maine would lead to negotiations for a
longer peace – they were wrong. In common with earlier agreements the
truce of Tours provoked rather than resolved hostilities. In August 1449
Charles VII launched the campaign that began the reconquest of Normandy.
In England in 1450 this precipitated Cade's Rebellion and the murder of
Suffolk, the man commonly seen as 'the architect of [Henry VI's] ... ill-
conceived policy of peace at any price'.[56] Jack Cade and his rebels demanded
punishment for those responsible for the surrender of the duchy. The
response revealed that while the English people had no wish to spend a
great deal of money on the war, they did not want peace with France either,
certainly not peace at any price. In his letter of 1450 to John Paston, John
Gresham lamented 'Today it is told Cherbourg is gone and we have now
not a foot of land left in Normandy.'[57] Soon afterwards Gascony was lost,
first in 1451 and finally in 1453.

However, although the Hundred Years War ended in 1453, Anglo-
French hostilities resumed soon after. As early as 1468 Edward IV was
planning an expedition to France; he continued to make alliances with
French principalities hostile to the Valois – with Brittany in 1472 and
Burgundy in 1474; and a year later an English army returned to France
forcing Louis XI (r.1461–83) to negotiate the treaty of Picquigny.[58] This,
however, was a different sort of conflict – the loss of Gascony changed the
nature of Anglo-French hostilities yet again, just as they had changed regularly over many years previously. By the later fifteenth century the sheer
length of the war created an intrinsic barrier to any resolution; it had
reshaped the national characters of England and France, establishing a
tradition of war and an identity defined by mutual hostility.

The attempts to secure peace in the Hundred Years War were determined in large measure by the respective personalities of the kings of England and France. Just as the treaty of Paris held strong for a time because of the personal relationship between Henry III and Louis IX, so a resolution would never have been possible during the reigns of Edward III and Charles V. The culture of the Valois and Plantagenet courts reflected the interests and priorities of their rulers. Consequently, the longest cessation of hostilities during the Hundred Years War followed the truce of Paris in 1396 when both Richard II and Charles VI were keen to secure some form of resolution. The truce foundered with Richard's deposition and in the political turmoil which Charles's madness created. That turmoil put paid to any idea of peace. In France, powerful factions led by the dukes of Orléans and Burgundy struggled for control. Orléans's assassination in 1407 set the stage for a further conflict that would be fought within the greater struggle of the Hundred Years War.

CHAPTER 5

The Madness of Kings

KINGSHIP AND ROYAL POWER

1407

The whole of the French nation was saddened by the illness which the king [Charles VI] contracted . . . for he was till then high in the love and favour of his subjects, and because he was the head the distress was all the more deeply felt. When the head of a body is sick, all the limbs suffer.[1]

Jean Froissart, *Chroniques*

The five English and five French kings who contested the Hundred Years War were hugely significant in shaping the course and outcome of the struggle, and this despite the rise of professional armies and the increasing importance of state institutions, the growth of bureaucracies, representative assemblies and the greater intricacy of local government, and despite the emergence of gunpowder and a major restructuring of the social order. As the French jurist Jean de Terrevermeille (c.1370–1430) wrote, 'His [the king's] losses are our [the people's] ruin, and our safety within him lies.'[2] And yet this was also a period in which the institutions of monarchy and conceptions of kingship were placed under enormous strain. Just as kings shaped the outcome of the war, so the struggle reshaped many of the characteristics of kingship in England and France. The war was coloured by and led to the depositions of three English kings, while the madness of Charles VI all but destroyed France.

To a degree this had always been so; kings had always shaped national destinies and royal failure had often proved disastrous, but rarely were the consequences as crippling as those seen in the reign of Charles VI. The vacuum at the centre of France (at the head of the body politic) caused by the king's madness led to civil war. This, in turn, allowed Henry V to capture Normandy, and through the subsequent treaty of Troyes in 1420 he

almost seized the French throne. The treaty appeared to signal the extinc-
tion of the Valois line and the effective annihilation of French kingship.

The consequences of Charles's madness had become manifest long
before this. In 1407

> there happened in the city of Paris an event which was more pitiful than
> any that had occurred for a very long time in the Christian kingdom of
> France, and that event was the death of one man. Because of it the king
> and all the princes of his blood and indeed nearly all his people suffered
> greatly; the kingdom was for a long time divided against itself and much
> weakened by this strife ... I am speaking of the death of the Duc
> d'Orléans, only brother of the king of France, Charles the Well-Beloved
> and sixth of his name.[3]

The assassination of Louis, duke of Orléans, by agents of Duke Jean the
Fearless of Burgundy on 23 November 1407, was caused, in part, by King
Charles's insanity, and it proved critical in shaping the trajectory of the
remainder of the Hundred Years War. Twelve years of civil strife followed, at
the end of which Jean himself would be murdered. Killed on the dauphin's
orders on the bridge of Montereau (at the confluence of the Seinne and Yonne
rivers) in 1419, his death in its turn led to the Anglo-Burgundian alliance and
the Double Monarchy. Clearly, this was not the outcome Jean had intended in
1407. Leaving aside his own murder, he had no wish to place an Englishman
on the throne of Clovis (r.481–511), Charlemagne (r.768–814) and St Louis
(Louis IX; r.1226–70). Indeed, Jean had no real wish to lessen the French
king's authority, or to take his place; rather he aimed to wield essentially vice-
regal power by gaining control of the council that took charge during the
king's increasingly febrile 'absences' – the name given to the sometimes
protracted bouts of madness Charles VI suffered for thirty years of his reign.

The first indication that all was not well with Charles had come on 5
August 1392 when the king was en route to Brittany, at the head of an
army raised to chastise the recalcitrant Duke Jean IV de Montfort (1339–
99). In the forest outside Le Mans he suffered the first manifestation of the
illness, often diagnosed as paranoid schizophrenia, which would scar the
remainder of his long reign.[4] The day was said to have been very warm and
the king was wearied by periodic bouts of fever and lack of sleep. Charles,
his brother Louis, the recently appointed duke of Orléans, and a few
attendants entered a clearing near the village of Pontvillain. A page, perhaps
lulled into sleep, dropped his lance and it fell on another man's helmet.

Hearing the clash of metal, Charles reacted with extraordinary violence. Thinking he was attacked, he lashed out with his sword. None dared restrain him, and swiftly the page and three of his companions were killed. The king also struck Louis and pursued him through the forest. For more than an hour, until completely spent, the king assailed any who came near him before eventually collapsing and falling into a coma.[5]

Having only lately reached his majority, both the king and also his kingdom were wracked by this seizure. His father's death in 1380 had thrown court and country into conflict as Charles's uncles vied for control.[6] The two main protagonists in these early days of his reign were the deeply unpopular Louis of Anjou (1339–84), whose ambitions stretched beyond France into Italy, and Philippe the Bold of Burgundy, who wished to use the resources of the royal treasury to carve out an even greater principality for himself in the Low Countries. Courted by both these men were the other princes of the Blood Royal and the key power-brokers, Jean, duke of Berry (1340–1416) and Louis of Bourbon (1337–1410). Louis of Anjou soon left to pursue his Italian dreams, leaving Philippe in control of the government and its extensive resources. By means of some judicious alliances he soon established himself as one of the most powerful princes in Europe. Then, in 1387, Charles VI declared himself of age (he was twenty), ready to assume the duties of government, and he replaced his uncles on the council with men of his own choosing – a group known to Froissart as the *Marmousets* (men of the king's chamber). This group, which operated under the political leadership of Olivier de Clisson (constable of France, 1380–92) and the intellectual direction of Philippe de Mézières, sought reform in government and throughout the state.[7] France saw a new balance of power established. Alongside the *Marmousets* the king's younger brother, Louis, duke of Touraine, was the main beneficiary of the new regime. Through a great deal of patronage and his valuable marriage in 1389 to Valentina Visconti of Milan, Louis increased his political and territorial influence enormously. Then, just prior to the 1392 Brittany campaign, Louis exchanged ('upgraded') Touraine for the duchy of Orléans. When Charles's madness struck it allowed the rift at the heart of government to be reopened. Louis' political advancement meant that he now formed the main opposition to Burgundian ambitions, and growing hostility between these power blocs led to his assassination in 1407 on the orders of Jean the Fearless, duke of Burgundy since 1404.

Jean the Fearless (Jean sans Peur) did not (perhaps could not) distance himself from Louis's murder, but neither did he show any remorse for his actions. On the contrary, he acknowledged his involvement in the affair, defended himself robustly and, rather dramatically, rewarded the principal assassin, Raoul d'Anquetonville, with an annuity 'in consideration of notable services which . . . [he] had rendered to the king and [the duke of Burgundy]'.[8] The king, however, during one of his lucid moments, saw things differently: the murder of one of the Blood Royal could not be ignored because it was, in a sense, an attack on his own authority. Throughout the later Middle Ages increasingly grandiose claims, founded on legal argument and expounded in theological doctrine, were made for the extent and (divine) source of French royal power. These led not only to the near sanctification of the king but also conferred certain sacral qualities on his family – those of his blood.[9] The murder of one of the Blood Royal, there-fore, even though perpetrated on the orders of the duke of Burgundy, had to be explained or punished. Early in the new year (1408), Jean the Fearless took steps to justify himself. His lawyer Jean Petit drafted a now-famous apologia, claiming the murder had been a judicial execution made in the interests of the state: he accused Orléans of treachery, tyranny and dabbling in black magic. Duke Jean received a warm reception in Paris when he told the same story. Such accusations resonated in this period, and that of sorcery not necessarily the loudest.[10]

From the late thirteenth century the accusation of treason carried increasingly dangerous connotations and, as a result, increasingly brutal punishments in both France and England. Philippe VI had responded to Flemish revolts in 1328 and 1338 – actions he viewed as treacherous – with brutal retribution, torture and execution. It was because of this, in part, that Edward III claimed the French throne in 1340 – to prevent a charge of treason being laid against the Flemings: by pressing his claim they might pledge him their allegiance with fewer qualms.[11] The charge of treason took on greater significance in the later Middle Ages following the use of Roman law to bolster royal authority and elevate the status of the monarch. Capetian lawyers stated that the king was as an emperor (i.e. without superior) in his own kingdom (*rex in regno suo est imperator*) – a concept later adopted in England. Together with a developing if still abstract idea of the state, such concepts contributed to the greater political fury with which treason (to king and state) was punished. Hanging, drawing and quartering (with certain variations depending on the nature of the crime) was introduced as the sentence for high-profile individuals adjudged guilty of treason.[12]

Both Plantagenet and Valois kings used the threat of the charge of treason as a political weapon, albeit with mixed success. Rulers such as

Philippe VI, uncertain of their authority and desperate to prevent any dimi-
nution of their status, claimed *lèse-majesté* to be not only the 'sister of rebellion and ... an act of disloyalty', but also 'tantamount to sacrilege'.[13] In
England, Edward II and Richard II thought similarly and both used broadly
(or barely) defined notions of treason to exert their authority. In their cases
this strategy proved disastrously counter-productive and it contributed to
their eventual depositions. In 1398 Richard went so far as to declare that
'the mere allegation of a man's treason was notorious proof of his guilt'.[14]
When determined solely by royal whim, treason, with its threat to life, limb
and honour, posed a fundamental danger to the body politic. In particular it
inhibited the nobility from playing what its members saw as their proper
role, diminishing their opportunities to question, let alone criticise, the
king. In England the result of such political impotence might leave only a
more direct course of action, namely to dispose of the monarch altogether
since no lesser means of complaint remained.[15] In France, although treason
charges remained common throughout the period of the Hundred Years
War, the reaction against Valois kings tended to be less violent.

The opaque definitions of treason which Edward II and Richard II
employed soon came to be seen as tyrannical. Those kings more certain of
their positions or more sensitive to the potential divisiveness of such a
policy delineated the parameters of the crime much more precisely. Edward
III issued the Statute of Treasons (1352): to commit treason was to plot
the death of the king, queen, or heir-apparent; to violate the queen or
the king's eldest daughter; to wage war against the king in his realm; to
provide direct assistance to the king's enemies; to counterfeit the privy seal,
great seal, or the king's money; to murder the chancellor, treasurer, or the
king's justices. All other felonies that might be adjudged treasonous were to
be brought before Parliament. After the Lancastrian usurpation in 1399,
Henry IV returned to this definition.[16]

In France the quasi-divinity of royal power made accusations of treason
especially significant. When combined with certain political realities
and the spectre of sorcery, which gained even darker connotations in the
context of Charles VI's madness, the accusations which the duke of
Burgundy levelled against the murdered Duke Louis proved sufficiently
convincing, and on 9 March 1408 Charles offered Jean the Fearless a
formal pardon. Unsurprisingly this did nothing to lessen the enmity
between the houses of Orléans and Burgundy; indeed, it provoked civil war.
Charles's 'absences', therefore, led to a major crisis of kingship, as did the
Lancastrian revolution in England. Richard II's deposition in 1399 proved

much more significant than that of Edward II in 1327. Henry IV's coronation shattered the Plantagenet line of succession, brought turmoil to England and ruptured the Anglo-French truce of 1396, which had been sealed in the same year with King Richard's marriage to Charles VI's six-year-old daughter Isabella.

This was merely one occasion when kingship shaped and was shaped by the Hundred Years War. Matters of kingship guided the trajectory of the conflict from its inception. Royal rights lay at the heart of many of the disputes that ignited the war in 1337: the harbouring of Robert d'Artois, the mutual aggravation of Anglo-Flemish and Franco-Scottish relations, the status of Gascony, and the claim to the French throne itself. Some of these issues had been a source of simmering resentment for some time because of conflicting interpretations of the legal relationship between the Plantagenets and Capetians. However, Charles IV's death in 1328 marked the end of the Capetian dynasty and changed the nature of the Anglo-French struggle. A series of disputes that had centred on the comparative rights of kings over lands in France became, at least in theory, a conflict over the right to rule France itself.

The rumour of war, therefore, grew louder with Philippe VI's coronation in 1328. It was a ceremony that conferred enormous authority on him: far more than just a political act, in France it was little less than a beatification. In England, by contrast, the anointing of the king never seems to have carried quite the same significance. This was in spite of vigorous attempts to propagate a potent image of holy kingship resting on legal and theological foundations, and augmented by fanciful stories in which angels delivered vials of oil with which to anoint God's chosen monarch.[17] The spiritual authority conferred by the coronation and fostered by long years of ecclesiastical support meant that the French monarch was portrayed as more akin to a Christian Roman emperor than to other European kings, including his English counterpart.[18]

The more limited nature of English kingship is evident in the oath which the monarch swore at his coronation. In the revised oath of 1308 Edward II promised not only to confirm the laws made by his predecessors, as his forebears had done, but also 'to maintain and keep the laws and rightful customs which the community of the realm shall choose, and defend and enforce them to the honour of God, to the best of his ability'.[19] This created a new and different form of contract between ruler and ruled. It implied that a change had occurred in the complexion of the body politic and that a new relationship now existed between the constituent parts of that body. By this time a reference to the 'community of the realm' implied a more extensive political body than merely the magnates and Privy Council; rather the oath indicated that the king was now answerable, in some way, to his people as a whole. While Edward II and his successors gave no more than the most general considerations to the expectations of the English peasantry, the coronation oath reveals the growing importance of a widening political community – one that would soon begin to express its opinions in Parliament and, with the Peasants' Revolt of 1381, through mass action.[20]

Just as the king had to be aware of a changing political constituency, so the people were readjusting their relationship with the monarch. Following the change in the coronation oath the so-called 'Declaration of 1308' stated that homage was due to the Crown and the regal office, not to the person of the king. This distinction between office and individual – the notion of the king's 'two bodies' – represents an important change in the conception of English monarchy and it may have facilitated the rash of royal depositions that followed.[21]

The importance of coronations (of king-making) can also be seen in the manner in which they influenced major strategic decisions in the course of the Hundred Years War. In late 1359, after the French rejected the extortionate Second Treaty of London, Edward III landed with one of the largest and best-equipped English expeditionary forces to date and marched on Reims, the coronation city. At the beginning of the war the king may have hoped merely to gain Gascony in full sovereignty and stop French interference in Scotland. As the campaign unfolded his hopes grew; perhaps he envisaged a restoration of the Angevin Empire, and following the capture of Jean II at Poitiers in 1356 his ambitions may, briefly, have extended to the throne of France itself. The siege of Reims, however, failed, as did a subsequent assault on Paris, forcing Edward to come to terms at Brétigny in 1360. The treaty recalibrated English aspirations at least until the French civil war.[22]

An even more dangerous expedition was undertaken to Reims to ensure Charles VII's coronation. Because of the treaty of Troyes and the conditions appertaining when Charles VI died, his son had not received the crown. In 1429, despite the relief of the siege of Orléans and the dauphinist victory at Patay (18 June 1429), the road to Reims, deep in Burgundian territory, remained perilous.[23] The ceremony, however, was central to Joan of Arc's mission, and although propagandised and romanticised there is a measure of truth in the image of the halting, hesitant, uncertain dauphin transformed into Charles the Victorious by his coronation.[24] Similarly the immediate although ill-conceived English rejoinder of Henry VI's ceremony performed in Paris and by an English bishop showed a keen awareness of the political significance of royal investiture.[25]

The coronation – a true coronation, that is – invested a monarch with great political and spiritual authority. It was an office underpinned by legal argument and theological doctrine, both of which evolved and became more closely entwined throughout this period. After being anointed with the Holy Oil, first used to invest Clovis, French kings were permitted to take Communion in both kinds (wine as well as bread), and both French and English monarchs gained the power to heal the king's evil (the skin disease scrofula). A regular custom of touching those afflicted with scrofula developed in the French royal court under Louis IX. In England, although earlier monarchs claimed or were attributed with healing powers, there is no strong evidence of a similar practice in use before Edward I came to the throne (1272). These sacral powers continued to be utilised during the Hundred Years War and came to indicate a legitimate claim to the French throne. In 1353 one Jehan de Lions avowed Edward III to be the rightful king of France because he could cure scrofula – a declaration for which he was imprisoned. In the *Grandes Chroniques* Louis IX's miraculous powers as king were used not only to emphasise his devotion and humility, but also to demonstrate his Valois successors' political legitimacy.[26]

Such ceremonies were influenced by biblical, Greek and Roman works regarding the source and extent of royal power. In France, authors such as Nicole d'Oresme, Christine de Pizan and Philippe de Mézières emphasised the pre-eminence of royal power although they recognised the king had responsibilities to his subjects. At Edward III's court, various governmental theories were proposed in the *Speculum Regis*, written for him as a young man by either Simon Islip (archbishop of Canterbury, 1349–66) or William of Pagula (d.1332). Thomas Bradwardine (1290–1349) was another who argued in favour of autocratic kingship. In *De causa Dei* he used Aristotle's *Metaphysics* to emphasise the thaumaturgical powers of the English king.[27]

The influence of Roman law was of particular significance in advancing this conception of kingship and promoted strongly by authors such as Giles of Rome (c.1243–1316) and John Wyclif (in *De Civili Dominio* and *De Officio Regis*). Giles referred to the prince or the king as a demi-god (*semideus*), and writers at the court of Charles V used even more extravagant language to exalt royal power.[28] These influenced later practices in England such as Richard II's insistence in the 1390s on new ceremonial and the use of 'majesty' as a term of address. The veracity of the story that Richard demanded his courtiers kneel if he so much as glanced at them has been called into question, but there is little doubt that his reign was seen as tyrannical. In reality, however, his style of government was representative of changing European conceptions of kingship – ones that, at this stage, sat more comfortably in a French rather than an English context.[29] The Valois kings were buttressed in their authority by long years of thaumaturgical ritual and propaganda not evident to the same degree in England. In France the king was above the law and bound by no constraint but 'the fear of his own conscience'.[30] It is perhaps for this reason that the madness of Charles VI was not a cause for deposition, although, like Richard II, he was clearly thought of as *rex inutilis* (a useless king).

This combination of divine authority and legal rights offered kings a powerful protection against rebellion, at least in theory, since those who opposed the royal will could be deemed sacrilegious. Clearly, however, this was not sufficient to protect English kings from deposition, which suggests they were not judged as 'holy' as their French counterparts. Indeed, in the case of Richard II, he may have been deposed in part because he assumed a style of kingship that had a distinctly French, sacral and hence authoritarian quality. The distinction between the English king's 'two bodies' grew in this period: as the splendour and spiritual resonance of the monarch's office increased, his hold on that office grew more tenuous.

When Richard II suffered the same political fate as his great-grandfather Edward II, he was portrayed as wanting in both his personae (or bodies) as king – the body politic and the body natural. Richard's personal limitations and failures were emphasised: he was accused of perjury in respect of his personal and coronation oaths; of sacrilege and sodomy; his mismanagement of the government was said to have led to a loss of royal dignity; and he had failed to uphold the law and liberty of the realm. This included, most damningly, chapter 39 of Magna Carta, which originally stated: 'No free man shall be taken or imprisoned, or dispossessed or outlawed or exiled or in any way ruined, nor will we go or send against him except by the lawful judgement of his peers or by the law of the land.' Legal constraints such as Magna Carta prevented the extensive use of Roman law in England: its inferiority to common law ensured English kings could not use it to bolster their authority to the degree enjoyed by the French. It is deeply significant that in 1369 Edward III replaced the phrase 'no free man' with 'no man, of whatever estate or condition he may be'. He promised no one should be dispossessed, imprisoned or put to death without 'due process of law', which was the first use of that phrase in the statutes.[31]

Richard had ignored this and attempted to be the source of the law rather than its mouthpiece (*rex loquens* as opposed to *lex loquens*). His actions were in accordance with certain Roman legal concepts: *Princeps legibus solutus est* ('the king is not bound by laws') and *Quod principi placuit legis habet vigorem* ('what the prince decides has the force of law'),[32] but in an English political context in 1399 he could only be adjudged a tyrant. The rule of law, the status of the monarch, his ability to govern, implement justice and defend the country were linked inextricably. Kingship in order to be effective had to be strong, but that strength could be used with 'evil intent' and, should it be so, the aristocracy was obligated to defend the proper laws and customs of the realm against tyranny in just the same way as they were required to support a just ruler – by force of arms.

Richard's deposition, perhaps because he was Charles VI's son-in-law, was discussed widely in France and horrified the French court. It entrenched the English reputation for moral depravity symbolised by regicide. Guillaume de Rochefort, chancellor of France (d.1492), exaggerated more than a little when he alleged the English had endured twenty-six changes of dynasty since the foundation of their monarchy. Such a 'stigmata of crime', he said, could never have taken place in France. His words, however, reflected differing attitudes to kingship on either side of the Channel.[33]

The development of Capetian and Valois claims to monarchical supremacy had taken place over a long period and evolved still further during the Hundred Years War. John of Salisbury's thirteenth-century notion of the king as the image of God (*rex imago Dei*) became, by the end of the second decade of the fifteenth century, an avowal of little less than a divine right of royal succession. By comparison, the kings of England, notably Richard II, while at the apex of the political community were an intrinsic part of it and subject to its contractual principles.[34] It was a contract that resulted in the deposition of successive English kings.

The Valois, therefore, may have been vulnerable to attack from abroad but in general the French monarchy rarely gave the impression of being threatened at home. Despite the political and personal disasters of Crécy, Poitiers and Agincourt, no French ruler paid with his life or throne. The later Capetian and early Valois kings created a model of kingship that appeared all but invulnerable to domestic assault.[35] Indeed, growing pride in the king and the Valois dynasty prompted various French authors to delight in the comparative poverty of Plantagenet monarchy and in the degeneracy that led the English to 'kill their kings'.[36] For this reason, despite his madness, there was no significant attempt to remove Charles VI from the French throne. The civil war that followed the assassination of Louis d'Orléans in 1407 was not a struggle to seize the Crown, merely to control its resources.

The apparent incomprehensibility or impossibility of regicide in France is, though, easily exaggerated – one of many idealistic themes nurtured through long years in the abbey of Saint-Denis and at the University of Paris. The French crown did not rest as easily on the monarch as those propagandists suggested: Charles of Navarre, for one, had no qualms in seeking 'regime change' in France, while Charles VII had to face the revolt of the *Praguerie*.[37] Nonetheless, there is little doubt that the theoretical foundations on which the French monarchy stood – legally and spiritually, if not bureaucratically and financially – were considerably more robust than those that sustained the Plantagenets.

As this suggests, conceptions of royal power differed in England and France, certainly when the war began, and those differences grew as the struggle unfolded. This was in part because the Hundred Years War altered political and social structures in England and France, changes to which monarchies had no immunity. War led to an expansion of government and encouraged greater participation in it as bureaucracies and representative assemblies developed – these institutions vied for power with the monarchies. Furthermore, the war continued for so long that it became a national enterprise for successive generations. This reshaped the martial role of the king and engendered a new sense of national consciousness in England and France (see Chapter 10).

However, although the Hundred Years War wrought many changes, the basic requirements of late medieval kingship remained much as they had been for generations, which is no surprise since much of the glamour of royalty lay in its antiquity. For Sir John Fortescue, the fifteenth-century political theorist, the king's responsibilities were simple and twofold: 'the office of king is to fight the battles of his people and to judge them rightfully'.[38] Success in these areas should ensure a successful reign such as that enjoyed by Charles V. Known to posterity as Charles 'the Wise', he was wise enough to surround himself with capable men who ensured justice was done and the realm defended. According to Christine de Pizan, the king's biographer, 'The king desired to fill his court and his council with just and wise men . . . [and] for the good conduct of his wars he made men come from every country, seasoned knights wise and expert in the ways of war.'[39] The importance of seeking out and giving heed to good advice had long been recognised.[40] According to Jean Gerson, 'A king without prudent counsel is like the head of a body without eyes, without ears, and without nose.'[41] By that criterion (and others) Edward II and Richard II were both senseless. Edward 'resembled his father [Edward I] neither in wit nor valour, but ruled the country in an unbridled fashion, and relied on the advice of certain evil persons ... such a man was not worthy to wear the crown and be called king'.[42]

According to John Capgrave (1393–1464), Richard II's failures were due largely to his injudicious choice of advisers: 'King Richard was in the habit of promoting worthless and malicious characters, and without either regarding the advantage of the state, or attending to the advice of the lords, afforded a hearing only to those who used, as it were, to colour their faces with the pigment of flattery.'[43] Thomas Walsingham, similarly, described the members of Richard's household as

> knights of Venus rather than Mars, showing more prowess in the bedchamber than on the field of battle, defending themselves more with their tongue than with their lance, being alert with their tongues, but asleep when martial deeds were required. So those who were in the king's company made no effort to teach him the attributes that befit a great knight. I am not just speaking of skill in wartime but also to the pursuits which especially befit noble kings in peacetime such as hunting or falconry or similar things which increase a king's reputation.[44]

Such matters were of deep concern to the wider polity, especially the nobility who wished to have the ear of the king and for him to behave appropriately – to be a king was, in no small measure, to appear kingly. Part of Edward III's success stemmed from his ability to collaborate with the English aristocracy and to bring the political elite together in support of his domestic policies and continental ambitions. This was a policy born of necessity and the result of seeing the dangers of division at first hand in his father's court. It was also a policy recommended by authors concerned with theories of political governance such as John of Salisbury (c.1120–80), whose highly influential work on the body politic was translated for Charles V.[45] Christine de Pizan used the same image to project an idealised social model: she stressed the need for harmony between the estates, the importance of balance in aristocratic relations and the mutual obligations of ruler and ruled. A prince should care for his subjects, and take note of their wishes, although, Christine noted, this gave them no right to rebel against him.[46] Philippe de Mézières, in similar fashion, used the image of a great ship and its sailors working together under the command of the captain (king) to represent an idealised vision of unity among the French Estates General.[47]

The nature of the relationship between a king and his subjects remained an issue of importance for a long time. For Niccolò Machiavelli at the start of the sixteenth century a prince best controlled his subjects through fear. This idea was far from new; over a hundred years previously Christine de Pizan had reached the same conclusion,[48] as had Jean Froissart, although predictably he expected rather more of his heroes: 'a lord was to be loved, trusted, feared, served and held in honour by his subjects'.[49]

Charles V, by achieving a measure of national unity and through a judicious choice of counsellors and lieutenants, orchestrated a French military revival from 1369 until his death in 1380. Charles, though, was no great soldier himself, and for many the ideal king was also a warrior. The glamour gained by victory in battle could be a vital element in successful royal government but, in France at least, as the war progressed the importance of national military success outweighed a king's personal prowess. Throughout the war tactical developments and improvements in military technology intensified the dangers of the battlefield: casualty rates increased and the opportunity to take prisoners declined. This placed all combatants at greater risk, royalty included. For a king, however, capture might be more damaging politically than death. The consequences of the defeat at Poitiers and the imprisonment of Jean II were long remembered. As a result, certainly for Christine de Pizan, the military successes of Charles V's reign were not compromised by his limited personal involvement. Given the memory of Poitiers, the dangers of indiscriminate missile weapons and the growing threat posed by artillery, she preferred to emphasise prudence (*prudentia*) over prowess (*proèce*) as the key virtue of kingship.[50] While it was certainly the case, as Honoré Bonet wrote, that the king of France 'could not abstain from making war against the king of England without mortal sin for if he were to allow his men to be killed and his kingdom robbed and destroyed, who would pardon such negligence?',[51] he did not have to do so in person. Certainly, by the time Charles VII came to the throne in 1422, bravery in battle and skill-at-arms were not indispensable requirements of French kingship.[52]

In England, by contrast, it remained a clear political advantage to be recognised as a warrior. Military failure or perceived passivity played important roles in the depositions of English monarchs, while personal success in the field against the nation's traditional enemies, France and Scotland, added much to a king's reputation. As a result, Richard II's policy of peace towards France and failure to live up to the reputation of his father and grandfather, still less to that of the Lionheart, his namesake, undoubtedly compromised his authority. By contrast, Henry V was able to transform the prestige and authority of the English Crown at home and abroad.[53] Like Richard II, Henry VI suffered by comparison with his forebears: contemporaries could scarcely believe he was the son of the victor of Agincourt. Scrabbling for an explanation, they described him as 'his [French] mother's stupid offspring, not his father's, a son greatly degenerated from the father, who did not cultivate the art of war'.[54] This only worsened with the king's descent into madness, said by some to have been brought on by news of the defeat at Castillon in 1453.[55]

It is clear that numerous fourteenth- and early fifteenth-century authors such as Froissart, Chandos Herald and Thomas Walsingham, writing for English audiences, placed great value on royal martial prowess, and although others such as John Gower saw the main role of the king as that of a governor not a warrior, theirs appears to have been a minority view. In France, by contrast, as the war progressed the expectation lessened that the king would also be the epitome of knighthood, perhaps because, as Crécy, Poitiers and Agincourt showed, chivalry (in its traditional, mounted guise) was unlikely to bring victory in an age of infantry and missile weapons. Charles VII became Charles 'the Victorious' in large measure because of the potency of Jean Bureau's artillery train, not his own skill- at- arms. By the end of the war there was a clear distinction between the expectations the peoples of England and France had of their kings – 'Chivalry [came to] define the English regal style, just as sacramentalism did the French.'[56]

The differences in the military expectations of kings as well as other characteristics of French and English kingship can be seen in royal funerals.[57] Among the most distinctive aspects of services in both countries was the use of a lifelike effigy in place of the deceased king. In England this practice dated back to the funeral of Edward II (1327) and it may have come to French attention following Henry V's death in 1422; certainly, it was first adopted in France a few months later for Charles VI's funeral.[58] Thereafter the French rites associated with the effigy appear to have swiftly become more elaborate. In France and England both effigies were dressed in the royal regalia and adorned with the symbols of sovereignty; but in France the effigy was treated as though it was alive – meals were even served in its presence. Because the effigy retained the dignity of monarchy the dauphin – the new king – did not participate in the funeral since it was thought improper/impossible for two kings of France to inhabit the same space simultaneously. Again, the imperial connotations of rule are apparent in this ceremony: French royal funerals display many of the characteristics of Roman apotheosis ceremonies. Through the use of the effigy the illusion of continuity of rule was maintained until the new monarch acceded: *Le roi est mort! Vive le roi!* The old king, through the effigy, retained his sacred authority and so continued to bear his symbols of office until buried at Saint-Denis.[59] The body of the king was accompanied to his burial by the four presidents of the *parlement* of Paris – a practice going back to the funeral of Jean le Bon in 1364. They did so 'because they represent his person in matters of justice, which is the principal member of his crown, and by which he reigns and has seignory [sovereignty]'.[60]

The sacral nature of French kingship was, therefore, evident in royal funerals. By contrast, in England the service revealed the military and chivalric connotations of monarchical power. During the Hundred Years War the tradition began of a knight (or more than one) entering the chapel during the requiem mass. Riding one of the king's horses, bearing a shield emblazoned with the king's arms and carrying his standard, he and other knights of the realm offered these tokens at the foot of the royal tomb. This may have begun in 1377 (Edward III) and was certainly performed in 1422 (Henry V). By comparison it was not until 1498 that a French king's 'achievements' were offered up at his funeral. This indicates that English kings (at least the successful ones) conformed to that 'rather aggressive brand of chivalry' which differentiated English from French kingship in the later Middle Ages.[61]

Differences in the character of English and French kingship had been evident when the war began in 1337, and they became more apparent as the struggle progressed. The period of the war saw France make the painful transition from 'feudal' monarchy to the verge of early modern absolutism. Following an uneven process of disintegration and reconstruction, the power and prosperity of Capetian France were all but broken before the Valois were able to establish (and re-establish) systems of governance centred on the king. This gave the monarch extensive and potentially sole control over the nobility and matters of finance and law – a system that continued to evolve and endured until the end of the *ancien régime*.[62] In England, by contrast, the further development of the so-called 'war state' built on earlier constitutional foundations to create a realm in which the king was bound by the law and ruled with the assent of Parliament – what Fortescue described as a *dominum politicum et regale*. For Fortescue this did not mean the English king was weaker than his French counterpart; on the contrary, parliamentary support provided the king with enormous financial resources, but it created a political structure in which the king operated within rather than above the law.[63]

These different monarchical models reflect the clash, both intellectual and political, between England and France over the comparative authority of their kings, which was a major cause of the Hundred Years War. The treaties of Le Goulet (1200) and Paris (1259) had established what proved to be a fundamentally untenable and ultimately hostile relationship between the two monarchs and the nations they ruled. This, however, was not apparent immediately. At the Mise of Amiens (1264) Louis IX was called on to judge the legality of a dispute between Henry III and Simon de Montfort (the Provisions of Oxford), which suggests his judicial supremacy was accepted in England at that time. Louis certainly seemed to believe that when Henry III performed liege homage for his French lands in 1259, he subordinated himself as king of England as well as duke of Gascony; Henry may have agreed.[64] Subsequently, of course, the relationship would become much more uncertain as English lawyers sought to divorce later monarchs from this unhappy marriage of (in)convenience.[65]

The death of Charles IV (1328) and the ensuing succession dispute complicated matters still further. In the aftermath of the Valois accession Edward III paid homage to Philippe VI for Gascony and Ponthieu.[66] According to Valois lawyers, this showed an acceptance of the superiority of French kingship and of Philippe's claim to the French throne. The English later responded that Edward had been a minor at the time, which offered him protection under Roman law, and that he had given homage on condition that this did not harm any of his hereditary rights. Consequently, they argued, he had not renounced his claim to the French throne. This view is reflected in certain chronicle accounts. According to Froissart, 'The king Edward of England did homage by mouth [i.e. a kiss] and words only, without putting his hands between the hands of the king of France.' By contrast, this limited form of homage is not shown in illustrations from the *Grandes Chroniques*: Edward is depicted dressed in royal attire, which suggests he did homage not merely as duke of Gascony but as king of England too.[67]

Edward III himself seems to have acknowledged, quietly perhaps, the political and moral superiority of French kingship – certainly for a French and Flemish audience and certainly when claiming the French throne. Over the course of his reign Edward adjusted his title, proclaiming himself either king of France and England, or king of England and France, depending on circumstances. Similarly, after his usurpation in 1399, Henry IV reversed the title on his great seal to read *rex Anglie et Francie*, reflecting his need to emphasise greater concern for his English title. However, after 1340 when the claim to the French throne was first proclaimed heraldically, the fleur-de-lys were always given prominence on the royal arms.[68]

This, then, seems an acknowledgement that French kingship was considered in some way(s) superior to English kingship, certainly around the time the war began. Unsurprisingly, the authors of the *Grandes Chroniques* and various French theorists shared this opinion. Christine de Pizan and others promoted a potent image of sacred royal power. The 'most Christian king' (*rex christianissimus*) secured the nation's future. The Crown's superiority rested on its consistent defence of 'Holy Church', a link that the canonisation of Louis IX had strengthened, and on its antiquity, particularly its links to Charlemagne, which were embodied in the coronation sword (*Joyeuse*) and the royal banner (the *Oriflamme*). Later, Charles V would actively promote a cult of Charlemagne, even referring to him as a saint in 1378.[69]

Antiquity was a potent symbol of power, but monarchs on both sides of the Channel had to negotiate with more immediate political forces at home in order to protect themselves against attack from abroad. The power and status of English and French kings depended in part on the authority of their respective representative assemblies – Parliament and the Estates General. In England the burgeoning authority of Parliament restricted the extension of royal power. The Commons, because of its control over taxation, began to exercise greater influence over the king and the direction of royal policy. Although princely rights were proclaimed and defended with immense vigour throughout the fourteenth and fifteenth centuries, English monarchs were forced, increasingly, to respond if not accede to parliamentary demands. A series of renowned Parliaments in the last quarter of the fourteenth century showed the changing nature of the political relationship between the king and the 'community of the realm'. The Good, Wonderful, and Merciless Parliaments (1376, 1386, 1388) revealed the growing power of the Commons as it brought charges of impeachment and attainder against the Crown's ministers.

A different relationship existed in France between the king and the Estates General. Although subjected to regular military and political setbacks, French monarchical authority grew relatively unfettered, while English kings had to work within new parameters and subject to a new political relationship with the representatives of the 'community of the realm'. This was a political group that now extended beyond the traditional magnate power bloc. In France provincial loyalties and simple logistics inhibited a comparable rise in the authority of the Estates General. National assemblies had gained little influence in Capetian times, and apart from exceptional periods there was rarely a call for a general assembly of the whole kingdom during the Hundred Years War.[70] This did make it difficult to raise taxes, especially in the years before 1356, but it meant the Estates General gained little influence over the king. Only in the 1340s and 1350s did the Estates General appear to be growing in authority, but it soon succumbed to internal divisions and growing tensions. It became a forum in which individual animosities were fought out, while the revolt of the Jacquerie brought any political actions of the lesser Estates into suspicion. Because of this, once it secured regular and easy access to taxation, French royal power could develop relatively unchecked. This, however, was not a smooth process. Initial steps towards a system of semi-permanent taxation were taken in response to the need to ransom Jean II and, subsequently, to deal with the problem of uncontrolled mercenary activity after the treaty of Brétigny in 1360. This system collapsed with the Armagnac (Orléans)-Burgundian civil war and was only re-established around 1435. Thereafter taxation provided the means for Charles VII to deal with a renewed mercenary threat and drive the English out of France.[71] Taxation was vital for the extension of French royal power: it allowed for the 1445 *ordonnances*, which paved the way for a standing army, and provided resources to co-opt much of the nobility into the king's service.[72]

The resources available to kings, therefore, increased very considerably during the Hundred Years War, and they took full advantage of this. Royal households grew in size and complexity, and as the court became fixed in a single or small number of locations its features, luxury, status and the practices observed within its confines developed: in architectural terms, despite the war, military considerations gave way to matters of display and domestic comfort.[73] In the first half of the 1350s, Jean II settled the French court more permanently in and around Paris, and Charles V moved the royal household from the Palais de Justice to the Hôtel Saint-Pol. Around this time the ceremonial of royal visits to the *parlement* of Paris also became increasingly intricate. Royal space within the *grand-chambre* of the *parlement*, from which royal judgments might be passed, was to be clearly demarcated with the paraphernalia of the *lit de justice*: a canopy, cover, backdrop and pillows, all embroidered with *fleurs de lys* and the arms of France. This separation of the monarch through the use of draperies was extended to other locations including the Hôtel Saint-Pol, the Salle Saint-Louis of the Palais de Justice, and the Louvre.[74]

In the fourteenth century Paris provided the Valois kings with a degree of security from regular English raids and ensured French kings were in close contact with the institutions of government. As the machinery of national administration became focused on the capital so it was necessary for the king to be nearby. For the same reason, after 1360, once Edward III finished his campaigning career he resided in or around London. Windsor became a favoured residence, the new Camelot, home to the Order of the Garter and a public memorial to the monarchy. The king largely rebuilt the castle between 1350 and 1377 at a cost of over £51,000. He reconstructed the Great Hall and the royal apartments. Edward provided himself with seven chambers, a closet and private chapel; the queen had four chambers, one with an adjoining chapel. Guest quarters and lodgings for senior members of the household were also constructed and furnished to the highest standards. Such developments involved a new use of space within great households. A larger number of rooms with a wider range of functions were assigned and designed for individual use. Edward also undertook impressive redevelopments at Sheen (Richmond) and Eltham (Greenwich), to which Richard II and Henry IV added. These three properties were the chief focus of expenditure on English royal domestic housing in the later fourteenth and early fifteenth centuries and became the primary residences of the king, but they were not the only ones: King's Langley, Woodstock near Oxford, Henley-on-the Heath and Kennington were all improved and extended.[75]

Such new building served not only to demonstrate royal status but also the status of those who served the king. Many aspects of the household were not functional but concerned with 'religion, display, extravagance, courtesy, gesture and movement, indeed anything that underpinned status and magnificence'.[76] At Windsor one reached the royal presence by progressing through a suite of chambers of increasing quality. In Charles V's donjon at Vincennes near Paris the same hierarchical progress took place, although vertically rather than horizontally. Such buildings allowed for the performance of ever more complex court ceremonial. Meals and feasting provided opportunities to emphasise royal power as well as the hierarchy that existed beneath the king. Seating and the provision of different qualities of food and drink demonstrated status and played a part in the general ritual of the court. Such questions of status might also be disruptive. At Charles VI's coronation banquet a scuffle broke out between the dukes of Anjou and Burgundy over precedence and seating.[77] Such activities were a key way by which royal (and noble) power and authority were demonstrated and imposed and, in time, they became one of the main ways by which power and authority were defined.

The religious calendar regulated the court's annual and daily rhythms in accordance with saints' days, fasts and festivals, and so the Chapel Royal provided an important ritual setting and forum in which the king's power could be displayed. Matters of national and international politics also shaped religious ceremony and might influence the design and decoration of royal chapels. The Valois enjoyed the magnificence of the Sainte-Chapelle, built by St Louis (Louis IX) to house the Crown of Thorns and the other relics he had purchased from Emperor Baldwin II of Constantinople. In the extraordinary setting of the upper chapel with its breathtaking stained glass a clear symbolic link was presented between Christ and the French monarchs. Furthermore, the Capetians and their successors had taken on the imperial mantle as defenders of Christendom, a theme also emphasised in the glass. The chapel may well have served as a pilgrimage site designed to encourage devotion to the king as much as to the King of Kings.[78]

St Stephen's Chapel, Westminster, was completed under the patronage of Edward III and Philippa of Hainault in 1363. Religious, dynastic, domestic and political considerations are evident in the design. On the altar wall to the north, beneath a painting of the Adoration of the Magi, St George was depicted leading a line of royal males consisting of the king and his five sons; the queen and her daughters were shown on the south wall. This important early example of English dynastic portraiture celebrated the royal family and made a powerful political statement. The family were depicted in a French style and Philippa and her daughters were dressed in the French fashion. Perhaps based on a French example at Poissy commissioned by Philippe IV, the wall painting may have been 'overt display of English fecundity' – an important statement given the failure of the Capetian line. Just to underline the political intent the quartered arms of England and France were prominently displayed. Given the nature of the Hundred Years War the king's family, the blood royal, was rebranded in accordance with English political ambitions.[79]

By the end of the war changes in military tactics and technology had altered the nature of warfare, its funding and the composition of royal armies. This, in turn, altered the role and expectations of kings. While numerous guides for rulers ('mirrors for princes') show that the main duties of kingship remained the defence of the realm, the maintenance of order and the provision of justice, the means by which these ends were to be achieved, had changed considerably.[80] The war, therefore, placed new and different pressures on monarchs and an awareness of this influenced political and military strategy. For example, the English *chevauchées*, whatever else their aim, were an assault on French kings – a statement that they could neither defend their realm nor maintain law and order within it.

The changing nature of the Hundred Years War reshaped the contesting views of kingship in England and France. By the early fifteenth century the conflict had evolved from a dynastic and feudal struggle into a national war fought by two kings who claimed identical powers in France. And in some superficial ways the institutions had become more similar. Family ties, for example, had strengthened, a fact both sides emphasised independently through their assertions of links to the Capetians and especially to St Louis. The Milemete treatise, a consideration of the art of kingship, compared Edward III to the young Louis IX, and Edward himself stressed this connection in his letter to the French people in 1340.[81] Henry V was advertised as both a direct descendant of St Louis and a legitimate king of England. After the treaty of Troyes English rulers continued to use dynastic imagery centring on St Louis: the duke of Bedford and the Anglo-French chancery promoted this link on coinage, on posters hung in the city of Paris and in public ceremonies. In other ways, however, the institutions were evolving increasingly distinctly. The conception of the French king as *rex christianissimus* who governed a holy realm had formed part of French political theory since the later thirteenth century, but it emerged with renewed vigour as a consequence of the Hundred Years War.[82]

Although conceptions of kingship changed over the course of the Hundred Years War, and despite mounting differences between English and French views of ideal monarchs, defence of the realm and of royal rights remained central to the promotion and manifestation of royal authority in the later Middle Ages. The king himself may not always have been a soldier but his ability to put troops into the field was vital to the maintenance and demonstration of monarchical power. The connection between the king and his soldiers was, therefore, crucial – and at no time was its importance greater than in 1415.

CHAPTER 6

Soldiers

VIEWS FROM THE FRONT
1415

In the opinion of the French [that] which assured the English of victory [at Agincourt was] the continuous way in which they rained down on [them] – a terrifying hail of arrow shot. As [the archers] were lightly armed and their ranks were not too crowded, they had freedom of movement and could deal mortal blows with ease . . . They kept themselves with advantage in the middle of the bloody mêlée . . . fighting with so much passion for they knew that for them it was a matter of life or death.[1]
The *Religieux* of Saint-Denis, *Histoire de Charles VI* (c.1415–22)

It was the regular soldiery – infantry and longbowmen – who secured England's most famous victory in the Hundred Years War. The limitations of knights and cavalry, which had been clear from the opening engagements, were writ large in 1415. Henry V's first campaign to France began with the siege of Harfleur in August and September and the reckless march towards Calais. It concluded on 25 October with the extraordinary triumph at Agincourt that became legendary almost as soon as it had been won. Later, from Shakespeare's perspective, this last shining moment presaged the drab then bloody descent into civil war. It established Henry as perhaps the greatest of England's medieval kings and Agincourt as the pre-eminent example of English martial fortitude until the Second World War.

The shattering victory, not far from the Somme, was, however, not one that came like lightning from a clear sky. It was the product of a military evolution, perhaps even revolution that had begun with Edward I's campaigns to Wales, Scotland and France. For the French, we are told, the defeat at *Azincourt* revealed not only the poverty of native skill-at-arms but also the political canker at the heart of France that had grown out of the

Armagnac-Burgundian civil war. Agincourt was a disaster that dwarfed Crécy and one greater even than that suffered at Poitiers.

It is, though, far too easy to be swept up in this Shakespearean tide. Agincourt was an important battle certainly but less significant than Henry's subsequent conquest of the duchy of Normandy and the poisonous divisions in France that the Armagnac-Burgundian civil war had fashioned. This reached a critical point on 10 September 1419 when agents of the dauphin, Charles, murdered Jean the Fearless. His successor, Philippe the Good, was forced into an alliance with England which shifted the political balance in France to such an extent that Henry could, through the treaty of Troyes (1420), demand the throne itself. When King François I (r.1515–47) visited Dijon in 1521 and was shown the broken skull of the murdered duke of Burgundy, a Carthusian monk told him that this was the hole through which the English entered France.

However, even if Agincourt was not quite the crucial battle it has often been considered, and regardless of the fact that the odds were not stacked quite so highly against Henry's bedraggled army as once was commonly thought, the 1415 expedition provides wonderful examples of the experience of the regular soldiery on campaign. Like a succession of infantry victories before it, Agincourt clearly showed that the balance of military power had changed. Battlefield success in the Hundred Years War depended not on the once supreme power of the mounted aristocracy and the cavalry charge but on the skills of the infantryman, the archer and, over time, the support of gunpowder artillery. Like Agincourt, the English victory over the Scots at Humbleton Hill in September 1402 was achieved by 'unremarkable poor men and serfs!'[2] Their skills were hard won; success and survival depended on ability and training, and not only military but mental preparation. The 'poor, bloody infantry' had to maintain close-order discipline in the face of huge physical and psychological pressures. In addition to the adrenalin-fuelled fear and fury common to all battles, and the enormous determination required to stand fast in the face of a cavalry charge, the soldiers of the Hundred Years War also had to contend with changing tactics and new weapons. As a result of these developments fewer prisoners were taken and the death toll among the defeated army rose accordingly. Military changes such as these did not only take place on the field of battle. The sieges, which litter and in many ways characterise the Hundred Years War, were also transformed during the conflict. The balance of power in such engagements shifted from the defensive to the offensive. Driven by technological advances, particularly the use of gunpowder artillery, such changes revolutionised warfare over the course of the later Middle Ages.

These military developments had profound social implications. Archers and infantrymen drawn from the ranks of the peasantry and yeomanry of England and Wales, rather than mounted knights, came to form the backbone of English armies in the Hundred Years War, numerically and tactically. The yeoman joined the military community and, as Shakespeare suggested, the battles in which he fought did 'gentle his condition'.[3] This compromised the exclusivity of the military elite, the *bellatores* (those who fought). The social prestige associated with military prowess was fractured by victories won by the common soldier and achieved by such unchivalric qualities as discipline and collective action.

In France, too, the defeats at Crécy, Poitiers and Agincourt brought the role and status of the military aristocracy into question. Contemporaries scorned their apparent cowardice and their capitulation to *gens de nulle value* – men of no worth. Indeed, when the flower of French chivalry wilted at Poitiers the revolt of the Jacquerie followed.[4] It was, though, in many ways, unfair criticism. There was no sign of cowardice at Crécy, at least not among the cavalry which charged the English lines fifteen times in the face of a withering arrow storm, or at Poitiers where so many of the French aristocracy paid for their military naiveté with their lives.

The Hundred Years War saw service in arms in both countries become a professional business rather than an act of *noblesse oblige*. Although the aristocracy continued to command, common career soldiers won battles such as Agincourt. They fought for their country, pay and booty – not necessarily in that order. They also fought in a new way as the strategies, tactics, equipment, funding and means of recruiting soldiers changed fundamentally in England and France over the course of the Hundred Years War. These were the men who suffered the privations that accompanied campaigning: the dysentery that afflicted so many; the regular struggle to find food in enemy territory; the limitations of medical care for the sick and wounded. They were also the men who perpetrated the many horrors of a war waged, for the most part, on those least able to defend themselves. Indeed, it was deliberate policy that they should act in this way: the *chevauchée* strategy of the first half of the war aimed to deprive the Valois king of troops and taxes by depriving his people of their lives or livelihoods. Tactics changed when Henry V returned to France in the Normandy campaign of 1417–20 – he came to conquer, not merely to despoil. Those, however, who would not pay him homage were fortunate if they were merely thrown out of their homes.

One of the most significant changes in the dynamics of warfare is evident in a series of battles which revealed that while cavalry remained potent, its dominance was no longer assured. Even before the outbreak of the Hundred Years War the battles of Courtrai (1302), Bannockburn (1314), Morgarten (1315), Dupplin Moor (1332) and Halidon Hill (1333) had called into question long-held assumptions about the invincibility of mounted troops. The Anglo-French struggle shattered those beliefs utterly. Battles such as Crécy, Poitiers, Agincourt and Castillon showed that well-trained, cohesive, properly equipped and disciplined infantry were more than a match for cavalry, especially when supported by longbowmen, cross-bowmen or gunpowder artillery.[5]

Infantry, of course, had been vital in all armies from earliest times, but for much of the medieval period its role had been secondary to that of cavalry and primarily defensive. In the later Middle Ages and throughout the Hundred Years War foot soldiers began to be used strategically, as an attacking force, although tactically they remained most effective when deployed in a defensive formation. If they established such a position infantry could – and typically did – repel cavalry. Because of this, to attack first was often to lose the tactical advantage, something noted by luminaries such as John Chandos and Jean de Bueil (1406–77), who was known as *le Fléau des Anglais* (the 'plague of the English'). Equally important were discipline and order in the ranks because, as Sir Thomas Gray remarked, armies could easily be 'defeated through their own disarray'.[6] Both sides came to recognise this during the Hundred Years War and it was often political and economic pressures rather than military considerations that forced one side to begin an assault. A king had to show he was not impotent or unmoved should an enemy encroach on his sovereign territory – defending the realm was his most fundamental responsibility. And if an enemy commander, royal or otherwise, was unwilling to make the first move, as at Agincourt, long-bowmen or crossbowmen could be used to provoke him.

In England the major impetus to strategic innovation was a result of the crushing defeat at Bannockburn. When Edward III returned to Scotland in the 1330s he sought to lay to rest the spectre of that defeat and employed tactics similar to those which Robert Bruce had used so effectively against his father. The Scottish campaigns of the 1330s proved a fine training ground for the English forces, and once the war with France began the lessons learned in Scotland were quickly put to the test. At Morlaix in 1342, William Bohun, earl of Northampton (c.1312–60), led English troops in support of Jean de Montfort against Charles de Blois, his rival for the duchy of Brittany. Northampton defeated a substantially larger army by deploying infantry, making extensive use of the longbow and choosing a defensive position which he improved by digging a concealed ditch. Northampton's experience, and that of many of the soldiers under his command, was used to good effect four years later at Crécy.

In response to these defeats the French began to experiment with a range of counter-strategies. In encounters at Lunalonge (1349), Taillebourg (1351), Ardres (1351) and Mauron (1352) they made imaginative use of cavalry and deployed an increasing number of foot soldiers. Such tactics were put into action at Poitiers (1356), although without great success. There, as at Crécy, the relative paucity of missile troops was a major drawback, while poor discipline, a lack of cohesion and tactical inflexibility also limited Jean II's options. Further initiatives were attempted in the years that followed: in 1364 at the battle of Auray, Bertrand du Guesclin tried to counter the threat the English longbowmen posed by advancing heavily armed infantry behind *pavises* (large, usually rectangular shields that could be held in the hands or propped up by a wooden or iron brace). He did this successfully although his forces were defeated in the subsequent hand-to-hand combat. Du Guesclin tried similar tactics at Nájera three years later where political imperatives and a divided command structure again undermined the French (Franco-Trastamaran) effort.[7] French commanders continued to show considerable tactical ingenuity in the campaigns of the 1370s and 1380s when the 'army of the reconquest' overturned the English advances gained through the treaty of Brétigny. Indeed, the balance of power shifted so far in this period that those living on the south coast of England received a bitter taste of the reality of war, and invasion came close on two occasions in 1385 and 1387.

Stalemate followed, however. The innovations that Charles V and du Guesclin had promoted were forgotten; for a time internal feuds and rivalries superseded those with the Old Enemy. Most significantly, Charles VI's madness inhibited the governmental developments necessary to build the financial and bureaucratic foundations on which a professional military structure could stand.

Strategic innovation on any meaningful scale could be achieved only with sufficient resources and the right type of troops. It was recognised that, in order to be successful, armies needed to be properly equipped and comprised of experienced soldiers. The sheer length of the war ensured that a greater proportion of the resources of the state on both sides of the Channel came to be devoted to military purposes. The nature of service in arms changed as a result: sophisticated processes of recruitment, the implementation of innovative strategies and tactics and the use of new military technology all contributed to alter radically the experience of conflict for all those who fought – those who were the new *bellatores*. In England the process developed swiftly in the early years of the war, building on earlier advances. In France the development was slower and punctuated with long periods of stasis, but by the end of the conflict Charles VII had outstripped his English rival Henry VI and constructed a permanent, standing army.

At the outset of the war both sides relied, to varying degrees, on traditional means to recruit soldiers. Because of the defensive nature of the war in France, at least until the 1420s, the Crown regularly used the *ban* and the *arrière-ban*. The former was a call to military service of those who were royal fief-holders; the latter, introduced after the defeat at Courtrai in 1302, was a military summons of all those fit to bear arms regardless of their status.[8] This provided the bulk of the army – men either served in person or paid for a replacement. However, it proved to be a far from ideal system – slow, unreliable and lacking in uniformity. In part this was because it tended to be organised on a local level. Troops recruited in this way usually fought close to home, having been raised to combat a specific threat. As a result it was difficult to coordinate an effective defence against the English *chevauchées* that covered such huge areas. The *ban* was, essentially, an extension of the system of urban defence. Towns took responsibility for their own protection through the system of *guet* and *garde* (watch and ward). However, a proper national system could only be implemented with sufficient funds and these could only be acquired through taxation. Until the Crown developed a robust and regular means of raising money it could not develop a professional army.[9]

In England, the precocious development of institutional financial systems meant that kings gained access to regular taxation from almost the beginning of the war. This, however, was not without its problems as it placed greater power in the hands of Parliament and especially in those of the Commons. This increased the scope of royal authority but could restrict the direction royal policy might take. Nonetheless, as a consequence of this development, recruitment to English armies became increasingly professional in the early years of the Hundred Years War, and the same basic model of recruiting soldiers was retained from c.1350 until the end of the conflict. Hence, by the time of the Agincourt campaign, soldiers were contracted through the tried and tested indenture system. The system was named after the document that formed the military contract. The contract was copied twice onto a piece of parchment with an indented line cut between the two copies. Should a dispute arise, the two copies could be fitted together again showing that the documents (and the conditions of service they specified) matched.

Indentures had a long history prior to the Hundred Years War but they were employed in an ever more standardised way and in far greater numbers after it began. The indenture system offered a much more sophisticated approach to recruitment than the traditional feudal array. Indentures allowed commanders to specify the types of troops they wished to raise for their expeditionary forces, their number, the proportion of infantrymen to archers and cavalry (in the case of Agincourt approximately one man-at-arms to three archers), and conditions of service (including pay, equipment and regulations concerning booty).

The growing professionalism of military activity in England and in France was a direct (perhaps inevitable) consequence of the Hundred Years War, and it offered new avenues of employment for many. Military service with its (theoretically) regular pay offered a career path or, certainly, a means of supplementing their income for the common man. Other incentives might also be important: pardons for various offences, the potential for booty or the chance of promotion. Even during periods of truce there were opportunities to make a living through service in garrisons overseas or on the frontiers of Scotland and Wales. Calais often housed over a thousand men; after 1415 Harfleur was home to 1,200 men-at-arms and archers, and after about 1420 Normandy was garrisoned by between 2,000 and 6,000 troops.[10] However, English chancery records and private communications to commanders are littered with demands and sometimes desperate pleas for back pay. Often the best way to secure wages for the last campaign was to sign on for the next. This process probably encouraged soldiers to serve for long periods, although it did not ensure a comfortable retirement. In a petition for alms made to Henry VI between 1451 and 1453, one Walter Orpington claimed to have served in France for thirty-six years during which time he was stationed in various garrisons and fought in numerous armies. He fought first with Henry V at Harfleur in 1415 and later in 'divers and many places in France and Normandy'. During that time he had been 'taken prisoner and lost his goods so that now he had fallen in great age and poverty he had little to help and sustain him'.[11]

Orpington would have served in a retinue. The indenture system raised armies composed of a number of retinues – individual commanders were contracted to bring a retinue containing specific numbers of troops with them. For the aristocracy these might consist of existing household staff or those formally recruited throughout the country by commissioners of array. In the Agincourt campaign the size of retinues varied considerably. Some were very small: at least 122 men made contracts to serve with fewer than ten men, and some brought no additional troops at all. Those of high rank and those with the greatest military experience brought the largest retinues. Thomas, duke of Clarence (1387–1421), for example, recruited 240 men-at-arms and 720 archers; his retinue included an earl, two bannerets and fourteen knights.[12]

It was not only soldiers who had to be recruited for a campaign. Depending on an expedition's length and objectives – raiding or occupation – specialists of various sorts would be needed. Pavillioners, grooms, cooks, stablemen, cordwainers, wheelwrights, fletchers, bowyers, saddlers, armourers, clerks, tailors, miners, stonecutters, smiths, waggoners and physicians and surgeons might be required. Even on brief raids a man-at-arms would usually be accompanied by one or more servants. These could add as much as 50 per cent to the numerical strength (if not the fighting strength) of a raiding force, while an army of occupation might be doubled in size. For major operations in which the king participated the royal household was put under arms, and so the expeditionary force included members of the pantry, kitchen, buttery, napery, spicery, poultry, scullery, bakehouse, hall, chamber and wardrobe. Edward III even took thirty falconers with him on campaign in 1359–60.[13]

This level of recruitment resulted in many sections of English society becoming increasingly militarised. The remarkable discovery of the mass grave from the battle of Towton (1461) in Yorkshire and what has been uncovered from the wreck of Henry VIII's flagship, the *Mary Rose* (1545), provide fascinating glimpses of this process. The Towton soldiers had an average age of about thirty (considerably older than their modern counterparts) and they stood, on average, 5 feet 7 ½ inches tall; those from the *Mary Rose* were of a very similar height but a little younger (in their midtwenties). The skeletal evidence, revealing wounds received in much earlier conflicts, shows that many of these men, like Walter Orpington, stayed in or returned to military service over an extended period. One of the Towton soldiers, who was about fifty years of age when he died, had suffered a ghastly facial wound some twenty-five years previously, perhaps when he fought in France. Such men as this had made a military career for themselves.[14] Intriguingly, both sets of evidence also show a substantial number of soldiers with signs of abnormal muscular development and greater bone circumference on the left shoulder and upper arm. This probably suggests strenuous exercise, perhaps training with a longbow or unimanual weapon from a young age.[15]

In France, the Valois kings took some similar steps towards developing a professional army. Jean II instituted a substantial review of military structures following his accession in 1350, and Charles V made a series of major improvements in the 1360s and 1370s. The establishment of a relatively stable tax system, the military imperatives of the Hundred Years War and the support of a significant section of the French nobility allowed Charles to come close to gaining a permanent army of men-at-arms and (some mounted) crossbowmen by the end of his reign. Using *lettres de retenue* (similar to indentures) the system became centralised and organised by the king's officials. This 'army of reconquest' succeeded spectacularly in regaining the lands which Charles's father had ceded to the English by the treaty of Brétigny. It is by no means certain that Charles intended to continue with this military system in the long term, but it is certainly the case that when he (and Bertrand du Guesclin) died in 1380 the core of the army decayed. Then, because of Charles VI's minority and the power struggles in the royal court, calls for peace with England grew louder. Soon the only permanent military forces were garrisons in Normandy and the southwest. The feudal array was re-established, the nobility took charge of local defence and national political divisions became reflected in divisions in military structures that were disastrously evident at Agincourt. It would not be until some time into Charles VII's reign that serious attempts were made once more to establish a permanent force.

Consequently, as it progressed, the Hundred Years War was fought, increasingly, by paid professionals. In England after c.1350 and in France by c.1445 soldiering had become a job of work for the common man, not simply a feudal obligation. Yet it was also a means of social advancement, as Thomas Gray noted in the late 1350s. He wrote: 'many [men began their careers] as archers, then becoming knights, and some of them captains'.[16] Not all these captains fought in their king's 'regular' forces. The militarisation of society meant that independent mercenary companies or Free Companies became a common feature on the military landscape. These companies were composed of soldiers from throughout Europe such as the ill-fated Genoese crossbowmen who fought at Crécy.[17] Many were led by men from Britain and France such as Robert Knolles, Hugh Calveley (English), Bertrand du Guesclin, Perrinet Gressart (French), Owen Lawgoch (Welsh) and Jacques de Lalaing (Burgundian). Other companies, most famously that led by John Hawkwood, took service in Italy. The growth of the mercenary companies caused a great deal of upheaval. Thomas Gray noted the problems created by large bodies of professional soldiers during periods of truce. He stated that during the 'truce' following Jean II's capture at Poitiers:

> Many of the English *who lived off the war* [my emphasis] set out for Normandy, took castles, fortified manors and caused other such warlike mayhem in the country, with the support of men of the community of England, who came to [join] them day by day against the king's orders. They came in astonishing numbers, all of them on their own account without any leader, and inflicted great oppressions on the country, taking tribute from almost the whole of Normandy, and from the borders of many surrounding lands ... they achieved so much ... And yet they were nothing but a gathering of commoners, young men, who until this time had been of little account, who came to have great standing and expertise from this war.[18]

The Free Companies continued to pose problems after the treaty of Brétigny was sealed. Charles V addressed these by seeking to use them for his own political advantage in the Castilian civil war. It proved an effective short-term solution. Later his grandson Charles VII was faced with similar circumstances, in his case the *écorcheurs*. Charles VII co-opted the mercenary companies directly into royal service. He created a standing army from the ranks of those men-at-arms who were unoccupied after the truce of Tours was concluded in 1444. In 1445–6 Charles established the royal companies of the *gens d'ordonnance*: 1,800 *lances fournies* (a group comprising 1,800 men-at-arms, 3,600 archers and 1,800 *coutiliers* (infantrymen armed with a short sword called a *coustille*)). This was expanded in 1448 into the system of the *francs archers* who represented every community and formed the core of a permanent army. First designed to be used in a campaign to Italy, these companies eventually recaptured Normandy (1449–50) and Gascony (1451, 1453).[19] When they did so Charles VII ensured his troops were well equipped

> with good and sure armour and weapons ... the men-at-arms were all armed with good cuirasses, armour for their limbs, swords ... also with lances carried by pages of the men-at-arms, each of whom had three good horses for himself, his page and his varlet, being armed with a

salet, jacket, dirk, hauberk, axe or bill. And each of the men-at-arms had two mounted archers, armed mostly with brigandines, leg harness and salets.[20]

English (Anglo-Welsh/Anglo-Gascon) armies were never quite so well appointed, and what they did carry tended to be rather different.[21] In particular they relied heavily on the longbow. Originally a Welsh weapon, as Gerald of Wales (Giraldus Cambrensis, c.1146–c.1223) discussed,[22] longbowmen became prominent in most English armies from Edward I's later campaigns onwards. They were used to great effect at the battle of Falkirk in 1298 and then in successive encounters in Scotland and France – although not at Bannockburn. In the fourteenth century the use of the longbow spread to soldiers recruited from throughout England, although commanders such as Sir Gruffydd Llwyd, Sir Rhys ap Gruffydd, Sir Hywel y Fwyall (Hywel of the Axe) and Sir Gregory Sais continued to lead retinues to France composed chiefly of Welsh archers.[23]

While sometimes used in hunting, the longbow was chiefly a popular not an aristocratic weapon. Cheap to manufacture but difficult to master, it required a great deal of training from a young age. The national importance of archery was such that it became the subject of legislation. In 1357 and 1369 prohibitions were placed on the export of bows and arrows; in 1363 regular archery practice became compulsory, and in 1365 archers themselves were forbidden to leave England without royal licence. It is no co-incidence that this period saw the development of the Robin Hood legends. Archery was at the heart of national military success and Robin became the archer par excellence. Because of their military impact and their cost-effectiveness longbowmen became the most common soldiers in English armies. The proportion of longbowmen to other troops in expeditionary forces was regularly 3, 4, or 5:1 and sometimes as much as 20:1.[24]

Nonetheless, questions remain regarding these men and the weapon they used to (what appears to have been) such devastating effect. These range from the nature of the weapons themselves, their power and rate of accurate fire, to their impact on the enemy and the disposition of archers on the battlefield. There is little surviving literature on the subject written before the later fifteenth century, although various illustrated works, depict different uses of the bow and the stances adopted while shooting. These include the Queen Mary's Psalter (probably made for Edward II), the Holkham Bible Picture Book (c.1330) and the Luttrell Psalter (c.1340). No longbows survive that predate those excavated from the *Mary Rose*, but if these are indicative of the weapons used in the Hundred Years War then they were formidable indeed. Measuring about 6 feet in length, they were made of yew or sometimes ash, with draw weights between 80 and perhaps as much as 185 pounds. This provided archers with a range of perhaps 400 yards, although the bow's real killing power was probably considerably less than that. The string was usually carried separately in a pouch to keep it dry.[25] Typically, archers were protected by a padded jerkin or brigandine, which had metal plates sewn onto leather, a helmet (an open-faced bascinet or wide-brimmed pot helm), and perhaps some arm or leg protection. However, by no means all archers were equipped in this way and it is recorded that at Agincourt many had no armour, headgear or even shoes.[26]

Chronicle accounts certainly suggest that the impact of an arrow storm could be overwhelming, and clearly longbowmen were very effective against French cavalry (at Crécy) and dismounted men-at-arms (at Poitiers). At Agincourt the longbow was, again, critical. We are told that

> [b]ecause of the strength of the arrow fire and their fear of it, most doubled back into the French vanguard, causing great disarray and breaking the line in many places ... Their horses had been so troubled by the arrow shot of the English archers that they could not hold or control them. As a result the vanguard fell into disorder and countless numbers of men-at-arms began to fall. Those on horseback were so afraid of death that they put themselves into flight away from the enemy. Because of the example they set many of the French left the field in flight.[27]

By contrast with the longbow, the crossbow underwent considerable development throughout the period of the Hundred Years War. In the early battles its inferiority to the longbow was pronounced; it could shoot neither as far nor anywhere near as quickly – for every three crossbow quarrels (bolts) a bowmen might fire twenty arrows or more.[28] Crossbows were, however, particularly useful in sieges where they could be fired from protected positions. In battle a crossbowman was usually more heavily armed than an archer and, typically, equipped with a *pavise* type of shield. At Crécy the Genoese crossbowmen were ordered to attack without their *pavises*. Consequently, they had nowhere behind which they could reload when confronted with the English and Welsh longbowmen firing more quickly than they and over longer distances. These types of shield were also used in England and large numbers of them were stored in the Tower of

London. The French valued them so highly that the trees from which they were made were protected.[29] However, by the beginning of the fifteenth century there were major innovations in crossbow design. Steel bows were introduced that could match or even outdistance a longbow. Although they remained slow to reload, at close-range and firing a heavy quarrel (12–18 inches in length) the crossbow became all but unstoppable.

The crossbow, which had been a weapon used on European battlefields from the twelfth century, was, therefore, improved considerably in this period. The Hundred Years War also saw the first use of an entirely new form of weapon that would, in time, revolutionise warfare completely. In their first battlefield incarnations gunpowder weapons, such as those used at Crécy, did little more than frighten the horses and had no impact on the outcome at all. They were light and simple guns often as dangerous to those firing them as to their targets.[30] However, their potential in sieges swiftly became apparent. In 1300 Pierre Dubois, a French royal clerk, had written a military treatise for Philippe IV. In his *Doctrine of Successful Expeditions and Shortened Wars* he commented on the time and expense involved in a major siege, noting that 'A castle can hardly be taken within a year.'[31] Consequently, any innovation that reduced the time and cost of capturing enemy fortifications would be extremely valuable. Over time gunpowder weapons extended the scope and potential gains of military expeditions dramatically.

Edward III recognised the emerging possibilities when he brought at least ten cannon and materials for over 5,000 pounds of gunpowder to the siege of Calais, albeit the weapons do not appear to have contributed a great deal to the capture of the town. Nonetheless, the potential of artillery was being taken seriously. The Black Prince brought small cannon with him for his raid in 1356, and they were used to some effect in the siege of Romorantin. Then, in the period from 1360 to 1370, many towns and almost all the great powers in western Europe began to acquire their own arsenals. In 1369 the receiver of Ponthieu purchased 20 copper cannon for Edward III as well as five iron cannon; 215 pounds of saltpetre, sulphur and amber for making powder; and 1,300 large quarrels/bolts.[32] The French successfully used gunpowder weapons to bring down the town walls of Saint-Sauveur-le Vicomte in 1374, although gunpowder weapons did not supersede the trebuchet or mangonel as siege weapons, and on the battle-field they did not influence tactical thinking to any great extent.[33] Yet, these crude guns were evolving into formidable artillery, and soon they began to change the nature of warfare. At Harfleur (1415) the

guns and engines so pounded ... the walls ... that within a few days
when by their violence and fury the barbican was in process of being
largely demolished, the walls and towers ... were rendered defenceless
... and fine buildings, almost as far as the middle of the town, were
either totally demolished or threatened with inevitable collapse.[34]

The exact nature and quantity of Henry V's artillery at Harfleur are uncertain, but there is no doubt that these weapons caused enormous damage.

Such changes, however, did pose problems. Although a commander
might capture a fortification or a town more swiftly by using artillery, the
damage the guns could cause might render the site all but useless. This was
not quite the case at Harfleur, but rebuilding proved to be a long and
expensive process, and the condition of the town made it unattractive to
potential settlers for some time.[35] Despite its evolution artillery remained
far from fool-proof: at Agincourt it appears that French artillery accounted
for only a solitary archer during the battle;[36] and in 1431 the duke of
Burgundy fired 412 cannonballs into the town of Lagny and succeeded
only in killing a chicken. The Parisian Bourgeois who recounted the story
suggested the remarkable failure should be attributed to the fact that 'this
evil work' was undertaken during Holy Week.[37] The trend, however, was
clear – gunpowder weapons were becoming extremely important.

At Orléans in 1428–29 both sides deployed artillery on a grand scale.
Joan of Arc's initial attack on the English besieging force concentrated
on an assault on the Tourelles – a gunnery emplacement. When captured
this added a substantial number of artillery pieces to the French arsenal,
which were used in the subsequent, devastating attacks on Jargeau, Meung
and Beaugency. Joan herself was considered particularly adept in sighting
the weapons. Gunpowder artillery would also be used effectively against
La Pucelle. The Maid's failure to take Paris was due, in part, to the capital's
own gunpowder defences and the improvements to the fortifications
that had been made to counter such weapons. Furthermore, when defeated
and captured at Compiègne, Joan had faced the Burgundians, who were
furnished with what was, at that time, Europe's most potent gunpowder
ordnance.[38]

The French took major steps to match the Burgundians in the late
1430s when the full resources of the state were made available to put in
place a professional artillery train. French artillery was completely reorgan-
ised, both administratively and tactically, by the Bureau brothers – Jean, the
king's Master Gunner, and his brother, Gaspard. The available weapons

grew in number and efficiency, and the artillery train proved its worth in northern sieges at Montereau in 1437, Meaux in 1439 and Pontoise in 1441. In 1437 the castle of Castelnau-de-Cernès in Gascony was 'broken down . . . by cannon and engines, and a great part of the walls were thrown to the ground'. Gunpowder weapons allowed the French to eject the English from Normandy and Gascony with astonishing speed. In some cases, as at Bourg north of Bordeaux in 1451, the mere presence of guns was sufficient to bring about an immediate surrender. Similarly, in July 1453 the French entered Castillon in Gascony through breaches in the walls 'made by artillery'.[39] Charles VII's arsenal included 'a very great number of great bombards, great cannons, veuglaires, serpentines, crapaudins, culverins and ribaudquins . . . well furnished with powder, shot [with] carriages to drag them [and] gunners experienced to handle them'.[40]

Gunpowder weapons also began to be deployed as effective field artillery in the final engagements of the Hundred Years War. Formigny (1450) in Normandy may have been the first battle decided by gunpowder artillery. The engagement began with a predictable cavalry assault on the English infantry and longbowmen, with predictable results. Soon afterwards, however, the Bureau brothers arrived with artillery, probably two breech-loading culverins on wheeled carriages. These were capable of a high rate of fire and could outdistance the longbowmen. Although it required the arrival of further reinforcements to decide the battle, gunpowder artillery played a telling role. It seems somewhat prescient that the final battle in the war – at Castillon – was, undoubtedly, determined by artillery. It marks a deeply significant change in the nature of warfare. Two armies, perhaps 20,000 strong, marched into Gascony in the spring of 1453. One of these, perhaps numbering 7,000 men, laid siege to the town of Castillon. John Talbot (c.1387–1453) received a petition from the inhabitants of the town to relieve the siege and he arrived outside the French camp on 17 July. Talbot enjoyed some initial success against a detachment of *francs archers*, but Jean Bureau had deployed some 300 cannon for the siege and these were soon turned on the Anglo-Gascons. The battle turned into a rout; Talbot's horse was killed by gunfire and, trapped under his mount, the earl was killed by an axe blow to the head.[41]

Developments in technology, therefore, revolutionised warfare, but armies still had certain basic requirements, particularly when it came to provisions. As armies became professional and soldiers began to receive wages, so the theoretical requirement lessened for commanders to provide their troops with provisions, as they had in the past. However, if left to their own devices, soldiers seeking to feed themselves on campaign could be extremely disruptive both to local populations and to military strategy, creating political and logistical problems. This was particularly evident during the Agincourt campaign, despite Henry V's extensive planning. Large quantities of provisions were collected by the English government to supply its armies using the system of purveyance, but soldiers usually had to acquire additional supplies while abroad either through payment or plunder. Various estimates have been made to try and establish soldiers' diets, which suggest that in order to function effectively in a campaign situation they would need to consume between 3,000 and 5,000 calories per day – the upper estimate is likely to be high and certainly in excess of what most troops enjoyed. According to a French campaign plan for 1327 a combatant subsisted for a day on 0.106 gallons of wine, 107 grams of meat and 1.039 kilograms of grain from which, theoretically, 1.385 kilograms of bread could be baked.[42]

The acquisition of food could well be part of an expedition's overall strategy, since deliberate devastation formed an intrinsic element in a *chevauchée*. When Edward III's army laid waste to 174 parishes between 9 and 22 October 1339, he could feed his army and implement his military objectives simultaneously. However, living off the land was often difficult, and it became more so as the war progressed. One could not guarantee the availability of sufficient supplies, and raided populations soon became adept at hiding food. Nor could one rely on such extraordinary days as the Scots enjoyed on 15 October 1346 when they plundered 295 cattle and 348 sheep from eight English settlements. Furthermore, effective pillaging took time, which meant an army had to spread out and move slowly, leaving it susceptible to attack. During the 1359–60 campaign Thomas Gray recounts that knights and esquires from the Black Prince's company 'were killed at night in their lodging, and foraying valets were taken in the field'.[43] Expeditions such as this were designed to be swiftly moving raids. This limited the size of any accompanying supply train. Even when small in number carts and wagons reduced an army's freedom of movement, although the Black Prince's 1355 campaign showed supply trains could ford rivers and travel at a good pace. Supply trains, nonetheless, were vulnerable to attack, and undoubtedly slowed down large armies.[44]

Successive campaigns could denude the countryside of supplies, especially if an army occupied an area for an extended period. Invading forces might also have to contend with a scorched-earth policy, as in 1359 (the Reims campaign) and in Castile in 1380. Henry V's army in 1415 was

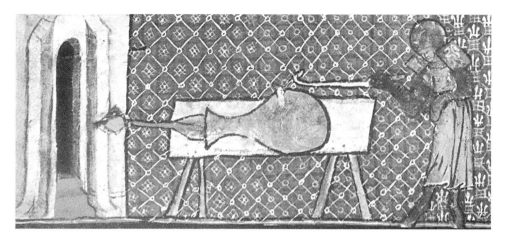

1 Walter de Milemete's treatise on kingship, *De nobilitatibus, sapientiis, et prudentiis regum* (c. 1326), includes what is probably the first illustration of a gunpowder weapon. Crude cannons such as this would evolve into formidable siege weapons by the end of the Hundred Years War and they also began to influence the outcomes of battlefield engagements such as Castillon (1453).

2 Commissioned by Sir Geoffrey Luttrell of Irnham, Lincolnshire, the magnificent Luttrell Psalter (c. 1330) is most famous for its extraordinary grotesques and *babewyns* but it also contains fascinating images of everyday life. Here, the increasing significance of archery can be seen. Tactically and numerically, archers became the most significant soldiers recruited for English armies in the Hundred Years War and they made a vital contribution to the victories at Crécy, Poitiers, and Agincourt. Such was its importance that in 1363 archery practice became compulsory.

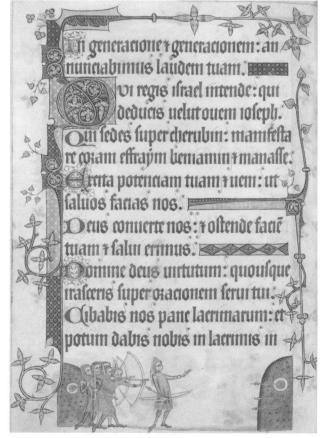

3 Victory at the battle of Sluys (1340) was all Edward III had to show for the enormous political and financial capital he expended in his first campaign to France. Fought using tactics developed for land battles, English archers were crucial in this engagement.

4 On 6 June 1329, Edward III gave homage to Philippe VI at Amiens for Gascony and Ponthieu. This image from the *Grandes Chroniques* suggests a deeply formal ceremony took place in which the young English king offered liege homage for his ancestral lands in France. Other accounts of the event, such as that recorded by Jean Froissart, differ and indicate that he paid only simple homage and, consequently, the relationship between Valois and Plantagenet was not so binding.

5 The victory at Crécy (1346) completely rehabilitated England's military reputation, which had been so damaged by the defeat to the Scots at Bannockburn (1314). In this encounter, Edward III and his commanders employed tactics which had been tried and tested in earlier engagements in Scotland and France to defeat the French cavalry and Genoese crossbowmen.

afferte domino gloriam nomini eius.
Collite hostias 7 introite in atria
eius: adorate dominum in atrio
sancto eius
Commoueatur a facie eius uniuer
sa terra: dicite in gentibus quia do
minus regnauit
Etenim correxit orbem terre qui nõ
commouebitur: iudicabit populos
in equitate
Letentur celi et exultet terra: com
moueatur mare et plenitudo eius.
gaudebunt campi 7 omnia que in
eis sunt

6 The Luttrell Psalter (c. 1330) includes a series of images that show the major events of the agricultural year. During the Hundred Years War, disruptions to farming took place in England along the south coast and the northern border because of French and Scottish raiding. However, this was nothing compared to the devastation visited upon the French peasantry in the course of successive English *chevauchées*. The somewhat idealised relationship between lords and vassals depicted in the psalter was also disturbed by repeated visitations of the Black Death.

7 This profile of Jean le Bon (c. 1350) may well have been painted prior to the king's accession in 1350, with the appellation 'Jehan Roi de France' added subsequently. It is the oldest extant portrait in France and may have been modelled on an imperial medal.

8 This fifteenth-century illustration shows Edward III as a knight of the Order of the Garter. Founded in 1348 to commemorate the Crécy-Calais campaign and to promote both the legitimacy of the king's claim to France and unity among the military aristocracy, the Garter became the pre-eminent chivalric fraternity in England.

9 Despite the declining role of cavalry on the battlefield both Plantagenet and Valois kings recognised the continuing political importance of the chivalric ethic. As a result, monarchical military Orders and Companies were founded on both sides of the Channel during the Hundred Years War. Jean II established the Company of Our Lady of the Noble House, more commonly known as the Company of the Star, in 1350. This proved to be a short-lived enterprise, however, and many of the founder members of the Company died or were captured at the battle of Poitiers (1356).

10 Edward III (1327–77), tomb effigy, Westminster Abbey. Although the English position in France had been in decline since the war reopened in 1369, that decline seemed terminal when Edward III died in 1377 after fifty years on the English throne. The Hundred Years War saw both coronations and royal funerals involve increasing religious intricacy and political symbolism.

11 Bertrand du Guesclin (d. 1380), tomb effigy, Abbey of Saint-Denis, Paris. Du Guesclin's reputation was based on military service in royal and mercenary ranks. After numerous campaigns he became constable of France in 1370 and was largely responsible for the recapture of those territories lost by the Valois in the treaty of Brétigny (1360). The low-born Breton knight was eventually buried alongside the kings of France in the abbey of Saint-Denis.

12 Richard II (1377–99), Westminster Portrait. Richard II's reign saw the continuing deterioration of the English position in France, which had begun when the Hundred Years War reopened in 1369. After dealing with the vicissitudes of the Peasants' Revolt (1381), Richard sought to expand his authority within the British Isles while also trying to achieve an accord with Charles VI. This brought him into conflict with his own nobles, which eventually led to his deposition in 1399.

13 Richard II's conception of his royal status evolved over the course of his reign. In the Wilton Diptych (c. 1396) he is shown in almost messianic fashion being presented to the Virgin, Christ Child, and the heavenly host by John the Baptist, Edward the Confessor, and St Edmund. The angels are shown as members of the king's household, wearing his personal device, the white hart, and one carries the banner of St George (England).

14 Honoré Bonet's *Tree of Battles* (c. 1390) was an extremely influential guide to military conduct heavily based on John of Legnano's *Tractatus de Bello*. Bonet lauded traditional military virtues but also decried the terrible consequences of war for the French peasantry. This image from a frontispiece to his work also indicates the importance of fortune (Blind Lady Fortuna and her wheel) and the terrible spiritual implications of the misuse of military strength (the hell mouth).

15 The coronation of Charles VI in 1380 marked the beginning of a long period of domestic strife in France. The young king's uncles struggled for control during his minority and, later, his madness. Of enormous symbolic and political importance, the coronation of French monarchs was said to invest those who received the holy oil with sacral powers including the ability to heal the skin disease, scrofula – 'the king's evil'.

16 Jean the Fearless, duke of Burgundy (1404–19) stood at the centre of the Armagnac-Burgundian civil war which ravaged France in the latter stages of Charles VI's reign. Jean orchestrated the assassination of Louis d'Orléans in 1407 and was himself murdered by soldiers loyal to the dauphin in 1419.

17 Fortunate to escape the slaughter at the battle of Agincourt (1415), Charles, duke of Orléans, spent the next twenty-five years in captivity as a political prisoner in the Tower of London. During this extended period he honed his very considerable literary talent and wrote acclaimed works of poetry in French and English.

18 A gold noble from the reign of Henry V. On the obverse the king is shown crowned, wearing armour and holding a sword and a shield quartered with the arms of England and France. He is standing in a ship which may signify English naval power or may be a reference to his command of the 'ship of state'.

19 Disinherited by the terms of the treaty of Troyes (1420), Charles VII, 'the Victorious', eventually re-established Valois power in France. First, with the aid of Joan of Arc, he stemmed the English advance, and then through political skill and the establishment of a professional army he oversaw the recapture of Paris, the reconquest of Normandy, and the final defeat of the English at Castillon (1453).

20 Shown here as the Virgin in Jean Fouquet's extraordinary *Melun Diptych* (c. 1452), Agnès Sorel rose to cultural and political prominence as mistress to Charles VII. After bearing him three daughters she died in mysterious circumstances and may have been poisoned on the orders of Jacques Coeur, the king's finance minister.

21 One of the most important authors in the later middle ages, Christine de Pizan wrote a wide range of works for various members of the French court. Her interests were extensive and included books on the roles of women in society, matters of high politics, and even a military guide.

22 Joan of Arc's remarkable career was short-lived. Convinced she had received divine inspiration, she revitalized the faltering Valois military effort by relieving the siege of Orléans in 1429 and led the campaign to Reims which concluded with the coronation of Charles VII. Burgundian forces captured her in 1430 and sold her to the English who handed her over to Church authorities for trial as a heretic. After an extensive trial and brief recantation she was found guilty and executed in Rouen in 1431. No contemporary portraits of Joan exist. This artist's interpretation from c. 1485 was painted after her Rehabilitation trial (1455–56).

23 As the coronation site of French monarchs Reims Cathedral played a major role politically and symbolically in the Hundred Years War. It was the target of major military campaigns in 1359–60 (led by Edward III) and 1429 (led by Joan of Arc).

brought to the verge of starvation despite moving through rich country. 'There were scarcely supplies for eight days for the king. The French devastated the farms, the vineyards and food supplies. They were keen to harry the people by hunger so that they might ruin them completely by making them weak without even fighting.'[45]

Although often essential and, usually, militarily useful, plundering created an inherent political tension. It was a little difficult to render one's potential subjects destitute while at the same time projecting an image of good lordship and a legitimate claim to the French throne. As a result, according to Jean le Bel, when Edward III launched the Reims campaign and made a serious bid for the French throne he attempted to do so without recourse to plunder. In order to feed the army between 6,000 and 12,000 carts were brought on the expedition. In the event it was not, primarily, a lack of food for the soldiers but shortage of fodder for the horses that forced the king to break off the siege of the coronation city. Feeding horses and other pack animals created enormous logistical problems and greatly increased the weight and volume of foodstuffs an army needed to carry.[46]

Baggage wagons had to carry foodstuffs, ammunition, weapons and equipment, while supply trains might also include animals, especially cattle. In addition to specifically military items, an army needed a great many utensils such as pans, goblets, leather buckets, cooking pots, spoons, bowls, barrels and bellows. Boots and warm clothing were needed as well given that the soldiers were likely to be sleeping outside. Armies also had to carry with them the means of producing food and cooking, particularly mills and ovens to make bread, oatmeal or biscuit.[47] If they did not bring such equipment with them they might have to try and find it. During the Reims campaign English soldiers were assaulted several times while they were trying to make flour. On one such occasion five English squires 'who were unarmed except for their helmets and shields ... were in a mill to grind some corn. Fifty French men-at-arms came to attack them.' The consequences were not what one would expect. According to Thomas Gray these five defeated the fifty, capturing eleven of them. On another occasion men from Edward Despenser's (1336–75) retinue were guarding some millers who were preparing flour for them when they were attacked by soldiers from a local French garrison.[48]

Conditions for French soldiers operating in France were different but not completely so. The Crown relied on a requisition system called the *prise* to raise supplies, chiefly cereals, wine and animal fodder. In general French soldiers were less likely to face opposition to the collection of food than the

English, and they tended to be more knowledgeable about local communities and so were able to anticipate the availability of supplies. However, as
Christine de Pizan noted, there were still problems associated with French
armies seeking foodstuffs while on campaign. She asked whether, 'if men-
at-arms are given wages and there is no irregularity in their payment, can
they take supplies from the countryside, and take anything else, as they
commonly do nowadays in France?' She was categorical in answering her
own question: 'I assure you absolutely not, for such things have nothing to
do with war but are wicked and violent extortions.' And if circumstances
were such that it became essential to take supplies, the soldiers 'should not
be like wolves, who are not satisfied with one sheep but must kill the whole
flock'.[49] Although the following account no doubt puts a fine gloss on
reality, Charles VII's military reforms did improve the situation. A royal
chronicler suggested that because 'they were paid each month [French
soldiers] did not dare ... to take any of the people prisoner nor to take or
ransom any beast ... nor seize any victuals ... without paying for them,
except only from the English or their adherents, in which case they could
take the victuals lawfully'.[50] Presumably it was sometimes difficult to establish who might be an adherent of the English.

Clearly the impact of an army on the countryside and its inhabitants could
be devastating. Even English apologists acknowledged that among expeditionary forces there were 'thieves ... who are more given to pillage than to
pity and care nothing for the tears of the innocent as long as they can lay
their hands on plunder'.[51] The despoliation of the French countryside and
those who lived there was characteristic of the quotidian brutality of life on
campaign. However, commanders sometimes tried to mitigate the destruction
their forces caused. There was a careful balance to be maintained in this regard.
On the one hand, a key purpose of a *chevauchée* was to despoil the French
countryside, demonstrating the pitiful weakness of the Valois monarchy; on
the other hand, English kings wished to present their credentials as legitimate
and benign rulers of France. In order to control behaviour English commanders
issued military ordinances. The first extant example dates from 1385, although
it was probably based on earlier regulations. The 1415 ordinances laid down
general rules to limit pillaging while taking account of the wider purpose
of the expedition. The regulations were extensive: in addition to prohibitions
on attacks on clergymen, women and certain other non-combatants, they
dictated a wide assortment of military duties including keeping watch, finding
quarters and supplies, the division of spoils and ransoms, and orders to maintain camp hygiene and control camp followers.[52]

Conditions for soldiers on campaign were rarely comfortable. The Reims campaign (1359–60) was, to take one example, a bleak experience for all those involved. The siege of the French coronation city ended when the English were forced to leave in search of supplies, particularly fodder for their horses. The subsequent assault on Paris was then halted by the weather:

> The King [Edward III] took his leave, and putting fire to everything along his route, set up camp near Montlhéry with his army round him. On Sunday 13 April [1360] it was agreed to make a very long march towards Beauce, due to a lack of fodder for the horses. The weather was desperately bad with rain, hail and snow, and such was the cold that many weakened men and horses perished in the field. They abandoned many carts and pack horses on account of the cold, the wind and the wet, which happened to be the worst weather in living memory.[53]

Similarly, the conditions suffered by Henry V's army during the siege of Harfleur and then on the march to Agincourt were terrible, as were the deeds they perpetrated, despite the king's orders.[54] The siege began on 23 August 1415 when Henry imposed a blockade on Harfleur and the town fell some four weeks later. It was, therefore, not a long siege at all, but conditions for all worsened swiftly. The army's food supply was precarious from the beginning of the operation and although foraging parties were sent out, the sheer size of the army meant these could achieve little. Henry made immediate requests to England and Gascony for supplies. Nor was hunger the only problem. The concentration of so many men in such a small area meant that living conditions soon deteriorated. The land around Harfleur, inevitably, was damp and rapidly became deeply unpleasant. Human waste, which could not easily be buried, soon polluted the water supply. Animal carcasses and other rubbish contributed to a growing stench; shellfish was relatively plentiful but posed a number of health risks; dysentery soon killed many and invalided more. Nor did it help that it was unseasonably warm. No doubt the aristocracy enjoyed more comfortable conditions, but even they were not immune to the problems and there were a number of high-ranking casualties. Richard Courtenay, bishop of Norwich, and Michael de la Pole, earl of Suffolk, both died. The duke of Clarence and the Earl Marshal, John Mowbray, fell ill and had to return home when the siege finally ended. Thomas, earl of Arundel, died shortly after his return. In total perhaps as many as 2,000 soldiers died from dysentery during the siege of Harfleur and perhaps as many again were invalided back to England.[55]

Although the siege had been short, the citizens of Harfleur did not simply capitulate. They manned the walls and employed several innovative defensive measures. Jars full of burning powders, sulphur and quicklime were placed on the town's walls ready to be thrown in the eyes of the attackers. Burning fat was hurled at the siege towers and those who manned them. In response the English soldiers spent much of their time digging: trenches to protect the attacking forces and mines to undermine the town's walls. The siege weapons pounded the walls throughout the day and the citizens of Harfleur struggled to make repairs overnight. Eventually the pressure from outside began to tell, the outer defences fell, and with that came the realisation that there was no hope of rescue. The leaders of Harfleur, including Raoul, sire de Gaucourt, surrendered on 22 September. Alongside a large proportion of the civilian population, Gaucourt and the members of the garrison were expelled/permitted to leave on condition that they did not take up arms against Henry again during this campaign.

Once he had control of the town Henry installed a very substantial garrison consisting of 300 men-at-arms and 900 archers under the command of Thomas Beaufort, earl of Dorset. The king then left with what remained of the army to march to Calais, a distance of approximately 150 miles. They were said to be a 'trifling band, now weakened by hunger, dysentery, and fever'.[56] In reality they were hungry and ill but not quite so few in number. From the beginning of the march a French contingent, under the command of Marshal Boucicaut (Jean II le Maingre, 1366–1421), shadowed the English. Boucicaut had observed events at Harfleur without seeking to intervene, since he not been able to raise a sufficiently large army to guarantee success in battle. However, as time passed, French recruitment continued, and as Henry lost men to the garrison, to dysentery and to death, the French chances seemed better. The dauphin, Louis of Guienne, arrived at Vernon, on the borders of Normandy, and the constable, Charles d'Albret, took up position first at Honfleur and then at Rouen, which many considered Henry's next likely target.

Henry's progress was delayed as the French tried to block his path across the Somme, including the ford at Blanchetaque, which Edward III had used to escape from Philippe VI in 1346. Supplies began to run perilously low as the English were driven away from Calais and towards the main body of the French army. Finally ways were found across the river at Voyennes and Béthencourt (near Péronne) – the English crossed only one

or two men at a time. Heading north once more Henry was finally intercepted by the French at Agincourt.

We cannot know for certain what the soldiers felt in the hours before
battle was joined. We have little in the way of personal letters and reminiscences and so there is a great deal that we can only surmise. Some must
have been terrified. Others may have relished the prospect of killing. Much
would have depended on a soldier's experiences and whether he had been
in a battle before. The psychological aspect of combat was crucial. Perhaps
because violence was an everyday part of medieval life, the shock of combat
may have been reduced for the uninitiated.[57] Whatever the case, dealing
with fear and the threat of injury, dismemberment or death was central to
success in battle, individually and collectively. Infantrymen had to contend
with the impact, literal and psychological, of attack, and if they were inexperienced or could not cope with that fear – if they fled instead of fought
– it could prove fatal individually or collectively. Indeed, it had been
precisely this discipline among groups of battle-hardened infantrymen that
accounted for a succession of English victories in Scotland and France.
Prior to this the shock of a cavalry charge often proved decisive. Cohesion
and solidarity (emotional and physical) in the ranks were vital. At Agincourt
the knowledge that the French had greatly superior numbers, which the
English could see for themselves by the 'forest of spears' across the field, did
not break the will of Henry's troops. Nonetheless, it was partly for psychological reasons that the king ordered his army to begin the attack, believing
that to delay any further would result in the English soldiers being 'infected
with fear' at the size of the French army.[58]

The structure of retinues may have contributed to the greater resolve of
the English. Some of those recruited for the Agincourt campaign were
experienced, professional soldiers, but others were novices who had been
offered no choice but to accompany their masters overseas. However, they
were recruited alongside and would fight next to friends, relatives and
colleagues, which could bolster morale: these were no 'Pals' Brigades', but
shame and solidarity were powerful forces. The presence of a substantial
proportion of the nobility and the general militarisation of society ensured
that English domestic social networks became linked to military service
overseas. Consequently, a local collective feeling became associated with an
emerging national *esprit de corps*. At Agincourt, as at Crécy and Poitiers,
experienced soldiers commanded these retinues, maintained order and gave
heart to their troops. Edward, duke of York (c.1373–1415), and Thomas,
Lord Camoys (c.1350–1421), commanded the vanguard and rearguard

respectively – both had seen a great deal of military action. Henry V himself had served a harsh military apprenticeship during the Glyn Dŵr revolt and he had seen battle at Shrewsbury in 1403. Furthermore, even though some of the soldiers had little military experience before arriving in France, they gained a good deal at Harfleur and on the march to Agincourt. In this way, as was the case in the Crécy campaign, 'virgin' soldiers acquired a taste of (for) fighting before the battle and they could also turn to veterans for guidance. Such retinues, built around an experienced and tempered 'core', were central to English military successes from 1346 to 1415 and beyond. At Verneuil (1424), for example, the vanguard in the army led by John, duke of Bedford, was broken by a French cavalry charge, but the English soldiers regrouped and there was no rout.[59]

The presence of the king or a member of the royal family might also help maintain order, discipline and morale. Henry certainly seems to have played an important role at Agincourt. When Sir Walter Hungerford (1378–1449) bemoaned the lack of archers in his company, Henry reprimanded him in a speech remarkably similar to that familiar from Shakespeare ('If we are marked to die, we are enough/To do our country loss; and if to live,/The fewer men, the greater share of honour'). Henry's 'humble few' with the aid of the Almighty would 'overcome the opposing arrogance of the French'.[60] In a similar fashion the Black Prince had rallied his troops before the battle of Poitiers. According to his biographer, Chandos Herald, Edward had prayed:

Father, as thou art true God, true man,
Deign by thy most holy name
Me and my folk to protect from harm,
Because true God in Heaven on high,
You know that my right is good.[61]

This was recognition that for all one's preparation, divine favour would ultimately determine the outcome. Battles had deep religious significance. Not only was victory or defeat an indication of divine judgment, but for many it might bring one decidedly closer to divine judgment of a very personal nature. Before Agincourt, as was common, there were prayers and every soldier 'who had not previously cleansed his conscience by confession, put on the armour of penitence; and there was no shortage then save only one of priests'. When the English viewed the bloody refuse of the battle at its conclusion, the outcome was judged inevitable because 'St George was seen fighting in the battle on the[ir] side'.[62]

The battle of Agincourt began at about 11 o'clock on the morning of 25 October (the feast day of Saints Crispin and Crispian). It had not been a pleasant night: heavy rain had turned the ploughed field between the two armies into a quagmire. The English and French forces had deployed before dawn and several hours passed without any move being made to attack. Eventually, Henry ordered an advance, perhaps fearing that his soldiers' nerve would not hold much longer. But before they moved forward an extraordinary act took place: each man knelt, kissed the ground and took a little earth in his mouth. This was clearly a ritual, a personal ceremony with sacramental connotations, combining something of the Eucharist with a memento of the burial service. The archers then pulled up the stakes with which they defended their positions and advanced.[63]

The size of the armies that fought at Agincourt remains a matter of contention. The Shakespearean myth suggests that the English were outnumbered by at least ten to one in 1415. Such an assumption is based on contemporary and near-contemporary English chronicles, which estimated the French army as between 60,000 and 160,000 men. Such grossly inflated numbers were designed to exaggerate the scale of Henry's victory. More recent work suggests the French army was more modest in size, perhaps 20,000–30,000 troops (including 10,000 men-at-arms, 10,000 *gros valets* – lightly armed soldiers who each accompanied a man-at-arms – and approximately 4,000 archers, crossbowmen and others). And it is even possible that the French army was smaller still, numbering 12,000 soldiers or fewer. By comparison the English army numbered between 6,000 and 9,000 soldiers – the author of the *Gesta Henrici Quinti* suggested 5,000 archers and 1,000 men-at-arms. The French, therefore, outnumbered the English by at least two to one, but by no more than four to one. However, the composition of each army differed significantly: about 65 per cent of the French soldiers were men-at-arms, whereas these accounted for fewer than 25 per cent of the English troops – the remainder were archers.[64]

In the event the French assault at Agincourt was disorganised, arrogant and naive, but it did not begin that way. The French commanders had a clear plan of action on the eve of the battle. Boucicaut (the marshal) and the Constable of France, Charles d'Albret, intended to use – essentially – English tactics against Henry by dismounting the main body of men-at-arms, dividing them into three 'battles' (divisions), and advancing them with the support of archers and crossbowmen deployed on the flanks. Artur de Richemont and Louis, count of Vendôme, commanded two cavalry wings which were to be held in reserve until the English had been engaged.

They would then launch a surprise flanking attack on the English archers and perhaps also on the rear of the English infantry.[65] The plan, however, could not be implemented. First, the terrain proved thoroughly unfavourable – there was no room for a flanking manoeuvre. Prior to its advance the English army had been defended by the Agincourt and Tramecourt woods, and thereafter the archers secured their defensive position with stakes. Second, and more significantly, there was a breakdown of discipline in the French ranks. Many of the French nobility would not wait for the missile troops to begin the engagement and jockeyed among themselves for a prime position in the vanguard.

Given their numerical disadvantage it is surprising that the English began the assault when Sir Thomas Erpingham's archers launched their first volley. It proved effective, however, by disrupting the French and goading them into a poorly organised attack. The French may well have known the condition of the English army – weary, hungry and sick – and so prolonging the agony could only be to their advantage.[66] The French heavy cavalry charged but was slowed by the sodden soil and then driven back by a punishing volley of arrows. At close range the longbowmen's arrows were deadly and could punch through even plate armour: 'by their very force [they] pierced the sides and visors of their helmets'.[67] Forced to retreat into the advancing French infantry, the cavalry caused chaos.

Because of the English longbowmen, those French troops who did reach the enemy lines were disorientated and, in some cases, wounded. Despite this their superior numbers began to tell and the English were pushed back. The king himself was caught up in the intense exchange and Edward, duke of York, was killed, but the line held. The French, however, now began to tire and the lightly armed English archers attacked from the flanks: 'seizing axes, stakes and swords and spear-heads that were lying about, they struck down, hacked and stabbed the enemy'.[68] In the heavy conditions the archers were extremely mobile. Many wore no armour at all and some even removed their headgear and boots so they might have better vision and grip underfoot. Barrels of wine were kept nearby so they could drink when they had a moment. The more nimble among them may have been sent out at intervals onto the battlefield to retrieve arrows.[69]

The ferocious pressure from the front and flanks, and the weight of numbers from behind, prevented an organised French retreat:

[S]o great was the undisciplined violence and pressure of the mass of men behind that the living fell on top of the dead, and others falling on top of the living were killed as well [leaving] such a great heap of the slain and of those lying crushed in between that our men climbed up those heaps, which had risen above a man's height, and butchered their enemies down below.[70]

At this point many of the French nobility were forced to surrender and offered themselves for ransom. However, perhaps two hours later, the English baggage train came under attack as French reserves under Waleran, count of Fauquembergues, launched a final assault. In response, fearing he would be encircled and that he might also be attacked by the captives, Henry ordered all but the most important prisoners executed.

On the English side there were remarkably few casualties. Many men, however, must have been wounded, some gravely. One Thomas Hostell suffered an extraordinary range of injuries over the course of the 1415 expedition, which left him in a dreadful condition after his return to England. At the siege of Harfleur he was 'smitten with a springald through the head, losing one eye, and his cheekbone broken; [while] at the battle of Agincourt [he was] sore hurt, maimed and wounded'. As a consequence he became 'enfeebled and bruised [and when] fallen to great age and poverty, and greatly indebted he [could] not help himself'.[71] Whether much could have been done for Thomas, throughout the war English commanders recognised that they needed to provide medical assistance for (at least some of) their troops. At Crécy Edward III had dressing stations available to soldiers during the battle, although medical care centred on the elite.[72] Henry V certainly took medical matters seriously and recruited a team of doctors for the 1415 expedition. Having been wounded in battle himself, at Shrewsbury in 1403, the king recognised the value of medical assistance on the battlefield. He had been struck by an arrow in the face and, while the shaft was removed, the arrowhead remained deeply embedded. Eventually, the king's surgeon, John Bradmore, devised a mechanism for safely enlarging the wound and extracting the arrowhead before cleansing the area. Consequently, when he left for the Agincourt campaign, Henry was accompanied by a medical team of twenty-one surgeons which included Thomas Morstede, Nicholas Colnet and William Bradwardine. These were skilled doctors and Morstede would later write the *Fair Book of Surgery*, which became a standard textbook. He and Bradwardine served on the Normandy campaign which departed England in 1417.[73]

The consequences of battle might, however, go beyond wounds to the body; physical trauma can also lead to mental incapacity. During Edward I's

reign there are two examples of this: one Bartholomew Sakeville suffered
an acute fever following a blow to the head from which he never fully
recovered, and another soldier, Nigel Coppedene, was pardoned of murder
as he was judged mentally incompetent following his treatment as a prisoner of war.[74] Some medieval soldiers, like their modern counterparts, must
have suffered from combat trauma (or post-traumatic stress). It is difficult
to know what Thomas Gray implied when he described the battle of
Poitiers as *hidouse* (hideous or fearsome), but no doubt it was a gruesome
experience. Evidence for the emotional and psychological impact of such
encounters is sparse but not non-existent. The sight of the piles of the slain
at Agincourt certainly did not enrapture all the victors. Rather, there were
tears at the 'terrible deaths and bitter wounds of so many Christian men'.[75]
Similarly, during the siege of Rouen (1419) an English soldier, John Page,
recalled the plight of those trapped between the city walls and the encir-
cling forces:

> There ne was no man, I understand,
> That saw that but his heart would change,
> And [if] he considered that sight
> He would be pensive and no thing light.[76]

Although he was a soldier, and one committed to Henry V's cause, Page
was deeply moved by the hellish conditions which the desperate civilians
suffered.

Buoyed by the triumph but exhausted and hungry, the bedraggled
English army trudged from Agincourt to Calais. There they were delayed
for a fortnight awaiting a favourable wind to bring them home. However,
the authorities at Calais would not allow the bulk of the army to enter the
town, fearing disruption and a threat to their own food supply. Consequently,
many of the English soldiers sold their prisoners and plunder for little
profit in order to buy what they could. '[M]ost of them had spent eight to
ten days without eating bread, and of other victuals, meat, butter, eggs,
cheese only the little they could find . . . there was such a shortage of bread
that [by the time they reached Calais] they did not bother what it cost, but
only that they should have some.'[77]

When he finally returned to England and London in November 1415,
Henry was greeted with a magnificent celebration – almost a Roman
triumph. The success at Agincourt practically sanctified Henry in English
eyes; the victory was divine confirmation of the righteousness of his claims

in France and of the rights of the Lancastrian dynasty to rule in England (and France). There would be no lack of popular support for his next expedition, the recapture of Normandy.

In preparation for this new invasion Henry needed a secure and safe passage to France, and a bridgehead from which to advance. He had two bases in the north of the country, Calais and Harfleur; the latter, though, was exposed and under constant threat of attack from land and sea. It did, nevertheless, offer the king a fine strategic vantage-point from which to enter the duchy of Normandy. During the Hundred Years War, because of the nature of communications and the limitations of maritime technology, one could not take 'command of the sea', but one could establish a maritime 'zone of control' for a short period of time.[78] Henry needed this before he could launch the Normandy campaign, and he achieved it through two major naval battles, at Harfleur in 1416 and off the Chef de Caux in the following year. The first encounter saw the duke of Bedford command an English force against a Franco-Genoese fleet that blockaded the port. The English had fewer ships but more troops, many of them archers. Although wounded in the battle himself, Bedford broke the blockade and captured three Genoese carracks in the process. The second battle, to clear the immediate path for the invasion fleet, took place close to Honfleur, a port near the mouth of the River Seine. Again, a Franco-Genoese fleet was operating in the area. John Holland, earl of Huntingdon (1395–1447), led an English flotilla to victory on this occasion.[79] Less than a month later the king sailed at the head of an invasion force of around 10,000 men in a newly built ship of 1,000 tons, the *Jesus*. Once it landed the army continued to be reinforced and resupplied on a regular basis by ship.

In this and other ways the sea played a vital role in the Hundred Years War. Both a barrier and a means of transportation, it lay at the heart of all logistical problems and potentialities. Its moods determined the success or failure of every expedition at the outset. Because much of the war was socio-economic in character, attacks on trade vessels by both sides were common. Maritime raiding was also common practice and a tactic both sides used extensively. It proved financially profitable, psychologically useful and an effective means of disrupting daily life, trade, shipping and fishing. In a war fought predominantly in France it was one of the few ways the French could retaliate against the enemy at home. Although not comparable to the terror of the *chevauchées*, the southern and eastern coasts of England were subjected to regular assault. These caused widespread destruction, some deaths and, at times, a profound climate of fear.[80]

This was almost tangible during the raids launched by Jean de Vienne, Admiral of France, in the 1370s and 1380s, when there was also a major threat of invasion. The initial plan involved the simultaneous landing of two forces, one led by Vienne in Scotland, the other commanded by Olivier de Clisson on the south coast of England. Vienne arrived at Leith on 1 June 1385 with a force of 1,300 men-at-arms and 250 crossbowmen. He led a raid into the Borders, but Richard II acted decisively and drove him back. Vienne returned to the West March and plundered Cumberland, but the invasion failed mainly because Clisson's force was delayed. In 1386–87 Vienne assembled a vast second invasion force at Harfleur, with perhaps 30,000 troops. Again the plan failed, and again because of Clisson, who fell into the hands of the duke of Brittany. Thereafter Charles VI's illness and growing tension in the Valois court curtailed the French naval effort.[81]

Because of the centrality of the sea in the prosecution of the Hundred Years War, it is not surprising that in terms of total costs naval and maritime expenditure were often greater than those incurred by land forces. In England ships were requisitioned in vast numbers and the scale of maritime operations was formidable from the outset. During the 1340s and 1350s at least a thousand 'arrests' of merchants ships were made. Estimates for the size of the English fleet at the battle of Sluys in June 1340 vary between 147 and 300 vessels. In 1347 Edward III used over 700 ships and about 15,000 sailors for the siege of Calais.[82] In France more substantial shipyards were available to the Valois kings to construct vessels; this was necessary since the Capetian and Valois kings could not press vessels into service in the same numbers as the Plantagenets. In 1295 Philippe IV had established the Clos des Galées, a base for French royal vessels on the left bank of the Seine at Richebourg, outside Rouen. This centre, modelled on the naval arsenal at Seville, was active in building and repairing ships in the early years of the Hundred Years War. It specialised in galleys – large, oared fighting ships, sometimes with two masts, based on a Mediterranean design rather than on the northern European model descended from Viking long-ships.[83] In the opening phase of the war the French may have had a slight edge over the English in terms of naval construction techniques, but for much of the war there was little to choose between the two sides in terms of maritime technology.

As well as transports, ships served as fighting platforms and in this way they reflected the military prejudices of each side. As one would expect, the English favoured the longbow and the French the crossbow as long-range naval weapons. Although there is some evidence of torsion artillery (catapults powered by highly tensioned and twisted ropes) in the early years of the Hundred Years War, most sea battles were decided by individual boarding actions in which ships were grappled to one another. There were many such encounters throughout the war. In the opening exchanges there were three recognised battles (Sluys in 1340, Winchelsea (Les Espagnols sur Mer) in 1350 and La Rochelle in 1372), and numerous smaller engagements.[84] Edward III, it seems, had a fondness (weakness) for ramming the opposition; his tactics at Winchelsea in 1350, against a Castilian force sailing home, have been likened to 'a demented ten-year-old on the dodgems'.[85]

When Henry V acceded to the throne in 1413 he recognised that his French ambitions relied on an expansion in English naval strength. He clearly 'understood the use of sea power as a primary weapon of war'.[86] New ships were built, others were refitted; the design of many of these was influenced by Genoese carracks with high-sided hulls. This made them difficult to board and provided good platforms for the use of missile weapons, which by this time included some rudimentary guns. It was during Henry's reign that Southampton became a major naval base. The king's expeditionary fleet in 1415 consisted of an extraordinary 1,500 ships which were needed to carry the 12,000 soldiers for the siege of Harfleur and the subsequent expedition to Agincourt. The invasion force in 1417 was a little smaller, but it still constituted a very sizable army – perhaps 10,000 soldiers. The conquest of the duchy followed. French attention was focused on the Burgundian threat to Paris while in the series of sieges Henry systematically took control of the duchy, capturing Caen in 1417 and Rouen in 1419.

Once completed, the reconquest of Normandy ensured that French access to the English coast was much reduced. It was, however, very expensive to maintain even a small group of ships in good repair, and once Normandy was in English hands (which provided greater control of the Channel), naval priorities declined and ships were sold to pay the king's debts after Henry V died in 1422. Thereafter English naval power gradually decayed – a state of affairs the author of the *Libelle of Englyshe Polycye* lamented. Recognising the collapse of the position in France, he argued strongly that the sea lanes around England should be kept open in order to maintain trade links with Calais (the location of the wool staple), Wales and Ireland. In reality, as English control in France crumbled, attacks on the south coast of England resumed. In 1448 the French burned Rye and Winchelsea, and the loss of Gascony did not mark the end of such activity.

In 1457 Pierre de Brézé, seneschal of Normandy, sacked Sandwich.[87] Such events would have seemed incomprehensible in Henry V's reign. Agincourt, the reconquest of Normandy and, lastly, the Burgundian alliance finally brought sufficient pressure to bear on Charles VI's doddering regime to compel the treaty of Troyes in 1420 and with it the prospect of a Dual Monarchy. In the concluding years of Henry V's reign what had been a war of raids and sieges became a war of occupation.

CHAPTER 7

Occupation
COEXISTENCE, COLLABORATION AND RESISTANCE
1423

*In the last week of August the Duke of Burgundy arrived in Paris, which did
no one any good as he had a great many troops with him who took everything
from the villages around Paris; the English were there too. Wine was then
very much dearer than it had been for a long time, and there were moreover
very few grapes on the vines, yet these English and Burgundians destroyed
even these few, just as pigs would have done and no one dared say anything
about it.*[1]

Anon., *Journal of the Parisian Bourgeois*, 1423

The journal of the so-called Parisian Bourgeois provides one of the most
vivid pictures of life in Paris before, during and after the Anglo-Burgundian
occupation (1420–36). His comments (such as the above) provide a familiar,
rather stereotypical view of occupation, characterised by brutal and destructive troops (here described as 'pigs'), a cowed population both in the city
and its hinterland, and concern over food shortages. But the anonymous
author was anything but stereotypical, and his attitude to the occupiers far
from simplistic. In a period for which monastic and aristocratic evidence
predominates, his journal provides a genuine 'voice' beyond the ranks of
the elite. His remarkable account of life in Paris covered more than forty
years (1405–49), and few subjects escaped his attention. His concerns
ranged from national and international events to the weather, the price of
food and drink and other events in the French capital both mundane and
extraordinary.

The Bourgeois' experiences offer a clear reflection of the changing
character of the Hundred Years War in the fifteenth century. English military strategy had shifted from the *chevauchées* and raids characteristic of the

campaigns of the 1340s, 1350s and 1370s to territorial conquest – to sieges and the widespread occupation of land. Technological developments as well as political circumstances impelled these strategic changes. Firstly, English commanders took advantage of increasingly effective gunpowder artillery, which made sieges a more practicable proposition. Secondly, they were driven by events in France, not least the opportunities provided by the political fracture at the centre of government which Charles VI's madness caused and the Armagnac-Burgundian civil war tore open. The victory at Agincourt and the subsequent conquest of Normandy are attributable to Henry V's military genius and the weapons he could employ, as well as to the deep fissures at the heart of the French polity. It was Normandy, re-established under English control for the first time since 1204, which provided the most important locus of occupation and colonisation in the Hundred Years War. Then, following the treaty of Troyes (1420), in addition to the duchy, Paris and much of northern France came under English (Anglo-Burgundian) authority. The murder in 1419 of Jean the Fearless, duke of Burgundy, had forced his successor, Philippe the Good, into an English alliance that laid the foundations for the Dual Monarchy and brought about the effective partition of half the country. Therefore, in the fifteenth century, the Hundred Years War, which had been, to differing extents, a dynastic and feudal conflict, a civil war, an economic struggle and a clash over the French throne, also became a war of occupation.

For the English this was a familiar situation. They had a long history of occupation and of 'colonial' government stretching back through the Angevin Empire to the Anglo-Norman realm established in 1066. Indeed, the Hundred Years War was fought, at least in part, to restore and reoccupy those lands the Plantagenets believed were theirs by birthright. When the war began what remained of that birthright, the English foreign lordships, was far from negligible; it comprised Wales, much of Ireland, the Isle of Man, the Channel Islands, Scotland (in theory) and, of course, Gascony. Lands in France, therefore, were already under English occupation at the start of the war in 1337, and England's political presence in France had been chiefly responsible for the outbreak of the conflict. Within ten years of the beginning of the struggle the first additions were made to the English dominions with the conquest of Calais in 1347 and its surrounding marches. Then, after the treaty of Brétigny in 1360, nearly a third of France fell into English control in what became the principality of Aquitaine. Much of this territory was lost soon after the resumption of the war in 1369, and in response the English resorted to a tried, tested and, in the 1370s, an almost completely ineffective raiding strategy. When Henry V led English forces back to France in 1415 he, too, embarked on a *chevauchée*, although he was not reluctant to besiege Harfleur. There was, however, a clear shift of policy in 1417 when Henry began the assault on Normandy and the conquest of land, not merely of men, became the primary objective.[2]

English policy towards the inhabitants of captured territories in the early part of the 1417–19 campaign tended to be brutal; indeed, some native populations were deliberately displaced, to be replaced with more trustworthy settlers. This became a common feature throughout the period of English control: an immigration policy was enforced that aimed to ensure political and military security by implanting the king's 'loyal subjects'. For those native populations that did find themselves under English dominion conditions varied greatly. For some it proved a devastating experience; for others a reasonably comfortable *modus operandi* was achieved. In either case, however, English occupation might be no worse than exploitation by French nobles, *écorcheurs* and *routiers* or garrison warfare, *petite guerre* (guerrilla warfare), or excessive demands for *patis* (extortion money) and uncontrolled taxation. Indeed, each in their own way formed a different sort of occupation, and might entail a comparable level of oppression.[3]

Any occupation presents the occupied with a number of possible responses: populations or individuals may resist; they may acquiesce, either passively or indignantly; or they may collaborate. Few of these were black-and-white decisions in the Hundred Years War because of fluctuating circumstances and the mutability of national identities and allegiances.[4] Consequently, reactions to occupation varied widely between and among those options. The nobility, while suffering less than most from occupation, were often faced with difficult political choices, nonetheless. This was certainly the case for many in Brittany, Gascony, Aquitaine, Normandy and Paris at different stages of the war. In May 1360, with the sealing of the treaty of Brétigny, many of the Aquitainian nobility were forced to offer their allegiance to England. Some, such as Guichard d'Angle, did so and remained loyal to the English. Lord of Angle-sur-l'Anglin and Pleumartin, and a substantial landowner in the northern march of Poitou, Guichard had fought for Jean II at Poitiers, but he became such a trusted member of the Black Prince's household that he was appointed tutor to the young Richard of Bordeaux (later Richard II). For others, however, such as Jean d'Armagnac, the former lieutenant of the king of France in Languedoc, this proved an uneasy alliance at best. Although he fought for the Black

Prince at the battle of Nájera in 1367, Armagnac was instrumental in instigating the revolt against the English regime that began in 1368. A more complex situation involved the shifting allegiances of the Albret clan. Members of the family had long formed a bulwark against Valois ambitions in the duchy of Gascony, but in 1368 some of them were induced to support the French king, and Arnaud-Armanieu d'Albret joined the count of Armagnac in leading the revolt against the Black Prince.[5]

In this way families could become politically divided as a consequence of occupation. Guillaume de Clinchamp offered his allegiance to Henry V in 1419 in order to retain his lands in Normandy, and one of his sons entered the service of John Kemp, the bishop of London. Two others, however, joined the French garrison of Mont-Saint-Michel. In 1433 the daughter of Guillaume le Tavernier, a rich bourgeois from Rouen, who had grown wealthy during the English occupation, married Jacques de Calais, an important member of the Council of Normandy. Their three sons, however, all refused to pay allegiance to the English and settled in the kingdom of Bourges.[6] Such stresses were evident throughout the war and loyalties might not be divided only between Plantagenet and Valois. The conflicting ambitions of the lords of Navarre and Brittany, and political strains between the other Princes of the Blood, especially during the Armagnac-Burgundian civil war, placed great stresses on individual and collective allegiances. Georges de La Trémoïlle (c.1382–1446), for example, was a favourite of Charles VII, whereas his brother, Jean (1377–1449), was chamberlain and counsellor to Philippe the Good of Burgundy. The family estates fell under both French and English jurisdictions in the 1420s. Despite this the brothers remained on good terms and sought to maintain their joint interests. They managed to do this but under unfortunate circumstances: in 1427 the English authorities confiscated Georges's property and handed it over to Jean.[7]

In general, however, occupation created somewhat more pressing problems for the peasantry. As Jean Juvénal des Ursins wrote, to describe the sufferings of the French people following the English invasion of 1415 would take a book as long as the Bible.[8] It is, however, difficult to assess precisely what determined peasant responses to occupation and certainly to judge if it truly mattered whether the oppressor was English, French, Scottish or the leader of a mercenary company. For example, while some of the revolts against the English in the latter stages of the occupation of Normandy have been characterised as nationalist uprisings, this is a difficult case to prove conclusively. It is certainly the case that a national consciousness developed in both England and France over the course of the Hundred Years War, and Charles VII does seem to have benefited from local support when he began the reconquest of Normandy. There is, for example, evidence of collusion with French royal forces in a number of towns, even strongholds as significant as Cherbourg. Nonetheless, by this stage it was in the self-interest of the peasantry to support the Valois – the political tide had clearly turned in France's favour. Prior to this, in the midst of the struggle, individuals and communities took advantage of circumstances as they presented themselves, sometimes changing allegiance as opportunities arose or as various factors became significant. Influences were often local rather than national. For others stability was an end in itself. Many valued a peaceful existence regardless of the identity of their lord.[9]

The alternative, endemic warfare, led to a breakdown of law and order, although there was usually a governmental vacuum in the early stages of occupation also. This certainly happened following the treaty of Brétigny when the English annexed nearly a third of France, and again following the conquest of Normandy. In this political void companies of brigands (described variously as *tuchins*, *brigans* or *godins*) often formed among the French peasantry. This was partly a response to governmental collapse and partly an act of self-defence. The peasants felt they were being robbed and harassed to such an extent by their fellows and their new lords that they were forced to take matters into their own hands. This led to a spiral of violence. In the 1360s one Jean le Jeusne, who was forced by such circumstances into brigandage in the Oise region north of Paris, claimed that because of the lawless activities of soldiers and others 'no labouring man, or any other subject in the kingdom, dared venture securely or go about their business in the district for fear of being killed or taken for ransom'. As a consequence, Jean claimed, he had been forced out of self-preservation to take up brigandage and robbery.[10] The same situation developed in the 1420s in the context of the ongoing civil war and the partition of France. In 1422, while Henry V fought his final campaign at Meaux north-east of Paris, English forces pillaged much of Brie. According to the so-called Parisian Bourgeois, the peasantry complained that

> because of them and the other lot no one could get any ploughing or sowing done anywhere . . . Then most of the labourers stopped working in despair, abandoned their wives and children and said to each other: What shall we do? Let it all go to the devil, what do we care what

becomes of us? We may as well do the worst we can instead of the best. We'd be better off working for Saracens than for Christians, so let's do all the damage we can . . . It's our rulers who are the traitors, it's because of them that we must . . . escape to the woods like strayed animals.[11]

A collapse of law and order in the immediate aftermath of conquest was, therefore, not uncommon, but it was unwelcome and costly both politically and financially, and not a situation that occupying forces wished to tolerate for long. Occupation inevitably involved changes of government, although these were not wholesale. Typically some administrative revisions took place, and new officials were almost always employed, but local governmental structures were usually retained whenever possible. Furthermore, measures were often taken to try and ensure that the transfer of power was not overly provocative. So, while occupation brought with it immediate demands to pledge loyalty to the new regime,[12] the Plantagenets made considerable efforts to emphasise their legitimacy. The 'natural and rightful' descent of the English ruling house from the Capetian dynasty was stressed and with it the lawful English claim to French territories. In spite of efforts to ease the transitions, however, it was abundantly clear that a new political dispensation had been introduced: areas under English occupation and authority became subject immediately to the English Crown (*pays subgiet au royaume d'Angleterre*) and those who lived in these areas were, thereafter, considered the king's subjects. As such they came to share, or had imposed upon them, a common identity.[13]

Within the lordships groups and individuals recognised their membership of this wider collective – as subjects of the king of England – certainly when it suited them to do so. In 1341 Edward III received a letter containing a range of colonial grievances from members of the English lordship in Ireland. They wrote to him stating 'whereas various people of your allegiance, as of Scotland, Gascony and Wales often in times past have levied war against their liege lord, at all times your English liege people of Ireland have behaved themselves well and loyally'.[14] Over the course of the Hundred Years War this political identity – or at least a veneer of it – was extended throughout those territories that came under English occupation.

Throughout the English lordships in France, the British Isles and Ireland that veneer was polished by a certain amount of governmental standardisation. This resulted from the replication of various policies and legal approaches. As state institutions developed and personnel circulated between the Plantagenet dominions, English experiences in the British

Isles and Ireland influenced the government of occupied territories in France. Similarly, many Englishmen who served in the colonies in France subsequently took up offices in the British lordships or on the Marches of Scotland and Wales. In this way what might, anachronistically, be described as a 'colonial staff' transferred its experience and approach to government throughout the English lordships.[15] This is especially evident among the upper echelons of the administration. John Fastolf (c.1378–1459), for example, served in Bordeaux, Normandy and Ireland.[16] John Talbot held senior offices in Wales, Ireland and France between 1404 and 1453.[17] Richard, duke of York (1411–60), served as lieutenant of France (1436, 1440) and Ireland (1447), and because of his extensive estates he also had connections with Wales.[18]

Nonetheless, despite these similarities, the experience of occupation and English attitudes towards the lordships they occupied varied considerably. Political and military circumstances differed as did cultural traditions, social customs, languages and dialects. The character of occupation might also be shaped by the nature of the area's historic relationship with England. Gascony, for example, had been under English control for nearly two hundred years by the time the Hundred Years War began – although major outbreaks of political unrest and violence had regularly punctuated this period. However, although often described as England's first colony, there was little English settlement in Gascony and few attempts to expropriate land or to build a new society on an English model. Few Englishmen apart from those performing eminent military or administrative service settled in the duchy, although it is possible more substantial settlement took place during the lifetime of the principality of Aquitaine (1362–71).[19]

Gascony, therefore, was not 'occupied' per se but, clearly, nor was it independent: its government was in the hands of a prince, lieutenant or chief governor appointed by the king of England and acting with vice-regal authority. Governing conditions, which had always been problematic as governors of the duchy from Simon de Montfort (1248–52) onwards had found to their cost, became even more difficult when the treaty of Brétigny appended a considerable swathe of southern and central France to the duchy, totalling nearly a third of the country. Placed in the care of Edward of Woodstock (the Black Prince), appointed prince of Aquitaine in 1362, the occupation of this greater Aquitaine resulted in rebellion after some six years caused in part by a style of government which, although far from oppressive by English standards, took little account of local traditions and culture. In particular, the imposition of a range of Anglo-Gascon governing practices did not sit well with those Aquitainian nobles who had been forced into English allegiance by the 1360 treaty. In a letter designed to foment revolt, Louis d'Anjou, Charles V's lieutenant in Languedoc, wrote to the Aquitainian nobility in 1368 reminding them of the 'Ordonnances, indictions et exactions de fouages [hearth taxes] et autres griefs et nouveletés' which the Black Prince had exacted and introduced. Because of this the revolt against the prince's administration may be seen, chiefly, as a failure of 'good lordship', one caused, in the main, by mutual misunderstanding over what good lordship entailed.[20] One must also acknowledge that the man responsible for the devastation of the 1355 *grande chevauchée* was hardly likely to be popular with those whose lands and property had been burned and pillaged so horrifically.

By contrast, most of the Gascons (as opposed to those from the greater Aquitaine) valued their connections with England, although they almost certainly preferred a less active political representative and a more distant relationship. When Richard II, as part of his peace negotiations with France in the 1390s, proposed that his uncle, John of Gaunt, be made duke and hold Gascony of the French Crown, the scheme foundered because of the Gascons' reaction: they claimed they would not be ruled by anyone other than the king of England or his heir apparent. Gascon representatives who visited the English court stated 'that from times long past they had been accustomed to be governed by the English crown and not by third parties set in authority over them by the exercise of the king's will, with the single exception of the prince of Wales as the true heir to the English throne'.[21]

Because Gascony (if not the greater Aquitaine) had long been an English dominion it was something of a special case in the Hundred Years War. The conflict also created circumstances in which the English came to occupy other parts of France, not through direct conquest but as a consequence of political alliances: Brittany was one such area. The outbreak of the Breton civil conflict in 1341 between Jean de Montfort (1295–1345) and Charles de Blois (1319–64) provided another theatre in which to fight the Hundred Years War: the ducal struggle became subsumed under the Anglo-French hostilities. This was not surprising since the dukes of Brittany held land in both France and England and paid homage to both kings, something that had presented Duke Jean III with a major problem when the war began in 1337 – to whom should he offer his allegiance? Matters then became even more complex when Jean died in 1345, leading to a succession crisis and an opportunity for both France and England to strengthen their political influence over Brittany and its lord – one of the peers of the realm. The duchy was geographically as well as politically important: it offered a potential English bridgehead to the French interior and a modicum of control over the vital sea route between Gascony and England. Edward III as guardian of the future Jean IV de Montfort (ruled 1364–99) offered support to him; while Charles de Blois, a claimant to the duchy through his wife, Joan de Penthièvre, allied with the Valois. With Jean (IV) only an infant, King Edward appointed an English lieutenant to care for his ward's interests and assume control in the Montfortist areas of Brittany. Consequently, English troops were active in the duchy from 1342. The civil war soon became localised, usually taking the form of siege and counter-siege. This gave individual captains and commanders a great deal of independence, and certain English garrisons effectively occupied the areas under their control.

Many took advantage of the situation to demand *patis* (collective ransoms or protection money). The three principal English fortresses – Vannes, Bécherel and Ploërmel – shared between them the *patis* of 124 parishes by 1359.[22] Walter Bentley, the English lieutenant (appointed in 1350), tried to control the practice, denouncing it in 1352, but it only came to an end, and then only briefly, in 1365 with the treaty of Guérande. This confirmed de Montfort's victory in the civil war, which had been secured by his triumph at the battle of Auray. When the war reopened in 1369, de Montfort's attempts to play Plantagenet and Valois off against each other, and the new involvement of a number of Breton captains, most notably du Guesclin and Olivier de Clisson, led to many towns paying ransoms to English and French troops, sometimes simultaneously. In the 1370s the *apatisation* of the countryside was widespread and conditions worsened for the inhabitants.[23]

Gascony, the principality of Aquitaine and Brittany provide varying models of English 'occupation', but the examples offered by English dominions in the British Isles are also important in the context of the Hundred Years War. English approaches to occupation in France were informed, in large measure, by experiences in Wales, Ireland and, to a lesser extent, Scotland in the late thirteenth and early fourteenth centuries. In turn the Hundred Years War reshaped attitudes in England to the Welsh, Irish and Scots. The financial and military demands of the conflict ensured that these British and Irish lordships had to be exploited for the English war effort. Welsh troops, for example, were recruited in substantial numbers and played highly significant roles in a number of campaigns to France. This, clearly, was not indicative of an entirely harmonious relationship as

English colonial policies, many of them the consequence of war and some implemented by Welshmen, contributed directly to the Glyn Dŵr revolt that began in 1400. An attempt to throw off colonial control, this led to brutal reprisals and the introduction of draconian measures aimed further to limit the political, economic and military influence of Welshmen in Wales.[24] The revolt certainly made Henry V wary of using Welsh soldiers on his French expeditions: by comparison with the thousands of Welshmen recruited for the Crécy-Calais campaign, only 500 soldiers were recruited for the Agincourt expedition, and all of these were from south Wales, distant from the epicentre of the rising.[25]

The repressive legislation implemented by the English in Wales in the early years of the fifteenth century reinforced measures Edward I had taken to impose his conquest just over a hundred years earlier. Similar action had been taken around the same time to maintain the political and social integrity of the lordship of Ireland: in 1297 the Dublin parliament denounced and prohibited the adoption of various Gaelic-Irish habits and traditions by English settlers, describing them as 'degenerate'. Such measures were clarified and extended in the Statute of Kilkenny (1366), perhaps the most famous official condemnation ever written of the Irish and their way of life. The statute sought to prohibit certain interpersonal and intercultural links between the Gaelic-Irish and Anglo-Irish populations: marriages were banned as was the use of the Irish language by the settler community; so too was the adoption of Irish clothing, hairstyles, means of riding (i.e. without a saddle). One should not give patronage to a Gaelic Irish poet or clergyman without licence to do so.[26] It has been suggested that action of this sort in Wales and Ireland, as well as the attempts made to establish English authority in Scotland, indicates either a racist or certainly an anti-Celtic mentality. Consequently, it is argued that there was a complete contrast between English attitudes to governing Celtic countries and French dominions – the distinction being between those areas that had been conquered rather than inherited.[27]

Such a distinction, however, is called into question by events in the Hundred Years War. Calais, much of the principality of Aquitaine and many of those lands in Normandy and northern France acquired by Henry V were the product of conquest or, at the least, of a diplomatic settlement secured through military force. Indeed, those areas Henry had captured prior to the treaty of Troyes in 1420 were explicitly described as *pays de conquête*.[28] In many of these areas 'colonial' government might be, and was often viewed as, oppressive and exploitative – that is when there were no major expulsions of the French population. Furthermore, the prosecution of the war, the developments associated with the rise of the so-called 'war state' and the transfer of officials throughout the king's lordships ensured increasing similarities of policy and practice in all areas under English control. This mimicked the situation in England itself where markedly more restrictive legislation in the post-plague period brought about the Peasants' Revolt: clearly, the heavy hand of the state proved no more welcome to the English than to those in the foreign lordships.

The two main periods of English colonisation in the Hundred Years War were founded, in part at least, on battlefield successes: at Poitiers and Agincourt, and the treaties that followed – Brétigny and Troyes respectively. The first of these, eventually, produced the short-lived principality of Aquitaine, a colonial experiment that ended in rebellion and the resumption of the war in 1369. Some thirty years later the Glyn Dŵr rebellion again altered English attitudes to occupation. The revolt hardened opinions about the Welsh, and also provided the future Henry V with valuable practical military experience before he embarked on the next major colonial programme in the Hundred Years War: first, the capture of Harfleur in the Agincourt expedition and, second, the conquest of Normandy.[29]

The Normandy campaign was shaped, in part, by Henry's and England's historic claim to the duchy.[30] As the *Gesta Henrici Quinti* had it, Henry 'prepared to cross to Normandy in order to recover his duchy of Normandy, which belongs to him by a right dating from the time of William the first, the Conqueror'. At the same time he also aimed to make good 'his divine right and claim to the duchy of Aquitaine'.[31] Military success and the vicissitudes of the French civil war ensured Henry secured this and more in the treaty of Troyes, although the treaty also changed the colonial character of Henry's French estates now he was to be their king. Prior to 1420 it had been politically expedient to promote the concept of an independent Normandy within France; after 1420 Henry ceased to do this. The duchy now was to be considered part of the kingdom and the king ceased to style himself duke of Normandy.[32]

The occupation of Normandy provides the most important example of English colonisation during the Hundred Years War, one that involved a major settlement programme, especially at Harfleur, Cherbourg and Caen. Henry's lands in northern France, which he claimed by right of conquest (*par droit de conquête*), were settled with those men whom the king trusted to defend, maintain or augment those conquests: English, Irish, Welsh and Gascon – again, manpower and other resources from all of the king's lordships were used and transferred between them. Strategic settlement was seen as important in establishing and maintaining control over an acquired territory. This had been an approach the English had adopted regularly in the foreign lordships throughout the British Isles and Ireland. By the end of 1420 some five thousand grants of properties had been made.[33]

Following the treaty of Troyes further lands became available to Henry and John, duke of Bedford, which could be used to reward and needed to be held and protected. Property was confiscated from the dauphin's followers and parcelled out to English loyalists.[34] The settlement programme received a further impetus after the battle of Verneuil (17 August 1424), when a substantial number of small grants were made to Englishmen of all ranks. More settlers were then brought in following the Congress of Arras to bolster the position in Normandy after the Burgundian defection and the loss of Paris (1435–36).[35] Henry V, Bedford, their lieutenants and successors gave these colonists a personal stake in maintaining *La France Anglaise* and at the same time ensured they had specific responsibilities to fulfil if they accepted the proffered lands or offices. The grants, then, were closely tied to the Crown's military objectives, and many were made in tail male in an attempt to ensure continuity of 'English' ownership over successive generations. Among the recipients of major grants were Thomas, duke of Clarence, who, after the fall of Falaise in 1418, received three *vicomtés*;[36] Thomas Montague, fourth earl of Salisbury, who, in addition to various territories and numerous offices, became count of Perche in 1419;[37] and Edmund Beaufort, first duke of Somerset (c. 1406–55), became count of Mortain in 1427, captain-general and governor of Maine in 1438 with title to the county in 1442. In 1447 Edmund succeeded Richard, duke of York, as lieutenant of France and of the duchies of Normandy and Gascony.

Those who benefited chiefly from the settlement programme were, however, not the great nobility, but lesser knights – having most to gain they were most willing to fight to defend those gains. '[T]he receipt of land bound the recipient not only to defend it but to contribute through his own military service and that of others, towards the provision of an army ready to fight and conquer in the king's name.'[38] This was, in effect, an extension of the usual recruitment policy. The chance of financial advantage had drawn most regular soldiers into the army in the first place, and because wages were rarely generous and often paid erratically other profits of war became attractive. In earlier campaigns these had included plunder and booty from raiding, demands for protection money or the promise of a plump ransom. However, the chance to gain land of one's own was a new and enticing incentive.

In all these colonies, in Britain, Ireland and France, the main concern of English administrations was to establish then maintain political control, especially in urban centres either through settlement or other means. Either a substantial proportion of the native population would be displaced or attempts were made to establish good relations with that population. The latter policy was particularly difficult to achieve if the campaign preceding the capture of the territory or town had been especially harsh. The campaign to take Calais (1346–47) is well known in this regard; indeed, the siege was so harsh and Edward III's temper so violent that no attempt was made to establish good relations. The inhabitants were expelled and the town repopulated with English settlers, although the population of the surrounding marches remained largely unchanged.[39]

By contrast, in the principality of Aquitaine the Black Prince sought to establish good relations with urban communities by confirming the privileges of many towns and gaining support among politically important families and individuals. However, having been subjected to the *chevauchées* of 1355 and 1356, many in the new principality were less than well disposed to the new regime and, notoriously, the prince had particular problems securing the loyalty of the Aquitainian nobility, although his record in this regard is not one of complete failure.[40] The policy which his brother, Lionel of Clarence, employed as lieutenant of Ireland at precisely the same time (September 1361–April 1364; December 1365–November 1366) was similar and, similarly, proved problematic.[41] Later English settlement policies in Normandy and northern France followed a comparable pattern and focused on securing support in urban centres. In Normandy, the towns formed the economic and administrative centres of the duchy, and so gaining control over them and support within them was considered essential by the new administration. It was particularly important to ensure residents fulfilled their military responsibilities, such as keeping watch and defending the town's walls (*guet et garde*).[42] If these responsibilities continued to be fulfilled, then fewer English soldiers were required.

The English experience in Ireland may well have shaped approaches to the colonisation of Normandy. It has been suggested that the English feared the creation of a 'middle nation' in Normandy such as developed across the Irish Sea – a settler community distanced and different politically and culturally from both the mother country and the local population.[43] Such concerns are fascinating from a sociological perspective but they do not seem to reveal the reality of the situation as it developed in Normandy. Rather than the hybrid, independent culture which the English administration faced in the 'degenerate' Anglo-Irish lordship, a much simpler pragmatism can be seen at work in northern France. In establishing the colony in Normandy, Henry V's policy had shifted between brutality and leniency. His early campaigns, at Harfleur and Caen (captured 4 September 1417), for example, were characterised by hostage-taking, mass expulsions, pillage and the imposition of martial law. Town archives and centres of civic government were often destroyed as a statement made to demonstrate the end of the old regime. At Harfleur, as at Calais, a large proportion of the local population was expelled after a long siege and English settlers were invited to take their place. Merchants were prominent among those offered property in the town, as they had been in Calais, in the hope this would stimulate the economy.[44] Henry's initial policy at Harfleur and Caen was designed to ensure he faced little opposition elsewhere. It proved reasonably successful, although certain towns did resist tenaciously. Later, once the conquest was complete, Henry and his successors sought to foster a spirit of conciliation although they maintained an intimidating military presence. Certain towns such as Bayeux, which had offered Henry no resistance, and Rouen, which surrendered after a long siege on 19 January 1419, both had their privileges confirmed. Townsmen were encouraged to view the king as a legitimate ruler and Henry invited them to petition him through English legal channels, conditioning them to view the new regime as the ultimate arbiter of justice. Circumstances changed with the treaty of Troyes: once recognised as the heir-apparent, Henry swore to govern France according to its ancient laws and maintain all rights and privileges in the kingdom.[45]

The success of English regimes in France depended on the ability to communicate with the local population: administrators and military commanders needed some grasp of the French language. This proved somewhat problematic because in England, just at this time, Henry V was promoting the use of English for political and nationalistic purposes. Consequently, the use of French in England diminished while the use of French by Englishmen in France became increasingly necessary. French (or Anglo-French) therefore had to be used extensively by Englishmen as part of the process of conquest and occupation. Differences in pronunciation no doubt existed and most were almost certainly not sophisticated in their use of language, but communication could usually be achieved. Garrison troops and lower-level administrators often struggled with the language, especially in the early months of an occupation. There are several reports of violence (on both sides) when the English could not make the inhabitants understand what they wanted. For example, in Rouen in 1427, English soldiers were recounted as shouting at the French inhabitants to 'speak English' (as the evidence is recorded in French it is not certain in what language they yelled), and in 1425 there were complaints that the commanders used 'mots etrangers' – presumably English words – as passwords so the townsmen who were forced to serve in the watch could not understand.[46]

In occupied areas levels of antagonism varied and were subject to a range of factors, many connected with the number and behaviour of foreign soldiers. The number of troops deployed varied according to military and political circumstances, but in general most towns only had small garrisons other than in times of crisis.[47] For example, during the period from 1419 to 1449 the size of the English garrison in Mantes (Normandy), a town of around 3,000 people, fell to as few as 21 in 1428 prior to the reverse at Orléans, and rose to as many as 480 after the fall of Paris in 1436. It seems that for much of this time relations were reasonably cordial between the occupying force and the local population. The maintenance of such an atmosphere often depended on the character of the captain and/or his lieutenant. Circumstances, however, often dictated that captains and garrison commanders rarely held their positions for long. In Mantes eleven men held the office in the first ten years of occupation after 1419. However, although the captain of a garrison was usually English, his lieutenant might not be and nor, indeed, might all the soldiers – up to an eighth of a garrison could be of French origin.[48] This could influence the atmosphere of an occupation considerably.

If relations remained cordial it allowed for the development of personal relationships, friendships and indeed marriages. Marriages between colonists and colonised were by no means uncommon, although in Normandy royal permission might be required for unions between settlers and natives. Some marriages, no doubt, were influenced by the opportunity they offered Norman women to preserve their property and livelihoods, and perhaps even their lives. Other unions were clearly the products of genuine affection, and when the Lancastrian position in Normandy collapsed, a number of Englishmen (and at least one Welshmen) remained in France with their wives.[49]

In this regard, as in others, successful relations between England and the occupied territories depended on integration as well as domination. Most administrations found it best to work with existing power structures and employed local men in official positions when possible. Nonetheless, it required careful diplomacy to avoid showing favouritism and antagonising the various feuding noble houses. In Lancastrian Normandy, apart from the creation of a *chambre des comptes* at Caen, many Valois administrative structures remained in place. Although some new practices were introduced, where possible the English sought to use established systems and exploit existing obligations rather than introduce new methods of governance and taxation.[50] Generally, Englishmen were appointed to the senior offices while lesser positions stayed in native hands, but there is no doubt that daily government relied heavily on the support of the indigenous population.

Conciliation and negotiation were also sought by maintaining representative assemblies and allowing meetings of the regional Estates to take place. English administrations used such meetings mainly to try and ensure taxes were raised with little opposition, but they also offered an opportunity for the occupied population to air complaints about the governing regime. In Aquitaine, the Estates was closely involved with granting taxes and its role and remit developed over the course of the war. This may well have influenced English approaches to the Estates of Normandy, which was first summoned (to Rouen) in January 1421. In Normandy that first meeting of the Estates signalled an end to martial law and the beginning of a period of greater local consultation. During the English occupation there would be some sixty-four meetings of the full Estates and local assemblies.[51] Such meetings may have reduced political friction; certainly orders regularly followed them, seeking to prevent illegal and excessive activities by soldiers and garrisons. However, they were not sufficient to prevent rebellion. In Aquitaine, the hearth tax (*fouage*), despite being granted by the Estates in 1368, encouraged a rebellion, albeit one fuelled by the activities of the Valois court. In a similar fashion the taxes demanded by the Anglo-Burgundian administration in fifteenth-century Paris proved extremely unpopular.[52] Peasant rebellions also shook English-occupied Normandy in the years either side of the Congress of Arras (1434–36) and in 1443. These have often been characterised as nationalist revolts; certainly they were repressed severely for fear that was the case, but taxation was, again, a major cause of the uprisings rather than just loyalty to Charles VII.[53]

Nonetheless, there was no great love for the English regime in Normandy. Just as Henry V had been able to capture many towns without resistance, so they returned equally willingly to French allegiance.[54] Any loyalty to the English regime in 1449–50, as to the Valois in 1417–19, was outweighed by fear of assault, pillage and slaughter. Mantes, for example, the last English bastion to fall in the *pays de conquête*, had been placed on a war footing after Charles VII declared war on 17 July 1449. It surrendered, apparently by common consent of the residents, to the advancing French army and the townspeople begged forgiveness for some thirty years of 'disloyalty'. The English garrison had already withdrawn without attempting a defence, perhaps persuaded to leave by the townspeople as they were at Lisieux, Coutances and Avranches. By this stage there was little hope that English reinforcements would be sent. While Normandy retained a special place in the English popular imagination, few Englishmen were willing to fund its defence.[55]

Among the main concerns of English regimes in France were military and political security, the maintenance of law and order and the collection of taxation. In addition to these they tried to ensure resources and information were not passed to the enemy. In Wales and Ireland legislation was enacted to prohibit native entertainers performing, as they were believed to be spying out English defences, although special licences to perform in English areas were often granted.[56] In the same fashion strict attempts were made to regulate contact between Lancastrian/Burgundian France and the 'kingdom of Bourges' in the fifteenth century. In particular there were concerns about the activities of French clergymen, many of whom were believed to be spies. In 1432 the abbess of Saint Antoine in Paris and some of her nuns were imprisoned when she was accused of collaborating with her nephew to betray the city.[57] In England there were, similarly, long-standing concerns about the activities of members of alien priories. In a petition of 1373 the Commons in the English Parliament requested

> that no French alien prior shall dwell within twenty leagues of the sea coasts; considering that they are French in their bodies, and from time to time spy upon the secrets and ordinances at parliaments and councils; and they send their spies and messengers to their abbots and superiors in the realm of France as well as bows and arrows, gold and silver, and other weapons, in comfort of [the king's] enemies and to the detriment of the country.[58]

Such concerns also recognised the importance of the Church and clergy in gaining and maintaining control throughout the English lordships. Restrictions on Gaelic Irishmen holding ecclesiastical offices in the Anglo-Irish colony had been introduced early in the thirteenth century and continued to be enforced, albeit patchily. In Wales, too, rather counter-productive attempts were made to exploit patronage rights over church offices.[59] Henry V also used the Church and its members to bolster his regime in Normandy. Many Norman churchmen were, it seems, relatively comfortable with political change, and the new regime may well have offered them greater independence than they had enjoyed in the past. Clearly, though, this did not inculcate a deep sense of loyalty to England and her kings as many rallied to Charles VII in 1449–50. In Paris and nearby Saint-Denis the English made particular attempts to secure the support of the local clergy. The ideological importance of these places, so central to the identity and spiritual and political authority of the French state, ensured that they were at the heart of English attempts to project an image of legitimate rule and to solicit support for the new regime. Ecclesiastical ritual, processions and ceremonies were used widely in the French capital, as they were in England, as a vehicle for propaganda:[60]

> ... in September [1424] the Regent [John, duke of Bedford] arrived in Paris. The city was decorated everywhere he was to go and the streets decorated and cleaned ... some of Paris's processions went out into the country to meet him ... When they met, they sang loudly Te Deum laudamus and other praises to God. Wherever he passed by, everyone shouted 'Noel!' When he came to the corner of the Rue aux Lombards there was an acrobat there performing as cleverly as anyone had ever seen. In front of the Châtelet there was a very fine Mystery of the Old and New Testaments done by the children of Paris ... [Then] he went onto Notre Dame, where he was received as if he had been God ... In short more honour was never done at a Roman triumph than was done that day to him.[61]

Paris, though, from the outset was considered a very different sort of colony. After the treaty of Troyes the capital saw relatively few changes in its government, which had been in Burgundian control since 1418. Because of the city's political and ideological significance it was vital to secure the allegiance of the most important officers of the central government, espe-cially members of the *parlement* and the *chambre des comptes*.[62] Although the duke of Bedford was a regular and important presence, there was limited English influence over Paris's day-to-day administration. No more than three Englishmen held office in the Paris Chancery, while the *prévôt*, responsible for order in the city, tended to be a Burgundian. And although the military governorship of Paris was often held by an Englishman, this was not always the case. Thomas, duke of Clarence, held the office in 1420, Thomas Beaufort, duke of Exeter, in 1421, and Humphrey Stafford, duke of Buckingham, in 1430–32.[63]

After the murder of Jean the Fearless in 1419, it seems that most of those Parisians who remained were ready, albeit reluctantly, to ally themselves with the Lancastrians. Their chief loyalty, however, was to Burgundy, though even this was not unquestioning and there were a number of plots to deliver the city to the dauphinists. In the main, however, Anglo-Burgundian rule seemed to offer the best opportunity for peace and a secure future in the city and its environs. Conditions were, however, far from calm for much of this period. The Parisian Bourgeois, famously, described the endemic lawlessness in Paris and its hinterland – for example, merchants were said to need an armed guard before they brought cattle to the town's butchers. The limited support for the new regime and tensions within that regime were evident from early in the occupation and not helped by dreadful food shortages: 'In the year 1420 you might see all over Paris here ten there twenty or thirty children, boys and girls, dying of hunger and of cold on the rubbish heaps ... yet the poor householders could do nothing to help them – no one had any bread, corn, firewood, or charcoal.'[64]

Sadly, this was not an isolated incident. During the Anglo-Burgundian occupation Parisians had to cope with a string of brutal winters, wet springs and poor harvests. In 1421, even the wolves were starving: 'they used to uncover with their paws the bodies of people buried ... for wherever you went, in the town or the country, you found people dead of the dreadful poverty that they suffered because of scarcity and famine caused by the accursed war'.[65] In early 1427 the ground was said to have been frozen for 36 days. The ordinary citizen could buy nothing to eat for less than two pence, which was beyond many. When the frosts finally ended, the rains began and seemed unceasing.[66]

In response to political ambivalence and climatic hostility the new regime made strenuous efforts to bolster its image and slander the enemy. A wide range of propaganda was employed – songs were sung, symbols and badges displayed, processions and various rituals took place; suitable information was disseminated, successes publicised, an image of an ordered purposeful society was projected.[67] But despite Bedford's 'bread and circuses' policy, attitudes to the English remained mixed. As the Parisian Bourgeois wrote in February 1423, 'all Parisians took an oath ... to be loyal and true to the Duke of Bedford, Regent of France ... to obey him in all things and all places and to do all they could to harass Charles who called himself King of France and all his allies and associates. Some were glad to do this, others most reluctant.'[68] There was, therefore, a grudging acceptance of the need for an alliance, but generations of enmity were not quickly forgotten. And while there was a significant number of marriages between the English and Parisians, and certain members of the English nobility became major patrons of art and luxury goods, on the whole the English were seen as arrogant and belligerent (and bad cooks). Disputes may also have been encouraged by a growing language barrier, exaggerated by a particular Parisian cant. However, as insults seem to have caused a number of arguments, issues of language were clearly not insurmountable. In Paris, as elsewhere, there was a good deal of racially abusive language – the English were regularly referred to as 'Goddons' (God-damns) because they swore so often.[69]

Although the occupation received far from unanimous support, in the main Paris maintained its allegiance to Burgundy and her ally. This is seen most clearly in the resistance to Joan of Arc and it explains why there was only a token English military force in situ. In a city of perhaps 80,000 people, the garrison never exceeded 2,000 troops. The main English presence was at the Bastille. When Sir John Fastolf was appointed captain of the Bastille in January 1421, he commanded a miserly 8 men-at-arms and 26 archers. Under Thomas More in 1431 it did not number in excess of 50 men, including servants. Indeed, it appears to have been deliberate policy to keep the garrison as unobtrusive as possible.[70] Similarly, in Saint-Denis, the town housing the abbey, north of Paris, it was only Charles VII's approach in August 1429 that led to a garrison being deployed. Like Paris, Saint-Denis came under English control through the treaty of Troyes and so was never considered part of the *pays de conquête*. The townspeople, however, were even less committed in their political sympathies than the Parisians. Once the garrison of Saint-Denis had proved ineffective, they capitulated immediately to Joan and Charles, who established their headquarters in the town. Then, when Charles withdrew, having failed to take Paris on 13 September 1429, Anglo-Burgundian control was restored in Saint-Denis alongside heavy fines imposed as punishment for the townsmen's lack of loyalty.[71]

The attack on the capital, however, made Parisians increasingly doubtful about the merits of the alliance. Costs were rising to support the defence and, clearly, the English were not providing the stability that so many wanted. As elsewhere, people tended to take a pragmatic approach to such matters. Practical concerns and basic survival instincts took priority over 'national' allegiances, which, in the fifteenth century were further complicated by the French civil war.[72] Indeed, who was 'foreign' in such circumstances? For many Frenchmen, Bretons, Burgundians or Gascons might be no less foreign than the English. Political conditions meant that one might be occupied by a foreigner who was also a political ally. Charles VII's grants of high office to various Scotsmen in the 'kingdom of Bourges', for example, caused considerable animosity. John Stewart, third earl of Buchan (c.1380– 1424), received Châtillon-sur-Indre and became constable of France in 1421 as a reward for leading the Franco-Scots army to victory at Baugé in March of that year. Archibald, fourth earl of Douglas (c.1369–1424), received the duchy of Touraine in 1424 and was named lieutenant-general of the king for the war against England, an unprecedented position for a non-royal foreigner. The city of Tours clearly resented the authority he wielded there until his death at the battle of Verneuil in August 1424. Douglas's son, the fifth earl (also Archibald; c.1391–1439), succeeded his father as duke of Touraine – he had previously been endowed with the lands of Dun-le-roi in Berry and the title of count of Longueville (then in English hands). However, such foreign appointments tended to be driven by extreme circumstances; and foreign recruitment both military and to high office lessened thereafter. Royal gifts made in times of desperation might quickly be revoked when the crisis had passed. By contrast Orléans had a Scottish bishop, John Carmichael, a substantial Scottish presence in its university and there relations appeared to be amicable.[73]

Any mention of Orléans inevitably draws one's thoughts to Joan of Arc whose own experience of occupation shaped her extraordinary life. Raised in a region on the very limits of the realm, close to Burgundian and pro-Burgundian territory, she was born into a world in which the threat of violence and occupation was a daily reality. Her village of Domremy was menaced regularly by mercenaries, English soldiers and Burgundian forces. Members of the village community often herded their animals onto an island in the River Meuse, which offered some protection from attack. But the accounts from Joan's trials (both of Condemnation and Nullification) reveal that village life certainly did not collapse despite these conditions. Joan was able to make her little pilgrimages to the nearby hermitage of Notre-Dame de Bermont; she fed the animals, occasionally helped with the ploughing, prepared hemp and wool and continued to follow the rituals of rural life. Clearly, Joan's early life was influenced by military activity, political instability and struggles for local control, but until about 1424 there is relatively little evidence of major disturbance in the region. However, about that time a series of border raids began and there were serious attacks on Domremy – the church was set on fire and pillaged. Mercenaries and Anglo-Burgundian forces assaulted the right bank of the Meuse and many of the villagers were forced to flee with their livestock to Neufchâteau. It was amidst these attacks in 1425 that Joan began to hear her 'voices'.[74] The consequence of this would change the course of the Hundred Years War.

CHAPTER 8

Women and War

POWER AND PERSECUTION

1429

A certain Pucelle [maiden] *named Joan has entered into the kingdom of France. She only arrived when the kingdom was on the verge of complete ruin, and at the moment when the sceptre of the realm ought to have passed to a foreign hand. This young girl accomplishes actions which appear more divine than human.*[1]

Jean Dupuy, *Collectarium historiarum*, 1429

A young girl arrived in the city of Orléans on 29 April 1429, riding at the head of a French army. On that Friday the outlook seemed very bleak for the people of Orléans and for King Charles VII of France, still commonly known as the dauphin. Despite the death of Henry V in 1422, two months before the demise of his father-in-law Charles VI, the English position had not collapsed. Indeed, it had strengthened in the intervening years. Under the ministrations of John, duke of Bedford, and with the continuing, if now faltering support of the duke of Burgundy, the territorial boundaries of the Dual Monarchy in France had been driven south to the Loire. Orléans was all that seemed to stand in the way of a major advance into the so-called kingdom of Bourges, where the dauphin's authority was recognised. Yet by early May, within a week of Joan of Arc's arrival, the English had withdrawn. Within two months English garrisons had been forced from Jargeau, Meung-sur-Loire and Beaugency and an army commanded by John Talbot, Thomas Scales and John Fastolf had been crushed in battle at Patay.

Bolstered by these successes Joan led an expedition that penetrated deep into Anglo-Burgundian territory and which culminated with Charles VII's coronation at Reims on 17 July 1429. This proved to be the high point of her brief, almost miraculous life. Thereafter her career stuttered, an assault on Paris failed, leaving Joan wounded and increasingly distanced from the royal court. When Charles agreed to a brief truce with England her talents were redirected against lesser prey, namely the mercenary captain Perrinet Gressart. During the winter of 1429–30 she fought a series of incidental campaigns before leading a small force against an Anglo-Burgundian offensive advancing along the River Oïse. In the course of this, forces under the command of Jean, count of Luxembourg, lieutenant of the duke of Burgundy, captured Joan at Compiègne on 14 May 1430. She was ransomed first to the English and then handed over to the Church to be tried. Then, after a protracted trial, she was executed for heresy by being burned at the stake.

Joan of Arc provides a fascinating example of a woman at war in the later Middle Ages. She was and remains an extraordinary and extraordinarily seductive figure. Her career and experiences were unique and, consequently, far from representative. Nonetheless, her remarkable intervention in the Hundred Years War reveals so much about changing attitudes to women in a period when female roles were scrutinised and re-evaluated in wholly new ways. One of those delighted and fascinated by Joan and her astonishing intervention at the siege of Orléans was Christine de Pizan, herself a remarkable figure. Arguably the first female professional author, Christine was hugely significant, and her 'Song of Joan of Arc' was merely the last in a long list of important works.[2] She wrote extensively and on diverse subjects ranging from guides for rulers ('mirrors for princes') and works of political theory to military manuals. Many of these works were directly inspired by the Hundred Years War and were intended to ameliorate the suffering of the French people. Her patrons included dukes Philippe and Jean of Burgundy, Louis of Guienne (then the dauphin), and Marie of Berry, duchess of Bourbon. She wrote a biography of Charles V and dedicated works to Charles VI and Jean, duke of Berry. Christine remains, though, most famous for her works directed at women, some of which suggested how they should conduct themselves, their affairs and their estates in the midst of war while their menfolk were away on military service.[3] By the end of the fourteenth century this set of circumstances had become commonplace: the protracted nature of the Hundred Years War meant women were often required to take charge of affairs that had typically been seen as inherently masculine.

As this suggests, the position of women in later medieval society was transformed during the course of the Hundred Years War. But war was not the only factor bringing about that change. The carnage of the Black Death also played a highly significant role and, for a while, it helped reposition women within the workforce. War and plague, those twin forces of Apocalypse, worked shoulder to shoulder, therefore, to affect women's lives in the later Middle Ages. Together these forces brought about major social and economic change not only because of the appalling number of casualties but also because of their impact on the gender balance in the general population. More men than women died in war and the Black Death struck down males more frequently than females. Children also suffered more than adults and male children most of all, especially in the terrible plague outbreaks that struck from 1361 onwards, the so-called 'malaise des enfants'.[4]

The physical and psychological impacts of war and plague were horrific and often seemed horrifically inexplicable. Yet, for a time, their consequences benefited those oppressed groups that survived them. The implications of these influences were profound and contributed to a major redefinition of the status of and roles played by women in France and England. Indeed, the century after the Black Death first struck (the century of the Hundred Years War) has typically been seen as something of a golden age for women when they gained greater social, economic and political autonomy. There were new opportunities to travel, a better chance to choose one's husband; one could marry later in life or indeed not marry at all. Such prospects were hugely beneficial although they could, collectively, exaggerate the already dreadful impact of war and plague. Later and fewer marriages, for example, could lower the birth rate which, allied with repeated outbreaks of plague, did nothing to restore the population.

War and plague created a socio-economic environment that improved women's opportunities to enter a growing range of professions, increased the value of their labour and gave them the chance to invest in land and property. Many were able to move away from their manors and offer their services elsewhere: the shortage of men provided unique opportunities for female workers, especially in those urban areas to which women migrated. Previously restricted, for the most part, to textile and cloth-making industries, women now found employment in a new range of businesses, as smiths, tanners, carpenters, brewers and tilers. Some of these professions were directly connected with the war effort. Women made scabbards for swords and knives, they sharpened tools and some worked in the arms trade (making chain mail and fletching arrows). Indeed, women were actively engaged at the centre of the English arms industry. While Walter of Bury, Edward III's smith at the Tower of London, was absent in France during the Crécy campaign of 1346, his mother Katherine carried on his work at the forge. Later, in Henry V's reign, Margaret Merssh also worked alongside her husband William, the king's smith, making fetters and manacles.[5]

Peasant women had, of course, always worked – in the fields alongside their menfolk, especially at harvest time – just as townswomen helped their husbands in business. Their work, however, had always been viewed as less valuable than that done by men. This continued to be the case despite the plague's impact: women did gain a higher standard of living and better working conditions over the period of the Hundred Years War but they faced continuing prejudice. As this suggests, the picture of a golden age for women may be a little too rosy: attitudes to women remained discriminatory; fighting continued to be more highly regarded than child-bearing; ploughing more important than spinning.[6] Women's wages increased but they did not rise to a level equivalent to men's, and nor were these gains maintained in the longer term. In the mid to late fifteenth century a deep economic recession, population growth and a slump in demand for various goods revived social pressures on women which they proved unable to resist. Any benefits for women gained in the golden age did not outlast the Hundred Years War as they had neither been institutionalised nor given legal status.[7]

War, then, was not responsible for all the major changes to the condition and position of women in the fourteenth and fifteenth centuries. Women were, however, responsible for the Anglo-French war, at least in one sense. The Hundred Years War was fought, ostensibly, over the question of female rights, and whether women could bequeath power and authority to their children. After 1328 Anglo-French relations became increasingly tense because of a dispute that centred on the nature of female power. When Charles IV of France died that year without a male heir the issue of whether a claim to the French throne could be passed down the female line became crucial. Could Edward III of England succeed to the French throne by virtue of the fact that his mother, Isabella, had been the late king's sister? For the English this claim remained a crucial diplomatic weapon throughout the war, even (perhaps especially) at those times when it was clear that they had no way of making it good. The situation in France was completely reversed; the security and legitimacy of the Valois dynasty relied on the total renunciation of such an assertion, and royal apologists launched a series of campaigns to 'prove' the absurdity, indeed the impossibility that a mother could bequeath power to her children. In order to make this case a range of biblical, classical and legal authorities were marshalled. Aristotle, for example, had claimed that males were naturally superior to females, a belief St Paul had reinforced. Medical theories also stated that women were inferior to men and subject to intemperate moods which made them unsuitable to rule and capable only of managing domestic affairs. The key element in the Valois legal arsenal was, however, Salic law, which the royal historiographer and monk Richard Lescot (1329–58) conveniently 'rediscovered' in the middle of the fourteenth century. Composed originally in the reign of Clovis, this was redeveloped in the context of the Hundred Years War to justify the exclusion of women from the royal succession and, thereby, invalidate the claims to the French Crown asserted by Edward III, Charles of Navarre and their successors.[8]

Such a (misogynistic) position aligned closely with wider social opinions.[9] As a result, despite changing circumstances after the Black Death, women continued to be barred from most civic and public offices and were routinely excluded from positions of power. Women's social position remained marked by a structured inferiority to men of their own 'class' in terms of inheritance, property ownership, economic opportunities, access to education, legal rights and enjoyment of formal political power.[10] In such an environment the tenets of Salic law found a receptive audience.

Certain women – queens, abbesses and noblewomen, for instance – did, however, wield considerable authority and there are numerous examples of women living long, self-reliant and politically important lives, although often only after they were widowed. Furthermore, the examples of Christine de Pizan, Margery Kempe and Chaucer's 'Wife of Bath' do suggest a certain shift in attitudes; certainly, they give the lie to the chivalric image of the woman who was only complete if she had a male defender. Circumstances in the Hundred Years War also forced women to take an active political role and many became deeply involved in the struggle. Indeed, some women were instrumental in shaping the way the conflict unfolded. Of these, royal women were most conspicuous, and throughout the war queens, naturally, played important roles both practical and symbolic. Some queens might be little more than pawns – their marriages arranged to secure alliances, treaties or truces; their primary function being to provide an heir to carry on the conflict. Others, however, became key figures in the war effort, often as diplomats and intercessors. A queen had a vital place in the socio-political hierarchy and many became much more active at the heart of government than tradition dictated. This might be caused by the absence of a king. Such circumstances redefined a queen's position and purpose, and many kings were absent regularly from the centre of power during the Hundred Years War – on campaign, diplomatic missions or in captivity. Queens might also have to face different sorts of absences: Isabeau of Bavaria and Margaret of Anjou, for example, were required to take the reins of power during the periods of madness suffered by their respective husbands – Charles VI and Henry VI.

Women of less eminent status also shaped the war; some of these, while not queens, were close to the king nonetheless. Alice Perrers and Agnès Sorel as mistresses to Edward III and Charles VII respectively gained considerable influence – 'soft power' – for which they were much maligned. Other women played important military roles. Noblewomen such as Jeanne de Montfort (c.1295–1374), Agnes Dunbar (1312–69) and Julienne du Guesclin (1330–1404) marshalled troops and/or took up arms themselves, and many more were required to protect their homes. Christine de Pizan advised women to become familiar with weapons and military strategy in order better to defend themselves and their estates. Alongside this military role women also became increasingly politically aware as the Hundred Years War progressed. This was especially so in major urban centres in which information was most abundant and propaganda distributed most assiduously. To take one admittedly exceptional example, in 1414, according to the Parisian Bourgeois, over four thousand women attended the bonfire rallies in Paris held to celebrate the Armagnac attack on the Burgundian city of Soissons.[11] In these ways and others the roles of women were reshaped, if only temporarily, over the course of the war. The all-encompassing nature of the struggle meant women could not avoid being caught up in Anglo-French hostilities; the impact upon them was often devastating but also, on occasion, empowering.

The queen played a central but intrinsically problematic role in later medieval France and England. There was something almost subversive about a woman filling an important office at the heart of an intensely patriarchal political system. This became increasingly complicated by the nature of the Hundred Years War. The very existence of the Valois monarchy was a testament to the French claim that women could not (and should not) rule in France. Nonetheless, queens on both sides of the Channel had important responsibilities throughout the war and not only as figureheads. As Christine de Pizan remarked:

... whilst we're on the subject of queens ... If you recall Queen Joan, wife of Charles IV ... think about the fine way she ran her court and exercised justice and the virtuous manner in which she lived her own life. Of no prince has it ever been said that he maintained the rule of law and safeguarded his lands and powers better than this lady did ... The same could be said of Queen Blanche, the late wife of King Jean [II], who retained control of her lands and enforced law and order.[12]

This situation was not entirely new. It had not been uncommon for French queens to serve as regents in earlier years. Blanche of Castile (d.1252), mother to (St) Louis IX, had set the standard for this role and almost from the outset of the war her successors were required to take on the office. In 1338 Philippe VI ordered that his wife, Jeanne of Burgundy (1293–1348), should serve as regent should he, at any stage, be occupied elsewhere. A very active politician, Jeanne was 'like a king [who] caused the destruction of those who opposed her will'. She led a Burgundian faction at court and because of her patronage many of her countrymen found high office during Philippe's reign.[13] Similarly, after his first bout of madness, Charles VI ensured his queen, Isabeau of Bavaria (1385–1422), would play a major role in government if he succumbed again or died. He appointed her principal guardian of the dauphin and granted her a position on the regency council. After the turn of the century she became one of the chief mediators in the ever more bitter struggle between the dukes of Orléans and Burgundy. Then in 1403, when Charles's ongoing madness necessitated a more permanent solution, she led the regency council. Her position, however, became increasingly difficult as the civil war progressed and she was forced, finally, to agree to the treaty of Troyes and the disinheritance of her son, Charles (VII).[14]

Isabeau's mediatory role was one commonly expected of a queen on both sides of the Channel. Various commentators, Christine de Pizan among them, argued that the queen should serve as a stabilising force in the nation, providing a balance in relations between the king and his people, both commoners and nobles. This was explicit in the French coronation ceremony, which made it clear that with her accession a queen accepted the obligation to act as an intercessor on behalf of the people. The coronation ceremony also demonstrated the unique character of female royal power, showing that although women could not hold temporal authority in their own right, a queen should exercise certain political functions. In token of these she received a sceptre and a ring symbolising her responsibility to be just and combat heresy; she also had the right to pardon certain criminals.[15]

It was in such an intercessory role, one shaped by the politics of the Hundred Years War, that Jeanne d'Évreux, third wife of King Charles IV, and Blanche d'Évreux, second wife of Philippe VI (nicknamed *Belle Sagesse* or 'Beautiful Wisdom'), acted on several occasions. Twice they intervened on behalf of Charles II, king of Navarre (Blanche's brother). In 1354 they helped obtain a pardon from Jean II for Charles's involvement in the murder of Charles de la Cerda, the constable of France (also known as Charles d'Espagne), and in 1357 they helped to reconcile Charles to the dauphin (the future Charles V), then serving as regent due to King Jean's imprisonment in England.[16] Yolande of Aragon (d.1442), Charles VII's mother-in-law and wife to Louis II d'Anjou, also worked as a mediator throughout the civil war, seeking a rapprochement between the houses of Armagnac and Burgundy. Yolande also stage-managed many of Joan of Arc's early meetings with Charles VII and ensured she had (and was seen to have) the necessary political and theological credentials. Yolande organised Joan's official introduction to the French king and recognised that she needed a suitably orthodox and virtuous reputation. It was Yolande who made certain that Joan's virginity was clearly established, and it was she who instigated the process of 'training, outfitting [Joan] as a knight, giving her a background knowledge of politics and the military situation, and spreading prophecies [which] were essential to her successes in 1429'.[17]

Yolande managed to acquire a remarkable degree of political autonomy, but when acting as an intercessor a queen did not always act independently; she could be 'played' for the king's advantage. She might serve as a vehicle for reconciliation, providing an opportunity for a king to show mercy when a masculine sense of honour would otherwise demand vengeance or punishment. Her pleas allowed men to be gracious without losing face.[18] This may well have been the case during one of the most famous intercessory scenes of the war, at Calais in 1347. Then, Jean Froissart recorded, the heavily pregnant Queen Philippa begged her husband Edward III for clemency for the six burghers of the town whom the king had decided would take personal (and fatal) responsibility for the cost and length of the siege that had taken a good deal of the sheen from his victory at Crécy the previous year. Seemingly moved by her pleas, after all others had failed, Edward handed the condemned men over to his wife to do with as she pleased. They were fed, clothed, given six *nobles* each and then permitted to go on their way. This dramatic episode may have been deliberately contrived to enhance the king's reputation, to emphasise his clemency, which could not be guaranteed if similar circumstances arose again, and to heap further humiliation on his enemies. Whether or not her intercession was feigned, and there is no doubt that the chronicler overemphasised Philippa's pregnancy, the queen's role was vital to the (staging of the) event.[19]

In a similar fashion Anne of Bohemia, Richard II's queen and Philippa's successor, was often cast in the role of intercessor. During the Merciless Parliament (1388) she pleaded with the Appellants for the lives of certain condemned men who had sided with the king. Later she interceded, on this occasion in vain, for the life of Sir Simon Burley, the king's favourite, and in 1392 she petitioned her husband to show mercy to the Londoners, who had given offence by refusing to make him a loan.[20]

Female political involvement at a high level was, therefore, frequent and significant in the first half of the Hundred Years War. This forced a number of authors, particularly in France, to reframe their dismissive attitudes to women. Misogyny had been at the core of Valois political doctrine for much of the fourteenth century; the claim to the throne which the Valois acquired in 1328 depended on disparaging women and scorning their ability to transmit, let alone wield political power. In the fifteenth century, however, given the frequent use of female regents and the prominent role played by queens and noblewomen, the more overt prejudice had to be tempered. It was replaced by a clear emphasis on Salic law, which provided a simple legal prohibition on women taking the throne. In addition, by this time, Valois propagandists were attributing a greater sacral nature to French kingship, and since a woman could not be consecrated as a priest, nor could she exercise power like a king.[21]

The dispute over the nature and character of female power which ignited the Hundred Years War began, in a sense, with a wedding. The union of Edward II and Isabella of France (1308), together with many of the royal marriages that followed, charts the struggle's political trajectory. The marriages of successive kings of England – of Richard II to Isabella of France (1396), of Henry IV to Joan of Navarre (1403), Henry V to Katherine de Valois (1420) and Henry VI to Margaret of Anjou (1444) – were shaped by political ambition or necessity within the context of the conflict with France. A number of these marriages sealed treaties or truces in the war: the 28-year truce of Paris (1396), the treaty of Troyes (1420) and the truce of Tours (1444). Indeed, there were few marriages that English kings contracted during the period of the war which the conflict did not influence. The exceptions to this are easily explained. Edward III's marriage to Philippa of Hainault pre-dated his accession and was shaped by the particular and peculiar circumstances of his mother's need to secure support in her challenge to young Edward's father. The other main exception, Richard II's union with Anne of Bohemia in 1382, was the most distanced politically from the French war and the most criticised. After his accession in 1377 Richard was perhaps Europe's most eligible bachelor and his court became deluged with offers from prospective fathers-in-law including Charles V of France, Charles of Navarre, Charles IV the Holy Roman Emperor, Robert II of Scotland and Duke Bernabo Visconti of Milan. Given the range of female suitors the final decision to marry Anne seems surprising. The political benefits gained from a link to the Holy Roman Empire are not and were not immediately apparent. Different forces, however, took precedence at this point in the war. Pope Urban VI played a major role in encouraging the union, and the outbreak of the Great Schism explains his eagerness. Urban hoped to unite his supporters in common cause against the (schismatic) Avignonese papacy: a marriage between England and the Holy Roman Empire seemed a useful mechanism to achieve this. Anne's arrival, however, aroused little enthusiasm in England; rather it was roundly condemned. There were immediate complaints about the cost of the marriage alongside sly comments about the obvious financial advantages that could have been gained through an alliance with the Visconti. Indeed, there seemed little benefit of any kind to king or country through the king's wedding to this little scrap of humanity. And the marriage itself certainly proved very expensive, especially as the embarrassingly small dowry agreed was never paid. Richard even ended up lending his impecunious brother-in-law 80,000 florins – roughly £12,000. But the couple soon developed a genuine affection for one another. They often travelled together; Richard only undertook one itinerary of the country without Anne. Certainly, when she died at Sheen, probably of plague, in 1394, the king was so distraught he had the palace demolished. Furthermore, it is possible that Richard's second and ultimately fatal conflict with the Appellants only took place once Anne's restraining influence disappeared. If so, Anne of Bohemia played a central role in the second half of the Hundred Years War – without the Lancastrian usurpation it would have been very different.[22]

Henry IV's marriage to Joan of Navarre may also have been motivated, at least in part, by a strong mutual attraction. Henry had first married Mary Bohun (d.1394), a match very much in accordance with his status in 1381 as heir to the Lancastrian estates. His second marriage, to Joan in 1403, is explained by his then recent usurpation of the English throne. As the daughter of Charles 'the Bad' of Navarre and Jeanne de Valois (daughter of Jean II of France), and as the widow of Jean de Montfort of Brittany, Joan gave the new ruling dynasty a plethora of diplomatic advantages. Joan had often played this role; her father, 'one of the most active and devious of European statesmen ... like all medieval rulers, used his own children as diplomatic pawns'.[23] Joan had first been betrothed to Juan, heir to the kingdom of Castile, but when nothing came of this Charles arranged a marriage for her to the duke of Brittany. Before Jean IV's death in 1399 she bore him eight children and then took on the responsibility of the ducal regency before her marriage to Henry. It was not, initially, a popular union in England or Brittany. A papal dispensation was required, which proved extremely awkward to arrange because of the ongoing Schism, and the Breton nobility were deeply concerned that the younger heirs to the duchy would relocate with their mother to England. Indeed, their wariness could not be assuaged and the children were forced to remain behind. Joan was suitably compensated, at least in financial terms. Henry gave her an immense dower – 10,000 marks – in addition to the queen's traditional manors and castles of Woodstock, Langley, Rockingham, Bristol, Nottingham and Leeds. This more than generous provision eventually led to a dispute between Joan and her stepson, Henry V.

When 'Prince Hal' acquired the regency in 1410, Joan was again coming to political prominence because of the Armagnac-Burgundian civil war. Brittany had long been at odds with Burgundy and the queen's son, Duke Jean V (1389–1442), was a staunch Armagnac supporter. After assuming the crown in 1413, Henry V took advantage of these divisions in France to reopen the war. This placed Joan in a difficult position. Brittany stood against England in 1415 at Agincourt where Joan's son Artur de Richemont was captured and her son-in-law Jean d'Alençon was killed. Meanwhile, the expense of Henry's French expeditions soon led him to cast a covetous eye on his stepmother's wealth.

Henry V's victory in 1415 changed the political landscape radically. The king's ambitions in France expanded considerably and they became closely linked to his marriage. From the beginning of his reign Henry had placed a marriage with Charles VI's daughter Katherine high on his list of diplomatic priorities. The subject was discussed at least as early as November 1413 and it became central to the negotiations in 1419–20 that resulted in the treaty of Troyes. This, clearly, was no love match and regardless of whether she had 'witchcraft in her lips' the marriage must have marked the beginning of a difficult and lonely transition for Katherine. Aged just eighteen, the new queen of England was thrust into a hostile environment as the symbolic representation of all Henry had fought for and won in France. Her new household, composed almost entirely of English personnel, reflected the new political reality. Her only French companions were three ladies-in-waiting and two maids. Katherine's status, however, was not in question – her ceremonial entry into London was very grand and she sat in pride of place at the feast following her coronation. Given her position she required a substantial dowry, some 40,000 crowns. It seems more than fortuitous that at just this time the dowager queen's dowry became available to Henry when his stepmother was arrested on suspicion of witchcraft. Joan of Navarre was neither tried nor convicted, but her fall from grace was immediate and precipitous. She spent the next several years confined in various castles, saving the Exchequer a more than convenient £8,000 a year. The incident indicates the potential vulnerability of even the most powerful of women.[24]

Joan was released from captivity a little before Henry's death in 1422, which marked the end of her successor's brief reign. Katherine (the new queen dowager) took charge of raising her infant son (Henry VI) until he was seven years old. She accompanied the young king on ceremonial events and diplomatic missions when and where his presence was necessary. She also found comfort with various members of the aristocracy. An affair with Edmund Beaufort, duke of Somerset became something of a scandal, and then at some point between 1428 and 1432 she secretly married Owen Tudor (c.1400–61). This became public not long before her death in 1437.[25]

Katherine's successor, Margaret of Anjou, also came from France to England as part of a treaty in the Hundred Years War, albeit a treaty of a very different sort to that of 1420. Although significant during the last decade of the Hundred Years War, she gained real political prominence in her own right only after her husband's mental collapse, which mirrored the decline of the English position in France. Margaret had been well schooled to seize and wield political power, having received a first-rate object lesson from her grandmother, Yolande of Aragon. Despite such august ancestors, she had been offered in marriage to Henry VI because she was a relatively minor figure in French royal society – a further indication of the changed political circumstances since 1420. Although she was Charles VII's niece, her father René, duke of Anjou and count of Provence, had been personally and politically broken by his attempts to secure, first, his wife's inheritance in Lorraine and, second, the kingdom of Naples. Given the political successes of the years since Joan of Arc's intervention, Charles VII was now in a position to offer Henry the lesser prize of Margaret's hand, rather than that of one of his daughters, and despite her meagre dowry the English had little choice but to accept. In the event the marriage only secured a truce (the truce of Tours, 1444) that lasted 23 months, and within eight years of the resumption of hostilities the Hundred Years War had been lost.[26]

The Hundred Years War did not only affect the marriages of kings and queens; the changing demands of the Anglo-French conflict also determined the marriages of lesser members of the English royal family. The flurry of alliances with Castile in the later fourteenth century is indicative of the growing importance of the Iberian Peninsula in the Hundred Years War. In 1371 John of Gaunt married Constanza of Castile (1354–94), daughter of Pedro the Cruel's mistress, Maria de Padilla, and Edmund of Langley married her sister, Isabella (1355–92).[27] The Black Prince had held Pedro's daughters as surety for obligations which the deposed king of Castile accepted but never fulfilled when he sealed the treaty of Libourne in 1366. Gaunt's marriage seems to have been amicable enough although he spent a good deal of time in the company of his mistress, Katherine Swynford. Isabella, contrastingly, seems to have found her husband rather dull. Certainly, she became the subject of scandalous rumours before her premature death in 1392 – she was only thirty-seven. She is reputed to have had an affair with Richard II's half-brother, John Holland, first earl of Huntingdon and duke of Exeter (c.1352–1400). The never objective Thomas Walsingham described her as a 'lady of sensual and self-indulgent disposition [who] had been worldly and lustful'.[28]

By contrast with the Plantagenets, the concerns of Valois monarchs lay with domestic matters, which reflects the different implications of the Hundred Years War in France. From 1328 onwards the need to secure the position of the Valois dynasty within France influenced successive royal marriages. Marriages were contracted with the aim of strengthening the position of the princes of the Blood Royal within France and extending the area under Valois control. This proved, eventually, to be a success, although the development of a series of semi-autonomous *apanages* posed a number of problems for the monarchy in the interim. The independence of certain territories, Burgundy in particular, came to pose a major threat. Philippe VI married first Jeanne of Burgundy and second Blanche d'Evreux-Navarre. Jean (II), as duke of Normandy, married Bonne of Luxembourg and then, as king, Jeanne de Boulogne. The second marriage ensured the king became *jure uxoris* (by right of his wife) count of Auvergne and Boulogne. Of Jean II's eight children one, Marguerite, became a nun, and another, Isabelle, married Gian Galeazzo Visconti, but the remainder married within the French aristocracy or those close to it politically and geographically, such as members of the houses of Flanders and Navarre. The most significant marriage – that of the future king, Charles V – was to Jeanne of Bourbon.[29] The exception to this pattern is the union of Charles VI with Isabeau of Bavaria, which Philippe the Bold of Burgundy orchestrated chiefly to cement his own growing influence in the Low Countries.[30]

The outbreak of the civil war in France added a further dimension to the calculations that had to be made when arranging a royal marriage. On 18 December 1413 Charles (VII) was betrothed to Marie d'Anjou, daughter of Duke Louis II of Anjou and Yolande of Aragon. Charles's elder brothers had been married to children of the house of Burgundy, but changing political conditions in the civil war made an alliance with the Angevins attractive. The match proved to be of great importance to the future dauphin: it furnished him with the personnel who would form his governing circle when he 'acceded' to the throne in such difficult circumstances in 1422.[31]

Lesser members of the French royal family, some already mentioned, were used to fashion or strengthen diplomatic links with or against the English as circumstances dictated and this was a policy that a number of France's allies in the Hundred Years War also adopted. For example, in the 1440s a number of Stewart princesses – sisters of King James II of Scotland (r.1437–60) – were found French husbands or husbands with French links in order to strengthen the Auld Alliance. Isabella married François, duke of Brittany (1414–50). Her sisters, Mary and Annabella, married respectively Wolfaert van Borselen, Philippe of Burgundy's admiral, and Louis, count of Geneva. In reality these matches proved of little political value. More significant was James II's own marriage to Mary of Gueldres. Early in 1448 James wrote to Charles VII asking for assistance in finding a bride. The French king recommended sending an embassy to the Burgundian court to negotiate a marriage with the houses of Burgundy, Gueldres or Cleves. The resulting marriage formed part of the treaty of Brussels (1449), which renewed the Franco-Scottish alliance.[32]

If queens posed a problem in a patriarchal society, then women wielding power but holding a much less formal position raised even more questions. Throughout the period of the Hundred Years War royal mistresses received coruscating criticism for the power they exercised over kings. In turn the monarchs in question had opprobrium poured on them for permitting this unnatural state of affairs. Because the royal court was a domestic as well as political setting, domestic, personal and political concerns overlapped constantly. Within the court those who might manipulate or control access to the king, or who had the king's ear in the council chamber or the bedchamber, had the potential to exert a great deal of power. A royal mistress could, therefore, manipulate policy and personnel in the court and so influence matters of wider political import. The loathing such influence might generate is especially evident in the case of Alice Perrers, Edward III's mistress, who came to prominence around 1364, some five years before the death of Queen Philippa:

> ...there was a woman in England called Alice Perrers. She was a shameless, impudent harlot, and of low birth, for she was the daughter of a thatcher . . . elevated by fortune. She was not attractive or beautiful, but knew how to compensate for these defects with the seductiveness of her voice. Blind fortune elevated this woman to such heights and promoted her to a greater intimacy with the king than was proper, since she had been the maidservant and mistress of a man of Lombardy, and accustomed to carry water on her own shoulders from the mill-stream for the everyday needs of that household. And while the queen was still alive, the king loved this woman more than he loved the queen.[33]

So wrote Thomas Walsingham with characteristic venom. While there is no doubt that Alice Perrers was at the centre of much of the corruption and casual embezzlement which characterised Edward III's court in the 1370s, she also became the chief scapegoat for the king's decline. She may well have been of relatively humble origins but little can be said with certainty about her beauty or lack of it, her good fortune or of how she spoke. The monk from St Albans may not have been the best judge of such things, when he is to be trusted on the subject of Alice at all. He later argued that she was forced to rely on various potions and enchantments to seduce the king. Although she probably became the king's mistress in or around 1364, the relationship did not become common knowledge until after Philippa's death in 1369. Alice certainly took advantage of her relationship with the king to advance her own financial and business interests. This, no doubt, was a major cause of her unpopularity – by the time of the king's death she had acquired some 50 manors and £20,000 in jewels.[34] Her significance in the context of the Hundred Years War lies in an event that took place a year earlier, in the Good Parliament of 1376. On this occasion the Commons launched its first major attack on the king's ministers following a demand for taxation. In return for funds the Commons demanded a redress of grievances that centred on poor government by the king's ministers and the pernicious influence of evil counsellors, including Alice herself. The allegations were widespread and damning and led to the first cases of impeachment in Parliament. Mistress Perrers was accused of embezzling funds worth between £2,000 and £3,000 a year since the time she first gained influence over the king. She was banished from court and the realm, although the king orchestrated her return by the end of the year.[35]

It was not always the case that a king's mistress was criticised. In the case of Charles VI, who was provided with an official mistress in 1405 because his wife could no longer cope with the mad king's sexual demands, the criticism fell on the queen. This formed a central element in the centuries-long character assassination of Isabeau of Bavaria: she was charged with abandoning her poor insane husband, taking advantage of his illness to seize control of France and of indulging in a life of decadence and iniquity.[36] It is hardly surprising that Isabeau could not cope: Charles VI's madness, unlike that of his grandson Henry VI, was often violent and always unpredictable. He would foam at the mouth, howl like a wolf, run naked through the palace, eat from the floor and was prone to setting objects on fire, including the queen's gowns, although only once he had urinated on them. Famously, at one stage he believed he was made of glass and his enemies wished to shatter him.[37]

Female influence was particularly notable during the reign and at the court of Charles VII, and not only in the form of Joan of Arc. According to the Milanese ambassador the king was 'entirely ruled by women'. In February 1425 Charles had taken into his protection the public whorehouse at Toulouse, but these were not the women the ambassador had in mind. Nor was it Marie d'Anjou, Charles's queen. She played a very limited political role and, indeed, had little time for one between her 14 pregnancies. Four of her children died in the three years between 1436 and 1439, after which she habitually wore black and retreated into a life of devotion and domesticity. Charles's mother-in-law Yolande of Aragon was, as we have seen, much more influential in shaping French politics than her daughter. Prior to her promotion of Joan of Arc, the dowager countess of Anjou had won Breton support for Charles VII and she also began to manipulate the strains in the Anglo-Burgundian alliance to his advantage.

Charles met another woman who proved to be extremely significant in his life soon after Yolande's death in 1442. Agnès Sorel rose from a relatively lowly position in the household of Isabella of Lorraine, wife of René d'Anjou, to become the king's mistress. Charles became besotted with her in 1443 and she probably gave birth to his daughter, Marie, in the following summer. He showered Agnès with gifts, grants and lands, and her friends and relatives benefited greatly from her close association with the king; many secured offices within the royal household, some even found their way into the episcopacy. In this way Agnès acquired a good deal of political influence. For example, it was because of her that Pierre de Brézé came to prominence as a royal favourite. Already a successful soldier, he became the king's chamberlain through Agnès's support, and his decline from power followed her death on 9 February 1450. She was rumoured, without substantiation, to have been poisoned by Jacques Coeur, the royal *argentier*, whose remarkable personal wealth made him Charles VII's key financier in the later phases of the Hundred Years War.[38]

As was often the case with royal mistresses, Agnès was criticised for the power she exercised, over everything from politics to fashion. Jean Juvénal des Ursins suggested that because of her influence the court became a place of 'whoredom and ribaldry' where women wore clothing through which one could see their 'nipples and breasts' (one of Agnès's breasts was displayed in Jean Fouquet's extraordinary Melun Diptych, *Virgin and Child Surrounded by Angels*, c.1450). She was said to have encouraged the ladies of the court to follow her example and wear 'great furred trains, girdles and other things . . . displeasing to God and the world'.[39] Such criticism, though, was commonplace. Clothing was a regular cause of concern for secular and ecclesiastical commentators. Immoderate dress had been held accountable for every disaster from the French defeat at Poitiers to the return of the Black Death. According to the chronicler John of Reading, the plague manifested divine wrath brought on by those who wore their hose so tight they could not kneel down to pray. The Goodman of Paris (the author of a text written between 1392 and 1394 by an elderly Parisian merchant for his new bride) urged his young wife to dress with 'great care' and without 'too much frippery'.

Joan, the Fair Maid of Kent (the Black Prince's wife and mother to Richard II), seems to have become a sartorial icon in Aquitaine and many followed her style of dressing in tight-fitting garments of silk and ermine with low-cut necklines and wearing pearls and precious stones in her hair. Not unlike her husband's political and courtly regime, Joan's fashionable excesses delighted some and scandalised others. A Breton lord, Jean de Beaumanoir, noted he wanted his wife to dress as 'an honest woman' and not adopt the 'fashions of the mistresses of the English or the Free Companies'. He was 'disgusted by those women who follow such a bad example, particularly the princess of Wales'.[40] Whether this was a reflection of her wardrobe or her sexual reputation is difficult to judge, since the stolid Philippa of Hainault also spent very significant amounts on fashion and jewellery – £20,000 over the last ten years of her life. It was after all expected that a queen should use her appearance to enhance the regal image. Nonetheless, there is no doubt that Joan developed a 'reputation as a sexual libertine', and references made by contemporaries to her as the 'virgin of Kent' may have been somewhat sarcastic.[41]

Queens (and dowager queens) might, very occasionally, find themselves involved in the practicalities of warfare. For those of lesser status it could be a more immediate and pressing concern. Throughout the Middle Ages women had always been involved in war. Usually this was in a civilian capacity: sometimes wives and female servants accompanied their husbands and masters on campaign, and there may well have been substantial numbers of female camp followers who cared for the troops, washing clothes, finding and preparing food and tending wounds. Some women were also involved in other, less conventional activities. It seems likely that brothels existed in some expeditionary forces; they were certainly common in Italy in this period.[42] Henry V commanded that 'open and common strumpets' should not be permitted in his army. And in the 1420s Thomas Montague, fifth earl of Salisbury, drew up ordinances for an expedition to Maine that included a clause 'For women that use Bordell [brothel] the which lodge in the Host', which suggests prostitutes continued to gather around armies – this decree aimed to prevent them lodging in the camp. These ordinances were not passed for moral reasons, as with the regulations enforced in Joan of Arc's armies where prostitutes were also forbidden, but to maintain order and discipline. There was also a fear, common to both sides, that women could be employed as spies.[43]

While references to women playing a formal military role are less frequent, they are not unknown.[44] Women were undoubtedly involved in a range of military activities during the war, and aristocratic women's responsibilities might extend beyond the domestic milieu. In 1335 Edward III wrote to Margaret, widow of Edmund, earl of Kent; to Marie de St Pol, widow of Aymer de Valence, earl of Pembroke; and to Joan, wife of Thomas Botetourt. The king, who was then fighting in Scotland, commanded these women to gather trusted advisers together in London to 'treat and ordain on the safe custody and secure defence of our realm and people, and on resisting and driving out the [French] foreigners' who Edward believed were massing troops and ships for an invasion. The women were then ordered to 'arm and array your people . . . to repel powerfully and coura- geously the presumptuous boldness and malice of our same enemies . . . if those enemies invade'.[45] In this case, although women were not consulted directly on military matters, their social position was such that they were expected to take responsibility for the defence of the realm while their husbands were elsewhere.

More commonly, aristocratic women took responsibility for protecting their own estates during a husband's or son's absence. It was for this reason that Christine de Pizan, drawing on the writings of Vegetius (in the later Roman Empire), Giles of Rome and Honoré Bonet, counselled that an aristocratic woman

> ought to have the heart of a man, that is, she ought to know how to use weapons and be familiar with everything that pertains to them, so that she may be ready to command her men if the need arises. She should know how to launch an attack or to defend against one, if the situation calls for it. She should take care that her fortresses are well garrisoned.[46]

There are numerous examples of women following such advice – knowingly or unknowingly – and it is clear that such a role was expected: certain women, clearly, needed to be prepared to organise the protection of their property. Agnes of Dunbar ('Black Agnes') successfully coordinated the defence of Dunbar Castle against the English in 1338, holding out for five months. According to Sir Walter Scott, she also had her maids dust the walls where the missiles from the siege engines struck.[47] Jeanne, wife of Jean, the future duke of Brittany, played a critical role in the siege of Hennebont (1342) during the Breton civil war. When Charles of Blois, the rival claimant to the duchy, laid siege to the town, Jeanne led the defence, riding through the streets urging the townsfolk to take up arms, encour- aging women to 'cut short their kirtles [gowns]' and carry 'stones and pots full of chalk to the walls', so that they might be thrown down on their enemies. The countess then rode out armed at the head of 300 horsemen to charge the French camp before setting it on fire and returning to Hennebont to defend it from another assault.[48] Julienne du Guesclin, said to be Bertrand's sister, may have taken an even more active role while defending her convent against an attack on Pontorson in Normandy in 1427. She is said to have donned her brother's armour and assisted with hurling back the scaling ladders as the English attacked, delaying them so that they were trapped against the walls when her brother returned.[49]

While this specific incident is likely to be apocryphal, women clearly did play important roles in the defence of towns, villages, farms and castles – stone-throwing, occasionally handling weapons and in many auxiliary roles. Hence, according to Thomas Walsingham, in 1404 when Dartmouth was under attack from French raiders, the townswomen 'laid low the enemy, inflicting dire damage with the missiles from their slings. And so several Frenchmen were killed or captured by women.'[50] Women in the besieged city of Orléans in 1428–29 are also recorded as assisting with the defence, carrying items such as water and oil, fat, lime and ashes; some were engaged more actively and pushed the attackers from the walls.[51] Such actions would seem to be at odds with expected female behaviour in this period. However, contemporaries could explain and condone female military activity if it took place within the domestic sphere – if a woman protected her home she followed a natural inclination. As Giles of Rome said:

> If we consider birds that live from rapine, such as sparrow hawks, goshawks, and eagles, the females have larger bodies, bolder hearts, and greater strength than the males. The names of all those birds are feminine and the males are worthless compared to the females. Since we see that among other animals both males and females fight, it would seem that the city would be especially ordained according to nature if both women and men were ordained to the practice of war, since it seems that this is especially in accord with the natural order, in which both we and the other animals take part.[52]

Joan of Arc, however, took such behaviour far beyond the domestic sphere and so polarised opinions from the beginning of her career. She was the most notable woman to take up arms in the Hundred Years War and arguably in the entirety of the Middle Ages. Born around 1412 in Domrémy in eastern France, Joan came from wealthy peasant stock. Aged thirteen she began to receive visions and hear the words of saints Michael, Catherine and Margaret, who charged her with driving the English from France and seeing the dauphin Charles crowned king. That a girl from such a background should even countenance taking on such monumental tasks is astonishing; that she succeeded is almost beyond belief. In May 1428 she made her way to her local castle of Vaucouleurs, which was under the command of one Robert de Baudricourt. Initially (and understandably) he was extremely sceptical and rebuffed her, but Joan's persistence and her growing support among the local townspeople eventually won him over and early in the following year he sent her under escort to meet Charles VII at Chinon.

When Joan arrived there, however, not all at the Valois court in exile were well disposed towards her. Regnaut de Chartres, archbishop of Reims, was especially suspicious. For a churchman, a woman who had not taken the veil and who claimed to have regular, direct contact with the divine was troubling at the very least. She was examined physically to ensure her virginity – this proved she was not in league with the devil – and examined theologically to establish her orthodoxy. However, others at court recognised her potential value. The precise reasons why Charles VII and Yolande of Aragon saw fit to trust or at least make use of Joan remain uncertain. Charles is reported to have been delighted by what Joan said to him in private at their first meeting, and he may have been convinced that she had, indeed, been sent by God to deliver him the crown and the kingdom. Yet it was also fortuitous that Joan's appearance coincided with the circulation of a number of political prophecies, which suggested the nation would be saved from the ravages of the English by a maiden. Her arrival may, consequently, have provided Charles with a wonderful opportunity to campaign for political and military support throughout the country. Or it may simply be the case that all other means the dauphinists had tried had, essentially, failed. Although Artur de Richemont (younger son of Jean V, duke of Britanny, and Joan of Navarre) had enjoyed some minor successes (for example, at Pontorson in 1427), Charles's forces had not experienced a significant victory since Baugé. Charles, therefore, took this opportunity to prepare a force to send to the relief of Orléans, and he presented Joan with arms, armour, a horse and a banner of her own design. Her impact at Orléans was immediate and astounding, and she contravened nearly every contemporary gender stereotype. This would bring about both her triumph and her execution.

From the outset of her political career – if so it can be called – Joan (or perhaps her supporters) recognised that she needed to present a particular image in order to be taken seriously by both the French army and the English. Consequently, it appears that she was educated in various martial skills prior to her arrival at Orléans. Fortunately, she had a natural aptitude for riding and using a lance and sword. She also learned a good deal about troop dispositions and the use of artillery. By the time she appeared at Orléans, Joan had been crafted into an ideal figure to shape political opinion – the virgin on horseback, leading her troops, clad in armour, bearing a standard and wielding a sword. This striking image proved extraordinarily effective in the short term, but it was also inherently dangerous, and it is not surprising that after she had secured his coronation Charles began to distance himself from Joan and made no great effort to secure her release after she was captured at Compiègne in May 1430.[53]

In 1431 English military commanders wrote a letter to churchmen, nobles and urban communities in France describing Joan's activities:

> It is commonly reported everywhere how the woman who had called herself Jehanne la Pucelle, a false prophetess, had for more than two years, against divine law and the estate of her sex, dressed in men's clothes, a thing abominable to God ... and presumptuously boasted that she often had personal and visible communication with St Michael and a great host of angels and saints of Paradise ... She dressed herself also in arms worn by knights and squires, raised a standard, and in very great outrage ... demanded to have and carry the very noble and excellent arms of France, which she entirely obtained, and carried in many conflicts and assaults ... In such a state she went to the fields and led men-at-arms and commanded great companies to commit and exercise inhuman cruelties in shedding human blood, in causing popular seditions and disturbances, inciting them to perjuries and pernicious rebellions, false and superstitious beliefs, in disturbing all free peace and renewing mortal war, in permitting herself to be worshipped and revered by many as a holy woman, and working other damnable things ... which in many places are recognised always to have greatly scandalised almost all of Christianity.[54]

Central and intrinsic to Joan's image were her clothing and her military role, both of which contravened contemporary expectations of women. For a woman to fight, apart from in exceptional circumstances, was to usurp a fundamental aspect of masculinity. In Joan's case her youth and humble background compounded this transgression. Defence of one's property, such as Christine de Pizan advocated, could be seen as an extension of female domesticity. However, Joan took the battle to her enemies and, in addition, flaunted (and flouted) many characteristics of chivalry and knighthood – her horse, clothing, weapons and the armour given her by Charles VII. Yet she also referred to herself as 'La Pucelle', meaning a 'young, female virgin', perhaps a 'maiden or maid', and her maidenhead had been established. It had been important, politically and symbolically, to prove Joan's virginity in order for her to fulfil the requirements of the various prophecies. Furthermore, virginity had powerful spiritual connotations that imbued Joan with a certain sacred power and gave her a degree of self-determination not available to married women. This also was awkward in a woman who had not taken the veil. These elements, taken together, made for a deeply incongruous mix and raised dangerous questions about Joan's position in society. In the end it would be her transvestism that resulted in her execution: it was an abomination according to the church court, and her actions were portrayed as a wilful contravention of divine law.[55]

Through her capture and execution Joan became merely the most notorious victim of the Hundred Years War. Although few women took part in major battles, they were far from immune from the war's worst excesses. The war affected women's lives in many ways; not least it caused the absence of fathers, brothers, lovers and husbands on military campaigns. Such absences, if not permanent, might last for months. It is hardly surprising that the image of the woman who 'weeps and waits' became common in many contemporary works. After the disaster of Agincourt, Christine de Pizan wrote *La prison de la vie humaine* (*The Prison of Human Life*), a letter dedicated to Marie de Berry, duchess of Bourbon, whose husband had been taken captive in the battle. The letter was written to console the women of France mourning the dead and those held prisoner. As Christine put it, she sought

> to find a remedy and a cure for the grievous illness and infirmity caused by a bitter heart and sad thoughts ... among so many honourable women struck by ... the many deaths or captivity of those close to them, such as husbands, children, brothers, uncles, cousins, and other relatives and friends.[56]

The children Christine mentioned also suffered in the course of the war and played a part in it too. They also lost fathers and brothers; they endured the depredations of war, English *chevauchées*, mercenary attacks, French coastal raids and all the panoply of devastation. Some children also fought, participating in military expeditions and battles. The Black Prince was sixteen when he fought in the vanguard at Crécy (1346). Froissart suggests that he was 'too young to bear arms but [his father, Edward III] had him with him on his ship, because he much loved him'.[57] John of Gaunt was only ten when he found himself on board ship during the naval battle of Winchelsea (1350). This seems almost inexplicable. Jean II's son, Philippe, was fourteen when he was captured alongside his father at Poitiers (1356) – his service there resulted in his *nom de guerre*, Philippe the Bold. Many less eminent children also found themselves in the forefront of the conflict. Boys were instructed in arms from a young age – in England especially in the use of the longbow – and many went on campaign. Presumably they were a common sight. In 1415 Henry V prohibited the participation of children under the age of fourteen in the Agincourt expedition, which suggests that in the past youngsters had regularly been involved.[58]

Children and women also suffered some of the worst excesses of war. Following the French victory at Cassel in 1328, men, women and children were put to the sword as an act of revenge for the Flemish victory at Courtrai more than twenty years previously.[59] At Caen in 1346, Epernay, and Vailly-sur-Aisne in 1358 and Beauvais in 1359, Jean de Venette described the abuse, capture and murder of women during mercenary raids and English *chevauchées*.[60] Accounts of the revolt of the Jacquerie were similarly violent. Various chroniclers recounted horrific scenes of the capture, murder and rape of noblewomen. Peasants were described as having 'killed, slaughtered and massacred without mercy all the nobles whom they could find ... and, what is still more lamentable, they delivered the noble ladies and their little children upon whom they came to an atrocious death'.[61]

This suggests that women might also be victims of war in a particular fashion – as victims of rape. While it is likely that men too were raped, no evidence survives concerning this. There is evidence, however, that boys were forced to serve as pages for military companies and it is not unlikely that, as such, some were compelled to provide sexual services. The rape of women was, as letters of remission indicate, appallingly common and committed by all sides. Martial Soubout, who served with the *routier* captain Guiot de Pin in the 1360s, admitted that rape was customary 'amongst the men of the Companies'; and the Parisian Bourgeois recounted, among several incidents, the actions of the Armagnacs at Le Mans in 1428 where 'they plundered, stole, raped women and girls, and did to those who thought them friends all the harm that anyone could do to an enemy'.[62] Women were also vulnerable during longer periods of occupation when they could fall prey to garrison forces. Evidence is abundant of women being forced to leave their homes and being held prisoner in fortresses by soldiers: one account tells of a woman held in the castle of Saint Fargeau for five years. More commonly soldiers broke into houses: Jean le Comté, a member of the French garrison at Falaise in 1372, made a practice of throwing husbands out of their homes for a night while he abused their wives.[63]

In modern conflicts rape has often been used as a weapon of war, and perhaps this was also the case in the Hundred Years War. Like pillage, it may have served as a means of asserting dominance in enemy (or sometimes 'friendly') territory. If so, there is no evidence that this was officially endorsed. It is possible, however, that sex was seen as one of the potential benefits of war, and a form of plunder. Assaults on the body politic of one's enemy might easily become equated with an assault on their physical bodies. Changing legal attitudes to rape in the later Middle Ages might also encourage such thinking. The English Statute of Westminster (1275) 'downgraded' rape from a felony to a trespass: it was no longer to be punished with loss of life or limb but by a fine or imprisonment. The crime also became closely associated with abduction, and in legal terms the concern shifted away from the women affected directly and focused on the implications of rape for families – chiefly aristocratic families. While the Statute of Westminster II (1285) restored greater penalties for rape, these were rarely imposed. Consequently, by the late fourteenth century the distinction between rape (forced coition) and abduction had become blurred. This can be seen in literary works as well as in law. John Gower, for example, in *Confessio Amantis*, saw rape as an example of the sin of Avarice not Lechery – he depicted the rape of a shepherdess by a knight not as the abuse of the woman but as the theft of another man's property. Consequently, in England in the later Middle Ages rape became a crime as much against a man (husband, father, and so on) as it was against a woman.[64] Within the context of the Hundred Years War English authorities might, tacitly, have viewed rape as an attack on property or viewed it as an act of domination, similar to the *chevauchée*, with its implication that the French could not defend their land and property.[65]

This, clearly, contradicted both military ordinances and the dictates of chivalry. For numerous authors of romances and chivalric chronicles the mistreatment of women made the darkest stain on one's honour. For authors such as Froissart the mistreatment of women was utterly reprehensible, a quintessential act of dishonour. By comparison, those who protected women were the most worthy of praise. Thomas Malory would crystallise chivalric attitudes to women in the later Middle Ages in *Le Morte d'Arthur*.

Malory makes it apparent that among a knight's fundamental responsibilities was the defence of women. In the *Morte*, Malory's knights swear an oath that requires them to pledge service to God, king, ladies and their fellow knights, and rape was described as the most dishonourable of acts and a betrayal of chivalric duty. It is clear, however, that the author's main concern was with attacks on noblewomen.[66]

A number of knights took such advice to heart. When the English attacked the French at Caen in 1346, Froissart lauded the English commander Sir Thomas Holland, who rode into the town before it was captured: 'He was able that day to prevent many cruel and horrible acts which would otherwise have been committed, thus giving proof of his kind and noble heart. Several gallant English knights who were with him also prevented a number of evil deeds and rescued many a pretty townswoman and many a nun from rape.'[67] Then, once the town was taken, another knight fighting for the English, Sir Godfrey Harcourt, commanded his men not to kill anyone or 'violate any women'. By contrast, Froissart asserted that the foreign captains who were supposed to enforce the accord reached between the English and French in 1360 'despoiled many a damsel', and also that roving bands of mercenaries terrorised the French countryside 'without any cause . . . and violated and despoiled women, old and young, without pity, and slew men, women and children without mercy'.[68]

And yet despite chivalric prohibitions the laws of war suggested that in some circumstances rape was permissible. When he began the siege of Harfleur in 1415, Henry V had one of his heralds read to the townspeople an extract from Deuteronomy Chapter 20, which stated that a town which refused to capitulate abrogated all chance of mercy: all men would be put 'to the sword, but the women and the children, the cattle and everything else in the city, all its spoil, you [the attackers] shall take as booty for yourselves; and you shall enjoy the spoil of your enemies'. This proved not to be their fate, however, and when the town capitulated the women and children along with the poorer inhabitants of the town (perhaps 2,000 people) were simply expelled. Furthermore, each was given a small sum of money and allowed to take with them what they could carry.[69]

Such actions were not uncommon. Women often received safe-conducts to leave conquered towns from both French and English, although they usually had to leave their homes swiftly and sometimes with few of their possessions. Following the reconquest of Normandy many of the displaced women who had crossed the Channel to be with their husbands were English. Others were French who had married English settlers for reasons of the heart or of the purse. Under these circumstances not all women were compelled to leave and nor were their husbands. A number of Englishmen, many of them soldiers, who had settled in France during the English occupation, married French women and remained with them once the war was over. John Edward, for example, the captain of La Roche-Guyon, married a French heiress. On the expulsion of the English from Normandy in 1449–50, he surrendered the fortress and offered his allegiance to Charles VII. Richard Merbury, captain of Gisors, acted similarly.[70] In this way female influence shaped individual destinies at the end of the Hundred Years War just as it had from the beginning.

Joan of Arc's intervention at the siege of Orléans changed the balance of power in the Hundred Years War at a crucial stage. If the city had fallen to the English, the position of Charles VII would have been greatly weakened, perhaps fatally so. As it was, the relief of the city paved the way for Charles's coronation in Reims and a very significant change in his authority and its appearance. The impression of English near invincibility established at Agincourt and reinforced in a succession of battles and campaigns had been undermined. Together these changes weakened the already fragile Anglo-Burgundian accord and laid the foundations for a rapprochement between Charles VII and Philippe the Good. When this was concluded at the Congress of Arras in 1435, it marked the beginning of the end of the Hundred Years War.

CHAPTER 9

Prisoners of War

GILDED CAGES

1435

> *And I, Charles, Duke of Orléans,*
> *Have wished to write these verses in the time of my youth;*
> *I shall admit it before everyone,*
> *For I made them while in prison, I confess,*
> *Praying God, that before I am old*
> *The time of peace may everywhere have come,*
> *As I heartily desire,*
> *And that I may soon see an end to all your woes,*
> *Most Christian, freeborn realm of France!*[1]
>
> Charles d'Orléans, 'La complainte de France'

Charles d'Orléans wrote those lines in captivity. He had been taken prisoner in 1415 at the battle of Agincourt and spent the next 25 years in English custody. His experience was both remarkable and yet commonplace. Many were taken prisoner during the Hundred Years War but very few were deprived of their freedom for so long. Because of his political value it was only in the 1430s, when the fortunes of war began to change – and change decisively, that Charles's hopes for release had a chance of becoming reality.

The decline in the English position had become clear by the time the Congress of Arras met in August 1435.[2] Joan of Arc had rejuvenated the French cause with her victories at Orléans, Jargeau and Patay (1429), and the former dauphin, now King Charles VII, had grown in status and political stature by virtue of military success confirmed by his consecration in Reims Cathedral.[3] Beside him Henry VI, still a minor and only king of France based on a dubious coronation ceremony performed in Paris by an

English bishop, was a childish, pale and ineffectual leader. The English position deteriorated further when Philippe the Good and Charles VII sealed a truce in December 1434, leaving the Anglo-Burgundian alliance on the verge of collapse. By this stage many Lancastrian territorial gains had been reversed, and although the duke of Bedford and his lieutenants, notably John Talbot, stabilised the situation, another Valois offensive in the opening months of 1435 led to the loss of Etaples and Le Crotoy (neither far from Calais) and the death of John FitzAlan, earl of Arundel, at Gerberoy. In this political climate it is not surprising that some elements at the English court warmed to the idea of a diplomatic settlement to the war. Negotiations of various sorts had, in any case, been ongoing since 1430 and with greater enthusiasm following Henry VI's return from France in 1432. The eventual outcome of this series of discussions was a major diplomatic gathering, one of the largest of the Middle Ages, the Congress of Arras. The congress lasted nearly a month, from 12 August to 4 September 1435. Although in principle a peace conference, it proved chiefly an opportunity for both sides to try to seize the political initiative by securing the support of the increasingly influential duchy of Burgundy.

Although his situation had now vastly improved, in order to consider himself truly king, Charles VII needed to retake Paris. However, the financial and military resources of the 'King of Bourges' were limited and certainly insufficient to allow him to contemplate a major assault on the capital. His only option, therefore, was a reconciliation with Philippe the Good and Burgundy. Philippe had not found the English alliance greatly advantageous for a number of years and he had left the door open for negotiations with the Valois court. These negotiations took on a greater significance in 1432 following the death of Philippe's wife Anne. As the duke of Bedford's sister she had formed an important link in the Anglo-Burgundian alliance. The removal of this link was followed by the fall from power of Charles's grand chamberlain, Georges de la Trémoïlle, in 1433. One of those taken prisoner at Agincourt, he had risen to high office after his release and became one of the most powerful figures at King Charles's court. He had also been bitterly opposed to a reconciliation with Burgundy.

Therefore, at the Congress of Arras the French and English were more concerned with maintaining or securing an alliance with Burgundy than with resolving their own quarrel. In the opening discussions one of the few sources of political leverage available to Henry VI's representatives were those French noblemen held as prisoners of war in England, the most important of whom was Charles d'Orléans. For many years after 1415 his political significance was such that the English refused to countenance his release, but by 1433 it had become necessary to use him and his fellow captive, Charles d'Artois, count of Eu, to secure a favourable settlement.[4]

Despite the efforts of Pope Eugenius IV and his representatives, the congress failed to resolve the Anglo-French war. It did lead ultimately, however, to the English defeat because of the Franco-Burgundian rapprochement. The French participants managed to convince the papal ambassadors that the treaty of Troyes had been fundamentally flawed; that Henry V, as he had never been king of France himself, could not bequeath the title to his son; and that Philippe could in good conscience renounce his alliance with England. He and Charles VII formally ended the (Armagnac-Burgundian) civil war some weeks later, on 21 September 1435. Their reconciliation followed shortly after another blow to the English – the death of John, duke of Bedford, earlier that month. Thereafter, although the English did not capitulate immediately, the political tide clearly ran in favour of the Valois for the remainder of the Hundred Years War. Charles d'Orléans, meanwhile, would not be released until 1440.[5]

The duke of Orléans was, in some ways, extremely fortunate even to be the subject of negotiation. He was discovered alive, but barely recognisable, drenched in blood, under a pile of corpses towards the end of the battle of Agincourt. The changing nature of warfare in the later Middle Ages, with the increasing significance of infantry, archery and artillery, meant that a smaller percentage of captives was taken than had previously been the case. At the same time the proportion of battlefield fatalities grew considerably. Earlier in the Middle Ages, for economic and political reasons it had been common practice to take prisoner those of knightly rank, but as changes took hold in military strategy and technology this became more difficult. As a result battlefields in the late Middle Ages became ever bloodier places for the military aristocracy. Consequently, at Halidon Hill, Northumberland, in July 1333, a battle in which the English rehearsed tactics they would later employ in France, so many nobles were killed that, according to the *Liber Pluscardensis* (a fifteenth-century chronicle written at Pluscarden Abbey in Scotland), 'it would be tedious to give all their names'.[6] Similarly, at Crécy in 1346 approximately 1,500 nobles died; while 2,500 fell at Poitiers ten years later; and perhaps as many as 6,000 at Agincourt.[7] And even if captured one might not survive. At Agincourt, fearing a French counter-attack, Henry V felt compelled to order the execution of many of his prisoners: an order from which the duke of Orléans was fortunate to be exempted. However, the impact of such trends should not be exaggerated;

many were still taken prisoner in the Hundred Years War, non-combatants as well as soldiers, and men of lesser as well as high rank. Indeed, because of the extent and duration of the conflict, the period of the Hundred Years War has been dubbed the 'golden age of private ransoms'. And so, in spite of the fatalities, perhaps more than a thousand soldiers were captured at Agincourt.[8]

Because of the political importance of certain prisoners, issues of ransoming were extremely significant throughout the conflict. They influenced the course of the Hundred Years War, they could shape the political and financial fortunes of nations and they often dominated debate in courts of law and chivalry.[9] Throughout the war goodly numbers of politically sensitive individuals were captured. The most valuable of these from France and from among the ranks of France's allies were King David II of Scotland (captured at Neville's Cross, 1346); Charles de Blois (claimant to the duchy of Brittany, captured at La Roche Derrien, 1347); Jean II of France (taken at Poitiers, 1356); Bertrand du Guesclin (captured at Auray, 1364, and Nájera, 1367); James I of Scotland (captured 1406); Charles d'Orléans (made prisoner at Agincourt, 1415); and Joan of Arc (taken at Compiègne on 23 May 1430).

Among the English and their allies, although no one as august as a king was taken captive, many with royal connections were made prisoners of war, including Ralph, first earl Stafford (at Vannes, 1342); Thomas Percy, earl of Worcester (at Soubise, 1372); John Beaufort, duke of Somerset, and John Holland, earl of Huntingdon (both captured at Baugé); John Talbot, earl of Shrewsbury (at Patay, 1429); and William Neville, earl of Kent (at Pont de l'Arche, 1449).

There were many potential benefits to be gained from taking a high-ranking prisoner. First, that prisoner could be financially valuable; second, while in captivity the prisoner could play no part in the war and his release might be dependent on his agreement not to take up arms again in the struggle; and, third, a captive might present a political or diplomatic advantage. For the lesser soldiery on both sides the chance to take an important prisoner provided a major incentive to participate in a campaign. Ransoms were potentially the most valuable of the many profits of war, although there were a number of problems associated with taking prisoners. To begin with, as with all booty, soldiers did not keep everything they captured – they were required to pass a percentage of all their ill-gotten gains on to their commander, and he in turn was bound to pass a proportion of this on to the king. This might be as much as a half, more commonly a third, of the value, although the actual sum delivered might not match initial expecta-tions.[10] Furthermore, because of the potential value of a prisoner arguments often broke out over who was the legitimate captor. These could lead to the deaths of prisoners before they had even been taken into captivity. The fact that English military ordinances mention this and attempted to address the problem indicates it was far from uncommon. For example, after the fall of Jargeau to Joan of Arc's troops in June 1429, many of the English garrison were killed because of a violent argument between those claiming to be their 'masters'.[11] And, finally, once a prisoner was properly secured, protracted negotiations might follow and, commonly, there were difficul-ties associated with securing payment. Money often passed through a number of hands and suffered deductions en route. This meant the process of collection could be expensive and, in the interim, the captor might have to pay a considerable sum for the upkeep of his hostage. Consequently, the final sum might be considerably less than that first agreed.

The celebrated case of the count of Denia offers an object lesson in some of the other dangers that could come with taking an important prisoner. The esquires Robert Hawley and John Shakell captured Denia (a prince of the Aragonese Blood Royal) at the battle of Nájera in April 1367. The count subsequently returned home to raise funds for his ransom, leaving his son, Alphonso de Villena, as a hostage. The case became politically charged because of the increasing importance of Iberian affairs in the Hundred Years War, and in 1377 the English Crown demanded Hawley and Shakell hand over Alphonso. When the captors refused they were imprisoned in the Tower of London, from whence they escaped and sought refuge in Westminster Abbey. What followed constituted one of the worst cases of breach of sanctuary in the Middle Ages. Thomas Walsingham described it as 'a sacrilege unknown in our history . . . [and a] pollution of the temple of God'. Fifty armed men, despatched by the Crown, entered the abbey church, captured Shakell and dragged him back to the Tower. Hawley, meanwhile, was discovered hearing mass; he tried to escape but was surrounded in the choir. The abbey monks, it seems, sought to prevent the soldiers from dragging the men from the church, but tempers flared and both Hawley and one of the monks were killed. Walsingham described the perpetrators, the 'agents of sacrilege', as 'heralds of Antichrist . . . [and] raving bacchanals, neither fearing God nor showing reverence to men'.[12] The abbey had to be reconsecrated after the incident. Soon afterwards the count negotiated his son's freedom, but this did not end the matter. Payment for Denia had not been received by 1390 when Maud Hawley, Robert's sister and heir, ceded her rights in the ransom to John Hoton, a London fishmonger. He, in turn, sued Shakell for his share, the latter having argued that the whole ransom now belonged to him. A protracted legal case followed. By the time payment was agreed and made, the principal claimants do not appear to have received more than one-eighth of the £32,000 originally due to them.[13]

Despite such potential dangers, especially in the middle years of the fourteenth century, campaigning offered English soldiers highly profitable opportunities. According to Jean le Bel, after the Anglo-Gascon *chevauchée* of 1355, 'Chevaliers, escuiers, brigants, garchons' were overloaded with 'leurs prisonniers et leurs richesses'.[14] Indeed, it has been suggested that at the height of English military success in the mid-fourteenth century the profits of ransoming paid for the war effort, perhaps several times over. And even greater claims have been made for the financial impact of ransoms – that they revived England's entire post-plague economy.[15] This, however, is a huge exaggeration. Members of the soldiery (famously John Fastolf) might enrich themselves in the ransom business, but the true value of high-ranking prisoners was political not financial.[16] For this reason the English Crown had and enforced rights over all prisoners taken in battle or on campaign and so controlled the time and manner of their release. The Valois kings had similar powers. It may have been Charles V who established the precedent that the king of France could purchase any prisoner, regardless of his ransom value, for 10,000 francs. However, the Valois tended not to enforce their authority as frequently as the Plantagenets. For instance, in the 1420s, at a time when Charles VII had to rely heavily on Scottish support, he did nothing to seek to exercise his rights to prisoners captured by his allies at Baugé. Nonetheless, although they were often content to allow prisoners to remain in private hands, the Valois kings did purchase prisoners of note from their captors on occasion. And unlike lesser prisoners such men might spend many years in captivity.[17]

Prisoners of note provided their captors with considerable political bargaining power, a diplomatic advantage that is reflected in the number of treaties negotiated in exchange for a prisoner's release. The capture of Charles de Blois, for example, led to the treaty of Westminster (1356) and that of Jean le Bon to the treaty of Brétigny (1360).[18] Discussions concerning the release of Charles d'Orléans and other prisoners from Agincourt became a major aspect of peace negotiations in the 1420s and 1430s, although these failed. There were also enormous political implications following from the capture of the Scottish kings, David II and James I. In addition to using a prisoner to gain diplomatic leverage over an enemy, princes might also take the opportunity to seek to change his political allegiance. Charles V did this to some effect with various Gascon lords captured in the 1370s.

No such attempts were made to 'turn' Joan of Arc, captured at Compiègne on 23 May 1430 by troops under the command of Jean, count of Luxembourg, lieutenant of the duke of Burgundy. Her case, of course, was extremely unusual. Having altered the political dynamic and shifted the balance of power in France, Joan was of enormous political value; she was also worth a great deal financially to her initial captor. According to Georges Chastellain, the man in Luxembourg's company who captured her was 'more joyful' at doing so 'than if he had had a king in his hands'.[19] Joan spent the initial part of her captivity in the fortress of Beaulieu-en-Vermandois; she was then transferred to the castle of Beaurevoir, where she spent four months. She clearly recognised the danger. She attempted to escape from both places, on one occasion by jumping from a tower, partly because she knew the Burgundians were likely to sell her and she 'would rather have died than to be in the hands of the English'. Joan asked her 'voices' (Saints Michael, Catherine and Margaret) if she could die and be spared 'the long torment of prison'. Although evidence of her conditions of imprisonment is limited, it was not a comfortable experience. Haimond de Mascy, a Burgundian in Luxembourg's service, noted during the Rehabilitation trial that he had tried 'several times, *playfully*, to touch her breasts'. Famously, Charles VII made no attempt to free her before she was sold to the English on 21 November 1430. The English in turn handed her over to the Inquisition to be tried and finally executed for heresy at Rouen on 30 May 1431.[20]

Prisoners could, therefore, be used to make a political statement, as with Joan, or as leverage in a range of situations. The continued safety of captives might depend on maintaining an agreement. They also offered a means of exchange that might sweeten a deal or prevent one losing too much face when handing over territory or property: a castle, say, might be lost but prisoners were returned in exchange. This last became common practice in the 1370s when the French overturned the territorial settlement agreed at Brétigny, and in the final phases of the war when the Valois reclaimed Normandy and Gascony. Another way in which prisoners might be used for political advantage was to delay an assault on a town or fortress. This occurred in the cases of William Neville and William Bruys. With ten others they were handed over to the French in 1373 as hostages by John,

Lord Neville, who had agreed to surrender the fortress of Brest if it was not relieved within one month. Three years later Edward III and the Privy Council received a petition from the captives' wives. Neville and Bruys were said to be confined 'in a harsh prison, often on point of death ... and their ransom has been [set] so high that it cannot be paid'.[21]

Prisoners might also be exchanged for one another, and because of various vested interests such deals could be very complex. This can be seen in the interlinked cases of Gui, count of Namur, John Randolf, third earl of Moray,[22] and William Montague, earl of Salisbury. The series of events that entwined the destinies of these men began before the outbreak of the Hundred Years War. In August 1335, Moray defeated a force under the command of the count of Namur, a cousin of Queen Philippa, who had brought troops to assist Edward III at Edinburgh. At this time the king was involved in his final expedition to subdue the Bruce faction in Scotland. Gui and his men surrendered to Moray, who agreed to free the count on condition that he took no further part in Edward's campaign. However, while escorting Gui to the border, Moray was himself surprised and captured by an English force. He was held first in York and then transferred between several locations, including Nottingham Castle, Windsor, Winchester and the Tower of London. He remained a prisoner until 1342 when Edward III ransomed him in exchange for William Montague, earl of Salisbury, who had been captured by the French early in 1340.[23]

Montague had served alongside Edward III in the Low Countries in the early exchanges of the Hundred Years War, and he had remained there when the king returned to England to deal with the political and financial fracas that unfolded after the failed siege of Tournai (1340). Montague's presence and that of Robert Ufford, earl of Suffolk, was required to promote Edward's 'provincial strategy', by which he sought to develop a body of support in France, and they both stood as surety for the king's debts to his continental allies. During Edward's absence, however, they launched an attack with Jacques van Artevelde on the French-allied town of Lille. It was a rash assault, one undertaken without infantry support, and as a result they were taken captive and handed over to Philippe VI.[24] The king, it seems, intended to kill Salisbury but was dissuaded by John of Bohemia for reasons of chivalric convention and because of the political leverage he might afford; instead, Salisbury was imprisoned in the Châtelet in Paris, on the right bank of the Seine. Montague was soon released on parole as part of the truce of Esplechin (September 1340), and he negotiated a further settlement with Philippe VI in May 1342 on condition that he never fought in France again. This obligation, however, was overturned in return for the release from English custody of the earl of Moray and other captives.[25]

John Talbot was another who was released only as part of an exchange. He spent four years as a prisoner after his defeat at the battle of Patay (18 June 1429). Faced with an 'unresonable and importable raunceon' (perhaps as much as £25,000), which was far in excess of Talbot's own resources, funds began to be raised in England by public subscription. In addition, the Crown offered £9,000, and a petition was presented in Parliament suggesting an exchange with a French nobleman of high status, the sire de Barbazan.[26] Unfortunately for Talbot, before the exchange could take place, Barbazan was rescued from captivity at Château Gaillard (a castle over-looking the River Seine in Normandy) on 24 January 1430. After the Maid of Orléans's trial began in March 1431, Charles VII exercised the royal prerogative to acquire Talbot as a prisoner of note and it may be that the French king contemplated offering an exchange for Joan of Arc. Clearly, this did not take place: Joan went to the stake and Talbot only secured his freedom after the earl of Salisbury captured Poton de Xaintrailles – Talbot's original captor – at Savignies in August 1431. Even then negotiations were protracted and Talbot only returned to England in the spring of 1433.[27]

Some prisoners, those of royal blood in particular, could be of immense political significance. Two Scottish kings found themselves detained in England in the course of the war: David II (captured at Neville's Cross, 1346 and released in 1357) and James I (held between 1406 and 1424). The extensive periods both spent in captivity had considerable implications for Anglo-Scottish relations and Scottish domestic politics. The consequences of the Scottish defeat in 1346 were especially severe because alongside David II three earls (Duncan of Fife, William of Sutherland, Malcolm of Wigton), William Douglas of Liddesdale and at least 20 major barons were taken prisoner. Another of those taken captive that day, John Graham, earl of Menteith, had earlier sworn allegiance to John Balliol and, consequently, was executed as a traitor. He was hanged, drawn and quartered, and the remains of his body were despatched to four major cities in the north.[28]

David II was taken to York and thence, in the care of Thomas Rokeby, to the Tower of London. The king's capture radically changed the political relationship between England and Scotland, if for two somewhat contra-dictory reasons. First, David's capture effectively neutralised Scotland as a French ally, which was clearly to England's advantage. However, Edward III had denied the legality and validity of the Bruce claim to the Scottish throne for 15 years, offering support to the rival Balliol family instead. In order to benefit from David's capture Edward would have to recognise John Balliol as king. Edward would face a similar situation after the capture of Jean II in 1356.

David II spent 11 years in captivity. The authorities in Scotland, led by Robert Stewart, earl of March, were in no hurry to bring the king home. The negotiations foundered over the size of the ransom and a demand that one of Edward III's sons succeed to the Scottish throne should David die childless.[29] Eventually the parties agreed the treaty of Berwick in October 1357. David's ransom was set at 100,000 marks (£66,666 13s. 4d.) to be paid over 10 years. Financial gain, however, does not appear to have been Edward's main priority; rather he aimed to ensure some political control over David and the other prisoners taken at Neville's Cross. The period of repayment was designed to guarantee a truce, which was of considerable importance given the forthcoming Reims campaign. Edward did not wish, as had happened in 1346, to set sail for France leaving his northern border exposed to Scottish attack.[30]

In fact the treaty of Berwick held for the remainder of David II's reign because repayment did not follow the agreed schedule. It was only with Edward III's death in 1377 that Robert II of Scotland stopped paying his predecessor's ransom. Then, with English dominions under pressure in France and the opportunities afforded by Richard II's minority, the Scottish border magnates once again began raiding English territory and seeking to extend their power southwards. In these circumstances the Auld Alliance now offered the French a chance to press their advantage home. In the 1380s the French admiral Jean de Vienne coordinated a series of attacks on the English coast, culminating in an attempted invasion of England on two fronts – one force marching south from Scotland. In the event it came to nothing and the treaty of Leulingham, which followed soon after (1389), formally included Scotland in an Anglo-French truce for the first time. That, along with the accession of the feeble Robert III in 1390, ensured the beginning of a period of calm in Anglo-Scottish relations.[31]

However, as the century turned, matters did not remain tranquil in Scotland itself. In 1406, in order to escape growing political instability, Robert III sent his heir, the future James I, to France. En route, however, and in violation of the truce with England, he was captured by pirates and sold to Henry IV. Aged just twelve, he began a period of imprisonment that would last almost 18 years. Although James succeeded to the throne in 1407, he remained a captive until 1424, held at different times at the Tower of London, Nottingham Castle, Windsor, Pevensey, Kenilworth and Westminster, and even accompanying Henry V on campaign to France. King Henry sought to use his prisoner in a variety of ways. For example, James's presence among the English army in France brought into question the nature of Scottish support for the Valois. Henry hoped to use his prisoner to fracture the Auld Alliance and to force the Scots into paying a heavy ransom, but he also wished to reshape Scottish attitudes towards England. Consequently, James was well treated during his time in England. The young king was educated in knightly skills – jousting and swordplay. He maintained a small household and was visited regularly by his countrymen. Some of these established political and personal ties with him, which influenced royal policies after his release. James's closest contact before 1424 was with his fellow captive Murdoch Stewart, son and heir of Robert, duke of Albany, Scotland's governor during James's absence. While he made token efforts to secure James's liberation, Albany was much more concerned with obtaining his son's release. When Murdoch was released in 1415, negotiations ground to a complete halt for a period. Like Robert the Steward during David II's captivity, Albany saw no reason to hurry the king's return. Indeed, until 1411 he referred to James in correspondence as 'the son of the late king'.[32]

During his long captivity James wrote *The Kingis Quair* (or *King's Book*). This poem took the form of a recollection in which the narrator looks back over a period of imprisonment and misfortune. It owes a great deal to Boethius's *De Consolatione Philosophiae* and also shows the influence of Chaucer and Gower. Much of the poem follows a dream sequence, dedicated to an appreciation of a lady and the different forms of love, but the author also recounts the story of his capture by the English and his disbelief that Fortune should be so cruel to him. Beasts, birds and fish of the sea had freedom yet he lived in thraldom, 'without comfort, abandoned in sorrow', for nearly 18 years. *The Kingis Quair* reveals James's emotional suffering and feelings of impotence during his captivity. By the end, however, matters take a turn for the better and the author is freed from the sufferings of unrequited love and his captivity.[33]

When James's release eventually took place, it came as a result of English not Scottish action. His amicable relationship with Henry V, who knighted him on St George's Day 1421, created the impression in England that James had a good deal of sympathy for the country. This was further encouraged by his marriage to Cardinal Henry Beaufort's niece, Joan, in February 1424. The Beauforts hoped to make James an ally after his release,

and it was their influence and their willingness to offer terms that forced
Albany to reopen negotiations. Agreements made in 1423 at York and
London, and in March 1424 at Durham, secured James's freedom in return
for a ransom of £40,000 (reduced by 10,000 marks, the value of the new
Scottish queen's dowry).[34]

James's release, however, did not lead to entirely amicable Anglo-Scottish
relations, nor did it end the Auld Alliance. Scots continued to be prominent
in French armies and political ties with France remained strong: in 1436
James's daughter, Margaret, married the dauphin, Louis. (She died childless
in 1445.) But with the growing political ascendancy of Charles VII the
nature of the Auld Alliance did begin to change. As Charles grew in
strength he became less reliant on Scottish support. Meanwhile, although
the Scots continued to take advantage of England's preoccupation with
France, there were no major assaults south of the border while the Hundred
Years War continued.

Although very valuable, neither David II nor James I was the most
important prisoner to fall into English hands during the Hundred Years
War. This accolade falls to Jean II of France, captured at the battle of
Poitiers in 1356. The king, fighting alongside his youngest son, Philippe,
had eventually been overwhelmed by sheer weight of numbers. Denis de
Morbeke, a knight from Artois, was first to lay claim to him, although the
king refused to surrender until he was assured that de Morbeke was, indeed,
a knight. Then Jean gave up one of his gauntlets as a sign of surrender.
However, the king was then grabbed by several other soldiers who wished
to claim him as their own, including a Gascon squire, Bernard de Troys.
The king clearly became concerned for his safety and that of his son at this
stage and is said to have called out 'I am a great enough lord to make you
all rich.' Just as things were getting out of hand the earl of Warwick and
Reginald Cobham, two of the Black Prince's chief lieutenants, forced their
way through the crowd on horseback and drove back the crowds before
conveying their prisoner to the prince.[35] Edward then treated the French
king with all the propriety due to one of his stature:

> The same day of the battle at night the prince made a supper in his
> lodging for the French king and for the most part of the great lords that
> were prisoners ... and always the prince served before the king as
> humbly as he could, and would not sit at the king's board for any desire
> the king could make, but he said he was not sufficient to sit at the table
> with so great a prince.[36]

As this suggests, Jean was by no means alone when taken in 1356; indeed, approximately two thousand of his comrades were also captured. Most of these had no political value and the great majority were soon released after payment or its promise. Seventeen prisoners were, however, considered to be of the utmost importance, and Edward III purchased these men from their captors at a cost of around £65,000. The most important of these by far was Jean II himself.[37]

After a period in Bordeaux in which frantic diplomatic negotiations took place, the Black Prince and his royal captive took ship for England. They landed at Plymouth and made a leisurely progress towards London. They arrived at the capital on 24 May 1357 and were met in the first of a major series of public events designed to emphasise the huge significance of what had happened at Poitiers. A thousand citizens dressed in the livery of the city guilds, and young maidens scattered gold and silver leaf; wine was freely dispensed. At a royal banquet Edward III was seated flanked by the two kings he held in captivity, David II and Jean II. It was the beginning of 'one of the most sustained and purposeful demonstrations of royal magnificence witnessed in medieval England'. King Jean was initially placed under house arrest in the Savoy, Henry of Grosmont's London residence. The Thames was patrolled to ensure he did not escape down the river. While in captivity the king was kept in a suitable style, but his entourage was quickly made aware that this generosity was limited and that many household expenses would have to be paid out of funds sent over from Paris. Edward III made sure that he 'displayed' his 'guest', alongside David II, in a series of public events. In the autumn of 1357 there was a great tournament at Smithfield, and a Garter feast in April 1358 at Windsor. Heralds were despatched to France, Germany and the Low Countries to proclaim the jousts, and many knights travelled to participate.[38]

Jean II's capture radically altered the political climate and the balance of power. The ransom negotiations first produced the treaties of London (8 May 1358 and 24 March 1359), but their extortionate terms were not implemented. Consequently, Edward III led a further expeditionary force to France in 1359. It was one the largest armies to assault France in the Middle Ages and its intention was appropriately grand. Edward marched on Reims with the aim of capturing the coronation city and being crowned king of France. He failed: he could not breach the walls and the citizens of Reims would not open the gates to him. Edward then marched on Paris, again to no avail. He did not have the means to implement an effective siege, and because of the experiences of Crécy and Poitiers the French would not be drawn into battle outside the walls. The result was a peace treaty sealed at Brétigny (8 May 1360). In addition to major territorial concessions and the (theoretical) renunciation of various claims and titles, Jean II's ransom was set at 3,000,000 *écus* (£500,000) – equivalent to five or six times the Crown's annual income from ordinary revenues, wool taxes and the lay and clerical subsidies. This was payable in annual instalments of 400,000 *écus*. As security a large number of hostages were sent to London, including certain princes of the Blood Royal – the dukes of Orléans and Bourbon, Louis d'Anjou and Jean de Berry. These hostages were treated in some style; they were accompanied by their households and found ample time for hunting and gambling. By 1362, however, many had, understandably, become extremely frustrated. Their freedom was conditional on the transfer of certain territories to English control, the payment of the second tranche of the king's ransom and the implementation of the renunciation clauses of the treaty of Brétigny. When it became clear that these terms would not be met for some time, the princes took matters into their own hands and negotiated a separate agreement with Edward III. Jean II felt duty bound to honour this and the princes were transferred to Calais to await the transfer of various securities. While there, however, Louis d'Anjou escaped, breaking faith with Edward, Jean and his fellow captives. As a consequence early in 1364 Jean felt compelled to return to London. It was an extraordinary step, to place himself, once again, in the hands of the king of England, but the French king feared for his honour and judged the risk worth taking to secure a more favourable settlement. Almost immediately he fell ill, and died in April, aged only forty-five. Edward III gave him a splendid funeral in St Paul's Cathedral before his body was returned to France for burial in Saint-Denis.[39]

Jean II's remarkable behaviour in returning voluntarily into potential captivity in England indicates the significance of honour and, by extension, of the chivalric ethic in matters of ransoming and prisoners of war. Its influence over the behaviour of the knightly community is evident throughout the war and especially in the pages of certain chroniclers. Jean Froissart's account of the siege of Caen in 1346 is a case in point:

> the Constable [the Count of Eu and Guines] and the Count of Tancarville . . . could see the battle was already lost. The English were now among them, killing as they liked without mercy . . . Looking out from the gate-tower where they had taken refuge and seeing the truly horrible carnage which was taking place in the street, the Constable and the Count began to fear that they might be drawn into it and fall into

the hands of archers who did not know who they were. While they were watching the massacre with dismay they caught sight of a gallant English knight called Sir Thomas Holand ... They recognised him because they had campaigned together in Granada and Prussia ... They were much relieved and called out to him ... On hearing his own name the knight stopped asked: 'Who are you sirs, who seem to know me?' They gave their names and said ... 'Come to us and make us your prisoners.' When he heard this Sir Thomas was delighted, not only because he could save their lives but also because their capture meant an excellent day's work and a fine haul of valuable prisoners.[40]

Froissart's account shows the close links that existed between Europe's military elite, certainly in the early stages of the Hundred Years War. However, it also reveals the growing strains placed on the ransom system as military tactics changed and fewer opportunities remained to capture a defeated opponent. Froissart described those who refused to take prisoners at the sack of Caen as 'gens sans pité',[41] but their behaviour was not so unusual and was becoming less so. Nonetheless, there are many examples of 'proper' treatment being meted out to prisoners of war. It is evident in an account of a duel that took place during the siege/sack of Limoges (1370). In the course of what was undoubtedly a brutal attack, however exaggerated by Froissart, John of Gaunt, duke of Lancaster, fought a spirited duel with a French knight, Sir Jean de Villemur. Eventually Villemur and his companions were forced to submit to Gaunt with the words: 'Sirs we are yours, you have beaten us. Treat us according to the law of arms.' 'By God, Sir John,' said the duke of Lancaster, 'we would never dream of doing anything else. We accept you as our prisoners.'[42]

Very similar attitudes can be seen at work in an incident which took place in the early 1430s. Then one Louis Bournel had been taken captive by Duke Phillippe the Good of Burgundy. He was well treated, kept in comfortable surroundings, and so he enjoyed accommodation appropriate to his station 'because he was a knight and a man of public standing.' Such treatment complied with chivalric convention but was not uncondi- tional − it would continue only so as long as he behaved 'properly' and followed the duke's instructions.[43]

The law of arms to which Sir Jean de Villemur appealed had become bound up with the chivalric ethic and it ensured ransoming became a key feature of chivalry. It mitigated the perils of the battlefield for those to whom it applied, but it only ever applied to the chivalrous – to those worth ransoming, as Anthoine of Burgundy, duke of Brabant, discovered to his cost at Agincourt. The duke was captured and died anonymously in the slaughter of prisoners because he wore the armour of one of his chamberlains and had not disclosed his identity, hoping to secure a low ransom.[44] A general valuation of soldiers' worth can be seen at the surrender of Pont-Audemer of 1449. Jean, count of Dunois, Charles VII's lieutenant, set the ransom of the English captain of the fortified town at 2,000 écus, that of each man-at-arms at 30 écus, and that of each archer at 12 écus.[45] However, the life of a regular soldier was never entirely safe when he fell into enemy hands. It was not at all uncommon for only the officers to be ransomed and the rest of the captured troops put to the sword. Often this depended on military circumstances and it was sometimes impossible or imprudent to take large numbers of regular soldiers captive. Nonetheless, as the war drew on, the ransom values of the lesser soldiery became increasingly standardised. This was an important development in the whole business of ransoming – its extension to the lower echelons of the military hierarchy. A scale of ransom prices for those below the elite became systematised. Alongside this process the costs associated with the maintenance of a prisoner (board and lodging) became fixed. Known as *les marz*, this was usually calculated as worth about a fifth of the ransom itself.[46]

For the aristocratic or valuable prisoner, convention dictated that their living conditions should not be too onerous, nor should their period of captivity be particularly extended, especially as they might be permitted to substitute a hostage for their own person. Such protocols, however, were often subject to political priorities and military realities. Over the course of the war the social composition of armies changed as the proportion of infantry and missile troops rose. As knights became less numerous on the battlefield, the manner in which the chivalric ethic operated altered: as noted above, when the count of Eu faced an English assault on Caen in 1346, the particular danger he faced was that he might fall into the hands of archers who did not recognise him. In addition, the need to maintain discipline in the ranks during a battle lessened the opportunities to take prisoners. In such circumstances it became more common to take no prisoners at all, at least until the fighting was done. The Flemish took no captives at Courtrai; the Swiss became renowned for offering no quarter to a defeated enemy.[47] The English also valued military cohesion more than chivalric convention. Although the Parisian Bourgeois suggested it was much better to be captured by the English than the French, the 'chivalrous' Edward III, founder of the Order of the Garter, had 100 Scottish prisoners beheaded on the morning after Halidon Hill.[48] At Crécy he ordered, on pain of death, that no one was to break ranks without his leave to pillage or take prisoners. This was necessary for tactical reasons but also a response to the deployment of the French war banner, the *Oriflamme*. The banner was a declaration of *guerre mortelle* – a fight to the death with no quarter given.[49] This also happened at Poitiers where 'Sire Geoffrey de Charny bore the scarlet standard, which is the token of Death, for the French king had issued an order that the life of no Englishman was to be spared except that of the prince himself.'[50] Although a ransom spree did take place in the later stages of the battle, the Black Prince had issued orders to try and ensure discipline in the ranks.[51] Charny himself was also well aware of the problems created by those men-at-arms who were 'too eager for plunder': they put themselves and their fellows at risk, their greed could cause disunity, and in battle 'they are more anxious to safeguard their captives and their booty than to help bring the battle to a good conclusion. And it may be that a battle can be lost in this way.'[52]

The changing military climate goes some way to explaining the lack of criticism that followed the slaughter of the French prisoners at Agincourt. Perhaps because it was widely believed that such a notable victory could not have been achieved without God's blessing, it would have been wrong to criticise the means of divine intervention. Perhaps such criticism as was voiced became submerged beneath the welter of self-recrimination that gripped France in the aftermath of the battle.[53] The English author of the *Gesta Henrici Quinti* described the event in the following, somewhat perfunctory terms:

But then . . . because of what wrathfulness on God's part no one knows, a shout went up that the enemy's mounted rearguard . . . were re-establishing their position and line of battle in order to launch an attack on us, few and weary as we were. And immediately, regardless of distinction of person, the prisoners, save for the dukes of Orléans and Bourbon, certain other illustrious men who were in the king's battle [division], and a few others, were killed by the swords either of their captors or of others following after, lest they should involve us in utter disaster in the fighting that would ensue.[54]

Nonetheless, the chivalric ethic continued to influence behaviour throughout the war and it could override political priorities in certain instances. The capture of Bertrand du Guesclin at the battle of Nájera (1367) is a vivid example of this. At this stage of his career du Guesclin was rising in Charles V's service and he had already gained a formidable military reputation, despite his defeat and capture at Auray in 1364. In 1367 he was purchased by Edward the Black Prince from his initial captor, Thomas Cheyne, and held for several months in Bordeaux without being offered terms for his release. The story of du Guesclin's ransom has been much embellished, and the details of the affair differ between the versions given by his biographer, Cuvelier, by Jean Froissart and by a number of other chivalric chroniclers; but it remains instructive nonetheless. Some accounts tell that du Guesclin accused the prince of cowardice, suggesting he was afraid to ransom him. The slight, according to Cuvelier, so affronted the prince that he immediately offered to release the future constable of France without charge – indeed, he offered to pay him 10,000 florins to re-equip himself – if in return he would swear not to take up arms again against the prince, his children or Pedro of Castile in whose name the prince had fought at Nájera. Du Guesclin refused these terms, at which Edward stated he should name his own price. Du Guesclin placed this at a staggering 100,000 francs (about £18,666). The Prince immediately remitted 40,000 francs and sent him back to France to find the remainder. Du Guesclin boasted that if King Charles and Enrique of Trastamara could not find the money, 'There is not a spinster in all of France/But would earn my ransom by her spinning.'[55] Du Guesclin was soon active again at the head of Charles V's armies, successfully recapturing the territory the French had ceded to England through the treaty of Brétigny and overrunning much of Aquitaine, which the Black Prince governed.

Such behaviour was by no means universal. During the reconquest of Aquitaine Charles the Wise chose not to bow to chivalric convention. Owen of Wales (Owain Lawgoc/Owain ap Thomas ap Rhodri, d.1378), a Welsh mercenary in Valois service, captured Jean de Grailly, captal de Buch (*dép* Gironde), a Gascon noble 'whom the French feared the most', at Soubise near the mouth of the Charente on 23 August 1372. De Grailly was never released. Charles V offered him numerous valuable incentives in return for his allegiance, but he refused them all. In 1374 Edward III purchased Waleran of Luxemburg, count of St Pol, in order to try and engineer an exchange for de Grailly, but Charles refused the deal and de Grailly died in captivity.[56] Similarly, for political reasons Henry V deliberately blocked all negotiations over the ransom of Charles d'Orléans. Both examples demonstrate the friction between obligations of honour and the pragmatism of national self-interest.

Chivalric convention also suggested that ransom demands should not be financially crippling (perhaps a maximum of three times a prisoner's annual income), but clearly this was not always the case. In reality, an earl or a count would rarely secure his freedom for less than £5,000, an annual income that only the wealthiest enjoyed. A man's reputation, his social and political connections, as well as his apparent wealth, were all taken into account when setting a ransom, as were the costs incurred during his captivity. Consequently, there was little uniformity when setting the ransoms of the elite, especially as political and military circumstances might also influence the amount demanded. Guillaume de Châteauvillain, a Burgundian nobleman, faced financial ruin when forced to sell a great deal of land to pay his ransom in 1430. This had been fixed initially at 22,000 crowns (approx. £5,000), but his expenses in prison, the cost of messengers and his responsibility for other captives meant that this soon rose to 31,000 crowns (£7,000).[57]

Because of such excessive ransoms kings and commanders on all sides often received petitions requesting assistance, and they often felt obliged to make some contribution.[58] Robert Langton, warden of Calais castle, in a petition of 1357, that asserted he was forced to sell all his lands, property and other goods to pay a ransom. The case was especially unfortunate because while he had travelled to England to collect the money his wife and son had been murdered.[59] In 1380, Ralph Lord Greystoke, a warden of the Scottish March and Roxburgh Castle, pleaded with John of Gaunt, in his capacity as the king's lieutenant in the Scottish Marches, for assistance after he had been seized by George Dunbar, the Scottish earl of March, and put to a 'heavy' ransom (1,000 marks): one 'so heavy', he claimed, 'that it w[ould] ruin him forever' and 'utterly destroy' him.[60] In 1426 Georges de la Trémoïlle (captured at Agincourt) received the lordship of Melle in Poitou from Charles VII in order to defray his ransom expenses.[61] In the final exchanges of the war, Sir Richard Frogenhale petitioned Henry VI for assistance in paying a ransom, having been captured while in service in France. He had already received contributions from Edmund Beaufort, earl of Somerset, and, interestingly, 'the gentlemen of Kent'. However, he had not been able to raise the remaining sum, meaning he would be forced to hand himself over to his captors again unless he received help.[62] The responsibility of a commander to assist with ransom expenses might have to be met in difficult circumstances. René d'Anjou, despite searching for the means to pay his own ransom after his defeat at the battle of Bulgnéville (Lorraine) in 1431, felt compelled to assist Jean de Rodemack who had also been taken prisoner.[63]

Soldiers were not the only group at risk of being captured during the Hundred Years War. Whole communities in France were held to ransom and forced to pay *patis* to mercenaries and troops of all sides. Merchants could also be taken captive. This was a concern not only to the individuals involved but also to governments because of the impact on trade. A petition made in the English Parliament of January 1390 noted the threat to the cloth trade that could result from merchants being taken prisoner.[64] The case of John Spencer, a London mercer, was far from unique. He sought restitution after having taken advantage of a safe conduct that Jean de Montfort offered to all merchants in 1371 to trade in the duchy of Brittany. Despite this Spencer had been captured close to La Roche-Maurice, near Brest; his goods were stolen, he spent nearly a year in prison and he was forced to pay a substantial ransom.[65]

Just as conventions regarding capture and the size of ransoms varied widely, so too did the conditions in which prisoners of war could be held captive. The majority of those taken prisoner were soon given parole in order to collect their ransoms and did not endure long periods of incarceration. The nature of the Hundred Years War, however, could create very difficult circumstances for a captive. Political conditions might mean that he was adjudged a criminal and executed rather than held as a prisoner of war. Also, the spread of undisciplined mercenary activity ensured that those captured by such men might receive treatment which fell far short of accepted 'chivalric' standards. Such standards demanded that captives be kept in a style appropriate to their rank. Capture should not be demeaning; as Charny noted in his *Livre de chevalerie (Book of Chivalry)*, 'Does not God show you great mercy if you are taken prisoner honourably, praised by friends and enemies?'[66] This, however, was not always the case. Following the Castilian victory over the English fleet at the battle of La Rochelle (23 June 1372), the *Chronique des quatre premiers Valois* describes how the prisoners were kept like dogs on a leash (*encoupples comme chiens en lesse en une corde*),[67] with the English commander, John Hastings, earl of Pembroke (1347–75), supposedly held in irons. Soon after the battle, the king of Castile, Enrique da Trastamara, sold Hastings to Bertrand du Guesclin, then constable of France, in return for certain Castilian estates. The subsequent negotiations with England were protracted: du Guesclin demanded

120,000 francs, a substantial proportion of which was to be paid before the earl would be released. Despite Hastings's royal connections little progress was made until early 1375; then, while du Guesclin was taking his prisoner from Paris to Calais, the earl died, on 16 April 1375. Walsingham recounts this happened because the Castilians had 'treated [him] monstrously'.[68]

Such examples, sadly, do not seem to be unusual. Some of those taken by Henry V at Harfleur were still being held seven years later in Fleet prison and were reduced to begging for food.[69] Captives might even be tortured in order to get them to agree to the most generous terms. Fettering, feeding on bread and water, beatings and even mutilations were not unknown. A case brought before the Châtelet of Paris in 1392 involved a torturer specifically employed to beat prisoners to force them to agree to the largest possible ransom. Perhaps the most horrific example was that of Henry Gencian, who during ten months of captivity in the 'care' of François de la Palu, lord of Varambon, had some of his teeth knocked out, his nose pierced like a bull, was beaten regularly and even forced, naked, into a pit full of snakes.[70]

A less extreme case is that of Jean d'Angoulême (Charles d'Orléans's brother, who, aged eight, had been used to guarantee a treaty made between the Armagnac faction and Thomas, duke of Clarence, at Buzançais on 14 November 1412). He remained in captivity in England until 1445. After Clarence's death at the battle of Baugé in 1421, Jean was given into the keeping of Margaret Beaufort (née Holland), Clarence's widow, and his living conditions appear to have deteriorated. Held at Maxey Castle (Northamptonshire), he complained he was not provided with enough to eat, and to support him his brother felt compelled to send him the proceeds of the *gabelle* (salt tax) in Orléans.[71]

Over the course of the conflict the position of prisoners of war shifted according to political circumstances. The ransom of prisoners in Lancastrian Normandy and the *pays de conquête* created particular problems for the English administration. Norman captives often paid their ransoms with the help of friends or family within the duchy of Normandy. This was intolerable, as these relatives and connections were now English subjects. Essentially, French prisoners were regaining their freedom with the assistance of subjects of the English Crown. In order to prevent this, Henry V forbade the issue of any safe conducts to Norman prisoners. Instead, they were to be handed over directly to the authorities – their captor would receive a third of the ransom. This situation changed somewhat when the treaty of Troyes was sealed in 1420 after which any French prisoner of war could be considered guilty of *lèse-majesté* and executed, although in practice this was very rare. Nonetheless, in English Normandy the distinction between a criminal and a prisoner of war became very uncertain.[72]

By comparison Thomas Gray had the leisure and means to begin his *Scalacronica* while held in Edinburgh Castle (1355–56). Gray was one of a number of notable authors who wrote in prison – a tradition Boethius fixed in the medieval mind when he wrote the *De Consolatione of Philosophiae* circa 524. During Gray's year in captivity he had access to Scottish sources and records, from Edinburgh castle's library and perhaps that at Holyrood Abbey.[73] Similarly, although long and psychologically onerous, Charles d'Orléans's imprisonment was physically comfortable, indeed, often luxurious. Having escaped the massacre of prisoners at Agincourt, Charles spent the next 25 years as a prisoner in England. He was of course not the only captive from Agincourt: a number of important individuals survived the slaughter, including Jean, duke of Bourbon, Charles d'Artois, count of Eu, Louis of Bourbon, count of Vendôme, Artur de Richemont and Jean le Maingre (Boucicaut II).[74] On returning from France Henry V made a genuine effort to ensure his prisoners' comfort and general well-being: he issued orders for the purchase of fine furnishings and bedding for their accommodation in and around London (at Westminster, Windsor,[75] the Tower of London and Eltham). Safe-conducts were also prepared for members of the captives' households in order that they might better administer their affairs and so personal possessions could be brought from France. While the duke of Bourbon asked for four falconers, Charles d'Orléans had nearly a hundred books delivered, including medical works and a large number of religious volumes – Bibles, breviaries, psalters, missals, Books of Hours, Lives of the saints, works by Sts Augustine, Gregory and Jerome.[76] Over the course of his captivity the duke acquired and commissioned many more books and built up a large library that included further devotional and theological writings, scientific and medical works, poetry and chronicles in both Latin and French.

During his captivity Charles d'Orléans not only read but wrote extensively. He became a noted poet and author, writing in both French and English. Some of his English works, influenced by Chaucer and other native poets, are now widely considered as among the finest English vernacular poetry of the first half of the fifteenth century. Appropriately, the poems the duke wrote in captivity (123 *ballades* and 89 *chansons*) have come to be known as *Le livre de prison*.[77] Twin themes emerge in his

writing – his longing for peace and for France. Ballade LXXV (written
about May 1433, after some 18 years in captivity) includes the verse:

Peace is a treasure one cannot praise too much;
I hate war, and should esteem it nothing at all;
It has hindered me a long time, rightly or wrongly,
From seeing France that my heart must love.

The duke endured such an extraordinarily extended captivity because of his
political significance. He was a central figure in the Armagnac-Burgundian
conflict, and hence became a vital element in the maintenance of England's
alliance with Burgundy. Furthermore, for a while he was second in line to
the French throne, while his half-brother, Jean, the Bastard of Orléans,
later comte de Dunois (1402–68), became a major figure in the dauphin's
retinue. Charles's son-in-law, Jean d'Alençon (1409–76), who was captured
aged fifteen at the battle of Verneuil in 1424, was also of great political
importance.[78] Therefore, during the first decade of his captivity, Charles's
political value was enormous, and although Henry V and his successors
ensured his comfort they also exploited that value.[79]

On 1 June 1417, as the king prepared for his second Normandy
campaign, Charles was moved from London into the custody of Robert
Waterton (d.1425), constable of Pontefract Castle (Yorkshire). Waterton
had great experience in such matters although his charges had not all ended
well; he had been Richard II's gaoler after the king's deposition and in 1399
the king had died in his care. In addition to Charles d'Orléans, Waterton
also took charge of Artur de Richemont, the count of Eu, and Marshal
Boucicaut. Pontefract was one of the largest castles in Yorkshire and
Waterton seems to have been a genial host: Charles was permitted to go
hunting and he spent time with Waterton's family at their home at Methley.
In return he was a generous guest. Records show he gave a number of gifts
to Waterton's wife and children. Restrictions, however, began to be placed
on Charles's freedom of action as fears grew of Scottish intervention,
especially after the formation of the Anglo-Burgundian alliance. At this
stage, although Waterton remained in royal favour he was relieved of his
most valuable charge. Charles passed into the care of Nicholas Montgomery
at Tutbury (Staffordshire) and then, soon after, to Thomas Burton, warden
of Fotheringhay (Northamptonshire), who also took responsibility for
Richemont, Eu and Boucicaut. Henry V continued to be concerned
about the possibility of his French prisoners contacting and plotting with

the steward of Scotland, Murdoch Stewart, duke of Albany (c.1362–1425). This seems unlikely in Charles's case, as for much of this time he appears to have been thoroughly absorbed with an array of financial problems, mainly concerned with raising the ransom for his brother, Jean of Angoulême.[80]

Circumstances again changed in 1420 with the completion of the treaty of Troyes. At this point some of Henry V's prisoners were freed (including Richemont),[81] and the duke of Bourbon received permission to travel to Dieppe to negotiate terms for his own freedom. But Henry prohibited the release of Charles d'Orléans while he could still prove politically valuable. This stipulation was repeated in the king's will of 1421 and it also extended to the count of Eu. Briefly, after the battle of Baugé in March of that year, in which the earls of Somerset (John Beaufort, 1404–44) and Huntingdon (John Holland) were captured, there seemed to be hope for the release of the duke of Orléans as part of an exchange, but this came to nothing. Holland, having been captured by the Scottish knight John Sibbald, spent five years in captivity in Anjou. Like Charles d'Orléans he faced daunting financial obstacles in paying his ransom and it took until 1426 before his stepfather, Sir John Cornwall, negotiated an exchange for the count of Vendôme (another of those captured at Agincourt). Huntingdon later claimed his captivity cost him 20,000 marks.[82]

With Henry V's death in 1422 and the continuing hostilities with the dauphin, the prospects for the release of Charles d'Orléans became ever more remote: by December he had passed into the custody of Sir Thomas Comberworth and was kept mostly at Bolingbroke Castle (Lincolnshire). His financial circumstances also grew increasingly bleak. First, because of the considerable costs involved in keeping the dukes of Bourbon and Orléans in captivity, the Privy Council decided in January 1424 that the captives should pay their own expenses. No information exists regarding how the new financial arrangements worked, although to lessen the pain of this Charles was permitted to have wine sent over from his own lands duty-free, which he immediately did.[83] Then in the second half of the decade the fighting in France spread to Charles's own lands: the devastation of his property had major financial implications.

Thereafter Charles d'Orléans was placed in the care of a succession of keepers. In 1429 he became the responsibility of Sir John Cornwall at Ampthill (Bedfordshire). In August 1432 he was entrusted to William de la Pole, earl of Suffolk, and his wife, Alice Chaucer, until in 1436 Charles was transferred to Sir Reginald Cobham at Starborough (Surrey). His final keeper, from 1438, was John, first Baron Stourton, who lived at Stourton in Wiltshire.

In this period, however, as the fortunes of war turned against the English, Charles's chances of freedom improved. He began to act as both a negotiator and as a subject for negotiation. In October 1433 he accompanied the earl of Suffolk to peace talks at Calais; in 1434 he was licensed to enter into negotiations with other French princes. In 1435 he returned to Calais but did not attend the Congress of Arras (where his release was debated), although he did hold discussions with Isabella, duchess of Burgundy, which produced proposals for a truce. In 1439 he was once again in Calais, playing a supporting role in ultimately abortive negotiations. By this time, with the French ever more successful militarily, the duke was being seen as an important agent for peace. However, his release remained strenuously opposed by various factions in England led by Humphrey, duke of Gloucester, who argued for the necessity of upholding Henry V's will and last wishes. Gloucester, eventually, was overruled by Cardinal Beaufort and by Henry VI himself, who ultimately took the decision to free the duke of Orléans. On 2 July 1440 the price of Charles's freedom was set at 100,000 nobles (£33,333), of which 40,000 (£13,333) were to be paid at once. The duke was also charged to exert all his influence to secure peace between England and France. The money was raised by contributions levied throughout France, and on 5 November Charles crossed to Calais. He was finally freed at Gravelines on 12 November, having solemnly sworn to observe the terms of his release.[84]

Ransoming, then, was deeply significant during the Hundred Years War; an integral element of the chivalric ethic and crucial to a number of vital political and diplomatic events, it also influenced the lives of ordinary soldiers. The increasing professionalisation of military activity had a major impact on the process of ransoming during this period. Changes in recruitment, strategy, tactics, payment and weaponry brought new pressures and possibilities. Changes in political circumstances also had a great effect on the position of prisoners of war – in certain conditions one might be adjudged a prisoner of war and in others a criminal. Efforts were made to systematise the process and to assert royal rights over those taken captive in the Anglo-French wars. Because of the changing nature of the battlefield, both Plantagenets and Valois established rules by which they could acquire prisoners of note or public standing.

Charles d'Orléans was one of the most significant of these prisoners. The chief legacy of his long incarceration were his writings. His literary career would have been impossible had he not been captured. In several ways his works of prose and poetry run counter to various cultural trends. In particular his remarkable facility with English was becoming uncommon among his countrymen, just as increasing numbers of Englishmen were struggling with French. His love for his homeland was, however, much more representative. Over the course of the Hundred Years War and as a direct result of the Anglo-French conflict a greater sense of national consciousness emerged on both sides of the Channel. As the war drew to a close an individual's conception of their political, cultural and national identity became increasingly defined.

CHAPTER 10

National Identities
ST GEORGE AND *LA MÈRE FRANCE*
1449

Thus King Charles of France . . . had by the Grace of God, and also by the skill and wisdom of his knights and counsellors and soldiers of all ranks, regained his duchy of Normandy which had been occupied . . . by his ancient enemies the English. He had placed the whole province under his power, and made provision for new government, and for police and military garrisons . . . all the while trusting in the grace and mercy of the King of Kings, who wills that every man should have his own, as it is written in a passage in Saint Matthew: 'Render unto Caesar the things which are Caesar's; and unto God the things which are God's'. Because of this he resolved to march into Guyenne, which had been occupied by the English since time immemorial . . . The nobles and people of that land have always been rebellious against the crown of France . . . although it forms part of the kingdom of France.[1]
Enguerrand de Monstrelet, *La Chronique*

When Charles VII invaded Normandy on 31 July 1449, he initiated the final act of the Hundred Years War. In March he had been provided with an excellent excuse for the invasion when the English-allied mercenary captain François de Surienne (known as 'L'Aragonais') launched an attack on the Breton *bastide* (fortified town) of Fougères, near the Norman border. Charles took the opportunity willingly, but his main concern at this stage of the war was political not military, not a concern for a *bastide* in Brittany but with the promotion of Valois authority throughout the realm. The king's main priority by 1449 was with his own people not with the English, and his chief aim to ensure the loyalty of his greater nobles, especially the Princes of the Blood. In a letter to the king of Castile and Leon dated 2 April 1451, Charles claimed he had been forced to take action in 1449 because the English had 'attempted by certain means to withdraw and attribute to themselves the subjection and obedience of our nephew of Brittany and of his lands and duchy, although, in truth, as is well known, he is our man, vassal and subject'.[2] Such an act, far more significant than the loss of a mere *bastide*, could not be countenanced. The invasion of Normandy, therefore, offered the king a chance to make a major demonstration of his power within his growing nation, and to offer decisive evidence of his sovereignty. It was a happy coincidence that the attack on Fougères also provided Charles with a reason to begin the series of campaigns that would end the Hundred Years War and see English territorial holdings in France reduced to nothing more than the port of Calais.

In many ways it is surprising that hostilities had not resumed before 1449. After the truce of Tours had been concluded on 28 May 1444, divisions became increasingly obvious in the English camp as Henry VI actively (and sometimes independently) pursued a peace policy with France. He agreed to the surrender of the county of Maine in December 1445, although this did not take place until 1448. English attention thereafter focused on the defence of Normandy, and the king even suggested that his claim to the French Crown might be traded for sovereign control of the duchy. At the same time various initiatives were undertaken to shore up the deteriorating English position. In particular, support was sought within France; steps were taken to fill the political void that had been left in December 1435, when Philippe the Good and Charles VII had made peace and sealed the treaty of Arras. To this end the English courted François I, duke of Brittany, and his brother, Gilles de Champtacé. Long after the conclusion of the Blois–Montfort civil war in 1364, dukes of Brittany had sought to avoid taking sides in the Hundred Years War, and François had maintained a studied neutrality when possible. Gilles, however, had wider ambitions, and he had spent the years 1432–34 in Henry VI's household, becoming close friends with the king.[3] When François paid homage to Charles VII in March 1446, divisions, already evident, widened in the ducal family, bringing about the arrest of Gilles in June – an act that appalled Henry. The English attack on Fougères, therefore, formed part of an extensive and intricate plan that aimed to pressurise Brittany into an alliance with England, free Gilles and force François to distance himself politically from Charles VII. In the event, it failed disastrously and gave Charles the opportunity to stamp his authority and re-establish his 'good lordship' throughout the realm.[4] Hence, the final phase of the Hundred Years War, like the first, would be a struggle for sovereignty – one to determine the extent and depth of the king of France's power within his realm.

Charles VII secured Brittany's allegiance swiftly and used the opportunity the English attack afforded to continue his campaign: Normandy and Gascony capitulated in short order in the face of bribery, political coercion and military force. Normandy was overrun within a year by French armies advancing on three fronts: Rouen surrendered on 10 November 1449; English reinforcements were crushed at Formigny on 15 April 1450; the capture of Caen (24 June) and Cherbourg (12 August) completed the conquest. In the summer of the following year, Charles sent an army south to Gascony under the command of Jean de Dunois (the 'Bastard' of Orléans, Charles d'Orléans's half-brother): Bordeaux and Bayonne submitted on 12 August and 20 August respectively. Henry VI's response – a paltry gesture of defiance – was, on 2 September 1452, to appoint John Talbot, earl of Shrewsbury, his lieutenant in Gascony. The French had expected an attack on Normandy and with their forces divided, on 23 October Talbot managed to recapture Bordeaux with the aid of Gascons loyal to England, or at least those preferring the distant government of London to a claustrophobic Valois presence. Over the next two months he re-established English control in the Bordelais, Médoc and Entre-deux-Mers. Talbot had, however, only delayed the inevitable; despite receiving reinforcements he and his army were destroyed by Jean Bureau's artillery at the battle of Castillon (17 July 1453), which marked the end of the Hundred Years War.[5]

Castillon was proclaimed a national victory, achieved through a national effort, and undoubtedly it proved to be a victory that enhanced an already flourishing sense of national identity. For Enguerrand de Monstrelet (quoted above) Charles VII triumphed over his 'ancient enemies' because he moulded the military potential of France into a powerful fighting force with the help and advice of wise representatives of the body politic. His conquests, underpinned in reality by new political, administrative and governmental initiatives, were seen as divinely inspired; they brought about the extension of Valois kingship within France to a point approaching its 'natural' geographical frontiers. And yet when Charles had turned, finally, to Gascony, it was not to liberate but to (re)conquer a duchy 'occupied by the English since time immemorial', whose people 'have always been rebellious against the crown of France'. Monstrelet gives a clear indication of the growth of a sense of French national identity over the course of the Hundred Years War, while simultaneously recognising some of the limitations of that identity. Even in 1453, many 'Frenchmen' had no wish to be governed from Paris, and Gascon exiles continued to exercise influence at the English court.[6]

The Hundred Years War had, nonetheless, reshaped both France and England substantially, and created or 'imagined' them into a new form – throughout the kingdom Frenchmen and women could now start to imagine themselves as part of a single community.[7] Indeed, France (herself) was now personified. The poet and political writer Alain Chartier, driven from his native Bayeux and then from Paris by the English invasion of 1417–20, coined the term *la mère France* (Mother France) in 1422. In his *Quadrilogue invectif* that same maternal figure entreats nobility, commons and clergy to unite in their efforts to save her from invasion and civil war. In a similar fashion St George emerged in the course of the struggle as England's patron saint and the very image of the nation. In 1351 it was said that 'the English nation ... call upon [St George], as being their special patron, particularly in war'.[8] By the end of the war men were willing to fight and die for those images and what they represented. Dying for one's country became redemptive. For some it was an almost Christ-like sacrifice, for others service in the name and for the honour of the nation brought with it a place in heaven, and glory and gratitude on earth. Furthermore, because the war had reshaped the institutions of government – the administrative and bureaucratic systems of the state – one could now serve the nation in many ways, not only on the battlefield. St George and *la mère France* also represented those who served the nation in Parliament or the Estates General, in the Exchequer and the *chambre des comptes*. These state institutions, in turn, helped determine the parameters of the nation. Its borders – geographical, cultural, social and political – were laid out much more clearly over the course of the war, and this process enshrined the differences between England and France.

Writing in various works in the aftermath of the fall of Bordeaux, Sir John Fortescue (Chief Justice of the King's Bench since 1442) emphasised what he saw as the clear constitutional differences between England and France. In particular, he concentrated on the superiority, as he saw it, of an English limited monarchy (*dominum politicum et regale*) over French 'absolute' kingship (*dominum regale*). English kings, unlike those in France, could not make laws or impose taxes without the consent of Parliament, but Fortescue argued that their power was at least the equal of their Valois counterparts because it was augmented with the support of the community of the realm. Writing, in part, as a response to such French polemicists as Jean de Montreuil and Jean Juvénal des Ursins, Fortescue described French justice as tyrannical, an arbitrary tool in the king's hands, not subject to the proper English procedures. As a result, he believed that in France, 'as soon as a man is adjudged to be guilty according to the king's conscience, he is thrust into a sack without any form of trial and is thrown into a river at night and drowned: a great many more men die in this way than stand convicted by due process of law.'[9]

Whether misguided, mischievous or mendacious, Fortescue's impression of French law, a defining criterion of French society, is instructive. The Hundred Years War emphasised and created differences between the two nations that soon became caricatured and exaggerated. By the end of the conflict both countries faced – or claimed they faced – a threat not only to their political integrity but also to a newly fashioned sense of national identity. Frenchmen and Englishmen, collectively, thought of themselves differently, and as very different from each other, due to the duration and nature of the Hundred Years War.

The evidence for such a development is considerable: a welter of propaganda proclaimed the justice of each side's cause, some of it the product of an intense intellectual debate between scholars and churchmen. Cultural slurs were exchanged with increasing frequency and vehemence; national stereotypes hardened. Over the previous hundred years the English had killed more Christians than any other people, according to Jean de Montreuil in about 1411. They wanted nothing more than to destroy the kingdom for which they had only abhorrence and hatred.[10] Both sides employed cartography to represent their national borders; patron saints embodied the nation on earth (as in heaven); and the church(es) disseminated the message of the state to the people. The appeal to serve the nation and to act for the common good became familiar refrains. The lower ranks of society began to invest in war personally, as taxpayers and as soldiers in national service.[11] The population at large became investors in a national enterprise.

Because of this, in 1450 'men [in England] began to protest about the sudden and complete loss of the king's lands in France'.[12] This politicisation resulted from the great effort both sides expended to justify new and near permanent levels of taxation. Those who paid their taxes expected their money to be used wisely and to good effect. In the phase of the war from 1340 to 1360, English military success had been proclaimed throughout the country, which ensured that Edward III's aspirations became those of the English political 'class' as a whole, and this group grew in size and social diversity as a consequence of the conflict and the national mobilisation of men and resources. The English population became accustomed to military success in this period, which meant that later failures could not easily be explained. Meanwhile in France similar processes were at work, galvanised not by victory but by devastation and occupation. After a time the sheer length of the conflict also began to influence attitudes; mutual antipathy became the normal state of affairs. And a range of other factors also played their part: the growth of chivalric and military orders, the central role of the monarchy and the importance of language, especially the increasing use of the vernacular, contributed a great deal to new and enhanced concepts of nationhood.

Therefore the Hundred Years War intensified and redefined a sense of national identity in England and France, but it did not create those identities *ex nihilo*. A French identity had been tied closely to the growth of royal authority over a long period, alongside a developing belief in the people's status as members of God's most favoured nation. The reality and theory of Capetian power had extended in breadth and depth from, perhaps, the reign of Louis VI, 'the Fat' (1108–37), whose deeds and dynasty were praised and commemorated by successive authors in the abbey of Saint-Denis from the time of Abbot Suger (c.1081–1151) onwards. Saint-Denis was the wellspring for the mythology of French royal power: home to the coronation regalia, the place in which the Capetians and their Valois successors were furnished with a historiographical foundation, polemical support and, most importantly, a sacral lustre. This spiritual celebrity, in turn, was conferred upon the members of the French nation – the most Christian people of the most Christian king. In this way the French came to view themselves as a Chosen People – a claim 'confirmed' by a series of miraculous events over long years including the conquests of Philippe II, 'Augustus' (r.1180–1223), and the extraordinary victory at Bouvines in–1214 that ended the Angevin-Flanders war. The sanctification of Louis IX at the start of the fourteenth century only served to strengthen this 'mystique of nationhood that was tied to the royal blood of the kings'.[13]

In England a conception of national identity was also bound up with royal status, although not so tightly. The extension and retraction of English authority within the British Isles and in France under the Norman, Angevin and Plantagenet kings had shaped the conceptual as well as the geographical borders of the nation, and hence its identity. This process may be traced through a series of phases and events. Prior to the outbreak of the Hundred Years War, the last major attempt to extend English authority in the British Isles had been in Edward I's reign when he sought to subdue his neighbours in Wales and Scotland. Edward's policies served to exaggerate the 'national' differences (political, cultural, legal and linguistic) that already existed between the countries of the British Isles and drove the Scots into the Auld Alliance (1295), which encouraged the outbreak of the Anglo-French war. Before this, the treaty of Paris (1259) had done much to redefine relations between England and France: it forced 'Englishmen' (some of whom might not have been resident in England) to declare their political allegiances more exactly, thus giving a new precision to a sense of national identity. The treaty was a confirmation that the bulk of the Angevin Empire had been lost, although this had been evident to many since Normandy fell to Philippe Augustus in 1204. In turn, the loss of French lands led to the construction of a new 'English' identity, even though a sense of 'Englishness', albeit of a different sort, can be discerned far earlier than this. It had been engendered by various expansionist projects in the British Isles and Ireland in the twelfth century, and these built upon a nascent, although not national, identity with roots in the Norman Conquest of 1066 and, indeed, reaching back to King Alfred's Wessex in the ninth century.[14]

A sense of national identity, therefore, was one shaped in part or perhaps chiefly through conflict with England's neighbours in the British Isles and with France. Prior to the outbreak of the Hundred Years War, although in the midst of Anglo-French hostilities, Parliament had heard accusations that the French were seeking to destroy both the English nation and the English language. First claimed by Edward I in 1295, the allegation was reiterated in 1344, 1346, 1376 and 1388. As the Parliament rolls of June 1344 put it, the king of France 'firmly intends, as our lord the king and his council fully comprehend, to destroy the English language and to occupy the land of England'.[15] French invasion plans discovered at Caen in 1346 suggested an intention 'to destroy and ruin the whole English nation and language'.[16]

Why a threat to a language commonly used only by a minority of the ruling elite at this time should prove so troubling is intriguing. Yet an association between identity, nation and language strengthened over the course of the later Middle Ages, not only in England and France but throughout Europe, much of which saw 'a growing intolerance of language diversity'.[17] During the Hundred Years War the increasing use of the vernacular in England emphasised and was used to express a growing cultural divide with France. Consequently, at the start of the fourteenth century the English aristocracy had been predominantly francophone (and often culturally francophile); however, by the end of the Hundred Years War its members spoke mainly English. This had begun before the outbreak of hostilities in 1337, but the war greatly accelerated the process.[18]

Language, therefore, long recognised as a key ethnic determinant, became an increasingly politicised subject (and object) in the later Middle Ages: a cause for conflict and a means by which conflict was described and furthered. At almost exactly the same time as Edward I addressed the English Parliament on the matter of the threat to the nation's political and cultural integrity, Philippe IV's officials claimed that individuals in English Gascony could be killed simply for speaking the *lingua Gallica* (northern/ Parisian French, the *langue d'oeil*). In England, as animosity towards France grew, the vernacular (the 'mother tongue') emerged as the language of administration, popular literature, history and political propaganda, and its use 'was a precondition of the process of deepening and consolidating the sense of national identity by harnessing the emotive energy of the association between language and nationalism'.[19] This process was enshrined in legislation: in 1362 the Statute of Pleading established English as the language to be used in debate in English royal and seigneurial courts (with some minor exceptions). After 1399 the Lancastrian dynasty made extensive use of written English in an attempt to win patriotic support for its claim to the throne. Henry IV and his successors followed the example set by the Capetian and Valois kings who had worked in such close alliance with the historians and propagandists of the abbey of Saint-Denis.[20] Consequently, the first half of the fifteenth century saw a rapid rise in the number of English-language chronicles as the Lancastrians attempted to appropriate vernacular historiography for their own ends.[21]

During the Council of Constance language was again emphasised as the prime characteristic of a nation. In 1417 the English ambassador, Thomas Polton, noted:

> Whether a nation be understood as a race, relationship, and habit of unity, separate from others, *or as a difference of language, which by divine and human law is the greatest and most authentic mark of a nation and the essence of it* [my emphasis] . . . or whether it be understood, as it should be, as an equality of territory with, for instance, the Gallic nation – in all these respects the renowned nation of England or Britain is one of the four or five nations that compose the papal obedience.[22]

Polton's chief concern at the council was to sustain England's claim to be one of the 'nations' (*nationes*) of the papal obedience, alongside France, Spain, Germany and Italy. These groupings were not nations in a modern sense but geographical collectives brought together for the purposes of ecclesiastical organisation. In order to make his claim, Polton equated England (*natio Anglicana*) with Britain (an ecclesiastical grouping comprising England, Ireland, Wales and Scotland), despite the fact that few of those additional peoples paid allegiance, willingly at least, to Henry V. The particular circumstances of the Council of Constance and the form of Polton's argument are a reminder that definitions of the 'nation' (in Latin variously described as *gens, patria* or *natio*) were not fixed in the late Middle Ages.[23] Indeed, without the institutional features of the modern nation state – capitalism, printing, industrialisation, mass education, and so on – it has been argued that France and England should not be considered as nations in this period. Or, if France and England were nations by the end of the Hundred Years War, they were not necessarily so in quite the same sense as the politico-cultural 'units' that followed.[24]

While such matters of precise definition are important, there is no question that the people of the fourteenth and fifteenth centuries were subjected to intense political, social and cultural pressures which both bound them together (as nations), yet also, at various times, placed enormous pressures on those same nations, threatening to fracture them. The Hundred Years War dismembered both countries militarily, governmentally, culturally and/or through disputes between members of the body politic. France was rent apart not only by English attacks, occupation and civil war, but by the Capetian-Valois *apanage* policy. In the *apanages* – areas partially divested of sovereign authority and given over to one of the Princes of the Blood – an already potent sense of regional identity was often exaggerated to the extent that it could supersede or undermine national loyalties. Edward III recognised and attempted to exploit this in the early stages of the war through what has been described as his 'provincial strategy', and the Lancastrian kings sought to manipulate the divisions of the Armagnac-Burgundian civil war in a similar fashion.[25] Such local loyalties and divisions inhibited the development of not only a sense of national identity, but also of the construction of some of the institutions of government that might provide a focus for such an identity and a means of communicating it throughout the realm. This is particularly evident in the regional Estates whose independence prevented governmental centralisation and Valois exploitation of France's full military and financial resources until late in the war.[26]

This sort of regional particularism was exemplified by and identified with such ambitious princes as Charles of Navarre, Gaston Fébus of Foix, Jean de Montfort of Brittany and successive dukes of Burgundy. The

Hundred Years War offered these men the opportunity to assert their independence and that of their principalities within France. Such political impediments to the construction of a national identity were strengthened by distinct linguistic and cultural characteristics in certain regions.[27] Political and cultural divisions of this sort could and did divide loyalties to a central authority and so inhibited the development of a sense of national identity, especially one primarily dependent on the monarch. Nonetheless, although the war allowed certain principalities to exploit French royal weakness, over a period of time it also provided French kings with some of the legal, administrative and military mechanisms to limit that same regional independence and eventually restore France to its 'natural' territorial borders. In the seventh century, Isidore of Seville (c.560–636) had defined Gaul as a country bounded by the Alps and the Pyrenees, the (Atlantic) ocean and the Rhine.[28] In part, the Hundred Years War was fought to justify the Capetian/Valois claim to sovereignty over that same area in the fourteenth and fifteenth centuries.

Conflicting regional identities and concerns regarding the legitimacy of the Valois succession ensured that royal claims to overlordship throughout the 'natural' geographic area of France were often questioned. After the death in 1328 of the last Capetian monarch, Charles IV, the Valois kings fought a constant battle to justify their claim to be the legitimate rulers of a unified France. They claimed to wield imperial power within the kingdom and argued that this descended from their Capetian and Carolingian forebears. They declared that their sovereign writ bound everyone within the realm and that there was nowhere their authority did not hold. Royal authority was, therefore, bound up with a concept of the inviolability of the French nation. Because of this, English counter-claims to territories within France such as Aquitaine and Normandy were, in some ways, more damaging than the Plantagenet demand for the throne of France itself. If the nation could be divided, then the myth of universal Capetian/Carolingian sovereignty within France could be discredited. If the theoretical foundations of Valois power were undermined, then the very concept of France could be invalidated. In this sense the French fought the Hundred Years War to substantiate a mythic concept of nationhood.[29]

The expansion and contraction of Capetian/Valois authority within France over a long period prior to and during the Hundred Years War is in striking contrast to the situation in England. There the geographical frontiers of the country changed very little throughout the medieval period, which accounts for certain differences in the process of nation-building between the two countries.[30] This is not to suggest, however, that England was politically or culturally homogeneous. Its diversity can be seen in the independent attitudes, distinctive political priorities and cultural differences of the English palatinates, marches, and in some counties: the political map of England (and certainly of the British Isles) revealed a great many regional variations.[31] The Hundred Years War, however, helped redraw that map, if not completely: England's internal frontiers became less apparent, although some political and cultural divisions remained. The long conflict saw the development of systems of permanent taxation, of a defined role for Parliament and of increasing control by central authorities over the localities as the so-called 'war state' emerged.[32] The demands of the Hundred Years War ensured that in England, as in France, albeit at different times and to varying extents, central authorities began to exploit national resources more fully. Regional identities diminished in the face of this assault and were replaced with something bearing a more national stamp. The gradual reincorporation of various *apanages* under the direct rule of the 'Most Christian King of France' and the assimilation of the duchy of Lancaster into the English royal demesne after Richard II's deposition in 1399 were the most obvious but by no means the only examples of this process.

Clearly, however, although the Hundred Years War encouraged a general process of political and cultural homogenisation, the conflict also subjected it to occasional, violent and potentially fatal punctuations. England and France suffered regular political divisions, the most spectacular of which led to depositions and civil wars. Since failures of what might, anachronistically, be described as 'foreign policy' often encouraged such divisions, the war should not be seen as a force that always engendered a sense of national consciousness, or national unity. Indeed, the conflict may be seen as a struggle brought on by differing interpretations of what constituted 'foreign policy', given the corporate or federal nature of the English king's domains, with claims to Wales, Scotland, Ireland, France (especially Aquitaine and Normandy), and the Channel Islands.

The outbreak of the Hundred Years War shifted England's political priorities and relations with those same 'nations' in the British Isles and Ireland: it ended an intense phase of Anglicisation that had begun following England's own colonisation ('Normanisation') after 1066. In the intervening years England claimed political sovereignty over the entirety of the British Isles and demanded, albeit unsuccessfully, the imposition of English legal, social and cultural norms throughout that area. Celtic laws and practices were denigrated; indeed, various Irish practices were described, explicitly, as degenerate by the Dublin parliament of 1297. In 1294 Peter Langtoft wrote: 'May Wales be accursed of God and of St Simon for it has always been full of treason. May Scotland be accursed of the mother of God! And may Wales be sunk down deep to the Devil. In neither of them was any truth.'[33] Such attitudes in Edward I's reign reflect an intense, unmatched and perhaps unrepresentative period of English colonial activity. Nonetheless, such activity did a great deal to shape Anglo-Celtic relations in the period just prior to the outbreak of the Hundred Years War. It also led to some of the most famous expressions of nationhood in Britain and Ireland in the Middle Ages: the Remonstrance of the Irish Princes (1317) and, in Scotland, the Declaration of Arbroath (1320), which stated 'for as long as but a hundred of us remain alive, never will we on any conditions be brought under English rule. It is in truth not for glory, nor riches, nor honours that we are fighting, but for freedom – for that alone, which no honest man gives up but with life itself.'[34]

Despite the fact that Scotland, Ireland and Wales were or were considered potential staging grounds for a French invasion, with the outbreak of war in 1337 English attention for the most part turned to France.[35] However, as the conflict progressed, although resources were employed throughout the British Isles only intermittently to try and enforce English power (and political and social norms), attitudes hardened to England's Celtic neighbours. Given a growing sense of national identity this is not surprising: 'the very Englishness of the [French] enterprise made [English] accommodations with Welsh and Irish society more difficult than they might otherwise have been'.[36]

The Hundred Years War, therefore, began with a sense of national and cultural superiority already evident on both sides of the Channel. This posed certain problems given the nature of English war aims in France. How could an English king seek to shape a distinctly francophobe national identity at home in order to gain the necessary resources to conquer the kingdom of France, while at the same time proclaiming he would allow France, once conquered, to be ruled according to those same customs that he described at home as so threatening and inferior? When Edward III first claimed the French throne in 1340 he swore to maintain 'the good laws and customs which existed at the time of [his] progenitor, St Louis, king of France'.[37] Edward's successors maintained the same policy and this required a certain political legerdemain: to their English subjects they needed to appear increasingly English as the war progressed; to their potential French subjects they could not appear distinctly foreign. Such concerns became particularly acute during the negotiations leading to the treaty of Troyes in 1420 when both sides demanded that the union of the Crowns should not lead to a closer political union that might compromise either nation's cultural integrity.[38]

Such concerns over national integrity, both political and cultural, were fought out and debated throughout the war in order to determine what, precisely, constituted the foreign or the alien. Given the context, it is not surprising that, in many cases, the chief criterion determining an individual's identity was political loyalty. Questions of allegiance lay at the heart of the Hundred Years War: uncertainties regarding political affiliations, loyalties and responsibilities had encouraged the increasingly febrile relationship between the kings of England and France since the treaty of Paris (1259), if not before. Hostilities developed because political allegiance and duty were defined differently, while expectations of service and responsibilities varied widely within and between English and French dominions. The conflict was fought over these differences, particularly in areas such as Normandy, Gascony and Burgundy. Because of the centrality of this issue the war may be seen as comprised of conflicting attempts to reforge a common sense of allegiance. This struggle to define and enforce political loyalty contributed to a sense of national identity in two ways: first, a unitary kingship – the typical focus of allegiance – formed a key element in establishing a nation and a sense of national identity; and, second, the intellectual debate bound up with the war and concerning the justice of a national cause revolved around the sovereign rights of individual monarchs.[39]

This route to political clarity was not a simple one. Over the duration of the conflict, kings might fracture national identities as effectively as fashion them. In England the limitations of Richard II and Henry VI brought about revolt and deposition, while Henry IV faced armed rebellions in England and Wales. In France military indignities were heaped on Philippe VI and Jean II, leading to the latter's capture at Poitiers in 1356 and his long English captivity. Charles VI's madness brought about a different form of 'absence', but both absences emphasised weakness at the centre rather than a strong foundation on which a national identity might stand. Consequently, even though kings were an important factor in forming national identities, during the Hundred Years War the stark contrasts between the strength and fragility of certain monarchs, accentuated by political divisions in both France and England, mean they were rarely a stable factor.

In spite of this, and despite the fact that individual kings failed their people, during the period of the Hundred Years War the realm and the nation grew increasingly synonymous. Indeed, there seems little doubt that at least by the fifteenth century the defence of royal rights – the primary cause of the Hundred Years War – had become equated with the defence of the nation, and not only the defence of territorial boundaries but also the defence of language, customs and a way of life. The emergence of a national sentiment was, therefore, cemented not always by individual kings but often by the institution of monarchy.[40] Loyalty to the nation meant loyalty to the monarchy, which, in England, allowed one to remove a failing king and not break faith with the nation. In France, conditions differed somewhat: the reigning monarch became explicitly associated with the identity of the nation as the head of the body politic, and the antiquity and sacral character of the monarchy did much to protect individual kings. The importance of good government and the well-being of the nation were, however, recognised at various times as distinct from the well-being of the monarch. As in England, the connection between a (French) national identity and the 'common good' could be used to attack the Crown. Even after the vindication of the Valois monarchy brought by the final victory at Castillon in July 1453, the French Crown was not entirely secure, and it is noteworthy that its first major challenge came in the form of the suggestively titled League of the Public Weal (1465).[41]

Nonetheless, when a French victory at Castillon brought the end of the war, however uncertain contemporaries were of the fact, it provided Valois propagandists with tremendous ammunition: it indicated divine approval for the dynasty and confirmed Charles VII's sovereignty over (much of) France. At Castillon, the Valois made real the 'myth' of French kingship. Charles VII became the true heir of the Capetians and Carolingians – the successor to Charlemagne and 'emperor in his kingdom'. In commemoration the king had a special medal struck. It bore the legend 'When I was made, everyone in France, without dispute, obeyed the prudent king, loved by God' – but it also carried the unfortunate coda, 'except at Calais, which is a strong place'.[42]

Such commemoration reflected and helped further construct a sense of national identity despite the minor embarrassment of English Calais, some Gascon resistance, Breton recalcitrance and continuing Burgundian aggression. The war itself, its memory and commemoration, became bound up with rituals of national identification and formed a key element in drawing individuals together and giving them a collective identity.[43]

Memorials to the war (if not war memorials in a modern sense) were constructed throughout and after the conflict in France and England: in the east window at Gloucester Cathedral (commemorating the English victory at Crécy); through the membership of the Company of the Star and Order of the Garter; in tomb effigies and monumental brasses; and through the invocation of Saints Michael and George, those slayers of the dragons of England and France respectively.

As the conflict unfolded, such memorials and icons became increasingly associated with the concept of sacrifice for the nation. In France, especially after defeat at Agincourt in 1415, it seems to have become important for a death in battle to be recorded on tombs or in epitaphs. This was certainly true by the end of the war, as the epitaph of Jean de Bueil (1477) shows:

> Pray for me, good people,
> For the lord of Bueil killed in the great war
> Fighting for France and for you.[44]

In tone and character it is reminiscent of nineteenth- and early twentieth-century war memorials that drew on Horace's maxim *Dulce et decorum est pro patria mori*. This was familiar during the period of the Hundred Years War, when a growing number of treatises and military orders urged knights to sell their lives dearly on the battlefield. Although authors such as Honoré Bonet suggested one might imperil one's soul dying in a war against Christians,[45] others, including Geoffrey de Charny, argued that death should hold no fear for a soldier who died in defence of the common good:

> [W]hen lords have wars ... their men can and should fight for them
> and move confidently and bravely into battle for such causes, for if one
> performs well there, one is honoured in life, and if one dies there, one's
> soul is saved, if other sins do not stand in the way of this.[46]

As Charny strove to galvanise French chivalry in the 1350s, so Thomas Walsingham despaired of England's military failures in the 1380s. His language, too, is indicative of the growth of a sense of national identity, of the need to serve the nation, and reveals his belief that those unwilling to place their lives at her disposal were cowards:

> Heavens above! The land which once produced and gave birth to men
> that demanded the respect of all men ... now spewed out men lacking

manly courage, who were a laughing stock to the enemy . . . For no one or hardly anyone, was found in the land who would dedicate himself to the service of the state, who would use his energies for the state's citizens.[47]

It is not surprising in this context of national sacrifice that French and English polemicists adopted certain aspects of crusade ideology leading to the emergence of a sort of 'sanctified patriotism'.[48] Crusading rhetoric began to be employed regularly in national service. The promise of a crusade had been used repeatedly from the early 1330s as both 'carrot and stick' to try and maintain or secure peace. The enemy's failure to agree terms for a settlement was often promoted as a grotesque unwillingness to recognise the need for a further campaign against the Turk. With the Great Schism and the devastating defeat at Nicopolis (1396) the prospect of successful international cooperation became increasingly difficult, despite the extraordinarily diligent efforts of Philippe de Mézières and others. Instead, the Hundred Years War was recast: it acquired some of the connotations of a crusade, and evolved from a dynastic struggle into one between chosen peoples.[49] Aspects of this were already evident and may be seen in Louis I d'Anjou's Apocalypse tapestries (c. 1373), which reflect the disasters of war and endemic plague. They provide a clear (and literal) example of the process by which the enemy was demonised. The tapestries portray the English, represented by Edward III and his sons, as monstrous and demonic, riding from the mouth of hell in a riot of devastation across France, while pitying saints can only look on in anguish. But, like the forces of the Apocalypse, they would be defeated eventually and with God's help.[50] Joan of Arc's activities and her own 'Letter to the English' (22 March 1429) should also be read in this same 'crusading' light. She claimed to have 'come from God to reclaim the blood royal'; to 'have been sent by God, the King of Heaven, to drive [the English] out of France'; and to assure the duke of Bedford and earl of Suffolk, to whom the letter was addressed, that they would 'never hold the kingdom of France from God, the King of Heaven, son of St Mary; for King Charles will hold it, because God, the King of Heaven, wishes it.'[51]

Later, certain French polemicists would depict Joan as a godsend – again, both literally and metaphorically. During her lifetime, matters were not so clear – certainly not for the people of Paris, which she assaulted in 1429. Even by the conclusion of the nullification trial in 1456 the reputation of this (soon-to-be) national icon remained uncertain. This

highlights the regional divisions and divided loyalties, as well as the sense
of sheer war-weariness that pertained at various times in the course of the
struggle and worked against the construction of a clear, encompassing
national identity. For the Parisian Bourgeois, for example, at several points
in his journal, any sort of peace, any cessation of 'this war, accursed of God'
was preferable to the continuance of a national struggle, whether sanctified
or not.[52] But as the war progressed and especially in its later stages, a
consensus seems to have emerged that dying for one's country was a sacrifice to be accepted willingly if the nation was at risk of occupation or annihilation, since such a sacrifice, like one made in a crusade, guaranteed
salvation. In France this became particularly evident after 1415 and the
defeat at Agincourt, *la maudite journée* (the accursed day). It is no coincidence that around this time a number of French works began to propound
the concept that the very identification of the nation, the name 'France',
derived from *franc* – meaning free from tribute. Hence to be French was to
be free and independent of any outside influence.[53]

War between England and France led to a growing sense of nationhood
in both countries. The struggle was chiefly a political one but it was also
galvanised by a series of socio-political and cultural changes that affected
much of Europe in the later Middle Ages. Trans-national institutions
began to weaken; the role of the Church changed and papal authority
declined. Cultural ties frayed as Latin lost its sway. Their replacements
were independent and vernacular. Consequently, the Hundred Years War
shaped and, as it concluded, entrenched new conceptions of national identity on both sides of the Channel.[54] For England, it was an identity shaped
by the shifting tensions between its 'British' and 'French' ambitions and
orientations. In France the growth of royal power in theory and actuality
formed the central core in an identity which, through the war and subsequently, came to encompass the 'natural' extent of the country.

Over the course of the war a theory of national identity was proposed
vigorously from court and capital in prose, in verse, in material form, in
processions and sermons. In 1370 William of Wykeham wrote to archdea-
cons in the diocese of Winchester stating that the French 'are preparing to
attack, invade and crush the borders of the realm of England ... with no
small multitude of ships and armed men'. In response to this he had 'ordered
and caused processions to be made and celebrated and devout prayers to be
said in all monasteries, churches and other sacred places'.[55] Through the
Church and various other channels a potent message was propounded
regarding the common good, a common enemy, the importance of a

common history, and the need for a national effort to defeat the perfidious enemy who threatens 'our' very way of life. St Denis (later St Michel) or St George would protect the nation. The English were regicides; the Valois and their Capetian predecessors were descended from a butcher; David II, the king of their Scottish allies, was an adulterer who had soiled the font at baptism, and so on. This programme gathered pace throughout the conflict aided by a process of cultural homogenisation and a growing awareness of the brutal realities of war.[56] Froissart remarked, 'since they wished to wage war, both kings found it necessary to make known to their people and set before them the nature of their dispute, so that they would be eager to support their lord. And by this means [the people] were aroused in each kingdom.'[57] But it is still difficult to know how that central message was received in the localities, on the frontiers of the kingdom and by the bulk of the population.

The journal of the Parisian Bourgeois, although produced in the capital, provides some insights regarding attitudes that may be a little more widely representative. His opinions changed over the long course of his account (1405–49) and his attitudes shifted regarding the various parties involved in the civil war and the nature of the Anglo-Burgundian occupation. As the tide of war turned in favour of Charles VII, 'the Victorious', so too the Bourgeois came to favour the Valois. Success (and failure) in the war made a final contribution to a sense of national identity. It shaped a collective memory of suffering, struggle and eventual victory achieved through a collective sacrifice. After 1453 there was a slow acceptance among the English that they were an island nation, no longer a power on the continent of Europe. In France, the chroniclers and lawyers constructed an 'official memory' of the war in which victory became a victory for the French nation. In the popular imagination this validated the propaganda, helped erase some of the discord of civil wars, the divisions caused by the treaty of Troyes and made at least some of the sacrifices worthwhile.[58]

Conclusion
1453 AND BEYOND

The English defeat at Castillon and the fall of Bordeaux in the summer of 1453 marked the end of the Hundred Years War. It was, though, a somewhat unsatisfactory conclusion, and not merely for the English and Henry VI. There was no treaty; Charles VII took control of Gascony but not Calais; Henry did not renounce his claim to the French throne, and nor would his successors do so until 1802. Even then, and following the battles of Trafalgar (1805) and Waterloo (1815), relations between England and France remained uneasy into the twentieth century. But in 1453 the nature of the hostilities that had coloured Anglo-French relations since the end of the Capetian dynasty changed radically. Contemporaries recognised this and imbued the events of 1453 with great political significance. The resonance surrounding the end of the war did not compare with the fall of Constantinople which happened in the same year, but for the English their humiliation marked a shattering change of circumstances, and together these events marked the beginning of a new order in Europe. The 'rebellion' of the duke of Aquitaine and the war for the throne of France were over, whatever the Yorkists, Tudors, Stuarts and Hanoverians might say. The end of the war, however, did not bring peace. In France, Charles VII may have become Charles the Victorious but he had to face the rebellions of his son Louis and the growing threat of Burgundy. The country and countryside had to be restored and tended. It had suffered horribly over successive generations and required a great deal of care and attention. Fortunately, the economy improved in the second half of the fifteenth century, as did the weather, leading to an upsurge in trade.

In England, by contrast, the scars of defeat covered the body politic and a bitter sense of betrayal and of national humiliation soon fed the flames of civil war. The losses between 1449 and 1453 had shaken the Lancastrian government and shocked the country at large. The fiasco had to be explained; those responsible had to be punished. At times war with France had bound the country together in a national mission; now, the end of that war tore it apart. Many who had fought side by side against the French would take up arms against one another in the Wars of the Roses at St Albans (1455), Towton (1461), Barnet (1471) and Tewkesbury (1471). One legacy of the Hundred Years War, therefore, was a France resurgent politically and economically, but an England faced with devastation as its leaders turned on one another to protect their power and pride, and to assuage the nation's shame.[1]

But the war did not only transform the political status of each nation; it effectively reforged their identities. England and France had been set on divergent evolutionary paths when the dispute began. The war accelerated their progression along those paths. The connections between England and France were virtually severed and their similarities were very much fewer in 1453 than they had been in 1337. The war began as a feudal and dynastic struggle between two monarchs; it ended as a national conflict. In many ways, of course, this left England weaker and clearly inferior to France. In another sense, however, it offered an opportunity for the English Crown, and perhaps also the English state, to conceive a new status for itself. Even though this new identity was the product of defeat, the feudal bonds between kings and countries that had encouraged hostilities in the first place and had always marked England as inferior to her neighbour across the Channel were erased. Rulers of England were now, finally, compelled to seek a new independent identity and a new political position for themselves within the British Isles, Europe and the wider world.[2] The Angevin Empire had been lost, irrevocably; the search for a new empire would begin.

Another legacy of the war was war itself: over the years of the struggle England and France and their people became shaped by war and organised for war. English and French society became increasingly militarised. More than a century of endemic warfare resulted in the establishment of governmental, bureaucratic and financial structures to support conflict on a wholly new scale. Without such structures the English indenture system and the French *ordonnances* of the 1440s would have been impossible. In England this formed part of the precocious establishment of a 'war state' in which much of government became shaped by and for military purposes. As a consequence of this, the army was placed on a semi-professional footing early in the struggle. In France the process was more protracted, but the

Crown was eventually able to acquire control over sufficient resources – financial and administrative – to enable it to construct a permanent standing army that formed a vital element in the emergent French state. These developments were deeply significant and not solely in military terms. They also altered the relationship between the king, the various representative assemblies (the Estates General and Parliament) and the aristocracy. In financial terms the changes driven by the need to wage war so regularly for so long meant that both monarchs enjoyed (potential) access to far greater resources than had their predecessors. In France, however, access to more extensive funds was acquired without a comparable rise in the influence of the representative assemblies: the French Estates, generally speaking, remained pliant and gained little influence over taxation. By contrast, members of the Commons in the English Parliament became increasingly aware of their authority and ability to influence the direction of royal policy now that this policy depended on the money which the Commons could grant.[3]

The professionalisation of warfare that drove these governmental reforms also brought about the end, in both countries, of 'feudal' service, or at least its widespread use. As a result, the role of the aristocracy altered very considerably, as did its position in relation to the Crown and the part it played in the business of the state. The establishment of a large standing army in France not only strengthened the position of the Crown and linked it directly to the development of the state but it provided a means of directly co-opting a small but significant proportion of the nobility into national service in a wholly new way. This, in turn, enabled the Crown to exercise increasing influence over the nobility.[4] As a consequence fighting became a career, one adopted by many outside the ranks of the aristocracy; it was no longer (or not merely) an act of *noblesse oblige*: this eroded the fundamental association between nobility and military service. This was also the case in England, although the new priorities of the Wars of the Roses ensured that the military function of the nobility could not be set aside for some time.

The militarisation of society in England and France also had the effect of drawing certain groups together through employment and shared experiences. With the end of the war came an end to some of those collective identities. For example, the intense phase of ransoming that had characterised and bankrolled much of the struggle concluded in 1453. The war had involved much of military society in the ransom business for the potential opportunity to ransom a prisoner of war had encouraged participation in the conflict, whereas capture, by contrast, could ruin a soldier. The Hundred

Years War had seen some major changes in the practice of ransoming. As military conduct became increasingly professional, so it became more difficult for individuals to take prisoners. Increasing levels of mortality on the battlefield reflected the growing importance of tactics that relied on order and discipline in the ranks. Despite this, ransoming continued to be important throughout the war. With the rise of professional armies, however, ransoming took on a more political character and it became more a priority for the Crown and the state rather than for the individual soldier. During the Hundred Years War the Crown had begun to exercise its rights to politically valuable captives; this became the predominant model in the sixteenth and seventeenth centuries.[5]

The transformation in the military role of the aristocracy and the changing experience of taking prisoners was also the result of technological and strategic developments. The greater use of infantry, missile weapons and the introduction of gunpowder artillery were among the most significant innovations, and they had widespread implications for the organisation and financing of warfare, as well as for the social connotations of military service. The military revolution that took place during the Hundred Years War marked the beginning of a new age, one which Don Quixote would lament in Miguel de Cervantes's novel of 1605:

> Blessed be those happy ages that were strangers to the dreadful fury of these devilish instruments of artillery, whose inventor I am satisfied is now in Hell, receiving the reward for his cursed invention, which is the cause that very often a cowardly base hand takes away the life of the bravest gentleman; and that in the midst of that vigour and resolution, which animates and inflames the bold, a chance bullet (shot perhaps by one who fled...) coming nobody knows how, or from where, in a moment puts an end to the brave designs and the life of one who deserved to have survived many years.

This was the type of death that Thomas Montague suffered at Orléans in 1428 and John Talbot at Castillon in 1453. Artillery, like the longbow before it, revolutionised military strategy and had immense repercussions on the ways in which campaigns were conducted; it forced a reassessment of the chivalric ethic and transformed the role of the aristocracy on the battlefield. Indeed, as a consequence of technological and strategic imperatives, by the end of the Hundred Years War the knights of England and France had relinquished their pre-eminent military positions. Longbows replaced lances, infantry replaced cavalry and the social contours of military service were redrawn.

Even among the command ranks, increasing numbers of leaders were drawn from those first found clinging to the lower rungs of the aristocracy, men such as Bertrand du Guesclin, John Chandos, Walter Mauny and the Bureau brothers. The social fluidity that the war promoted and which repeated outbreaks of plague encouraged meant that membership of the growing ranks of the aristocracy became more achievable for those who traditionally would have had no means of gaining acceptance. The development of sub-knightly ranks of the aristocracy – in England the gentry, in France the *petite noblesse* – and the emergence of a wealthy merchant class and upper stratum of the peasantry, allowed families and individuals to ease their way in and perhaps fall out of the ranks of the aristocracy. Furthermore, with the expansion of the state and a new conception of nationhood, men could now find careers away from the battlefield; there were new ways to serve in the governmental and bureaucratic institutions that had developed to promote, organise and bankroll the war. Men such as William de la Pole (d.1366), a merchant from Hull, founded a baronial dynasty because of his ability to lend money to the Crown, much as Jacques Coeur (c.1395–1456) became hugely significant because he could fund Charles VII.[6]

The changes in the ways in which war was prosecuted, financed and organised ensured that it became, to a new extent, a national business. The nation was investing its wealth and strength in a collective venture and it required a return on that investment. Central authorities did much to encourage this collective attitude and sought to engender a sense of community. Sophisticated systems of propaganda were employed at elite and popular levels to justify the war and encourage support for its prosecution. Partly as a consequence of this, new conceptions of national identity emerged on both sides of the Channel. The very meanings of *nationes, patria, res publica, status*, and so on, changed as both countries fought for domination and faced, or claimed they faced, destruction. The words and what they represented gained new connotations; they implied a greater sense of community and, perhaps it would not be too anachronistic to say, of fraternity.[7]

One product of this insistent stream of propaganda was the reification of the myth of a unified France. The dream of Valois hegemony within the 'natural' geographical area of France came to be realised through military success against England – all but completely achieved by 1453 – and over the following half-century by the Crown's reabsorption of the *apanages* and other independent estates into the royal demesne. This geopolitical process was a remarkable achievement given the sheer size of France and the long-standing links that many regions had with England. The extended southern shore of the 'English Channel', the area that stretched from Gascony, through Saintonge, Poitou, Brittany, Normandy and across to Flanders, had enjoyed close ties – economic, political and geographical – to the northern shore, many of them more important, historically, than those which bound them to Paris. A further problem took the form of the burgeoning power of Philippe the Good and his successor Charles the Bold who, in addition to the county and duchy of Burgundy, ruled Flanders, Brabant, Holland, Zeeland, Hainault and Luxembourg, and so formed a bloc to the extension of royal control within that natural geographic (hexagonal) area of France.[8]

Regional particularism also remained potent elsewhere. In some cases local loyalties had been accentuated over the course of the war by tensions such as the Armagnac-Burgundian struggle. Political differences generated by that conflict, and the various additional disputes that had combined to intensify the Hundred Years War, would take several generations to cool. There were also further areas of contention that had to be settled, such as those which arose from the trial and condemnation of Joan of Arc, hence the need for her rehabilitation (nullification) trial in 1455–56. In more general terms, despite ever greater political unity, a range of social, cultural and linguistic differences remained evident in France for some time. However, in *Rosier des guerres* (a work now widely agreed to have been dictated in 1481–82 by the king to his physician for the instruction of his son), Louis XI wrote a powerful statement of the loyalty to the nation that had been engendered by the Anglo-French war and which now character-ised attitudes to and in France: 'None may doubt the merit of death in defence of the common good. One must fight for one's country.' No doubt this represented an exaggerated vision of conditions and feelings in the country, but it reflected a new conception of the nation and of the respon-sibilities of all Frenchmen to fight in the motherland's defence.[9]

In England a comparable process of geopolitical unification took place during the war and thereafter, although it was fraught with difficulties. Henry Bolingbroke's usurpation of the throne in 1399 brought the Lancastrian 'apanage' within the royal demesne, and one of the few advantages of the Wars of the Roses was to continue this process – more estates returned to the king's direct control. Greater cultural unity was gained through the increasing use of the English language for governmental and popular purposes, although dialectical differences remained widespread throughout the country. The use of the language for official 'publications' encouraged an increasing politicisation of the population that did, at times, generate a powerful sense of national sentiment. However, it also led to divergent attitudes concerning the proper direction for the nation and what constituted the common good. The rise of the 'Commons' in Parliament, the various peasant revolts that punctuated the conflict and the civil war that grew out of its failure, are an indication of the problems involved with this growing sense of popular, political awareness. The assertion of the 1381 rebels that they were 'the true commons' reverberated through political society.[10]

A mounting political awareness was perhaps the most benign impact of the war on the populations of England and France. The direct effects of the conflict tended to be less abstract and more violent. Community life was seriously affected in many areas. Normandy, Paris and other areas of northern France had experienced foreign occupation with all its problems, and some of its benefits. Other regions, such as Gascony, would now have to adapt to a different sort of occupation – a new governing culture and political dispensation: rule from Paris would prove as foreign in its way as government from London. Throughout both countries taxation had become all but permanent. Indeed, few aspects of economic life had remained untouched by the conflict. For the French peasantry, in certain parts of the country, the series of attacks from English soldiers, foreign mercenaries and the exploitation of their own side must have felt unrelenting. Although certain merchants and manufacturers benefited a great deal from the war, in some (few) parts of England and (many in) France communities declined or disappeared because of raiding or the effects of war on trade. Plague also played a vital role in this process, exacerbating the misery and yet providing new opportunities for those who survived.[11]

Women were among those who could, if lucky, take advantage of the greater opportunities for social mobility in the century after the plague. It was a far from easy time, of course, especially in France where attacks on women were all too common, but acceptance into new trades and a greater level of personal independence were significant developments. The benefits, however, did not last. Although the war demonstrated the political abilities and great fortitude of many women in France and England, the treatment meted out to the most famous woman of the period, Joan of Arc, revealed the underlying levels of misogyny that would be reinstitutionalised when socio-economic conditions slowly reverted to 'normal' in the later fifteenth century.

Many ecclesiastical communities also suffered. Despite spiritual sanctions and certain military ordinances those churches and monasteries that were unfortunate enough to lie in the paths of English or French soldiers were rarely spared the horrors of war. The Church and its members were also co-opted by the Crown in both countries to legitimise their respective claims and to wage a propaganda war in support of their conflicting aspirations. Both sides were successful in this, although the focus of French and English propaganda differed. In general, however, the involvement of the Church in the struggle did little for its reputation. The period of the Hundred Years War saw the spiritual authority of the Church and many of its members compromised by a new awareness among congregations of its political corruption and worldliness. The power of the papacy waned in the context of the 'Babylonian Captivity' in Avignon, the Great Schism and the Conciliar Movement. Monarchs on both sides of the Channel took the opportunity to assert greater authority over their 'national' Churches while the impact of the Black Death seemed only to confirm the failures of the institutional Church. What emerged to fill the spiritual vacuum was a vibrant lay piety that, in time, encouraged further reform.

The peoples of England and France and the countries in which they lived were therefore changed in deeply significant ways by the experience of the Hundred Years War. No one realised that with the battle of Castillon and the fall of Bordeaux the war, in one guise at least, had ended; no one knew that they were witnessing the end of an age. However, in more than one way the Hundred Years War gave birth to a new era and to modern Europe.

Notes

Abbreviations

AN	Archives Nationales (Paris)
BEC	*Bibliothèque de l'École des Chartes*
BIHR	*Bulletin of the Institute of Historical Research* (later *Historical Research*)
BL	British Library (London)
BN	Bibliothèque Nationale (Paris)
BPR	*The Register of Edward the Black Prince Preserved in the Public Record Office*, ed. M. C. B. Dawes, 4 vols (London, 1930–33)
CCR	*Calendar of Close Rolls*
CPR	*Calendar of Patent Rolls*
EHD	*English Historical Documents*
EHR	*English Historical Review*
ODNB	*Oxford Dictionary of National Biography* (online edn, 2004–13)
PROME	*The Parliament Rolls of Medieval England*, ed. C. Given-Wilson et al. (cd-rom) (Woodbridge, 2005)
TNA	The National Archives (London)
TRHS	*Transactions of the Royal Historical Society*

Introduction (1337)

1. *English Historical Documents*, IV, *1327–1485*, ed. A. R. Myers (London, 1969), 271.
2. H. Martin, *Histoire de France* (1855). For a discussion of the Hundred Years War as a historiographical concept, see K. Fowler, *The Age of Plantagenet and Valois* (London, 1967), 13–14.
3. M. G. A. Vale, *The Ancient Enemy: England, France and Europe from the Angevins to the Tudors* (London, 2007), ix.
4. See further K. DeVries, 'The Hundred Years Wars: Not One but Many', *The Hundred Years War, II: Different Vistas*, ed. D. J. Kagay and L. J. A. Villalon (Leiden, 2008), 3–36.
5. D. Bates, 'The Rise and Fall of Normandy, *c.* 911–1204', *England and Normandy in the Middle Ages*, ed. D. Bates and A. Curry (London, 1994), 19–35.
6. Treaty of Le Goulet (1200): *Recueil des Actes de Philippe Augustus*, ed. H.-F. Delaborde, 4 vols (Paris, 1916–79), II, 178–85; T. Rymer, *Foedera, conventions, litterae etc*, rev. ed. A. Clarke, F. Holbrooke and J. Coley, 4 vols in 7 parts (London, 1816–69), I, i, 75–6; P. Chaplais, ed., *Diplomatic Documents*, I, *1101–1272* (London, 1964), no. 9; A. Curry, *The Hundred Years War* (Houndmills, 2nd edn, 2003), 29; J. Bradbury, *Philip Augustus, King of France, 1180–1223* (Harlow, 1998), 133–5.
7. G. P. Cuttino, *English Medieval Diplomacy* (Bloomington, IN, 1985), 49–51.
8. Treaty of Paris (1259): *English Historical Documents*, III, *1189–1327*, ed. H. Rothwell (London, 1975), 376–9. See also W. M. Ormrod, 'England, Normandy and the Beginnings

of the Hundred Years War, 1259–1360', *England and Normandy*, ed. Bates and Curry, 198; P. Chaplais, 'The Making of the Treaty of Paris (1259) and the Royal Style', *EHR*, 67 (1952), 235–53; E. Hallam and J. Everard, *Capetian France, 987–1328* (Harlow, 2nd edn, 2001), 283, 342–4.

9. F. Watson, 'Settling the Stalemate: Edward I's Peace in Scotland, 1303–1305', *Thirteenth-Century England*, VI, ed. M. Prestwich, R. H. Britnell and R. Frame (Woodbridge, 1997), 128; M. Prestwich, *Edward I* (New Haven, CT, and London, 1997), 275.

10. M. Prestwich, *Plantagenet England, 1225–1360* (Oxford, 2005), 165–8.

11. For further discussion of this in a wider context, see S. Gunn, 'War and the Emergence of the State: Western Europe, 1350–1600', *European Warfare, 1350–1750*, ed. F. Tallett and D. J. B. Trim (Cambridge, 2010), 50–73; R. G. Asch, 'War and State Building', *ibid.*, 322–37.

12. Curry, *Hundred Years War*, 35–7; J. R. Strayer, *The Reign of Philip the Fair* (Princeton, NJ, 1980), 318–24; Prestwich, *Edward I*, 376–400.

13. M. G. A. Vale, *The Origins of the Hundred Years War: The Angevin Legacy, 1250–1340* (Oxford, 1996), 227–9.

14. P. Chaplais, *The War of Saint-Sardos (1323–1325): Gascon Correspondence and Diplomatic Documents* (London, 1945).

15. S. Phillips, *Edward II* (New Haven, CT, and London, 2010), 512–16, 522–50.

16. W. M. Ormrod, *Edward III* (New Haven, CT, and London, 2011), 82–3; R. J. Knecht, *The Valois: Kings of France 1328–1589* (London, 2007), 1–2, 24; C. Taylor, 'The Salic Law and the Valois Succession to the French Crown', *French History*, 15 (2001), 358–77; *idem*, 'Edward III and the Plantagenet Claim to the French Throne', *The Age of Edward III*, ed. J. Bothwell (York, 2001), 156–7.

17. A. Ayton, 'The English Army at Crécy', *The Battle of Crécy, 1346*, ed. A. Ayton and P. Preston (Woodbridge, 2005), 200–29; C. J. Rogers, *War Cruel and Sharp: English Strategy under Edward III, 1327–1360* (Woodbridge, 2000), 27–76, esp. 28–33, 36, 54–5, 58–9, 63, 73–4; *idem*, ed., *The Wars of Edward III: Sources and Interpretations* (Woodbridge, 1999), 38.

18. H. Knighton, *Knighton's Chronicle 1337–1396*, ed. G. Martin (Oxford, 1995), 3. See also G. W. S. Barrow, *Robert Bruce and the Community of the Realm of Scotland* (London, 1965), 369.

19. M. Prestwich, 'Why did Englishmen Fight in the Hundred Years War?', *Medieval History*, 2 (1992), 63–4; P. Contamine, 'La Guerre de Cent Ans en France: Une approche économique', *BIHR*, 47 (1974), 125–49; E. B. Fryde, 'Financial Resources of Edward III in the Netherlands, 1337–40, Pt. 2', *Revue belge de philologie et d'histoire*, 45 (1967), 1,142–216; J. E. Ziegler, 'Edward III and Low Country Finances: 1338–1340, with Particular Emphasis on the Dominant Position of Brabant', *Revue belge de philologie et d'histoire*, 61 (1983), 802–17; J. F. Verbruggen, 'Flemish Urban Militias against the French Cavalry Armies in the Fourteenth and Fifteenth Centuries', trans. K. DeVries, *Journal of Medieval Military History*, I, ed. B. S. Bachrach (Woodbridge, 2002), 145–69; *idem*, *The Battle of the Golden Spurs: Courtrai, 11 July 1302*, ed. K. DeVries, trans. D. R. Ferguson (Woodbridge, 2002).

20. J. le Bel, *Chronique*, ed. J. Viard and E. Déprez, 2 vols (Paris, 1904), I, 119–20; J. Sumption, *The Hundred Years War*, I: *Trial by Battle* (London, 1990), 292.

21. T. Wright, ed., *Political Poems and Songs Relating to English History*, 2 vols (London, 1859–61), I, 1–25; M. G. A. Vale, *The Princely Court: Medieval Courts and Culture in North-West Europe* (Oxford, 2001), 213–18; Ormrod, *Edward III*, 189.

22. On the significance of the English claim to the throne and the seriousness with which it was viewed, see E. Perroy, *The Hundred Years War*, trans W. B. Wells (London, 1951), 69, and for a contrary view J. le Patourel, 'Edward III and the Kingdom of France', *History*, 43 (1958), repr. in Rogers, *The Wars of Edward III*, 247–64. For further comment, see C. T. Allmand, *The Hundred Years War: England and France at War, c.1300–c.1450* (Cambridge, 1988), 7–12; Curry, *Hundred Years War*, 44–58. For the treaty of Esplechin, see Sumption, *Trial by Battle*, 358–9.

23. K. A. Fowler, *The King's Lieutenant: Henry of Grosmont, First Duke of Lancaster, 1310–1361* (London, 1969), 46–66.

24. A. Grant, 'Disaster at Neville's Cross: The Scottish Point of View', *The Battle of Neville's Cross, 1346*, ed. D. Rollason and M. Prestwich (Stamford, 1998), 32–5; Sumption, *Trial by Battle*, 574–6.

25. Rogers, *War Cruel and Sharp*, 286–324.

26. D. Green, *The Battle of Poitiers, 1356* (Stroud, rev. edn, 2008), 38–69.

27. D. J. Aiton, ' "Shame on him who allows them to live": The Jacquerie of 1358', unpub. PhD thesis (University of Glasgow, 2007), esp. 97–147.
28. Treaty of Brétigny-Calais (1360): BL Additional MS 32097 fol. 108v; MS Stowe 140ff., 50v–56; E. Cosneau, *Les grands traités de la Guerre de Cent Ans* (Paris, 1889), 33–68; Rymer, *Foedera*, III, i, 202–9; *English Historical Documents*, IV, 103; C. J. Rogers, 'The Anglo-French Peace Negotiations of 1354–1360 Reconsidered', *Age of Edward III*, ed. Bothwell, 193–214; Ormrod, *Edward III*, 397–413.
29. The grant of the principality of Aquitaine (19 July 1362): TNA E30/1105; BL Cotton MS Nero D VI f.31; Rymer, *Feodera*, III, ii, 669. On the Free Companies, see K. Fowler, *Medieval Mercenaries*, I: *The Great Companies* (Oxford, 2001), 46–52; R. Delachenal, *Charles V*, 5 vols (Paris, 1909–31), III, 239ff.
30. Knecht, *Valois*, 33.
31. Treaty of Libourne (1366): Rymer, *Foedera*, III, ii, 799–807; C. A. González Paz, 'The Role of Mercenary Troops in Spain in the Fourteenth Century: The Civil War', *Mercenaries and Paid Men: The Mercenary Identity in the Middle Ages*, ed. John France (Leiden, 2008), 331–43; P. E. Russell, *The English Intervention in Spain and Portugal in the Time of Edward III and Richard II* (Oxford, 1955), 59–101; Clara Estow, *Pedro the Cruel of Castile, 1350–1369* (Leiden, 1995), 232ff; L. J. A. Villalon, 'Spanish Involvement in the Hundred Years War and the Battle of Nájera', *The Hundred Years War*, I: *A Wider Focus*, ed. D. Kagay and L. J. A. Villalon (Leiden, 2005), 3–74.
32. T. Walsingham, *The St Albans Chronicle: The Chronica Maiora of Thomas Walsingham*, I, *1376–1394*, ed. and trans. J. Taylor, W. R. Childs and L. Watkiss (Oxford, 2003), 37; D. Green, 'Medicine and Masculinity: Thomas Walsingham and the Death of the Black Prince', *Journal of Medieval History*, 35 (2009), 34–51.
33. Delachenal, *Charles V*, IV, 408–18; V, 5–37; F. Autrand, *Charles V, le sage* (Paris, 1994), 568–612.
34. J. B. Henneman, *Olivier de Clisson and Political Society in France under Charles V and Charles VI* (Philadelphia, PA, 1996), 172–88.
35. A. Curry, 'War or Peace? Philippe de Mézières, Richard II and Anglo-French Diplomacy', *Philippe de Mézières and His Age: Piety and Politics in the Fourteenth Century*, ed. R. Blumenfeld-Kosinski and K. Petkov (Leiden, 2011), 295–320; N. Saul, *Richard II* (New Haven, CT, and London, 1997), 205–34.
36. M. Bennett, *Richard II and the Revolution of 1399* (Stroud, 1999), 170–91; R. C. Famiglietti, *Royal Intrigue: Crisis at the Court of Charles VI, 1392–1420* (New York, 1986), 73–110; R. Vaughan, *John the Fearless: The Growth of Burgundian Power* (Woodbridge, new edn, 2002), 67–102; R. R. Davies, *The Revolt of Owain Glyn Dŵr* (Oxford, 1995), 102–28.
37. J. Barker, *Conquest: The English Kingdom of France, 1417–1450* (London, 2009), 3–30; Allmand, *Hundred Years War*, 27–9.
38. Treaty of Troyes (1420): Cosneau, *Grands traités*, 100–15; P. Chaplais, *English Medieval Diplomatic Practice, Part One: Documents and Interpretations*, 2 vols (London, 1982), II, 629–36.
39. C. T. Allmand, *Henry V* (New Haven, CT, and London, 1997), 61–150.
40. L. J. Taylor, *The Virgin Warrior: The Life and Death of Joan of Arc* (New Haven, CT, and London, 2009), 56–60, 92–4; M. G. A. Vale, *Charles VII* (London, 1974), 56–7.
41. R. Vaughan, *Philip the Good: The Apogee of Burgundy* (Woodbridge, new edn, 2002), 98–107.
42. Vale, *Charles VII*, 70–4, 79–84.
43. B. Wolffe, *Henry VI* (New Haven, CT, and London, new edn, 2001), 184–214; R. A. Griffiths, *The Reign of Henry VI: The Exercise of Royal Authority, 1422–1461* (London, 1981), 443–81; A. Corvisier, *Histoire militaire de la France*, 1: *Des origines à 1715* (Paris, 1992), 201–5.
44. M. Keen, 'The End of the Hundred Years War: Lancastrian France and Lancastrian England', *Nobles, Knights and Men-at-Arms in the Middle Ages* (London, 1996), 239–55; A. J. Pollard, *John Talbot and the War in France, 1427–1453* (Barnsley, 2nd edn, 2005), 131–8.

Chapter 1 Knights and Nobles: Flowers of Chivalry (1346)

1. Wright, ed., *Political Poems and Songs*, I, 6–7.
2. Vale, *Princely Court*, 213–18.
3. J. Huizinga, *Homo Ludens: A Study of the Play Element in Culture* (London, 1970), 17–18.

4. For further discussion of chivalrous writing in this period, see C. Taylor, 'English Writings on Chivalry and Warfare during the Hundred Years War', *Soldiers, Nobles and Gentlemen: Essays in Honour of Maurice Keen*, ed. P. Coss and C. Tyerman (Woodbridge, 2009), 65–70.
5. R. Vernier, *The Flower of Chivalry: Bertrand du Guesclin and the Hundred Years War* (Woodbridge, 2003), 5–6.
6. Honoré Bonet (sometimes called Bouvet) became prior of Salon, near Embrun. He studied at the University of Avignon and held various minor official positions. His book *L'arbre des batailles* is a treatise on war and the laws of war. Written in 1387 for a broad readership, it proved extremely influential: *The Tree of Battles of Honoré Bouvet*, trans. G. W. Coopland (Liverpool, 1949).
7. See further D. Crouch, 'Chivalry and Courtliness: Colliding Constructs', *Soldiers, Nobles and Gentlemen*, ed. Coss and Tyerman, 32–48.
8. J. Sumption, *The Hundred Years War*, II: *Trial by Fire* (London, 1999), 494, 497–8, 532; J. Viard, 'La campagne de juillet-août et la bataille de Crécy', *Le Moyen Âge*, 2nd ser. 27 (1926), 3–4.
9. R. Kaeuper, 'The Societal Role of Chivalry in Romance: Northwestern Europe', *The Cambridge Companion to Medieval Romance*, ed. R. L. Krueger (Cambridge, 2000), 99.
10. On the vexed question of the Blanchetaque crossing and whether Edward III was aware of the ford in advance, see A. Ayton, 'The Crécy Campaign', *Battle of Crécy*, ed. Ayton and Preston, 85–98.
11. For accounts of the battle of Crécy, see *Chronicon Galfridi le Baker de Swynebroke*, ed. E. M. Thompson (Oxford, 1889), 82–5; *Knighton's Chronicle*, 63; A. Murimuth, *Continuatio Chronicarum*, ed. E. M. Thompson (London, 1889), 246; J. Froissart, *Oeuvres*, ed. Kervyn de Lettenhove, 28 vols (Brussels, 1867–77), V, 33–8; J. Froissart, *Chroniques*, ed. S. Luce, G. Raynaud and L. Mirot, 15 vols (Paris, 1869–1975), III, 169, 405, 407, 409; Le Bel, *Chronique*, II, 99ff. For various interpretations, see Viard, 'Le campagne de juillet-août', 67, 70–1; Rogers, *War Cruel and Sharp*, 266–70; B. Schnerb, 'Vassals, Allies and Mercenaries: The French Army before and after 1346', *Battle of Crécy*, ed. Ayton and Preston, 269–70.
12. Ayton, 'The English Army at Crécy', 200–15; K. DeVries, *Infantry Warfare in the Early Fourteenth Century: Discipline, Tactics and Technology* (Woodbridge, 1996), 112–28 (on Dupplin Moor and Halidon Hill); P. Boitani, 'Petrarch and the "barbari Britanni"', *Petrarch in Britain: Interpreters, Imitators, and Translators over 700 Years*, ed. M. McLaughlin, L. Panizza and P. Hainsworth (Oxford, 2007), 9.
13. W. Shakespeare, *Henry V*, I. ii. 102–12.
14. M. Keen, *Chivalry* (New Haven, CT, and London, 1984), 18–43; D. Crouch, *The Birth of Nobility: Constructing Aristocracy in England and France, 900–1300* (Harlow, 2005), 46–86.
15. C. J. Rogers, 'The Military Revolutions of the Hundred Years' War', *Journal of Military History*, 57 (1993), 258–75; DeVries, *Infantry Warfare*, esp. 9–22, 66–85, 100–11.
16. According to Le Baker, French crossbows at Poitiers did inflict considerable damage: *Chronicon*, 151. For a cautionary note regarding the disparity between longbows and crossbows, see R. Mitchell, 'The Longbow–Crossbow Shootout at Crécy (1346): Has the "Rate of Fire Commonplace" been Overrated?', *The Hundred Years War*, II: *Different Vistas*, ed. L. J. A. Villalon and D. J. Kagay (Leiden, 2008), 233–57.
17. *The True Chronicles of Jean le Bel, 1290–1360*, trans. N. Bryant (Woodbridge, 2011), 180.
18. *BPR*, I, 14, 45; P. Morgan, *War and Society in Medieval Cheshire, 1277–1403* (Manchester, 1987), 182, 186.
19. *Froissart: Chronicles*, ed. and trans. G. Brereton (Harmondsworth, 1978), 92; J. Froissart, *Chroniques: Le Manuscrit d'Amiens*, III, ed. G. T. Diller (Geneva, 1992), 20. Despite Edward's comments, reported by Froissart, the bishop of Durham and the earls of Huntingdon and Suffolk may have sent reinforcements to assist the Black Prince: *Anonimalle Chronicle, 1333–1381*, ed. V. H. Galbraith (Manchester, 1927), 22.
20. Le Baker, *Chronicon*, 82–5; Froissart, *Oeuvres*, ed. Lettenhove, V, 37–8; R. Barber, *Edward, Prince of Wales and Aquitaine: A Biography of the Black Prince* (Woodbridge, 1978), 68; Sumption, *Trial by Fire*, 530.
21. *Anonimalle Chronicle*, 23, 160.
22. *Froissart: Chronicles*, ed. and trans. Brereton, 89–90.
23. J. Barker, *The Tournament in England, 1100–1400* (Woodbridge, 1986), 184.
24. Cited by Kaeuper, 'Societal Role of Chivalry', 102.

25. C. de Pizan, *The Book of the Body Politic*, ed. and trans. K. L. Forhan (Cambridge, 1994), 59, 63.

26. For examples of the mantra *qui plus fait, mieux vault* ('he who achieves most is the most worthy'), see G. de Charny, *The Book of Chivalry*, ed. and trans. R. W. Kaeuper and E. Kennedy (Philadelphia, PA, 1996), 87, 93, 95, 97, 99. Similarly, Chaucer and Dante judged individuals according to worth, although not only their military value: N. Saul, 'Chaucer and Gentility', *Chaucer's England: Literature in Historical Context*, ed. B. A. Hanawalt (Minneapolis, MN, 1992), 49.

27. In the foreword to Frontinus's *Stratagems*, translated for Charles VII, Jean de Rouvroy, dean of the faculty of theology at the University of Paris, noted 'more battles . . . have been won by ruses and subtleties . . . than by greater numbers': Vale, *Charles VII*, 195; C. de Pizan, *Book of the Body Politic*, 64.

28. Charny, *Book of Chivalry*, 11–13; Le Bel, *Chronicles*, trans. Bryant, 208; Froissart, *Oeuvres*, ed. Lettenhove, V, 220–51, 271–4; Y. N. Harari, *Special Operations in the Age of Chivalry, 1100–1550* (Woodbridge, 2007), 109–24.

29. M. Keen, 'War, Peace and Chivalry', *Nobles, Knights and Men-at-Arms*, 13–20.

30. For such arguments see J. Huizinga, *The Autumn of the Middle Ages*, trans. R. J. Payton and U. Mammitzsch (Chicago, IL, 1996); R. Kilgour, *The Decline of Chivalry as Shown in the French Literature of the Late Middle Ages* (Cambridge, MA, 1937).

31. R. W. Kaeuper, *Chivalry and Violence in Medieval Europe* (Oxford, 1999), 129–49.

32. Chandos Herald, *Life of the Black Prince*, ed. and trans. M. K. Pope and E. C. Lodge (Oxford, 1910), 136.

33. Jean Juvénal des Ursins, cited by J. Gillingham, 'Richard I and the Science of War in the Middle Ages', *War and Government in the Middle Ages: Essays in Honour of J. O. Prestwich*, ed. J. Gillingham and J. C. Holt (Woodbridge, 1984), 85.

34. A. Ayton and J. L. Price, eds, *The Medieval Military Revolution: State, Society and Military Change in Medieval and Early Modern Europe* (London, 1995); C. J. Rogers, ed., *The Military Revolution Debate: Readings on the Military Transformation of Early Modern Europe* (Boulder, CO, 1995), esp. ch. 3.

35. On the recognition of the need for discipline in French armies by the end of the war, see J. de Bueil, *Le Jouvencel*, ed. C. Favre and L. Lecestre, 2 vols (Paris, 1887, repr. Geneva, 1996), II, 32; M. Chan Tsin, 'Medieval Romances and Military History: Marching Orders in Jean de Bueil's *Le Jouvencel introduit aux armes*', *Journal of Medieval Military History*, VII, *The Age of the Hundred Years War*, ed. C. J. Rogers, K. DeVries, and J. France (Woodbridge, 2009), 126–34.

36. Keen, *Chivalry*, 221.

37. Walsingham, *The St Albans Chronicle: The Chronica Maiora of Thomas Walsingham*, II: *1394–1422*, ed. and trans. J. Taylor, W. R. Childs and L. Watkiss (Oxford, 2011), 687.

38. Sir T. Gray, *Scalacronica, 1272–1363*, ed. and trans. A. King (Woodbridge, 2005), 83.

39. A. King, 'The Ethics of War in Sir Thomas Gray's *Scalacronica*', *War, Government and Aristocracy in the British Isles c.1150–1500: Essays in Honour of Michael Prestwich*, ed. C. Given-Wilson, A. Kettle and L. Scales (Woodbridge, 2008), 153; *idem*, 'A Helm with a Crest of Gold: The Order of Chivalry in Thomas Gray's *Scalacronica*', *Fourteenth-Century England*, I, ed. N. Saul (Woodbridge, 2000), 22–4.

40. R. Barber, 'The Military Role of the Order of the Garter', *Journal of Medieval Military History*, VII, *The Age of the Hundred Years War*, ed. C. J. Rogers, K. DeVries, and J. France (Woodbridge, 2009), 1–11; D. A. J. D. Boulton, *The Knights of the Crown: The Monarchical Orders of Knighthood in Later Medieval Europe, 1325–1520* (Woodbridge, 1987), 127–8; J. Munby, R. Barber and R. Brown, *Edward III's Round Table at Windsor* (Woodbridge, 2007), esp. 77–99; P. R. Coss, *The Knight in Medieval England, 1000–1400* (Stroud, 1993), 91, 100.

41. H. Collins, *The Order of the Garter, 1348–1461: Chivalry and Politics in Late Medieval England* (Oxford, 2000), 1, 41; N. Saul, 'Introduction', *St George's Chapel, Windsor in the Fourteenth Century*, ed. N. Saul (Woodbridge, 2005), 1; J. R. Major, *From Renaissance Monarchy to Absolute Monarchy: French Kings, Nobles and Estates* (Baltimore, MD, and London, 1994), 68.

42. TNA E101/407/4, 17 (knighting of James I); M. G. A. Vale, *War and Chivalry: Warfare and Aristocratic Culture in England, France, and Burgundy at the End of the Middle Ages* (Atlanta, GA, 1981), 34, 36, 39–42.

43. M. Penman, *David II* (Edinburgh, 2004), 150–1; K. Stevenson, *Chivalry and Knighthood in Scotland, 1424–1513* (Woodbridge, 2006), 2, 170–9.
44. M. Keen, 'Coucy, Enguerrand (VII) de, earl of Bedford (*c*.1340–1397)', *ODNB* (online edn, 2004); Griffiths, *Reign of King Henry VI*, 512–13.
45. Boulton, *Knights of the Crown*, 181, 184–5, 197.
46. Le Bel, *Chronicles*, trans. Bryant, 217.
47. See *Book of Chivalry*, esp. 48–64. On the distribution and influence of Vegetius's text in the Middle Ages, see C. T. Allmand, *The De Re Militari of Vegetius: The Reception, Transmission and Legacy of a Roman Text in the Middle Ages* (Cambridge, 2011), esp. 121–32 (for its influence over C. de Pizan and Jean Juvénal des Ursins).
48. M. Bloch, *Feudal Society*, trans. L. A. Manyon, 2 vols (London, 2nd edn, 1971), II, 283–344; D. Crouch, *The Image of the Aristocracy in Britain, 1100–1300* (London, 1992), 153; *idem, Birth of Nobility*, 29–36, 222–52; G. Duby, *The Chivalrous Society*, trans. C. Postan (Berkeley and Los Angeles, CA, 1977), 75; *idem, The Three Orders: Feudal Society Imagined*, trans. A. Goldhammer (Chicago, IL, 1980), 293–307; P. R. Coss, *The Lady in Medieval England, 1000–1500* (Stroud, 1998), 37; *idem, Knight in Medieval England*, 50–2.
49. P. Contamine, 'Points de vue sur la chevalerie en France à la fin du Moyen Âge', *Francia*, 4 (1976), 256; P. R. Coss, *The Origins of the English Gentry* (Cambridge, 2003), 18, 239.
50. C. de Pizan, *Book of the Body Politic*, 50.
51. C. de Pizan's *Book of Deeds of Arms and of Chivalry* is first and foremost a military guide. While there is consideration of just wars (C. de Pizan, *The Book of Deeds of Arms and of Chivalry*, trans. S. Willard, ed. C. C. Willard [University Park, PA, 1999], 14–15), the perils of war and the consideration that a prince should give to the matter prior to setting out on a campaign (18–23), the bulk of the work is concerned with the appointment of military officers (e.g. 23–6), the qualities they should possess (37–9), the lodging of troops, procedures for marching, crossing natural obstacles, preparations for battle, the arrangement of soldiers on the battlefield, provisions, advice on storming and defending a fortress, soldiers' pay (153–5), the distribution of booty and similar matters. A section is devoted to the proper use of tricks and subtlety in combat (163–4). Consideration is also given to topics such as ransoms, judicial combats and heraldry.
52. H. Kaminsky, 'Estate, Nobility and the Exhibition of Estate in the Later Middle Ages', *Speculum*, 68 (1993), 701; H. Zmora, *Monarchy, Aristocracy and State in Europe, 1300–1800* (London, 2000), 22–3; J. Mourier, 'Nobilitas quid est? Un procès à Tain-l'Hermitage en 1408', *BEC*, 142 (1984), 255–69.
53. Major, *From Renaissance Monarchy to Absolute Monarchy*, 58–9. See also G. Prosser, ' "Decayed Feudalism" and "Royal Clienteles": Royal Office and Magnate Service in the Fifteenth Century', *War, Government and Power in Late Medieval France*, ed. C. T. Allmand (Liverpool, 2000), 180; *idem*, 'The Later Medieval French *noblesse*', *France in the Later Middle Ages*, ed. D. Potter (Oxford, 2003), 182–5.
54. P. Contamine, 'La Guerre de Cent Ans: Le xvᵉ siècle. Du "Roi de Bourges" au très victorieux Roi de France', *Histoire militaire de la France*, 1: *Des origines à 1715*, ed. A. Corvisier (Paris, 1992), 198–208; D. Potter, 'Chivalry and Professionalism in the French Armies of the Renaissance', *The Chivalric Ethos and the Development of Military Professionalism*, ed. D. J. B. Trim (Leiden, 2003), 152.
55. Jean de Bueil, *Le Jouvencel*, II, 100.
56. Alongside a number of translations of French works by Christine de Pizan, Alain Chartier and others Nicholas Upton wrote *De studio militari* for Humphrey, duke of Gloucester, in 1447; and William Worcester's *Boke of Noblesse* was later given to Edward IV: Taylor, 'English Writings on Chivalry and Warfare', *Soldiers, Nobles and Gentlemen*, ed. Coss and Tyerman, 68.
57. *The Chronica Maiora of Thomas Walsingham (1376–1422)*, ed. and trans. D. Preest and J. G. Clark (Woodbridge, 2005), 210; *St Albans Chronicle*, I, cv–cvi, 705.
58. Report of the battle of Poitiers by Robert Prite, clerk: BL Cotton Caligula D III f. 33. See also Froissart, *Oeuvres*, ed. Lettenhove, XVIII, 388; 'Complainte sur la bataille de Poitiers', ed. Ch. de Beaurepaire, *BEC*, 12 (1851), 257–63. French defeats were attributed 'à l'impéritie [incompetence] de la classe militaire par excellence, c'est-à-dire de la noblesse'. See also P. Contamine, 'De la puissance aux privilèges: doléances de la noblesse française envers la monarchie aux XIVᵉ et XVᵉ siècles', *La noblesse au Moyen Âge, XIe–XVe siècles. Essais à la mémoire de Robert Boutruche*, ed. P. Contamine (Paris, 1976), 250; *idem, Guerre, état et société*

à la fin du Moyen Âge. Études sur les armées des rois de France, 1337–1494 (Paris, 1972), 45, 175; F. Autrand, 'La déconfiture: La bataille de Poitiers (1356) à travers quelques textes français des XIVe et XVe siècles', *Guerre et société en France, en Angleterre et en Bourgogne, XIVe–XVe siècle*, ed. P. Contamine, C. Giry-Deloison and M. Keen (Villeneuve d'Ascq, 1991), 93–121.

Chapter 2 The Peasantry: *Vox Populi* (1358)

1. Bonet, *Tree of Battles*, 189.
2. *The Chronicle of Jean de Venette*, ed. and trans. J. Birdsall and R. A. Newhall (New York, 1953), 76.
3. D. Bessen, 'The Jacquerie: Class War or Co-opted Rebellion?', *Journal of Medieval History*, 11 (1985), 43–59.
4. N. Wright, *Knights and Peasants: The Hundred Years War in the French Countryside* (Woodbridge, 1998), 84–5; P. S. Lewis, *Later Medieval France: The Polity* (London, 1968), 283–6; S. K. Cohn, *Lust for Liberty: The Politics of Social Revolt in Medieval Europe, 1200–1425* (Cambridge, MA, 2006), 34–5, 220–1.
5. *Froissart: Chroniques*, ed. and trans. Brereton, 151–2. See further S. K. Cohn, *Popular Protest in Late Medieval Europe: Italy, France and Flanders* (Manchester, 2004), 143.
6. Further evidence can be found in petitions made to the king or English Parliament (collected chiefly in TNA SC8), and in *lettres des remission* which the French king offered as pardons for a crime or failure to comply with official instructions (found mainly in AN JJ).
7. See, for example, R. Boutruche, 'The Devastation of Rural Areas during the Hundred Years War and the Agricultural Recovery of France', *The Recovery of France in the Fifteenth Century*, ed. P. S. Lewis, trans. G. F. Martin (London, 1971), 23–59; J.-M. Tourneur-Aumont, *La bataille de Poitiers (1356) et la construction de la France* (Poitiers, 1943). The *Annalistes* took their name from the scholarly journal *Annales d'histoire économique et sociale*. They stressed the significance of long-term (*longue durée*) historical studies and promoted the use of social scientific methods, often emphasising social rather than political or diplomatic issues.
8. C. de Pizan, *Book of the Body Politic*, 16–17.
9. For the 1385 ordinances and those of Henry V, usually dated to 1419, see *The Black Book of the Admiralty*, ed. T. Twiss, 4 vols (London, 1871), I, 453–8; 459–72. For discussion of these see M. Keen, 'Richard II's Ordinances of War of 1385', *Rulers and Ruled in Late Medieval England: Essays Presented to G. L. Harriss*, ed. R. E. Archer and S. Walker (London, 1995), esp. 34, 37–8; A. Curry, 'The Military Ordinances of Henry V: Texts and Contexts', *War, Government and Aristocracy in the British Isles*, ed. Given-Wilson et al., esp. 227.
10. *Gesta Henrici Quinti. The Deeds of Henry the Fifth*, ed. and trans. F. Taylor and J. S. Roskell (Oxford, 1975), 69.
11. P. Charbonnier, 'The Economy and Society of France in the Later Middle Ages: On the Eve of Crisis', *France in the Later Middle Ages*, ed. D. Potter (Oxford, 2003), 55; O. J. Benedictow, *The Black Death, 1346–1353: The Complete History* (Woodbridge, 2004), 98. According to the 1334 English lay subsidy, allowing for two exempt counties and leaving the towns aside, about 13,000 villages paid tax. These were communities of 300–400 people; both size and number fell after the Black Death: C. Dyer, 'The Political Life of the Fifteenth-Century English Village', *Political Culture in Late Medieval Britain*, ed. L. Clark and C. Carpenter (Woodbridge, 2004), 139.
12. J. Dewald and L. Vardi, 'The Peasantries of France, 1400–1789', *The Peasantries of Europe from the Fourteenth to the Eighteenth Centuries*, ed. T. Scott (Harlow, 1998), 22–4.
13. G. Pépin, 'Does a Common Language Mean a Shared Allegiance? Language, Identity, Geography and their Links with Polities: The Cases of Gascony and Britanny', *Contact and Exchange in Later Medieval Europe: Essays in Honour of Malcolm Vale*, ed. H. Skoda, P. Lantschner and R. L. J. Shaw (Woodbridge, 2012), 79–101.
14. Charbonnier, 'The Economy and Society of France', 57–8; G. L. Harriss, *Shaping the Nation: England 1360–1461* (Oxford, 2005), 209–14, 222, 227.
15. G. Small, *Late Medieval France* (Basingstoke, 2009), 59–60.
16. *Chronicle of Jean de Venette*, 75–6.
17. Boutruche, 'Devastation of Rural Areas', 27–31.
18. T. Basin, *Histoire de Charles VII*, ed. C. Samaran, 2 vols (Paris, 1933, 1944), I, 84.

19. M. Bennett, 'The Experience of Civilian Populations during the Hundred Years War in France, 1330–1440', *British Commission for Military History Newsletter* (Spring 2009).

20. C. T. Allmand, 'War and the Non-Combatant in the Middle Ages', *Medieval Warfare: A History*, ed. M. Keen (Oxford, 1999), 260–1; D. Green, 'National Identities and the Hundred Years War', *Fourteenth-Century England*, VI, ed. C. Given-Wilson (Woodbridge, 2010), 115–29.

21. R. Barber, *The Life and Campaigns of the Black Prince* (Woodbridge, 1979), 52.

22. C. J. Rogers, 'By Fire and Sword: *Bellum Hostile* and "Civilians" in the Hundred Years War', *Civilians in the Path of War*, ed. M. Grimsley and C. J. Rogers (Lincoln, NB, 2002), 69 n. 34; H. J. Hewitt, *The Black Prince's Expedition of 1355–1357* (Manchester, 1958), 72–5.

23. This is also described in the 'Bergerie nouvelle, fort joyeuse et morale, de Mieulx que devant, à quatre personnaiges, c'est assavoir: Mieulx que devant, Plat Pays, Peuple Pensif, et la Bergière', *Ancien théâtre françois ou Collection des ouvrages dramatiques les plus remarquables depuis les mystères jusqu'à Corneille*, ed. Viollet le Duc, 10 vols (Paris, 1854–7), III, 213–31.

24. Wright, *Knights and Peasants*, 99–102. See further A. Blanchet, *Les souterrains-refuges de la France: Contribution à l'histoire de l'habitation humaine* (Paris, 1923), 176–7.

25. Wright, *Knights and Peasants*, 106–7.

26. M. Jones, 'War and Fourteenth-Century France', *Arms, Armies and Fortifications in the Hundred Years War*, ed. A. Curry and M. Hughes (Woodbridge, 1994), 108–10; N. Wright, 'French Peasants in the Hundred Years War', *History Today*, 33 (1983), 39–42.

27. This appears to be in spite of the orders of 17 August that 'under pain of death there should be no more setting fire to places (as there had been to begin with) and that churches and sacred buildings along with their property should be preserved intact, and that no one should lay hands upon a woman or on a priest or servant of a church, unless he happened to be armed, offered violence or attacked anyone': *Gesta Henrici Quinti*, 27, 61, 71.

28. Wright, *Knights and Peasants*, 77.

29. P. Champion, *Guillaume de Flavy, capitaine de Compiègne: contribution à l'histoire de Jeanne d'Arc et à l'étude de la vie militaire et priveée au XVe siècle* (Paris, 1906), 205.

30. *Le pastoralet*, ed. J. Blanchard (Paris, 1983), sections of this work are translated in A. Curry, *The Battle of Agincourt: Sources and Interpretations* (Woodbridge, 2000), 351–3. See also H. Cooper, 'Speaking for the Victim', *Writing War: Medieval Literary Responses to Warfare*, ed. C. Saunders, F. Le Saux and N. Thomas (Cambridge, 2004), 213–16, 222–8.

31. *Froissart: Chronicles*, ed. and trans. Brereton, 178.

32. P. Ducourtieux, *Histoire de Limoges* (Limoges, 1925, repr. Marseille, 1975), 53, 59; D. Green, *Edward the Black Prince: Power in Medieval Europe* (Harlow, 2007), 91–2; Barber, *Edward, Prince of Wales and Aquitaine*, 226 and n. 23; *idem*, *The Knight and Chivalry* (Woodbridge, rev. edn, 1995), 240.

33. S. McGlynn, *By Sword and Fire: Cruelty and Atrocity in Medieval Warfare* (London, 2008), 142–3, 151; M. Keen, *The Laws of War in the Late Middle Ages* (London, 1965), 120–1, 124; J. Bradbury, *The Medieval Siege* (Woodbridge, 1992), 161.

34. Allmand, *Henry V*, 81–2, 117.

35. 'Chronique de Ruisseauville': Curry, *Battle of Agincourt*, 123.

36. E. de Monstrelet, *La chronique d'Enguerran de Monstrelet: en deux livres, avec pièces justificatives: 1400–1444*, ed. L. Douët-d'Arcq, 6 vols (Paris, 1857); Curry, *Battle of Agincourt*, 144. See also *Gesta Henrici Quinti*, 55.

37. *The Historical Collections of a Citizen of London in the Fifteenth Century*, ed. J. Gairdner (London, 1876), 1–46; McGlynn, *By Sword and Fire*, 193–4; Allmand, *Henry V*, 123–7.

38. *Froissart: Chronicles*, ed. Brereton, 306; M. Hughes, 'The Fourteenth-Century French Raids on Hampshire and the Isle of Wight', *Arms, Armies and Fortifications*, ed. Curry and Hughes, 125–7.

39. Walsingham, *Chronica Maiora*, ed. Preest, 226; *St Albans Chronicle*, I, 753.

40. *Knighton's Chronicle*, 351.

41. C. Dyer, *Making a Living in the Middle Ages: The People of Britain, 850–1520* (New Haven, CT, and London, 2002), 236–9.

42. Boutruche, 'Devastation of Rural Areas during the Hundred Years War', 51. R. M. Smith, 'The English Peasantry', *The Peasantries of Europe from the Fourteenth to the Eighteenth Centuries*, ed. T. Scott (London, 1998), 360–1; Dyer, 'Political Life of the Fifteenth-Century English Village', 135–58.

43. A. Chartier, *Le quadrilogue invectif*, ed. E. Droz (Paris, rev. edn, 1950), 33–4; Curry, *Battle of Agincourt*, 349.
44. Lewis, *Later Medieval France*, 280.
45. *Statutes of the Realm*, ed. A. Luders et al., 11 vols (London, 1810–28), I, 307.
46. P. D. Solon, 'Popular Response to Standing Military Forces in Fifteenth-Century France', *Studies in the Renaissance*, 19 (1972), 88.
47. J. Barnie, *War in Medieval Society: Social Values and the Hundred Years War, 1337–99* (London, 1974), 38–40; C. Given-Wilson, 'Purveyance for the Royal Household, 1362–1413', *BIHR*, 56 (1983), 145–63; I. Krug, 'Purveyance and Peasants at the Beginning of the Hundred Years War: Maddicott Reexamined', *The Hundred Years War*, II: *Different Vistas*, ed. D. Kagay and L. J. A. Villalon (Leiden, 2008), 345–65; W. M. Ormrod, 'Murmur, Clamour and Noise: Voicing Complaint and Remedy in Petitions to the English Crown, *c.*1300–*c.*1460', *Medieval Petitions: Grace and Grievance*, ed. W. M. Ormrod, G. Dodd and A. Musson (York, 2009), 149–50. For a complaint by the 'king's liegemen of Devon' regarding the purveyance of food by Sir Robert Ashton in preparation for an expedition to Brittany in 1375, see G. Dodd, *Justice and Grace: Private Petitioning and the English Parliament in the Late Middle Ages* (Oxford, 2007), 150.
48. W. M. Ormrod, 'The Peasants' Revolt and the Government of England', *Journal of British Studies*, 29 (1990), 1–30; Dyer, *Making a Living*, 284.
49. *Anonimalle Chronicle*, 144–7; R. B. Dobson, ed., *The Peasants' Revolt of 1381* (London, 2nd edn, 1988), 155–211.
50. *St Albans Chronicle*, I, 425; W. M. Ormrod, 'In Bed with Joan of Kent: The King's Mother and the Peasants' Revolt', *Medieval Women: Texts and Contexts in Late Medieval Britain: Essays for Felicity Riddy*, ed. J. Wogan-Browne et al. (Turnhout, 2000), 277–92.
51. Cohn, *Popular Protest*, 89; Wright, *Knights and Peasants*, 85–7.
52. Vaughan, *John the Fearless*, 99; R. Fédou, 'A Popular Revolt in Lyon in the Fifteenth Century: The *Rebeyne* of 1436', *The Recovery of France in the Fifteenth Century*, ed. Lewis, trans. Martin, 243–6, 254.
53. I. M. W. Harvey, *Jack Cade's Rebellion of 1450* (Oxford, 1991).
54. The Proclamation of Jack Cade (June 1450): *English Historical Documents*, IV, 266–7.
55. D. Grummitt, 'Deconstructing Cade's Rebellion: Discourse and Politics in the Mid-Fifteenth Century', *Identity and Insurgency in the Late Middle Ages*, ed. L. Clark (Woodbridge, 2006), 107.
56. R. Almond and A. J. Pollard, 'The Yeomanry of Robin Hood and Social Terminology in Fifteenth-Century England', *Past and Present*, 170 (2001), 52, 77.
57. See P. R. Coss, 'Cultural Diffusion and Robin Hood', *Past and Present*, 108 (1985), 35–79. The first written reference to Robin occurs in 1377 but the first surviving ballad, *Robin Hood and the Monk*, only dates from about 1450, and the *Gest of Robyn Hode* appears about fifty years later. Internal evidence suggests that, at the latest, it was put together by 1400 and 'there are good reasons for thinking … the *Gest* is … a product of the first half of the fourteenth century'. J. R. Maddicott, 'The Birth and Setting of the Robin Hood Ballads', *EHR*, 93 (1978), 276. Andrew Ayton suggests a date for the *Gest* in or before the 1330s: 'Military Service and the Development of the Robin Hood Legend in the Fourteenth Century', *Nottingham Medieval Studies*, 36 (1992), 129–30.
58. C. Richmond, 'An Outlaw and Some Peasants: The Possible Significance of Robin Hood', *Nottingham Medieval Studies*, 37 (1993), 92, 96–7.

Chapter 3 The Church and the Clergy: Voices from the Pulpit (1378)

1. Walsingham, *Chronica Maiora*, trans. Preest, 64; *St Albans Chronicle*, I, 223.
2. J. G. Clark, *The Benedictines in the Middle Ages* (Woodbridge, 2011), 255–6.
3. A. K. McHardy, *The Age of War and Wycliffe: Lincoln Diocese and its Bishop in the Later Fourteenth Century* (Lincoln, 2001), 30–1; D. S. Bachrach, 'The Organisation of Military Religion in the Armies of King Edward I of England (1272–1307)', *Journal of Medieval History*, 29 (2003), 265–86.
4. See C. Beaune, *The Birth of an Ideology: Myths and Symbols of France in Late Medieval France*, ed. F. L. Cheyette, trans. S. R. Huston (Berkeley, CA, 1991), esp. 172–96; H. J. Hewitt, *The Organization of War under Edward III, 1338–62* (New York, 1966), 154 ff; P. S. Lewis, 'War

Propaganda and Historiography in Fifteenth-Century France and England', *Essays in Later Medieval French History* (London, 1985), 193–214; A. K. McHardy, 'Liturgy and Propaganda in the Diocese of Lincoln during the Hundred Years War', *Religion and National Identity*, ed. S. Mews (Oxford, 1982), 215–27; D. Pearsall, ' "Crowned King": War and Peace in 1415', *The Lancastrian Court*, ed. J. Stratford (Donington, 2003), 163–72; N. Pons, 'La Guerre de Cent Ans vue par quelques polémistes français du XVe siècle', *Guerre et société*, ed. Contamine, Giry-Deloison and Keen, 143–69. For examples of legislation against rumour-mongering, see Rymer, *Foedera*, II, ii, 775; III, i, 72; C. T. Allmand, ed., *Society at War: The Experiences of England and France during the Hundred Years War* (London, 1973), 149–50.

5. 'The Great Chronicle of London': Allmand, *Society at War*, 102–3.

6. Walsingham, *Chronica Maiora*, ed. Preest, 413; *Gesta Henrici Quinti*, 102–13; W. R. Jones, 'The English Church and Royal Propaganda during the Hundred Years War', *Journal of British Studies*, 19 (1979), 19, 22–3, 27; G. W. Bernard, *The Late Medieval English Church: Vitality and Vulnerability before the Break with Rome* (New Haven, CT, and London, 2012), 24.

7. A. Bossuat, 'La littérature de propagande au XVe siècle: la mémoire de Jean de Rinel, secrétaire du roi d'Angleterre, contre le duc de Bourgogne (1435)', *Cahiers d'histoire*, 1 (1956), 146; N. Pons, 'Latin et français au XVe siècle: le témoignage des traits de propagande', *Le Moyen français*, 3 vols (Milan, 1986), II, 71; J. Krynen, *L'empire du roi: idées et croyances politiques en France, XIIIᵉ–XVᵉ siècles* (Paris, 1993), 311; C. Taylor, 'War, Propaganda and Diplomacy in Fifteenth-Century France and England', *War, Government and Power in Late Medieval France*, ed. C. Allmand (Liverpool, 2000), 71.

8. C. Given-Wilson, *Chronicles: The Writing of History in Medieval England* (London, 2004), 153–4; G. M. Spiegel, *The Chronicle Tradition of Saint-Denis: A Survey* (Brookline, MA, and Leiden, 1978), 72–4, 121, 124–5; G. Small, *George Chastellain and the Shaping of Valois Burgundy: Political and Historical Culture at Court in the Fifteenth Century* (Woodbridge, 1997), esp. 128–61.

9. Walsingham, *Chronica Maiora*, ed. Preest, 210; Henry Knighton's chronicle, written between 1379 and 1396, is a history of England from the Norman Conquest to the last decade of the fourteenth century, with some introductory passages on events before 1066. Adam Usk began writing his chronicle in the spring of 1401. It is at its fullest for the years 1397–1402 and has valuable accounts of the Parliament of 1397, the revolution of 1399 and the first two years of Henry IV's reign. The years 1402–14 are sparse on English affairs, but contain a good deal of information on the Glyn Dŵr revolt and the politics of the papal court; Thomas Walsingham's main historical works include: *Chronica Maiora* (written 1376–1422, with a retrospective section stretching back to 1272), *Gesta Abbatum* (written in the 1390s) and *Ypodigma Neustriae* (a digest of English and Norman history covering the period from 911 to 1419); the anonymous author of the *Gesta Henrici Quinti* compiled his narrative of the Agincourt campaign and surrounding events between 1416 and 1417.

10. J. Gerson, 'Vivat rex' and 'De puella Aureliansi', *Oeuvres complètes*, ed. P. Glorieux, 10 vols (Paris, 1960–73), VII, 1137–85; IX, 661–5; J. Chiffoleau, 'La religion flamboyante (v.1320–v.1520)', *Du Christianisme flamboyant à l'aube des Lumières (XIVᵉ–XVIIIᵉ siècles)*, ed. J. Chiffoleau et al. (Paris, 1988), 60.

11. B. Guenée, *Between Church and State: The Lives of Four French Prelates in the Late Middle Ages*, trans. A. Goldhammer (Chicago, IL, 1991), 149–50.

12. Lewis, 'War Propaganda and Historiography', 201–2.

13. Chartier, *Le quadrilogue invectif*, esp. 10–19; see also J. Laidlaw, 'Alain Chartier and the Arts of Crisis Management, 1417–1429', *War, Government, and Power in Late Medieval France*, ed. Allmand, 37–53.

14. N. de Fribois, *Abrégé des Croniques de France*, ed. K. Daly (Paris, 2006); P. de Nesson, *Pierre de Nesson et ses œuvres*, ed. A. Piaget and E. Droz (Paris, 1925); J. Juvénal des Ursins, *Les écrits politiques*, ed. P. S. Lewis and Anne-Marie Hayez, 3 vols (Paris, 1978–92).

15. Wright, *Knights and Peasants*, 36.

16. H. Solterer, 'Making Names, Breaking Lives: Women and Injurious Language at the Court of Isabeau of Bavaria and Charles VI', *Cultural Performances in Medieval France*, ed. E. Doss-Quinby, R. L. Krueger and E. J. Burns (Cambridge, 2007), 213–15. See also T. Adams, *The Life and Afterlife of Isabeau of Bavaria* (Baltimore, MD, 2010), esp. 124–5, who argues that the attacks on Isabeau were politically motivated and not as widespread as has been commonly asserted.

17. Basin, *Histoire de Charles VII*, ed. C. Samaran, I, 220–2; M. Spencer, *Thomas Basin (1412–1490): The History of Charles VII and Louis XI* (Nieuwkoop, 1997), 104–5.

18. C. T. Allmand, 'The English and the Church in Lancastrian Normandy', *England and Normandy*, ed. D. Bates and A. Curry (London, 1994), 287–9, 292. On clerical resistance, see R. Jouet, *La résistance à l'occupation anglaise en Basse-Normandie, 1418–1450* (Caen, 1969), 73–7; J.Barker, 'The Foe Within: Treason in Lancastrian Normandy', *Soldiers, Nobles and Gentlemen*, ed. Coss and Tyerman, 314–15.

19. G. Llewelyn Thompson, *Paris and its People under English Rule: The Anglo-Burgundian Regime 1420–1436* (Oxford, 1991), 152–3, 174–5.

20. G. L. Harriss, 'Beaufort, Henry (1375?–1447)', *ODNB* (online edn, 2008); *idem, Cardinal Beaufort: A Study of Lancastrian Ascendancy and Decline* (Oxford, 1989); R. Cazelles, *Société politique, noblesse et couronne sous Jean le Bon et Charles V* (Paris, 1982), 125, 155, 175, 244. Over the course of the war thirteen of the twenty-five French chancellors were churchmen; D. Potter, ed., *France in the Later Middle Ages, 1200–1500* (Oxford, 2002), 257–8; F. Lot and R. Fawtier, *Histoire des institutions françaises au Moyen Age*, III: *Institutions ecclésiastiques* (Paris, 1962), 407–37. A huge preponderance of English lord treasurers and chancellors in this period were bishops – although the first lay chancellor, Robert Bourchier, served in 1340–1. In addition churchmen served as finance ministers and diplomats, e.g. Jean la Grange and Henry Burghersh, bishop of Lincoln; A. McGee Morganstern, 'The La Grange Tomb and Choir: A Monument of the Great Schism of the West', *Speculum*, 48 (1973), 52–3; N. Bennett, 'Burghersh, Henry (*c.*1290–1340)', *ODNB* (online edn, 2004). Others were involved in military matters such as defence, e.g. Hamo Hythe, bishop of Rochester (1320–52); M. C. Buck, 'Hythe, Hamo (b. c.1270, d. in or after 1357)', *ODNB* (online edn, 2009).

21. The French clergy were exempt from direct taxation, but indirect taxation affected them and their institutions in a variety of ways. In addition, clerical tenths (levies of one-tenth of clerical income) were granted to French kings by popes regularly up until c.1350 and then again after c.1420.

22. Anon., *A Parisian Journal, 1404–49*, ed. and trans. J. Shirley (Oxford, 1968), 147. See also T. Guard, *Chivalry, Kingship and Crusade: The English Experience in the Fourteenth Century* (Woodbridge, 2013), 193–6.

23. Bernard, *Late Medieval English Church*, 27–33.

24. P. de Mézières, *Letter to Richard II: A Plea made in 1395 for Peace between England and France*, trans. G. W. Coopland (Liverpool, 1975), 21.

25. Cited by Barnie, *War in Medieval Society*, 12. See also K. Plöger, *England and the Avignon Popes: The Practice of Diplomacy in Late Medieval Europe* (London, 2005), 23.

26. G. Barraclough, *The Medieval Papacy* (London, 1968), 153; D. Wood, '*Omnino Partialitate Cessante*: Clement VI and the Hundred Years War', *The Church and War*, ed. W. J. Shiels (Oxford, 1983), 179–89.

27. P. N. R. Zutshi, 'The Avignon Papacy', *The New Cambridge Medieval History*, VI: *c.1300–c.1415*, ed. M. Jones (Cambridge, 2000), 669–70.

28. J. J. N. Palmer, 'England, France, the Papacy and the Flemish Succession, 1361–9', *Journal of Medieval History*, 2 (1976), 339–64; Ormrod, *Edward III*, 442–4.

29. C. Given-Wilson, 'Parliament of October 1404: Introduction', *PROME*; Walsingham, *Chronica Maiora*, ed. Preest, 333–5; M. Wilks, 'Royal Patronage and Anti-Papalism from Ockham to Wyclif', *Wyclif: Political Ideas and Practice* (Oxford, 2000), 132–3; Bernard, *Late Medieval English Church*, 18–19, 27, 31–3.

30. B. P. McGuire, *Jean Gerson and the Last Medieval Reformation* (University Park, PA, 2005), 49–51.

31. H. Kaminsky, 'The Great Schism', *New Cambridge Medieval History*, VI, ed. Jones, 675–6. Cardinals usually numbered between 10 and 25. It was a matter of pride for the major states to produce at least one cardinal. The College of Cardinals elected a pope when the incumbent died, usually from among their own number.

32. J. Sumption, *The Hundred Years War*, III: *Divided Houses* (London, 2009), 493–510; R. Allington–Smith, *Henry Despenser: The Fighting Bishop* (Fakenham, 2003), 54–81.

33. H. Kaminsky, 'The Politics of France's Subtraction of Obedience from Pope Benedict XIII, 27 July, 1398', *Proceedings of the American Philosophical Society*, 115 (1971), 367–71.

34. Kaminsky, 'Great Schism', 696; J. H. Lynch, *The Medieval Church: A Brief History* (Harlow, 1992), 328–35.
35. Bonet, *Tree of Battles*, 189.
36. Walsingham notes that when Henry V's ordinances became common knowledge, many people began wandering through English encampments in France wearing clerical garb having shaven their heads, 'engaged in the transactions of the marketplace, and coming and going as they pleased with the English outwitted by their holy cunning', *Chronica Maiora*, ed. Preest, 423; *St Albans Chronicle*, II, 713–14.
37. *Chronicle of Jean de Venette*, 67.
38. Froissart, *Chroniques*, ed. Luce, V, 175; also see *ibid.*, XIV, 164.
39. Keen, *Chivalry*, 232.
40. Wright, *Knights and Peasants*, 65.
41. H. Denifle, *La désolation des églises, monastères et hôpitaux en France pendant la Guerre de Cent Ans*, 2 vols (Paris, 1897–99), II, 592–601.
42. Denifle, *La désolation*, 613, 615–16, 689, 731–3; Clark, *Benedictines*, 274.
43. Walsingham, *Chronica Maiora*, ed. Preest, 97–9.
44. A. K. McHardy, 'The Effects of the War on the Church: The Case of the Alien Priories in the Fourteenth Century', *England and her Neighbours, 1066–1453: Essays in Honour of Pierre Chaplais*, ed. M. Jones and M. G. A. Vale (London, 1989), 277–88.
45. Allmand, *Henry V*, 273–4; Bernard, *Late Medieval English Church*, 189–90, 200; Clark, *Benedictines*, 275.
46. A. Emery, *Greater Medieval Houses of England and Wales, 1300–1500*, II (Oxford, 2000), 370; McHardy, 'Effects of War on the Church', 278–84; A. McHardy and N. Orme, 'The Defence of an Alien Priory: Modbury (Devon) in the 1450s', *Journal of Ecclesiastical History*, 50 (1999), 303–4.
47. W. M. Ormrod, 'Parliament of Nov. 1373: Text and Translation', *PROME*, item 32.
48. John Cherlewe, prior of Lewes (c.1366–96), was captured during a French raid in 1377: Walsingham, *Chronica Maiora*, ed. Preest, 46.
49. McHardy, *Age of War and Wycliffe*, 36–7.
50. Walsingham, *Chronica Maiora*, ed. Preest, 36–7, 46, 110.
51. *Chronicle of Jean de Venette*, 64; *Gesta Henrici Quinti*, 44. Courtenay led embassies to France in 1414 and 1415.
52. G. E. St John, 'War, the Church, and English Men-at-Arms', *Fourteenth-Century England*, VI, ed. C. Given-Wilson (Woodbridge, 2010), 74–7, 83.
53. *Gesta Henrici Quinti*, 66, 78, 84, 89.

Chapter 4 Making Peace: *Blessed are the Peacemakers* (1396)

1. *The Major Latin Works of John Gower*, ed. E. W. Stockton (Seattle, WA, 1962), 207–8 (*Vox Clamantis*, Bk 5, ch. 8).
2. J. Campbell, 'England, Scotland and the Hundred Years War in the Fourteenth Century', *The Wars of Edward III*, ed. C. J. Rogers (Woodbridge, 1999), 207–30; G. Templeman, 'Edward III and the Beginnings of the Hundred Years War', *ibid.*, 233, 245.
3. A. Grant, *Independence and Nationhood: Scotland, 1306–1469* (Edinburgh, 1984), 32–57; K. Daly, 'The *Vraie cronicque d'Escoce* and Franco-Scottish Diplomacy: An Historical Work by John Ireland?', *Nottingham Medieval Studies*, 35 (1991), 106–33.
4. Anglo-Castilian treaty (1362): TNA E30/191; A. Goodman, 'England and Iberia in the Middle Ages', *England and her Neighbours, 1066–1453*, ed. Jones and Vale, 85–91; Russell, *English Intervention*, 1–11, 127; L. J. A. Villalon, 'Spanish Involvement in the Hundred Years War and the Battle of Nájera', *Hundred Years War*, I: *A Wider Focus*, ed. Kagay and Villalon, 53–6.
5. I. Aspin, *Anglo-Norman Political Songs* (Oxford, 1953), 104–15; *Wynnere and Wastoure*, ed. S. Trigg (London, 1990), ll. 265–7; N. Saul, 'A Farewell to Arms? Criticism of Warfare in Late Fourteenth-Century England', *Fourteenth-Century England*, II, ed. C. Given-Wilson (Woodbridge, 2002), 131–45. See also B. L. Bryant, 'Talking with the Taxman about Poetry: England's Economy in "Against the King's Taxes" and *Wynnere and Wastoure*', *Studies in Medieval and Renaissance History*, 3rd ser. 5 (2008), 219–48, esp. 230.

6. The extract dates to 1356, after the French defeat at Poitiers and the capture of King Jean II: *Chronicle of Jean de Venette*, 66.
7. F. Petrarca, *Le familiari*, ed. V. Rossi, 4 vols (Florence, 1933–42), IV, 138–9.
8. T. Meron, 'The Authority to Make Treaties in the Late Middle Ages', *American Journal of International Law*, 89 (1995), 7–10.
9. W. Langland, *The Vision of William Concerning Piers the Plowman: In Three Parallel Texts*, ed. W. W. Skeat, 2 vols (Oxford 1886; repr. 1965): A Text Passus, I, ll.137 ('that loue is the leuest thing that vr lord asketh, and eke the playnt of pees'); IV, 34ff; VI, 107–17: B Text, I, 150–6; III, 220ff.; B. Lowe, *Imagining Peace: A History of Early English Pacifist Ideas, 1340–1560* (Philadelphia, PA, 1997), 91–3.
10. G. Chaucer, 'The Former Age', in Lowe, *Imagining Peace*, 97–100; Saul, 'Farewell to Arms?', 134.
11. J. Gower, *Confessio Amantis*, ed. and trans. T. Tiller (Harmondsworth, 1963), 145–6.
12. J. Gower, *The Complete Works of John Gower*, ed. G. C. Macaulay, 4 vols (Oxford, 1899–1902), III, 313 (*Vox clamantis; Confessio amantis*).
13. J. Bromyard, *Summa Predicantium*, 24, cited by R. Cox, 'Natural Law and the Right of Self-Defence according to John of Legnano and John Wyclif', *Fourteenth-Century England*, VI, ed. C. Given-Wilson (Woodbridge, 2010), 154.
14. R. Cox, 'Wyclif: Medieval Pacifist', *History Today*, 60 (2010), 26–7.
15. Bonet, *Tree of Battles*, 154.
16. C. de Pizan, *Book of Deeds of Arms and of Chivalry*, 171.
17. C. de Pizan, *Book of Deeds of Arms and of Chivalry*, 14.
18. Jean Juvénal des Ursins, *Audite Celi* (begun in May 1435 prior to the Congress of Arras): *Ecrits politiques*, I, 93–281. Having witnessed the impact of the war on his see of Beauvais, Jean Juvénal clearly hoped for peace: see Taylor, 'War, Propaganda and Diplomacy in Fifteenth-Century France and England', 81. Jean Juvénal, the author of *Histoire de Charles VI Roy de France*, served as bishop of Beauvais (1433–44), bishop of Laon (1444–49) and archbishop of Reims (1449–73).
19. F. Autrand, 'The Peacemakers and the State: Pontifical Diplomacy and the Anglo-French Conflict in the Fourteenth Century', *War and Competition between States*, ed. P. Contamine (Oxford, 2000), 261–3 (regarding papal letters), 268–76 (on peace conferences). For further discussion of the peace conferences, see Plöger, *England and the Avignon Popes*, 203–9; E. Déprez, 'La conférence d'Avignon (1344): L'arbitrage pontifical entre la France et l'Angleterre', *Essays in Medieval History Presented to T. F. Tout*, ed. A. G. Little and F. M. Powicke (Manchester, 1925), 301–20; B. Guillemain, 'Les tentatives pontificales de médiation dans le litige franco-anglais de Guyenne au XIVᵉ siècle', *Bulletin philologique et historique du comité des travaux historiques et scientifiques* (1957), 423–32; P. Chaplais, 'Réglements des conflits internationaux franco-anglais au XIVᵉ siècle', *Le Moyen Âge*, 57 (1951), 169–302.
20. Sumption, *Trial by Fire*, 231–3, 236–8; Green, *Battle of Poitiers*, 43–5. The cardinal was one of several individuals driven in his search for peace by the possibility of a crusade: see C. Deluz, 'Croisade et paix en Europe au XIVᵉ siècle: Le rôle du cardinal Hélie de Talleyrand', *Cahiers de recherches médiévales*, I (1996), 53–61.
21. TNA SC 7/13/8; Wood, 'Omnino partialitate cessante: Clement VI and the Hundred Years War', *Church and War*, ed. Shiels, 179–89; *idem, Clement VI: The Pontificate and Ideas of an Avignon Pope* (Cambridge, 1989), 137–8.
22. Vernier, *Bertrand du Guesclin*, 129.
23. BL Cotton MS, Vitellius C XI, nos 2–3; J. J. N. Palmer, *England, France and Christendom, 1377–99* (London, 1972), 171–2; Sumption, *Divided Houses*, 827–9; Saul, *Richard II*, 226–8; C. Phillpotts, 'The Fate of the Truce of Paris, 1396–1415', *Journal of Medieval History*, 24 (1998), 61–80.
24. *Westminster Chronicle, 1381–1394*, ed. and trans. L. C. Hector and B. F. Harvey (Oxford, 1982), 484. See further J. J. N. Palmer, 'The Anglo-French Peace Negotiations, 1390–1396', *TRHS*, 5th ser. 16 (1966), 81–94; Saul, *Richard II*, 211–19. For events in Aquitaine, 2 March 1390 (the grant of the duchy to John of Gaunt)–21 March 1395, see TNA E30/1232.
25. C. de Pizan, *The Book of Peace*, ed. K. Green, C. Mews and J. Pinder (University Park, PA, 2008), 63.
26. C. de Pizan, *The Book of Peace*, 59–60.
27. *Parisian Journal*, 252.

28. AN, JJ 104, no. 231: cited by Wright, *Knights and Peasants*, 51–2; Autrand, 'The Peacemakers and the State', 252–3.
29. *Parisian Journal*, 290.
30. B. Ditcham, 'The Employment of Foreign Mercenary Troops in the French Royal Armies, 1415–1470', unpub. PhD thesis (University of Edinburgh, 1979), 229–60.
31. This can be seen throughout the *Chroniques*, but is perhaps most notable in the reminiscences of the mercenary captain, the Bascot de Mauléon: *Froissart: Chronicles*, ed. and trans. Brereton, 280–94. G. Pépin, 'Towards a Rehabilitation of Froissart's Credibility: The Non-Fictious Bascot de Mauléon', *The Soldier Experience in the Fourteenth Century*, ed. A. R. Bell and A. Curry (Woodbridge, 2011), 175–90.
32. De Mézières, *Letter to King Richard II*, 14.
33. De Mézières, *Letter to King Richard II*, 93–7, 139.
34. De Mézières, *Letter to King Richard II*, 86–7, 92. On de Mézières' role, see further Michael Hanly, 'Philippe de Mézières and the Peace Movement', *Philippe de Mézières and his Age*, ed. Blumenfeld-Kosinski and Petkov, 61–82; A. Curry, 'War or Peace? Philippe de Mézières, Richard II and Anglo-French Diplomacy', *ibid.*, 295–320.
35. Vale, *Origins of the Hundred Years War*, 14.
36. Rymer, *Foedera*, I, ii, 794; Prestwich, *Edward I*, 328–9.
37. Rymer, *Foedera*, II, ii, 150, 153–4. Philippe VI formally took the cross at a great ceremony in the Pré-aux-Clercs outside the abbey of St Germain (Paris) on 2 October 1333. See C. J. Tyerman, 'Philip VI and the Recovery of the Holy Land', *EHR*, 100 (1985), 25–52; E. Déprez, *Les préliminaires de la Guerre de Cent Ans. La Papauté, la France et l'Angleterre, 1328–1342* (Paris, 1902), 127–35; Sumption, *Trial by Battle*, 117–18, 132–3, 135–6, 155–8; Vale, *Origins*, 257–8; Guard, *Chivalry, Kingship and Crusade*, 17–19, 34.
38. See, for example, M. Keen, 'Chaucer's Knight, the English Aristocracy and the Crusade', *English Court Culture in the Later Middle Ages*, ed. V. J. Scattergood and J. W. Sherborne (London, 1983), 45–61; A. Luttrell, 'The Crusade in the Fourteenth Century', *Europe in the Late Middle Ages*, ed. J. Hale et al. (London, 1965), 122–54.
39. N. Housley, *The Avignon Papacy and the Crusades* (Oxford, 1986). On the Alexandrian crusade of 1365, see A. S. Atiya, 'The Fourteenth Century', *A History of the Crusades*, III: *The Fourteenth and Fifteenth Centuries*, ed. K. M. Setton and H. W. Hazard (Madison, WI, 1975), 3–26; P. Edbury, 'The Crusading Policy of King Peter I of Cyprus', *The Eastern Mediterranean Lands in the Period of Crusades*, ed. P. M. Holt (Warminster, 1977), 90–105.
40. N. Housley, '*Pro deo et patria mori*: Sanctified Patriotism in Europe 1400–1600', *War and Competition between States*, ed. P. Contamine (Oxford, 2000), 221–8, esp. 221–2; N. Housley, 'France, England, and the "National Crusade"', 1302–1386', *France and the British Isles in the Middle Ages and Renaissance: Essays by Members of Girton College, Cambridge in Memory of Ruth Morgan*, ed. G. Jondorf and D. N. Dumville (Woodbridge, 1991), 183–98; Tyerman, 'Philip VI and the Recovery of the Holy Land', 52.
41. R. Vaughan, *Philip the Bold* (Woodbridge, new edn, 2002), 59, 79.
42. For descriptions of the English in this fashion, see *Gesta Henrici Quinti*, 48, 151: 'God Himself, gracious and merciful to His people' (*suo populo*); 'God's chosen people' (*populum dei electrum*). See further M. Harvey, 'Ecclesia Anglicana, cui ecclesiastes noster christus vos prefecit: The Power of the Crown in the English Church during the Great Schism', *Religion and National Identity*, ed. S. Mews (Oxford, 1982), 230; A. Curry, 'War, Peace and National Identity in the Hundred Years War', *Thinking War, Peace and World Orders in European History*, ed. A. Hartmann and B. Heuser (London, 2001), 145.
43. E. C. Caldwell, 'The Hundred Years War and National Identity', *Inscribing the Hundred Years War in French and English Cultures*, ed. D. N. Baker (Albany, NY, 2000), 238–41.
44. *Gesta Henrici Quinti*, 110, 120, 146.
45. The 'Letter' was circulated widely and copied into various Burgundian, French and German chronicles: *Joan of Arc: La Pucelle*, ed. and trans. C. Taylor (Manchester, 2006), 74–6; D. A. Fraoli, *Joan of Arc: The Early Debate* (Woodbridge, 2000), 58, 71, 74, 119.
46. C. de Pizan, *Ditié de Jehanne d'Arc*, ed. A. J. Kennedy and K. Varty (Oxford, 1977); C. de Pizan, *The Epistle of the Prison of Human Life; with An Epistle to the Queen of France; and Lament on the Evils of the Civil War*, ed. and trans. J. A. Wisman (New York, 1984); C. de Pizan, *The Book of Peace*, 27.

47. *Gesta Henrici Quinti*, 100–12; Allmand, *Henry V*, 409–13; C. L. Kingsford, *English Historical Literature in the Fifteenth Century* (Oxford, 1913), 34.

48. See C. Given-Wilson, ed., 'Henry V: Parliament of 1420, Text and Translation', *PROME*, items 1, 25. See also D. McCulloch and E. D. Jones, 'Lancastrian Politics, the French War, and the Rise of the Popular Element', *Speculum*, 58 (1983), 100.

49. *The Chronicle of Adam Usk, 1377–1421*, ed. and trans. C. Given-Wilson (Oxford, 1997), 271, entry for 1421.

50. G. L. Harriss, 'Marmaduke Lumley and the Exchequer Crisis of 1446–9', *Aspects of Late Medieval Government and Society: Essays Presented to J. R. Lander*, ed. J. G. Rowe (Toronto, 1986), 143–78.

51. *The Libelle of Englyshe Polycye: A Poem on the use of Sea-power, 1436*, ed. G. Warner (Oxford, 1926). It has been suggested that Lydgate may have had a hand in the *Libelle*'s composition: Griffiths, *Reign of King Henry VI*, 236–7. See also J. Scattergood, 'The Libelle of Englyshe Polycye: The Nation and its Place', *Nation, Court and Culture: New Essays on Fifteenth-Century English Poetry*, ed. H. Cooney (Dublin 2001), 28–49; S. Rose, *The Medieval Sea* (London, 2007), 120; N. A. M. Rodger, *Safeguard of the Sea: A Naval History of Britain*, I: *660–1649* (London, 2004), 152.

52. Lydgate's *Troy Book* (1420) and *Siege of Thebes* (c.1422) referred to the treaty of Troyes and peace between England and France. Lydgate wrote 'On the Prospect of Peace' prior to Suffolk's mission to France to secure a marriage alliance for Henry VI: Wright, *Political Poems and Songs*, II, 209–15, and 'On the Truce of 1444', *ibid.*, 215–20; McCulloch and Jones, 'Lancastrian Politics', 112.

53. Lydgate, 'A Praise of Peace', ll.117–84: *The Minor Poems of John Lydgate*, ed. H. N. MacCracken (London, 1934), 786–91.

54. Harriss, *Shaping the Nation*, 576–7.

55. B. M. Cron, 'The Duke of Suffolk, the Angevin Marriage, and the Ceding of Maine, 1445', *Journal of Medieval History*, 20 (1994), 92–3.

56. J. Watts, 'Pole, William de la, First Duke of Suffolk (1396–1450)', *ODNB* (online edn, 2004).

57. *Paston Letters*, ed. J. Gairdner (London, 1872), I, no. 103; M. Keen, 'The End of the Hundred Years War: Lancastrian France and Lancastrian England', *England and her Neighbours*, ed. Jones and Vale, 297, 307.

58. Rymer, *Foedera*, V, iii, 65; M. A. Hicks, 'Edward IV's *Brief Treatise* and the Treaty of Picquigny of 1475', *Historical Research*, 83 (2009), 253–65.

Chapter 5 The Madness of Kings: Kingship and Royal Power (1407)

1. *Contemporary Chronicles of the Hundred Years War from the Works of Jean le Bel, Jean Froissart, and Enguerrand de Monstrelet*, ed. and trans. P. E. Thompson (London, 1966), 226.

2. Jean de Terrevermeille, born c.1370 at Nîmes, wrote the *Tractatus* in about 1418, a work divided into three parts, one being *Contra rebelles suorum regum*: J. Barbey, *La fonction royale. Essence et légitimité d'après les Tractatus de Jean de Terrevermeille* (Paris, 1983).

3. *La chronique d'Enguerran de Monstrelet*, ed. Douët-d'Arcq, I, 154–5.

4. *Froissart: Chronicles*, ed. and trans. Brereton, 392–401; Walsingham, *Chronica Maiora*, ed. Preest, 289; J. Capgrave, *The Chronicle of England*, ed. F. C. Hingeston (London, 1858), 254; Famiglietti, *Royal Intrigue*, 7.

5. Froissart, *Oeuvres*, ed. Lettenhove, XV, 29–30, 35–43; *Chronique des quatre premiers Valois (1327–1393)*, ed. S. Luce (Paris, 1862), 323–4; Sumption, *Divided Houses*, 798.

6. For Charles V's plans for his heir's minority rule, see *Ordonnances des rois de France de la troisième race*, ed. D. F. Secours et al., 23 vols (Paris, 1723–1849), VI, 45–9.

7. Knecht, *Valois*, 45; J. B. Henneman, 'The Military Class and the French Monarchy in the Late Middle Ages', *American Historical Review*, 83 (1978), 946–65; idem, *Olivier de Clisson*, 72–85.

8. See B. Guenée, *Un meurtre, une société: l'assassinat du duc d'Orléans, 23 novembre 1407* (Paris, 1992), 185–7; L. Mirot, 'Raoul d'Anquetonville et le prix de l'assassinat du duc d'Orléans', *BEC*, 72 (1911), 445–58.

9. M. C. E. Jones, 'The Last Capetians', *New Cambridge Medieval History*, VI, 421; Knecht, *Valois*, 8–9.

10. *Parisian Journal*, 47; Monstrelet, *Chronique*, I, 177–242; Vaughan, *John the Fearless*, 67–73.

11. S. H. Cuttler, *The Law of Treason and Treason Trials in Later Medieval France* (Cambridge, 1981), 145–6.

12. N. Saul, *The Three Richards* (London, 2005), 24–5; W. H. Dunham and C. T. Wood, 'The Right to Rule in England: Depositions and the Kingdom's Authority, 1327–1485', *American Historical Review*, 81 (1976), 744–6; B. Guenée, *States and Rulers in Later Medieval Europe*, trans. J. Vale (Oxford, 1985), 39; W. Ullmann, *Medieval Political Thought* (Harmondsworth, 1975), 81; W. R. Childs, 'Resistance and Treason in the *Vita Edwardi Secundi*', *Thirteenth-Century England*, VI, ed. M. Prestwich, R. Britnell and R. Frame (Woodbridge, 1997), 180–1. For further discussion, see J. G. Bellamy, *The Law of Treason in the Late Middle Ages* (Cambridge, 1970), 1–58; J. S. Bothwell, *Falling from Grace: Reversal of Fortune and the English Nobility, 1075–1455* (Manchester, 2008), esp. 36–46; J. Dunbabin, 'Government', *The Cambridge History of Medieval Political Thought c.350–c.1450* (Cambridge, 1988), 492; Krynen, *L'empire du roi*, 384–414.

13. J. Pitt-Rivers, 'Honour and Social Status', *Honour and Shame: The Values of Mediterranean Society*, ed. J. G. Peristiany (London, 1965), 37; Knecht, *Valois*, 8.

14. *Statutes of the Realm*, II, 98–9; *English Historical Documents*, IV: 406; C. D. Ross, 'Forfeiture for Treason in the Reign of Richard II', *EHR*, 71 (1956), 574.

15. S. J. T. Miller, 'The Position of the King in Bracton and Beaumanoir', *Speculum*, 31 (1956), 267, 293; J. Morrow, *History of Political Thought: A Thematic Introduction* (Basingstoke, 1998), 279; Cuttler, *Law of Treason*, 5, 21, 31.

16. *Statutes of the Realm*, I, 319–20; C. Given-Wilson, 'Parliament of Oct. 1399: Text and Translation', *PROME*, item 70; Ormrod, *Edward III*, 364–6.

17. C. Wilson, 'The Tomb of Henry IV and the Holy Oil of St Thomas of Canterbury', *Medieval Architecture and its Intellectual Context: Studies in Honour of Peter Kidson*, ed. E. Fernie and P. Crossley (London, 1990), 181–90; T. A. Sandquist, 'The Holy Oil of St Thomas of Canterbury', *Essays in Medieval History Presented to Bertie Wilkinson*, ed. T. A. Sandquist and M. R. Powicke (Toronto, 1969), 330–44.

18. Although the English service conveyed less authority, in liturgical terms it was very similar to the French. An interesting distinction between the two lies in a reference in the French ceremony to the king's right to rule over the 'Saxons, Mercians, and Northumbrians'. According to Theodore Godefroy in his compilation of French coronation *ordines* (1619), this clause was introduced after the election of the dauphin Louis to the throne of England in 1216 (during the baronial war against King John). E. S. Dewick, ed., *The Coronation Book of Charles V of France: Cottonian MS Tiberius B. VIII* (London, 1889), xvii; E. A. R. Brown, '"Franks, Burgundians, and Aquitanians" and the Royal Coronation Ceremony in France', *Transactions of the American Philosophical Society*, n.s. 82 (1992), 53, 85; Miller, 'Position of the King in Bracton and Beaumanoir', 288.

19. A. Harding, *Medieval Law and the Foundations of the State* (Oxford, 2002), 256; R. S. Hoyt, 'The Coronation Oath of 1308', *EHR*, 71 (1956), 353–83. There are a number of similarities with the 1308 coronation oath and various tracts on kingship circulating in King John's reign prior to the drafting of Magna Carta. See *Die Gesetze de Angelsachsen*, ed. F. Liebermann, 3 vols (Halle, 1903–16), I, 635–6. My thanks to David Crouch for drawing my attention to this.

20. In January 1327, prior to the coronation of Edward III, Archbishop Reynolds preached on the text 'Vox populi, vox Dei' ('the voice of the people [is] the voice of God'), and the medal struck to commemorate the coronation bore the motto 'Populi dat iura voluntas' ('the will of the people gives right'). M. Wilks, *The Problem of Sovereignty in the Later Middle Ages* (Cambridge, 1963), 190 n. 2; C. Valente, 'The Deposition and Abdication of Edward II', *EHR*, 113 (1998), 859.

21. R. S. Hoyt, 'The Coronation Oath of 1308: The Background of "les leys et les custumes"', *Traditio*, 11 (1955), 235–57; H. G. Richardson, 'The English Coronation Oath', *Speculum*, 24 (1949), 44–75. On the notion of the king's two bodies and many issues concerning medieval kingship, see E. Kantorowicz, *The King's Two Bodies: A Study in Mediaeval Political Theology* (Princeton, NJ, repr. 1997).

22. Rogers, *War Cruel and Sharp*, 385 ff. On Edward III's imperial ambitions, see Ormrod, *Edward III*, 414–45.

23. K. DeVries, *Joan of Arc: A Military Leader* (Stroud, 2003), 118–28.

24. Vale, *Charles VII*, 45, 51, 56–7, 195–7. At his coronation Charles VII heard Jean Juvénal des Ursins, archbishop of Reims, declare: 'au regard de vous mon Souverain Seigneur, vous n'êtes pas simplement personne Laye, mais Prélat Ecclésiastique, le premier en votre Royaume qui soit après le Pape, le bras dextre de l'Eglise'. Each successive king for generations heard his consecrator pray at the coronation that 'this our Prince ... be given Peter's keys and Paul's doctrine'. D. de Maillane, *Dictionnaire de Droit Canonique et de Pratique Bénéficiale conferé avec les maximes et la jurisprudence de France* (Paris, 1761), II, 759–60, cited by A. Guinan, 'The Christian Concept of Kingship as Manifested in the Liturgy of the Western Church: A Fragment in Suggestion', *Harvard Theological Review*, 49 (1956), 246.

25. Griffiths, *Reign of Henry VI*, 189–94; A. Curry, 'The "Coronation Expedition" and Henry VI's Court in France 1430 to 1432', *The Lancastrian Court*, ed. J. Stratford (Donington, 2003), 29–52.

26. F. Barlow, 'The King's Evil', *EHR*, 95 (1980), 3, 14, 17, 24–5; Guinan, 'Christian Concept of Kingship', 224; A. D. Hedeman, *The Royal Image: Illustrations of the Grandes Chroniques de France, 1274–1422* (Berkeley, CA, 1991), 71.

27. H. S. Offler, 'Thomas Bradwardine's "Victory Sermon" in 1346', *Church and Crown in the Fourteenth Century: Studies in European History and Political Thought*, ed. A. I. Doyle (Aldershot, 2000), 2–4; M. S. Kempshall, *The Common Good in Late Medieval Political Thought* (Oxford, 1999), 130–56; Ullmann, *Medieval Political Thought*, 124–5, 159–73; A. Black, *Political Thought in Europe 1250–1450* (Cambridge, 1992), 9–12, 20–1, 49–51, 77–8; A. D. Menut, 'Maistre Nicole Oresme: Le *Livre de Politiques* d'Aristote. Published from the Text of the Avranches Manuscript 223', *Transactions of the American Philosophical Society*, new ser. 60 (1970), 1–392. See also Guenée, *States and Rulers*, 37–9, 67; Morrow, *History of Political Thought*, 132.

28. A. S. McGrade, 'Somersaulting Sovereignty: A Note on Reciprocal Lordship in Wyclif', *Church and Sovereignty*, ed. D. Wood (Oxford, 1991), 261–8; Harding, *Medieval Law*, 266; J. H. Burns, *Lordship, Kingship and Empire: The Idea of Monarchy, 1400–1525* (Oxford, 1992), 57; Kantorowicz, *King's Two Bodies*, 134, 157.

29. J. Taylor, 'Richard II in the Chronicles', *Richard II: The Art of Kingship*, ed. A. Goodman and J. Gillespie (Oxford, 1999), 21–2; N. Saul, 'The Kingship of Richard II', *ibid.*, 40; C. M. Barron, 'The Deposition of Richard II', *Politics and Crisis in Fourteenth-Century England*, ed. J. Taylor and W. Childs (Gloucester, 1990), 145. See Vale, *Charles VII*, 194–228, for comparison with later Valois practice.

30. P. S. Lewis, 'France in the Fifteenth Century: Society and Sovereignty', *Europe in the Late Middle Ages*, ed. J. Hale, R. Highfield and B. Smalley (London, 1965), 279. 'The English development from the early thirteenth century onwards showed the preponderance of the feudal function of the king at the expense of his theocratic function.' Ullmann, *Medieval Political Thought*, 149.

31. N. Perkins, *Hoccleve's 'Regiment of Princes': Counsel and Constraint* (Cambridge, 2001), 137. On Richard's deposition, see Bennett, *Richard II and the Revolution of 1399*; J. Watts, 'Usurpation in England: A Paradox of State-Growth', *Coups d'état à la fin du Moyen Âge? Aux fondements du pouvoir politique en Europe occidentale*, ed. F. Foronda, J.–P. Genet and J. M. Nieto Soria (Madrid, 2005), 51–72; R. V. Turner, 'The Meaning of Magna Carta since 1215', *History Today*, 53 (2003), 29–35.

32. Dunham and Wood, 'Right to Rule in England', 744–6; Guenée, *States and Rulers*, 81.

33. M. Bloch, *The Royal Touch*, trans. J. E. Anderson (New York, 1989), 38; J. Le Goff, 'Le roi dans l'occident médiéval: Caractères originaux', *Kings and Kingship in Medieval Europe*, ed. A. J. Duggan (Exeter, 1993), 140; C. Taylor, 'Sir John Fortescue and the French Polemical Treatises of the Hundred Years War', *EHR*, 114 (1999), 124–5; A. Vauchez, *Sainthood in the Later Middle Ages*, trans. J. Birrell (Cambridge, 1997), 173.

34. Guenée, *States and Rulers*, 39; Burns, *Lordship, Kingship and Empire*, 40–5; Ullmann, *Medieval Political Thought*, 147.

35. See C. T. Wood, '*Regnum Francie*: A Problem in Capetian Administrative Usage', *Traditio*, 23 (1967), 136–9. 'Next to the King of France no monarch in Europe was of greater importance from a legal point of view than the Emperor of the Byzantine Empire': J. Goebel Jr, 'The Equality of States. II', *Columbia Law Review*, 23 (1923), 127.

36. P. S. Lewis, 'Two Pieces of Fifteenth-Century Political Iconography: (b) The English Kill their Kings', *Journal of the Warburg and Courtauld Institutes*, 27 (1964), 319–20.

37. Knecht, *Valois*, 88–91.
38. Sir J. Fortescue, *De laudibus legum Anglie*, ed. and trans. S. B. Chrimes (Cambridge, 1942), 3. See also E. Powell, *Kingship, Law and Society: Criminal Justice in the Reign of Henry V* (Oxford, 1989), esp. 30, 36; J. Krynen, *Idéal du prince et pouvoir royal en France à la fin du Moyen Âge (1380–1440): Étude de la littérature politique du temps* (Paris, 1981), esp. 109–36.
39. C. de Pizan, *Le livre des fais et bonnes moeurs du roi Charles V, le Sage*, ed. E. Hicks and T. Moreau (Paris, 1997), 64; K. Langdon Forhan, *The Political Theory of Christine de Pizan* (Aldershot, 2002), 97. See further D. Delogu, *Theorizing the Ideal Sovereign: The Rise of the French Vernacular Royal Biography* (Toronto, 2008), 153–83; Krynen, *Idéal du prince et pouvoir royal*, 144–54.
40. See II Chronicles: 10. See also *Fifteenth-Century English Translation of Alain Chartier's 'Le Traité l'Esperance' and 'Le Quadrilogue Invectif'*, ed. M. S. Blayney (London, 1974), 80–1; T. Hoccleve, *The Regiment of Princes*, ed. C. R. Blyth (Kalamazoo, MI, 1999), ll. 4858 ff.; J. Ferster, *Fictions of Advice: The Literature and Politics of Counsel in Late Medieval England* (Philadelphia, PA, 1996); J. Coleman, 'A Culture of Political Counsel: The Case of Fourteenth-Century England's "Virtuous" Monarchy vs Royal Absolutism and Seventeenth-Century Reinterpretation', *Monarchism and Absolutism in Early Modern Europe*, ed. C. Cuttica and G. Burgess (London, 2011), 19–31.
41. Cited by P. S. Lewis, 'Jean Juvenal des Ursins and the Common Literary Attitude to Tyranny in Fifteenth-Century France', *Medium Aevum*, 34 (1965), 119.
42. On Edward's deposition, see Phillips, *Edward II*, 529–31.
43. J. Capgrave, *The Book of the Illustrious Henries*, trans. F.C. Hingeston (London, 1858), 103. See also J. T. Rosenthal, 'The King's Wicked Advisors and the Medieval Baronial Rebellions', *Political Science Quarterly*, 82 (1967), 595–618.
44. *St Alban's Chronicle*, I, 815; W. M. Ormrod, 'Knights of Venus', *Medium Aevum*, 73 (2004), 290–305.
45. John of Salisbury, *Policraticus*, ed. and trans. C. Nederman (Cambridge, 1990); J. Bothwell, *Edward III and the English Peerage: Royal Patronage, Social Mobility and Political Control in Fourteenth-Century England* (York, 2004), 154–60.
46. C. de Pizan, *Book of the Body Politic*, 12–25; Guenée, *States and Rulers*, 39; Ullmann, *Medieval Political Thought*, 123–4.
47. De Mézières, *Letter to Richard II*, 60–2, 134–6.
48. C. de Pizan, *Book of the Body Politic*, 38–9; C. H. Clough, 'Late Fifteenth-Century English Monarchs Subject to Italian Renaissance Influence', *England and the Continent: Essays in Memory of Professor Andrew Martindale*, ed. J. Mitchell (Stamford, 2000), 301–2.
49. Froissart, *Chroniques*, ed. Raynaud, X, pt 2, 213. For further discussion, see P. Ainsworth, 'Froissardian Perspectives on Late Fourteenth-Century Society', *Orders and Hierarchies in Late Medieval and Renaissance Europe*, ed. J. Denton (Toronto, 1999), 56–73.
50. Forhan, *Political Theory of Christine de Pizan*, 31, 82–4, 103–8; Krynen, *L'empire du roi*, 204–24.
51. Bonet, *Tree of Battles*, 192.
52. Vale, *Charles VII*, 5.
53. C. D. Fletcher, 'Manhood and Politics in the Reign of Richard II', *Past and Present*, 189 (2005), 3–39; G. L. Harriss, 'Introduction: The Exemplar of Kingship', *Henry V: The Practice of Kingship*, ed. G. L. Harriss (Oxford, 1985), 1, 19.
54. J. Wheathamstead, *Registrum Abbatiae Johannis Wheathamstede*, ed. H. T. Riley (London, 1872), I, 415.
55. *Incerti Scriptoris Chronicon Angliae de Regnis Henrici IV, Henrici V et Henrici VI*, ed. J. A. Giles (1848), 44–7; Wolffe, *Henry VI*, 271; C. Rawcliffe, 'The Insanity of Henry VI', *Historian*, 50 (1996), 8–12.
56. Saul, *Three Richards*, 94.
57. Much of what follows has benefited greatly from Chris Given-Wilson, 'The Exequies of Edward III and the Royal Funeral Ceremony in Late Medieval England', *EHR*, 124 (2009), 257–82. The first English royal funeral *ordo* was written *c.*1360–70 (*De Exequiis Regalibus cum ipsos ex hoc seculo migrare contigerit*): P. Binski, 'The Liber Regalis: Its Date and European Context', *The Regal Image of Richard II and the Wilton Diptych*, ed. D. Gordon and L. Monnas (London, 1997), 233–46; R. E. Giesey, *The Royal Funeral Ceremony in Renaissance France* (Geneva, 1960); M. Gaude-Ferragu, *D'or et de cendres: La mort et les funérailles des princes dans*

le royaume de France au bas Moyen Âge (Lille, 2005), 239–50. For the first funeral of an enthroned monarch after the conclusion of the Hundred Years War, by which time English coronation services clearly had acquired great sacral connotations, see A .F. Sutton, L. Visser-Fuchs with R. A. Griffiths, *The Royal Funerals of the House of York at Wind*sor (London, 2005).

58. This may have been necessary for political or symbolic reasons: J. Burden, 'Re-writing a Rite of Passage: The Peculiar Funeral of Edward II', *Rites of Passage: Cultures of Transition in the Fourteenth Century*, ed. N. F. McDonald and W. M. Ormrod (York, 2004), 13–29; P. G. Lindley, 'Ritual, Regicide and Representation', *Gothic to Renaissance: Essays on Sculpture in England*, ed. P. G. Lindley (Stamford, 1995), 110.

59. R. E. Giesey, 'The Royal Funeral in Renaissance France', *Renaissance News*, 7 (1954), 130–1; *idem, Royal Funeral Ceremony*, 139–41; *idem*, 'The Presidents of Parlement at the Royal Funeral', *Sixteenth-Century Journal*, 7 (1976), 25–7. For views that suggest the effigy was used primarily for commemorative purposes, see Gaude-Ferragu, *D'or et de cendres*, 242–9.

60. *Chronique des règnes de Jean II et de Charles V*, ed. R. Delachenal, 3 vols (Paris, 1910–14), I, 343.

61. M. Keen, 'Chivalry and English Kingship in the Later Middle Ages', *War, Government and Aristocracy in the British Isles*, ed. Given-Wilson et al., 265. The display of Edward III's martial 'achievements' may have been influenced by the Black Prince's funeral in 1376: Green, *Edward the Black Prince*, 163–4.

62. Henneman, 'Military Class and the French Monarchy', 946; P. S. Lewis, 'The Failure of the French Medieval Estates', *Past and Present*, 23 (1962), 3.

63. On the 'war state', see G. L. Harriss, 'Political Society and the Growth of Government in Late Medieval England', *Past and Present*, 138 (1993), 28–57. For Fortescue's life, works and theories, see J. Fortescue, *The Governance of England*, ed. C. Plummer (Oxford, 1885); F. Gilbert, 'Sir John Fortescue's *dominium regale et politicum*', *Medievalia et Humanistica*, 2 (1944), 88–97; E. W. Ives, 'Fortescue, Sir John (c.1397–1479)', *ODNB* (online edn, 2005).

64. C. T. Wood, 'The Mise of Amiens and Saint Louis' Theory of Kingship', *French Historical Studies*, 6 (1970), 307, 309.

65. Vale, *Origins of the Hundred Years War*, 48–63.

66. Rymer, *Foedera*, II, iii, 9, 13, 27.

67. Froissart, *Chroniques*, ed. Luce, XVIII, 241–2, 246–7; C. Taylor, 'Edward III and the Plantagenet Claim to the French Throne', *Age of Edward III*, ed. Bothwell, 162.

68. See Krynen, *L'empire du roi*, esp. 345–414; P. Chaplais, 'English Diplomatic Documents to the End of Edward III's Reign', *The Study of Medieval Records: Essays in Honour of Kathleen Major*, ed. D. A. Bullough and R. L. Storey (Oxford, 1971), 50–4; M. Michael, 'The Little Land of England is Preferred before the Great Kingdom of France: The Quartering of the Royal Arms by Edward III', *Studies in Medieval Art and Architecture Presented to Peter Lasko*, ed. D. Buckton and T. A. Heslop (Stroud, 1994), 113–26; W. M. Ormrod, 'A Problem of Precedence: Edward III, the Double Monarchy and the Royal Style', *Age of Edward III*, ed. Bothwell, 135–6, 143, 153.

69. Beaune, *Birth of an Ideology*, 105–5; Hedeman, *Royal Image*, 1, 98.

70. J. Bradbury, *The Capetians: Kings of France, 987–1328* (London, 2007), 300; Lewis, 'Failure of the French Medieval Estates', 8–12.

71. J. B. Henneman, *Royal Taxation in Fourteenth-Century France: The Development of War Financing, 1322–1356* (Princeton, NJ, 1971); *idem, Royal Taxation in Fourteenth-Century France: The Captivity and Ransom of John II, 1356–1370* (Philadelphia, PA, 1976); *idem*, 'Military Class and the French Monarchy', 947–51, 955.

72. Vale, *Charles VII*, 18–19.

73. C. M. Woolgar, *The Great Household in Late Medieval England* (New Haven, CT, and London, 1999), 46–7.

74. S. Hanley, *The Lit de Justice and the Kings of France: Constitutional Ideology in Legend, Ritual, and Discourse* (Princeton, NJ, 1983), 15–27.

75. W. M. Ormrod, '*For Arthur and St George*: Edward III, Windsor Castle and the Order of the Garter', *St George's Chapel, Windsor*, ed. Saul, 14; John M. Steane, *The Archaeology of Power: England and Northern Europe AD 800–1600* (Stroud, 2001), 42–3, 108–9; S. Bond, 'The Medieval Constables of Windsor Castle', *EHR*, 82 (1967), 225–49, esp. 226–8, 234–6, 239, 248.

76. Woolgar, *Great Household*, 16, 48, 61, 68.
77. M. Whitely, 'The Courts of Edward III of England and Charles V of France: A Comparison of their Architectural Setting and Ceremonial Functions', *Fourteenth-Century England*, III, ed. W. M. Ormrod (Woodbridge, 2004), 153–66; Huizinga, *Autumn of the Middle Ages*, 50; C. Given–Wilson, *The Royal Household and the King's Affinity, 1360–1413* (New Haven, CT, and London, 1986), 30–3.
78. M. Cohen, 'An Indulgence for the Visitor: The Public at the Sainte-Chapelle of Paris', *Speculum*, 83 (2008), 840–83.
79. Vale, *Princely Court*, 220; V. Sekules, 'Dynasty and Patrimony in the Self-Construction of an English Queen: Philippa of Hainault and her Images', *England and the Continent in the Middle Ages*, ed. Mitchell, 167; L. Benz St John, *Three Medieval Queens: Queenship and the Crown in Fourteenth-Century England* (New York, 2012), 100–2. See also John Cherry and Neil Stratford, *Westminster Kings and the Medieval Palace of Westminster* (London, 1995), 28–49.
80. Fortescue, *De laudibus legum Anglie*, 17; Capgrave, *Book of the Illustrious Henries*, 150; C. de Pizan, *Book of the Body Politic*, 11. Walter de Milemete's treatise, *De Nobilitatibus Sapientiis et prudentiis Regum* (*c.*1326), offered a model of good kingship to the young Edward III: M. Michael, 'The Iconography of Kingship in the Walter of Milemete Treatise', *Journal of the Warburg and Courtauld Institutes*, 57 (1994), 36.
81. In the 1340 letter, posted in northern French churches, Edward III stressed he did not wish to overturn the rights of the French people, but to return the country to the 'good laws and customs which existed in the time of our ancestor [and] progenitor Saint Louis, king of France.' Rymer, *Foedera*, II, 1,108–9, 1,111.
82. Thompson, *Paris and its People*, 183; Michael, 'Iconography of Kingship', 38; Hedeman, *Royal Image*, 63, 143, 180.

Chapter 6 Soldiers: Views from the Front (1415)

1. 'Histoire de Charles VI', in A. Curry, ed., *The Battle of Agincourt: Sources and Interpretations* (Woodbridge, 2000), 107.
2. T. Walsingham, *St Albans Chronicle 1406–1420*, ed. V. H. Galbraith (Oxford, 1937), 333.
3. Henry V suggested, according to Shakespeare, that fighting at Agincourt was intrinsically ennobling for his soldiers: *Henry V*, IV. iii. 63.
4. *Knighton's Chronicle*, 62.
5. J. F. Verbruggen, *The Art of Warfare in Western Europe during the Middle Ages*, trans. S. Willard and Mrs R. W. Southern (Woodbridge, 2nd edn, 1997), 111, 199.
6. *Scalacronica*, 163; G. de Cuvelier, *La chanson de Bertrand du Guesclin de Cuvelier*, ed. J.-C. Faucon, 3 vols (Toulouse, 1990–91), ll. 5875–8; *Le Jouvencel*, I, 189; C. Rogers, 'Tactics and the Face of Battle', *European Warfare, 1350–1750*, ed. F. Tallett and D. J. B. Trim (Cambridge, 2010), 203–5.
7. M. Bennett, 'The Development of Battle Tactics in the Hundred Years War', *Arms, Armies and Fortifications*, ed. Curry and Hughes, 5, 10–13.
8. P. Contamine, *War in the Middle Ages*, trans. M. Jones (Oxford, 1984), 87.
9. Contamine, *Guerre, état et société*, 26–38; C. T. Allmand, *The Hundred Years War: England and France at War, c.1300–c.1450* (Cambridge, 1988; rev. edn, 2001), 92–3.
10. A. Curry, A. Bell, A. Chapman, A. King and D. Simpkin, 'What Did You Do in the Hundred Years War, Daddy? The Soldier in Later Medieval England', *Historian*, 96 (2007), 7; Prestwich, 'Why did Englishmen Fight in the Hundred Years War?', 58–65.
11. TNA C 1/9/407.
12. A. Curry, *Agincourt: A New History* (Stroud, 2005), 52–3, 57–8. Clarence contracted dysentery at Harfleur and did not take part in the battle of Agincourt: G. L. Harriss, 'Thomas, Duke of Clarence (1387–1421)', *ODNB* (online edn, 2010).
13. Y. N. Harari, 'Strategy and Supply in Fourteenth-Century Western European Invasion Campaigns', *Journal of Military History*, 64 (2000), 301–2.
14. V. Fiorato, A. Boylston and C. Knussel, eds, *Blood-Red Roses: The Archaeology of a Mass Grave from the Battle of Towton, 1461* (Oxford, 2000), 45–59, 94; A. J. Stirland, *The Men of the Mary Rose* (Stroud, 2005), 81–2; K. DeVries, 'Teenagers at War during the Middle Ages', *The*

Premodern Teenager: Youth in Society, 1150–1650, ed. K. Eisenbichler (Toronto, 2002), 207–23.

15. S. A. Novak, 'Battle-Related Trauma', *Blood-Red Roses*, ed. Fiorato, Boylston and Knussle, 116. See *ibid.*, 104, 107–9 for a survey of the skeletons of archers, which shows that the Towton soldiers were not especially tall or robust.

16. *Scalacronica*, 157.

17. K. DeVries, 'Medieval Mercenaries: Methodology, Definitions and Problems', *Mercenaries and Paid Men: The Mercenary Identity in the Middle Ages*, ed. J. France (Leiden, 2008), 54, 56, and n. 57.

18. *Scalacronica*, 153.

19. Contamine, *Guerre, état et société*, 277–319; *idem*, 'La Guerre de Cent Ans: le XVe siècle. Du "Roi de Bourges" au très victorieux roi de France', *Histoire militaire de la France*, ed. Corvisier, 201–8; Vale, *Charles VII*, 104–6.

20. 'Chronique française du roi de France Charles VII', *English Historical Documents*, IV, 262.

21. Ayton, 'English Armies in the Fourteenth Century', *Arms, Armies and Fortifications*, ed. Curry and Hughes, 34; R. Hardy, 'Longbow', *ibid.*, 161–3, 180.

22. Gerald of Wales, *The Journey through Wales*, ed. and trans. L. Thorpe (London, 1978), 112–13.

23. Curry et al., 'What Did You Do in the Hundred Years War, Daddy?', 12; www.medievalsoldier.org; Verbruggen, *Art of Warfare*, 117–21; A. Chapman, 'Welshmen in the Armies of Edward I', *The Impact of the Edwardian Castles in Wales*, ed. D. M. Williams and J. R. Kenyon (Oxford, 2010), 175–82.

24. J. Bradbury, *The Medieval Archer* (New York, 1985), 93; Ayton, 'Military Service and the Development of the Robin Hood Legend in the Fourteenth Century', 135; A. J. Pollard, 'Idealising Criminality: Robin Hood in the Fifteenth Century', *Pragmatic Utopias: Ideas and Communities, 1200–1630*, ed. R. Horrox and S. Rees Jones (Cambridge, 2001), 158–61.

25. P. V. Harris, 'Archery in the First Half of the Fourteenth Century', *Journal of the Society of Archer-Antiquaries*, 13 (1970), 19–21; Rogers, 'The Military Revolutions of the Hundred Years War', 249–51 and nn. 36–41; Novak, 'Battle-Related Trauma', 109; P. Marsden, *Sealed by Time: The Loss and Recovery of the Mary Rose* (Portsmouth, 2003), 121, 124–5. It has been proposed that rather than causing a great number of casualties, archer fire disorganised an enemy assault making them easy prey for infantry: C. Gaier, 'L'invincibilité anglaise et le grand arc après la Guerre de Cent Ans: un mythe tenace', *Tijdschrift voor geschiedenis*, 91 (1978), 378–85; J. Keegan, *Face of Battle: A Study of Agincourt, Waterloo and the Somme* (Harmondsworth, 1978), 78–116. For a different approach, see C. J. Rogers, 'The Efficacy of the English Longbow: A Reply to Kelly DeVries', *War in History*, 5 (1998), 233–42.

26. Chronicles of Jean Le Fèvre, Jean Waurin and Enguerrand de Monstrelet: Curry, ed., *Battle of Agincourt*, 160.

27. Le Fèvre, Waurin and Monstrelet: Curry, ed., *Battle of Agincourt*, 161. Also see M. Strickland and R. Hardy, *The Great Warbow: From Hastings to the Mary Rose* (Stroud, 2005), 318–38.

28. Mitchell, 'Longbow–Crossbow Shootout', 242–5.

29. K. DeVries, 'The Introduction and Use of the *Pavise* in the Hundred Years War', *Arms and Armour*, 4 (2007), 95, 98–9.

30. M. Prestwich, *Armies and Warfare in the Middle Ages: The English Experience* (New Haven, CT, and London, 1996), 293; T. F. Tout, 'Firearms in England in the Fourteenth Century', *EHR*, 26 (1911), 670–4, 676.

31. Cited by C. J. Rogers, 'The Age of the Hundred Years War', *Medieval Warfare: A History*, ed. M. Keen (Oxford, 1999), 136.

32. Froissart, *Chroniques*, ed. Luce, IV, 11; Contamine, *War in the Middle Ages*, 140; J. Bradbury, *The Medieval Siege* (Woodbridge, 1992), 159; S. Storey-Challenger, *L'administration anglaise du Ponthieu après le traité de Brétigny, 1361–1369* (Abbeville, 1975), 286.

33. R. D. Smith, 'Artillery and the Hundred Years War: Myth and Interpretation', *Arms, Armies and Fortifications*, ed. Curry and Hughes, 153–5; R. L. C. Jones, 'Fortifications and Sieges in Western Europe *c.*800–1450', *Medieval Warfare*, ed. Keen, 180–3; M. Prestwich, 'Was there a Military Revolution in Medieval England?', *Recognition Essays Presented to E. B. Fryde*, ed. C. Richmond and I. Harvey (Aberystwyth, 1996), 25.

34. *Gesta Henrici Quinti*, 39; K. DeVries, 'The Impact of Gunpowder Weaponry in the Hundred Years War', *The Medieval City under Siege*, ed. I. A. Corfis and M. Wolfe (Woodbridge, 1995), 228–30.

35. Curry, *Agincourt: A New History*, 83.
36. *Gesta Henrici Quinti*, 86–7 and n. 1; J. Barker, *Agincourt* (London, 2005), 296–7.
37. *Parisian Bourgeois*, 257.
38. K. DeVries, 'The Use of Gunpowder Weaponry by and against Joan of Arc during the Hundred Years War', *War and Society*, 14 (1996), 9–14; DeVries, *Joan of Arc*, 52, 56–8; R. D. Smith and K. DeVries, *The Artillery of the Dukes of Burgundy, 1363–1477* (Woodbridge, 2005), esp. 98–103.
39. Vale, *War and Chivalry*, 132–3.
40. 'Chronique française du roi de France Charles VII': *English Historical Documents*, IV, 262.
41. K. DeVries, *Medieval Military Technology* (Ontario, repr. 2003), 162–3; DeVries, 'Impact of Gunpowder Weaponry on Siege Warfare', 22; M. de Lombarès, 'Castillon (17 juillet 1453): première victoire de l'artillerie', *Revue historique de l'Armée*, 3 (1976), 7–31; M. Keen, 'The Changing Scene: Guns, Gunpowder and Permanent Armies', *Medieval Warfare*, ed. Keen, 272–3; A. H. Burne, *The Agincourt War: A Military History of the Latter Part of the Hundred Years War from 1369 to 1453* (London, 1956), 332–42.
42. Harari, 'Strategy and Supply', 302–3 and n. 10; Prestwich, *Armies and Warfare*, 247–8.
43. *Scalacronica*, 175.
44. Hewitt, *Black Prince's Expedition*, 47–8; P. Hoskins, *In the Steps of the Black Prince: The Road to Poitiers, 1355–1356* (Woodbridge, 2011), 21–2.
45. T. Elmham, 'Liber Metricus de Henrico Quinto': Curry, ed., *Battle of Agincourt*, 43; Harari, 'Strategy and Supply', 306, 308–10.
46. *Chronicles of Jean le Bel*, ed. Bryant, 256–7; R. Wadge, *Arrowstorm: The World of the Archer in the Hundred Years War* (Stroud, 2007), 75–7.
47. Harari, 'Strategy and Supply', 298, 304, 315–16, 318–19.
48. *Scalacronica*, 175, 185.
49. C. de Pizan, *Book of Deeds of Arms and of Chivalry*, 165–6.
50. 'Chronique française du roi de France Charles VII', *English Historical Documents*, IV, 262.
51. *Gesta Henrici Quinti*, 55.
52. Keen, *Laws of War*, 64–5, 104–6; Curry, 'The Military Ordinances of Henry V: Texts and Contexts', *War, Government and Aristocracy in the British Isles*, ed. Given-Wilson et al., 214–49.
53. *Scalacronica*, 185.
54. Curry, ed. *Battle of Agincourt*, 43–4, 129.
55. Curry, *Agincourt: A New History*, 85; Barker, *Agincourt*, 188–92.
56. Walsingham, *St Albans Chronicle*, II, 673.
57. Keegan, *Face of Battle*, 114–16.
58. *Gesta Henrici Quinti*, 81, 83. See further C. J. Rogers, *Soldiers' Lives through History: The Middle Ages* (Westport, CT, 2007), 169–74.
59. Ayton, 'English Army at Crécy', *Battle of Crécy*, 200–24; M. K. Jones, 'The Battle of Verneuil (17 August 1424): Towards a History of Courage', *War in History*, 9 (2002), 395–8.
60. *Gesta Henrici Quinti*, 79; Shakespeare, *Henry V*, IV. iii. 22–4.
61. Chandos Herald, *Life of the Black Prince*, 38. See also J. R. E. Bliese, 'When Knightly Courage may Fail: Battle Orations in Medieval Europe', *Historian*, 53 (1991), 489–504.
62. *Gesta Henrici Quinti*, 79; Elmham, 'Liber Metricus de Henrico Quinto': Curry, ed., *Battle of Agincourt*, 45, 48.
63. Barker, *Agincourt*, 289. On the religious preparations soldiers made prior to campaigning, see G. St John, 'Dying Beyond the Seas: Testamentary Preparation for Campaigning during the Hundred Years War', *Fourteenth-Century England*, VII, ed. W. M. Ormrod (Woodbridge, 2012), 177–96.
64. Both Contamine and Curry suggest that the French army was much smaller than is commonly accepted (9,000–12,000): P. Contamine, 'Crécy (1346) et Azincourt (1415): une comparaison', *Divers aspects du Moyen Âge en Occident* (Calais, 1977), 35; Curry, *Agincourt: A New History*, 187. Other recent works suggest a figure of around 24,000 is more accurate: C. J. Rogers, 'The Battle of Agincourt', *Hundred Years War*, II: *Different Vistas*, ed. Villalon and Kagay, 57–63; Barker, *Agincourt*, 227, 274; M. Bennett, *Agincourt, 1415* (Oxford, 1991), 72.

65. C. Phillpotts, 'The French Plan of Battle during the Agincourt Campaign', *EHR*, 99 (1984), 59–66.
66. Thomas Gray thought the French delay prior to beginning the battle of Poitiers had been instigated for much the same reason: *Scalacronica*, 145.
67. *Gesta Henrici Quinti*, 87.
68. *Gesta Henrici Quinti*, 89.
69. Monstrelet: Curry, ed., *Battle of Agincourt*, 160.
70. *Gesta Henrici Quinti*, 91.
71. C. Rawcliffe, *Medicine and Society in Later Medieval England* (Stroud, 1995), 4.
72. Ayton, 'English Army at Crécy', *Battle of Crécy*, ed. Ayton and Preston, 174.
73. Barker, *Agincourt*, 29–30, 142–6; M. Carlin, 'Morstede, Thomas (d.1450)', *ODNB* (online edn, 2004); Strickland and Hardy, *Great Warbow*, 279–86.
74. *Scalacronica*, 146–7; W. Turner, 'Mental Incapacity and the Financing of War in Medieval England', *Hundred Years War*, II: *Different Vistas*, ed. Kagay and Villalon, 388, 390. For the sparse and tantalising evidence for trauma arising from primitive combat, see L. N. Keeley, *War before Civilization: The Myth of the Peaceful Savage* (New York, 1996), 146.
75. *Gesta Henrici Quinti*, 92–3.
76. 'The Siege of Rouen', *The Historical Collections of a Citizen of London in the Fifteenth Century*, ed. J. Gairdner (London, 1876), 1–46, cited by A. Goodman, *The Wars of the Roses: The Soldiers' Experience* (Stroud, 2005), 29.
77. Le Fèvre and Waurin: Curry, ed. *Battle of Agincourt*, 167.
78. Barker, *Conquest*, 7; C. Richmond, 'The War at Sea', *The Hundred Years War*, ed. K. Fowler (London, 1971), 98–100.
79. Allmand, *Henry V*, 103, 107–8, 113; A. Curry, 'After Agincourt, What Next? Henry V and the Campaign of 1416', *Conflicts, Consequences and the Crown in the Late Middle Ages*, ed. L. Clark (Woodbridge, 2007), 23–51.
80. Rodger, *Safeguard of the Sea*, 91–2; S. Rose, *Medieval Naval Warfare, 1000–1500* (New York, 2002), 68; Richmond, 'The War at Sea', 103; G. R. Cushway, ' "The Lord of the Sea": The English Navy in the Reign of Edward III', unpub PhD thesis (University of Exeter, 2006), 264.
81. D. Green, 'Jean de Vienne', *The Oxford Encyclopedia of Medieval Warfare and Military Technology*, ed. C. J. Rogers, 3 vols (New York, 2010), II, 440.
82. M. M. Postan, 'The Costs of the Hundred Years' War', *Past and Present*, 27 (1964), 34–5, 39; T. J. Runyan, 'Ships and Mariners in Later Medieval England', *Journal of British Studies*, 16 (1977), 3–4, 8; J. W. Sherborne, 'The Hundred Years' War. The English Navy: Shipping and Manpower 1369–1389', *Past and Present*, 37 (1967), 163–75.
83. Rose, *Medieval Sea*, 112. By the end of the fourteenth century the *Clos des Gallées* had become little more than a scrapyard – it was destroyed when the English took Rouen in 1419.
84. I. Friel, 'Winds of Change', *Arms, Armies and Fortifications*, ed. Curry and Hughes, 185; Cushway, 'The Lord of the Sea', 11; Sumption, *Trial by Battle*, 215–16, 264, 404; Rogers, *Wars of Edward III*, 36.
85. Friel, 'Winds of Change', 187.
86. Rodger, *Safeguard of the Sea*, 145.
87. Rose, *Medieval Sea*, 118–20.

Chapter 7 Occupation: Coexistence, Collaboration and Resistance (1423)

1. *Parisian Journal*, 191.
2. Allmand, *Henry V*, 186–204.
3. D. Grummitt, 'Écorcheurs', *Oxford Encyclopedia of Medieval Warfare and Military Technology*, ed. Rogers, II, 13. See also Rogers, 'By Fire and Sword: *Bellum Hostile* and "Civilians" in the Hundred Years War', *Civilians in the Path of War*, ed. Grimsley and Rogers, 47–9, 53. In the fifteenth century, during Bedford's regime, the garrisons in Normandy on the Maine frontier derived an annual income of 25,000 *livres* in protection money by raiding across the border: Wright, *Knights and Peasants*, 78.
4. C. T. Allmand, *Lancastrian Normandy, 1415–1450: The History of a Medieval Occupation* (Oxford, 1983), 211.

5. J. Sumption, 'Angle, Guichard (IV) d', Earl of Huntingdon (c.1308/15–1380)', *ODNB* (online edn, 2006); D. Green, *The Black Prince* (Stroud, rev. edn, 2008), 181–7.
6. *Chronique du Mont-St-Michel (1343–1468)*, ed. S. Luce, 2 vols (Paris, 1879), I, 168 n. 2; J. Barker, 'The Foe Within: Treason in Lancastrian Normandy', *Soldiers, Nobles and Gentlemen*, ed. Coss and Tyerman, 310–11.
7. A. Bossuat, 'The Re-Establishment of Peace in Society during the Reign of Charles VII', *The Recovery of France in the Fifteenth Century*, ed. P. S. Lewis, trans. G. F. Martin (London, 1971), 65.
8. Juvénal des Ursins, *Les écrits politiques*, III, 109.
9. Barker, *Conquest*, 50–2, 65–71.
10. AN JJ 107, no. 11; cited by Wright, *Knights and Peasants*, 90.
11. *Parisian Journal*, 167.
12. For the oath of allegiance demanded by the English of Frenchmen after the treaty of Troyes, see TNA C 47/30/9/10; M. Mercer, *Henry V: The Rebirth of Chivalry* (London, 2004), 70–1.
13. A. Curry, 'Lancastrian Normandy: The Jewel in the Crown', *England and Normandy in the Middle Ages*, ed. Bates and Curry, 236.
14. R. A. Griffiths, 'The English Realm and Dominions and the King's Subjects in the Later Middle Ages', *Aspects of Late Medieval Government and Society*, ed. Rowe, 84–5.
15. D. Green, 'Lordship and Principality: Colonial Policy in Ireland and Aquitaine in the 1360s', *Journal of British Studies*, 47 (2008), 26–7 and nn. 116–18; A. J. Otway-Ruthven, 'Ireland in the 1350s: Sir Thomas Rokeby and his Successors', *Journal of the Royal Society of Antiquaries of Ireland*, 97 (1967), 47–9; R. Frame, 'Thomas Rokeby, Sheriff of Yorkshire, Justiciar of Ireland', *Peritia*, 10 (1996), 275, 285–6, 290, 294; *idem*, 'Rokeby, Sir Thomas (d.1357)', *ODNB* (online edn, 2008).
16. Among Fastolf's many offices he served the duke of Clarence in Aquitaine (1412–13); as deputy-constable of Bordeaux, captain of Soubise and Veyres (1413–14); captain of Harfleur and Fecamp (1417–21); and lieutenant in Normandy (1422): G. L. Harriss, 'Fastolf, Sir John (1380–1459)', *ODNB* (online edn, 2009).
17. John Talbot's official positions included: commander of the English garrisons at Montgomery and Bishop's Castle (1404); captain of Caernarfon (1409); lieutenant of Ireland (1414); lieutenant-general for the conduct of the war on the eastern front (1434); marshal of France (1436); lieutenant of Ireland (1445); commander of Lower Normandy (1448); lieutenant of Gascony (1452): A. J. Pollard, *John Talbot and the War in France 1427–1453* (Barnsley, 2nd edn, 1983); A. J. Pollard, 'Talbot, John, First Earl of Shrewsbury and First Earl of Waterford (c.1387–1453)', *ODNB* (online edn, 2008).
18. J. Watts, 'Richard of York, Third Duke of York (1411–1460)', *ODNB* (online edn, 2009); T. B. Pugh, 'Richard Plantagenet (1411–60), Duke of York, as the King's Lieutenant in France and Ireland', *Aspects of Late Medieval Government and Society*, ed. Rowe, 107–41.
19. M. W. Labarge, *Gascony, England's First Colony, 1204–1453* (London, 1980); R. Frame, 'Overlordship and Reaction, c.1200–c.1450', *Ireland and Britain, 1170–1450* (London, 1998), 77–8; R. Boutruche, 'Anglais et Gascons en Aquitaine du XIIe au XVe siècles. Problèmes d'histoire sociale', *Mélanges d'histoire dédiés à la mémoire de Louis Halphen* (Paris, 1951), 57.
20. *Histoire générale de Languedoc avec des notes et les pièces justificatives*, ed. C. de Vic and J. Vaissètte, rev. edn A. Molinier, 16 vols (Toulouse, 1872–1904), X, 1,404–6; Barber, *Edward Prince of Wales*, 213; Ormrod, *Reign of Edward III*, 36; Green, *Edward the Black Prince*, 134–5; Green, 'Lordship and Principality', 3–30. For a different interpretation of conditions in Aquitaine and of the nature of the prince's administration, see G. Pépin, 'Towards a New Assessment of the Black Prince's Principality of Aquitaine: A Study of the Last Years (1369–72)', *Nottingham Medieval Studies*, 50 (2006), 59–114; G. Pépin, 'The Parlement of Anglo-Gascon Aquitaine: The Three Estates of Aquitaine (Guyenne)', *Nottingham Medieval Studies*, 52 (2008), 133–45.
21. *Westminster Chronicle*, 484.
22. Wright, *Knights and Peasants*, 77.
23. M. Jones, 'Les capitaines anglo-bretons et les marches entre la Bretagne et le Poitou de 1342 à 1373', *La 'France anglaise' au Moyen Âge*, ed. R. H. Bautier (Paris, 1988), 357–75; M. Jones,

'Edward III's Captains in Brittany', *England in the Fourteenth Century*, ed. W. M. Ormrod (Woodbridge, 1986), 99–118; M. Jones, *Ducal Brittany, 1364–1399: Relations with England and France during the Reign of Duke John IV* (Oxford, 1970), 1–21.

24. Repressive legislation enforced in Wales in the early fifteenth century built on that first introduced in the 1284 Statute of Rhuddlan/Wales: *Statutes of the Realm*, II, 128–9, 140–1; I. Bowen, ed., *The Statutes of Wales* (London, 1908), 31–7; *CPR, 1399–1401*, 469–70; R. A. Griffiths, *The Principality of Wales in the Later Middle Ages: The Structure and Personnel of Government*, I: *South Wales, 1277–1536* (Cardiff, 1972), xix; R. R. Davies, *The Revolt of Owain Glyn Dŵr* (Oxford, 1995), 65–93.

25. A. Curry, 'Sir Thomas Erpingham: A Career in Arms', *Agincourt, 1415*, ed. A. Curry (Stroud, 2000), 66; Allmand, *Henry V*, 209; A. Chapman, 'The King's Welshmen: Welsh Involvement in the Expeditionary Army of 1415', *Journal of Medieval Military History*, IX, ed. A. Curry and A. Bell (Woodbridge, 2011), 41–63. Welsh troops continued to be recruited throughout Henry's campaigns, for example in 1420: TNA E403/645/6.

26. H. F. Berry, ed., *Statutes and Ordinances, and Acts of the Parliament of Ireland: King John to Henry V* (Dublin, 1907), 430–69; S. Duffy, 'The Problem of Degeneracy', *Law and Disorder in Thirteenth-Century Ireland: The Dublin Parliament of 1297*, ed. J. Lydon (Dublin, 1997), 87–106; J. Lydon, 'Nation and Race in Medieval Ireland', *Concepts of National Identity in the Middle Ages*, ed. S. Forde, L. Johnson and A. V. Murray (Leeds, 1995), 105.

27. J. Le Patourel, 'The Plantagenet Dominions', *History*, 50 (1965), 306.

28. For the approximate boundaries of the *pays de conquête*, see J. H. Wylie and W. T. Waugh, *The Reign of Henry the Fifth*, 3 vols (Cambridge, 1914–29), III, 235–7.

29. Allmand, *Henry V*, 16–38; Curry, *Agincourt: A New History*, 16–17.

30. Harriss, 'Introduction: The Exemplar of Kingship', *Henry V: The Practice of Kingship*, 29; Curry, 'Lancastrian Normandy: The Jewel in the Crown?', *England and Normandy*, ed. Bates and Curry, 241–52.

31. *Gesta Henrici Quinti*, 16–18; J. J. N. Palmer, 'The War Aims of the Protagonists and the Negotiations for Peace', *The Hundred Years War*, ed. Fowler, 54–5; Barker, *Agincourt*, 14.

32. Curry, 'Lancastrian Normandy: The Jewel in the Crown?', 237–8; Allmand, *Lancastrian Normandy*, 126.

33. R. E. Glasscock, 'Land and People c.1300', *A New History of Ireland*, II: *Medieval Ireland 1169–1534*, ed. A. Cosgrove (Oxford, 1987), 212–16; R. R. Davies, 'Colonial Wales', *Past and Present*, 65 (1974), 3–6, 11; C. T. Allmand, 'The Lancastrian Land Settlement in Normandy, 1417–50', *Economic History Review*, 2nd ser. 21 (1968), 463.

34. In retaliation Charles (VII), at the assembly of the Estates General held in Selles in January 1421, declared the property of those who had remained in English occupied territories confiscated and distributed it, in theory, to his own followers: Bossuat, 'Re-Establishment of Peace', 62.

35. R. Massey, 'The Lancastrian Land Settlement in Normandy and Northern France, 1417–1450', unpub. PhD thesis (University of Liverpool, 1987), 67–178; L. Puisseux, *L'émigration normande et la colonisation anglaise en Normandie au XVe siècle* (Paris, 1866), 66; Allmand, *Lancastrian Normandy*, 61–3; Curry, 'Lancastrian Normandy: The Jewel in the Crown?', 241.

36. These lands reverted to the Crown after Clarence's death at the battle of Baugé (1421).

37. Montague's offices and titles in France included captain of Honfleur (1419–20); lieutenant-general in Normandy and in the marches south of the Seine (appointed 26 April 1419), extended to the whole duchy of Normandy and Maine on 13 November 1420; governor of Alençon, Bonsmoulins and Verneuil (1420–23): A. Curry, 'Montagu, Thomas, Fourth Earl of Salisbury (1388–1428)', *ODNB* (online edn, 2008).

38. Allmand, 'The Lancastrian Land Settlement', 463–6; *idem*, *Lancastrian Normandy*, 52–6.

39. Sumption, *Trial by Battle*, 576–83; S. Rose, *Calais: An English Town in France, 1347–1558* (Woodbridge, 2008), 7–22.

40. Rymer, *Feodera*, III, i, 548; R. Favreau, 'Comptes de la sénéchaussée de Saintonge, 1360–2', *BEC*, 117 (1959), 76–8; *idem*, 'La cession de La Rochelle à l'Angleterre en 1360', *La 'France anglaise' au Moyen Âge*, ed. Bautier, 222–7; P. Chaplais, 'Some Documents Regarding the Fulfilment and Interpretation of the Treaty of Brétigny', *Camden Society*, 3rd ser. 19 (1952), 52–3 and nn. 1–2.

41. Green, 'Lordship and Principality', 8–9, 20–1; Delachenal, *Charles V*, IV, 18–20, 67; P. Boissonnade, *Histoire de Poitou* (Paris, 1941), 136–7; É. Labroue, *Bergerac sous les Anglais* (Bordeaux, 1893), 66; A. Higounet-Nadal, *Périgueux au XIVe et XVe siècles* (Bordeaux, 1978), 148.

42. A. Curry, 'Towns at War: Norman Towns under English Rule, 1417–1450', *Towns and Townspeople in the Fifteenth Century*, ed. J. A. Thomson (Gloucester, 1989), 149.

43. C. T. Allmand, 'La Normandie devant l'opinion anglaise à la fin de la Guerre de Cent Ans', *BEC*, 128 (1970), 355; J. Lydon, 'The Middle Nation', *The English in Medieval Ireland*, ed. J. Lydon (Dublin, 1984), 12–20.

44. Allmand, *Lancastrian Normandy*, 51.

45. Before 1420 Gisors, Dieppe, Caen, Falaise and Pontoise also had their privileges confirmed: Rymer, *Feodera*, IV, iii, 137, 146, 199; Curry, 'Towns at War', 149, 157–61.

46. A. Curry, A. Bell, A. Chapman, A. King and D. Simpkin, 'Languages in the Military Profession in Later Medieval England', *The Anglo-Norman Language and its Contexts*, ed. R. Ingham (York, 2010), 81–2, 85, 87–8.

47. For the garrison sizes at Bayeux, Caudebec, Coutances, Caen, Carentan, Verneuil and Pont-de-l'Arche in 1433–4, see J. Stevenson, ed., *Letters and Papers Illustrative of the Wars of the English in France during the Reign of Henry the Sixth, King of England*, 3 vols (London, 1861–4), II, ii, 540–6.

48. Captains of Mantes included: Sir John Grey (later count of Tancarville); Edmund, earl of March; John Handford; Richard Guethin; Ralph Grey; Thomas Hoo; and Richard Lowick. A. Curry, 'Bourgeois et soldats dans la ville de Mantes pendant l'occupation anglaise de 1419 à 1449', *Guerre, pouvoir et noblesse au Moyen Âge. Mélanges en l'honneur de Philippe Contamine*, ed. J. Paviot and J. Verger (Paris, 2000), 179–80, 183; *idem*, 'Towns at War', 148–50, 153, 156, 162; *idem*, 'The Nationality of Men-at-Arms Serving in English Armies in Normandy and the Pays-de-Conquête, 1415–1450', *Reading Medieval Studies*, 18 (1992), 157.

49. A. Curry, 'Isolated or Integrated? The English Soldier in Lancastrian Normandy', *Courts and Regions in Medieval Europe*, ed. S. Rees Jones, R. Marks and A. J. Minnis (York, 2000), 192; Allmand, *Lancastrian Normandy*, 80.

50. P. Crooks, 'Factions, Feuds and Noble Power in the Lordship of Ireland, c.1356–1496', *Irish Historical Studies*, 35 (2007), 434–6; P. Capra, 'Les bases sociales du pouvoir anglo-gascon au milieu du XIVe siècle', *Le Moyen Âge*, 4ème sér. 81 (1975), 276; *idem*, 'L'évolution de l'administration anglo-gasconne au milieu du XIVe siècle', *Bordeaux et les Iles britanniques du XIIIe au XXe siècle* (Bordeaux, 1975), 23; J. Given, *State and Society in Medieval Europe: Gwynedd and Languedoc under Outside Rule* (Ithaca, NY, and London, 1990), 154–66; Curry, 'Lancastrian Normandy: The Jewel in the Crown?', 250.

51. Pépin, 'Parlement of Anglo-Gascon Aquitaine', 135, 137–8, 145–9, 153–6. See also Palmer, *England, France and Christendom*, 152–65; C. J. Phillpotts, 'John of Gaunt and English Policy towards France, 1389–1395', *Journal of Medieval History*, 16 (1990), 363–86; Allmand, *Lancastrian Normandy*, 171–86; Curry, 'Towns at War', 159, 163.

52. *Histoire générale de Languedoc*, X, 1404–6; Thompson, *Paris and its People*, 28–9.

53. M. K. Jones, 'L'imposition illégale de taxes en "Normandie anglaise": une enquête gouvernemen-tale en 1446', *La 'France anglaise'*, ed. Bautier, 461–8; Wright, *Knights and Peasants*, 87.

54. Curry, 'Towns at War', 153, 155–8, 165–6.

55. Curry, 'Towns at War', 162. Mantes provides one of the best examples of the reconquest. The town's *Déliberations* have been used extensively by Anne Curry. They are found in Mantes-la-Jolie; Bibliothèque Municipale, Archives Communales de Mantes, Série BB 5ff.

56. Berry, *Statutes and Ordinances*, 447; E. Tresham, ed., *Rotulorum Patentium et Clausorum Cancellarie Hibernie Calendarium* (Dublin, 1828), Pat. 49 Edward III, 94 no. 164.

57. *Parisian Bourgeois*, 281; Vale, *Charles VII*, 122; Thompson, *Paris and its People*, 8–9.

58. W. M. Ormrod, ed., 'Edward III: Parliament of 1373, Text and Translation', *PROME*, item 32. See also A. K. McHardy, 'The Effects of War on the Church: The Case of the Alien Priories in the Fourteenth Century', *England and her Neighbours*, ed. Jones and Vale, 277–95.

59. F. X. Martin, 'John, Lord of Ireland, 1185–1216', *A New History of Ireland*, II, ed. Cosgrove, 153; R. R. Davies, *The Age of Conquest: Wales, 1063–1415* (Oxford, 1991), 398.

60. Allmand, 'The English and the Church in Lancastrian Normandy', *England and Normandy*, ed. Bates and Curry, 287–9; *idem, Lancastrian Normandy*, 218; Thompson, *Paris and its People*, 158–9, 171–5, 179ff.

61. *Parisian Journal*, 200–1.

62. J. Favier, 'Occupation ou connivence? Les Anglais à Paris (1422–1436)', *Guerre, pouvoir et noblesse au Moyen Âge Contamine*, ed. Paviot and Verger, 247; Thompson, *Paris and its People*, 151.

63. Stafford also served as constable of France, and lieutenant-general of Normandy. Clarence held the *vicomtés* of Auge, Orbec and Pont Audemer until his death in 1421. Beaufort served, briefly, as lieutenant in Aquitaine (1413–14), and as captain of some of Henry V's major conquests – Harfleur, Rouen, Conches and Melun, in addition to Paris.

64. *Parisian Journal*, 155. After the treaty of Arras the Burgundians played a crucial role in recapturing Paris for Charles VII: Thompson, *Paris and its People*, 10, 37–44, 149–50, 159, 208–9, 238.

65. *Parisian Journal*, 161.

66. R. R. Butler, *Is Paris Lost? The English Occupation, 1422–1436* (Staplehurst, 2003), 65–6.

67. G. Llewelyn Thompson, 'Le régime anglo-bourguignon à Paris: facteurs idéologiques', *La 'France anglaise' au Moyen Âge*, ed. Bautier, 53–60; *idem*, ' "*Monseigneur Saint Denis*", his Abbey, and his Town, under the English Occupation, 1420–1436', *Power, Culture, and Religion in France, c.1350–c.1550*, ed. C. T. Allmand (Woodbridge, 1989), 19.

68. *Parisian Bourgeois*, 185.

69. S. Roux, *Paris in the Middle Ages*, trans. Jo Ann McNamara (Philadelphia, PA, 2009), 59; Griffiths, *Reign of Henry VI*, 516; Thompson, *Paris and its People*, 208–9, 216–17; Favier, 'Occupation ou connivence?', 252; Barker, *Conquest*, 70.

70. G.L. Harriss, 'Fastolf, Sir John (1380–1459)', *ODNB* (online edn, 2004); Favier, 'Occupation ou connivence?', 249–50.

71. Charles d'Orléans's Italian secretary Antonio Astesano described conditions in Saint-Denis in 1451: Antonio Astesano, 'Éloge descriptif de la ville de Paris et des principales villes de France en 1451', ed. A. Le Roux de Lincy and L.–M. Tisserand, *Paris et ses historiens aux XIV–XV siècles* (Paris, 1867), 552. See also Thompson, 'Monseigneur Saint Denis', 15–18, 27–8.

72. This was certainly the case when Limoges renounced its loyalty to the Black Prince in 1370. See Paul Ducourtieux, *Histoire de Limoges* (Limoges, 1925, repr. Marseille, 1975), 53, 59; Barber, *Edward, Prince of Wales*, 224–6 and n. 23; Keen, *Laws of War*, 120–1, 124; Green, *Edward the Black Prince*, 90–3. The English regimes in Normandy and Paris faced similar problems after 1435 with the collapse of the Burgundian alliance at the Congress of Arras: see *Parisian Journal*, 318; Allmand, 'Lancastrian Land Settlement', 471.

73. B. G. H. Ditcham, ' "Mutton Guzzlers and Wine Bags": Foreign Soldiers and Native Reactions in Fifteenth-Century France', *Power, Culture and Religion in France*, ed. Allmand, 2–4, 6–8; Norman MacDougall, *An Antidote to the English: The Auld Alliance, 1295–1560* (East Linton, 2001), 59–77; M. H. Brown, 'Stewart, John, third earl of Buchan (*c.*1380–1424)', *ODNB* (online edn, 2006); *idem*, 'Douglas, Archibald, fourth earl of Douglas, and duke of Touraine in the French nobility (*c.*1369–1424)', *ODNB* (online edn, 2006); *idem*, 'Douglas, Archibald, fifth earl of Douglas, and duke of Touraine in the French nobility (*c.*1391–1439)', *ODNB* (online edn, 2006).

74. L. Taylor, *The Virgin Warrior: The Life and Death of Joan of Arc* (New Haven, CT, and London, 2009), 2, 11–12, 14–15, 21–2.

Chapter 8 Women and War (1429)

1. *Joan of Arc: La Pucelle*, ed. and trans. C. Taylor (Manchester, 2006), 89.

2. C. de Pizan, *Le ditié de Jehanne d'Arc*, ed. and trans. A. J. Kennedy and K. Varty (Oxford, 1997).

3. See C. de Pizan, *The Book of the City of Ladies*, trans. R. Brown-Grant (Harmondsworth, 1999). Other major works include: 'The Epistle of Othea' (*c.*1399); 'The Book of the Deeds of King Charles V, the Wise' (1404); 'The Book of the Body Politic' (1405); 'The Book of Deeds of Arms and of Chivalry' (*c.*1410); 'The Book of Peace' (*c.*1412); 'The Epistle of the Prison of Human Life' (1415–18); 'The Song of Joan of Arc' (1429).

4. J. Bolton, 'The World Upside Down: Plague as an Agent of Economic and Social Change', *The Black Death in England*, ed. W. M. Ormrod and P. Lindley (Stamford, 1996), 37–9, 51.

5. S. Shahar, *The Fourth Estate: A History of Women in the Middle Ages* (New York, 1983), 191–2; H. Nicholson, *Medieval Warfare* (Basingstoke, 2004), 185 n. 86; H. Swanson, 'The Illusion of Economic Structure: Craft Guilds in Late Medieval English Towns', *Past and Present*, 121 (1988), 39; J. M. Bennett, *Ale, Beer and Brewsters in England: Women's Work in a Changing World, 1300–1600* (Oxford, 1996); J. C. Ward, *Women in England in the Middle Ages* (London, 2006), 92; Barker, *Agincourt*, 92–3.

6. S. H. Rigby, 'Introduction: Social Structure and Economic Change in Late Medieval England', *A Social History of England, 1200–1500*, ed. R. Horrox and W. M. Ormrod (Cambridge, 2006), 16–17; M. E. Mate, 'Work and Leisure', *ibid.*, 276–7.

7. S. Bardsley, 'Women's Work Reconsidered: Gender and Wage Differentiation in Late Medieval England', *Past and Present*, 165 (1999), 3–16.

8. C. Taylor, 'The Salic Law, French Queenship, and the Defense of Women in the Late Middle Ages', *French Historical Studies*, 29 (2006), 543 and n. 2, 548. Comments/treatises on Salic law following Richard Lescot's rediscovery of the concept (*The Laws of the Salian Franks*, ed. and trans. K. Fischer Drew [Philadelphia, PA, 1991], 28–55) include Jean de Montreuil's *Traité contre les Anglois* (1411), the *Audite celi of* Jean Juvénal des Ursins (1435), the *Abrégé des chroniques de France* by Noel de Fribois (1459) and the anonymous *Grand traitis la loy salique* (c.1464): see K. Daly and R. E. Giesey, 'Noel de Fribois et la loi salique', *BEC*, 151 (1993), 5–27.

9. See, for example, the extremely misogynistic courtesy book written by Geoffrey de la Tour Landry in c.1380: *The Book of the Knight of La Tour-Landry*, ed. T. Wright (London, 1906).

10. Rigby, 'Introduction: Social Structure and Economic Change in Late Medieval England', *A Social History of England*, ed. Horrox and Ormrod, 9–10.

11. *Parisian Journal*, 88.

12. C. de Pizan, *Book of the City of Ladies*, 31–2.

13. *Chronique des quatre premiers Valois*, cited by Autrand, *Charles V*, 21. See also Small, *Late Medieval France*, 98.

14. R. Gibbons, 'Isabeau of Bavaria, Queen of France (1385–1422): The Creation of an Historical Villainess', *TRHS*, 6th ser. 6 (1996), 54. Among Isabeau's many children, a number died in infancy: Charles (d.1386), Charles (1392–1401), Philippe (d.1407), Louis of Guyenne (1397–1415). Jean, duke of Tourraine (1398–1417) preceded Charles (VII) as dauphin.

15. Taylor, 'Salic Law', 555; L. L. Huneycutt, 'Intercession and the High-Medieval Queen: The Esther Topos', *Power of the Weak: Studies on Medieval Women*, ed. J. Carpenter and S.-B. MacLean (Chicago, IL, 1995), 126–46; J. C. Parsons, 'The Queen's Intercession in Thirteenth-Century England', *ibid.*, 147–77; A. Musson, 'Queenship, Lordship and Petitioning in Late Medieval England', *Medieval Petitions*, ed. Ormrod, Dodd and Musson, 158–63.

16. *Chronicle of Jean de Venette*, 57–8, 69; Benz St John, *Three Medieval Queens*, 33–63.

17. Taylor, *The Virgin Warrior*, 35, 42–3, 51, 55.

18. P. Strohm, *Hochon's Arrow: The Social Imagination of Fourteenth-Century Texts* (Princeton, NJ, 1992), 95–119.

19. Benz St John, *Three Medieval Queens*, 99–100; Rose, *Calais*, 20–2; J.-M. Moeglin, 'Édouard III et les six bourgeois de Calais', *Revue Historique*, 292 (1994), 229–67.

20. *Westminster Chronicle* cited by A. K. McHardy, ed., *The Reign of Richard II: From Minority to Tyranny, 1377–97* (Manchester, 2012), 227, 73–5; J. L. Leland, 'Burley, Sir Simon (1336?–1388)', *ODNB* (online edn, 2011).

21. Taylor, 'Salic Law, French Queenship and the Defense of Women', 553, 557–60.

22. *Westminster Chronicle*, 25; Saul, *Richard II*, 83–4; *idem*, 'Anne (1366–1394)', *ODNB* (online edn, 2004).

23. M. Jones, 'Joan (1368–1437)', *ODNB* (online edn, 2008).

24. L. Hilton, *Queens Consort: England's Medieval Queens* (London, 2008), 307–20.

25. M. Jones, 'Catherine (1401–1437)', *ODNB* (online edn, 2008); C. Richmond, 'Beaufort, Edmund, first Duke of Somerset (c.1406–1455)', *ibid.* (online edn, 2008); R. A. Griffiths, 'Tudor, Owen (c.1400–1461)', *ibid.* (online edn, 2008); Allmand, *Henry V*, 66, 68, 131–2, 137, 140–1, 144–5; Wolffe, *Henry VI*, 45, 90.

26. H. Castor, *She-Wolves: The Women who Ruled England before Elizabeth* (London, 2010), 301–402; H. Maurer, *Margaret of Anjou: Queenship and Power in Late Medieval England* (Woodbridge, 2003), 1–38.

27. Estow, *Pedro the Cruel*, 265.
28. *St Albans Chronicle*, I, 963; A. Tuck, 'Edmund, First Duke of York (1341–1402)', *ODNB* (online edn, 2008).
29. Autrand, *Charles V*, 14–16; Delachenal, *Charles V*, I, 33–5.
30. Vaughan, *Philip the Bold*, 44.
31. Vale, *Charles VII*, 22–4.
32. MacDougall, *An Antidote to the English*, 83–6; idem, 'Mary (d.1463)', *ODNB* (online edn, 2004).
33. *St Albans Chronicle*, I, 43; cited by W. M. Ormrod, 'Who was Alice Perrers?', *Chaucer Review*, 40 (2006), 219.
34. C. Given-Wilson, 'Perrers, Alice (d.1400/01)', *ODNB* online edn, (2008); W. M. Ormrod, 'Alice Perrers and John Salisbury', *EHR*, 123 (2008), 379–93; Ormrod, 'Who was Alice Perrers?', 219–29; J. Bothwell, 'The Management of Position: Alice Perrers, Edward III, and the Creation of a Landed Estate, 1362–1377', *Journal of Medieval History*, 24 (1998), 31.
35. *St Albans Chronicle*, I, 12; G. A. Holmes, *The Good Parliament* (Oxford, 1975), 134–5, 137–8.
36. Gibbons, 'Isabeau of Bavaria', 57–8; Adams, *Life and Afterlife of Isabeau of Bavaria*, 113–48.
37. Famiglietti, *Royal Intrigue*, 1–21; B. Guenée, *La folie de Charles VI: roi bien-aimé* (Paris, 2004), 23–36.
38. Vale, *Charles VII*, 90–3, 129; P. Prétou, 'Les poisons de Jacques Cœur', *Cahiers de recherches médiévales*, 17 (2009), 121–40; P. Bernu, 'Le rôle politique de Pierre de Brezé au cours des dix dernières années du règne de Charles VII (1451–1461)', *BEC*, 69 (1908), 303–47.
39. Cited by Vale, *Charles VII*, 94. See also C. Schaefer, 'L'art et l'histoire. Étienne Chevalier commande au peintre Jean Fouquet le diptyque de Melun', *Art et architecture à Melun au Moyen Âge, actes du colloque d'histoire de l'art et d'archéologie* (Paris, 2000), 293–300.
40. *The Goodman of Paris: A Treatise on Moral and Domestic Economy by a Citizen of Paris c.1393*, trans. E. Power (Woodbridge, new edn, 2006), 37; John of Reading, *Chronica Johannis de Reading et anonymi Cantuariensis, 1346–1367*, ed. J. Tait (Manchester, 1914), 166–8; Green, *Edward the Black Prince*, 118–19; S. M. Newton, *Fashion in the Age of the Black Prince: A Study of the Years 1340–1365* (Woodbridge, 1988); M. Dupuy, *Le Prince Noir: Edouard seigneur d'Aquitaine* (Paris, 1970), 200.
41. V. Sekules, 'Dynasty and Patrimony in the Self-Construction of an English Queen: Philippa of Hainault and her Images', *England and the Continent in the Middle Ages: Studies in Memory of Andrew Martindale*, ed. J. Mitchell (Stamford, 2000), 167; P. Stafford, *Queens, Concubines and Dowagers: The King's Wife in the Early Middle Ages* (Leicester, 1998), 108–9; W. M. Ormrod, ' "In Bed with Joan of Kent": The King's Mother and the Peasants' Revolt', *Medieval Women: Texts and Contexts in Late Medieval Britain*, ed. J. Wogan Browne et al. (Turnhout, 2000), 277–92.
42. J. F. Verbruggen, 'Women in Medieval Armies', trans. K. DeVries, *Journal of Medieval Military History*, 4 (2006), 119; R. M. Karras, 'The Regulation of Brothels in Later Medieval England', *Signs*, 14 (1989), 399–433.
43. Goodman, *Wars of the Roses*, 148; A. Curry, 'Soldiers' Wives in the Hundred Years War', *Soldiers, Nobles and Gentlemen*, ed. Coss and Tyerman, 205.
44. M. McLaughlin, 'The Woman Warrior: Gender, Warfare and Society in Medieval Europe', *Women's Studies*, 17 (1990), 193–209.
45. J. Ward, *Women of the English Nobility and Gentry, 1066–1500* (Manchester, 1995), 146–7.
46. C. de Pizan, *The Treasure of the City of Ladies*, trans. S. Lawson (Harmondsworth, 1985), 129.
47. F. Watson, 'Dunbar, Patrick, Eighth Earl of Dunbar or of March, and Earl of Moray (1285–1369)', *ODNB* (online edn, 2008).
48. Sumption, *Trial by Battle*, 389–95. For a more sceptical view of her heroic role, see M. Jones, 'The Breton Civil War', *Froissart: Historian*, ed. J. J. N. Palmer (Woodbridge, 1981), 68–9.
49. *Dictionnaire de biographie Française* (Paris, 1967), XI, 1,526.
50. *Chronica Maiora*, trans. Preest, 331; *St Albans Chronicle*, II, 403.
51. Taylor, *The Virgin Warrior*, 58.
52. Giles of Rome, *De Regimine Principum, Libri III*, cited by J. M. Blythe, 'Women in the Military: Scholastic Arguments and Medieval Images of Female Warriors', *History of Political Thought*, 22 (2001), 253.
53. Taylor, *The Virgin Warrior*, 19–21, 49–50; M. Warner, *Joan of Arc: The Image of Female Heroism* (Berkeley, CA, 1981), 185, 188–9.

54. J. Quicherat, ed., *Procès de condemnation et de rehabilitation de Jeanne d'Arc dite La Pucelle*, 5 vols (Paris, 1841–9), I, 489–93, trans. DeVries, *Joan of Arc*, 1.

55. S. Crane, *The Performance of Self: Ritual, Clothing and Identity during the Hundred Years War* (Philadelphia, PA, 2002), 73–106; L. G. Edwards, 'Joan of Arc: Gender and Authority in the Text of the Trial of Condemnation', *Young Medieval Women*, ed. K. Lewis, N. Menuge and K. Phillips (Stroud, 1999), 139–40, 144; *Joan of Arc*, ed. and trans. Taylor, 46–9.

56. C. de Pizan, *The Epistle of the Prison of Human Life with An Epistle to the Queen of France and Lament of the Evils of the Civil War*, ed. J. A. Wisman (New York, 1984), 3.

57. A. Goodman, *John of Gaunt: The Exercise of Princely Power in Fourteenth-Century Europe* (Harlow, 1992), 31.

58. Curry, *Agincourt: A New History*, 207–9; Barker, *Agincourt*, 307–8.

59. W. H. TeBrake, *A Plague of Insurrection: Popular Politics and Peasant Revolt in Flanders, 1323–1328* (Philadelphia, PA, 1993), 33–4, 123.

60. *Chronicle of Jean de Venette*, 40–1, 85–6, 93.

61. *Chronicle of Jean de Venette*, 76; R. Hilton, *Bond Men Made Free: Medieval Peasant Movements and the English Rising of 1381* (London, 1973), 127.

62. *Parisian Journal*, 223.

63. Wright, *Knights and Peasants*, 73.

64. Gower, *Confessio Amantis*, ed. and trans. Tiller, 204–5; C. Saunders, 'A Matter of Consent: Middle English Romance and the Law of *Raptus*', *Medieval Women and the Law*, ed. N. Menuge (Woodbridge, 2000), 106, 109–10; K. Phillips, 'Written on the Body: Reading Rape from the Twelfth to Fifteenth Centuries', *ibid.*, 128, 138.

65. I. Mast, 'Rape in John Gower's *Confessio Amantis* and other Related Works', *Young Medieval Women*, ed. Lewis, Menuge and Phillips, 103–4, 108; D. Wolfthal, *Images of Rape: The 'Heroic' Tradition and its Alternatives* (Cambridge, 1999), 64–5; A. Ramsay, 'On the Link between Rape, Abduction and War in C. de Pizan's *Cité des dames*', *Contexts and Continuities: Proceedings of the Fourth International Colloquium on Christine de Pizan* (Glasgow, 2002), 693–703.

66. Sir Thomas Malory, *The Works of Sir Thomas Malory*, ed. E. Vinaver and P. J. C. Field, 3 vols (Oxford, 3rd edn, 1990), I, 120; Saunders, 'A Matter of Consent', 118–19. Rape clearly had 'class' connotations. There was greater abhorrence at the rape of noble women and greater shock when noble men were the perpetrators. See, for example, *La chronique d'Enguerran de Monstrelet*, III, 9–10 (on the capture of Soissons where noblemen joined the ordinary soldiers in indiscrimate rape); and S. Painter, *French Chivalry: Chivalric Ideals and Practices in Mediaeval France* (Ithaca, NY, 1957), 141–6.

67. *Froissart: Chronicles*, ed. and trans. Brereton, 75.

68. J. E. Gilbert, 'A Medieval Rosie the Riveter? Women in France and Southern England during the Hundred Years War', *The Hundred Years War*, I: *A Wider Focus*, ed. Kagay and Villalon, 345–6.

69. *Gesta Henrici Quinti*, 34, 54.

70. Curry, 'Soldiers' Wives', 201–3.

Chapter 9 Prisoners of War: Gilded Cages (1435)

1. E. McLeod, *Charles of Orléans: Prince and Poet* (London, 1969), 172.

2. See J. G. Dickinson, *The Congress of Arras, 1435: A Study in Medieval Diplomacy* (Oxford, 1955).

3. This despite the fact that the dauphin's coronation service had to be improvised because the royal insignia and crown were in English hands. Charles also lacked a copy of the most recent order of service and a Capetian coronation *ordo* had to be used instead. R. A. Jackson, *Vive le Roi! A History of the French Coronation from Charles V to Charles X* (Chapel Hill, NC, 1984), 34–6.

4. Griffiths, *Henry VI*, 198–9.

5. Knecht, *Valois*, 70–2; Vale, *Ancient Enemy*, 102–3; Harriss, *Shaping the Nation*, 566–7. For the proposed English response to the collapse of the Burgundian alliance and the failure of the Congress of Arras, see 'Sir John Fastolf's Report' (1435), in J. Stevenson, ed., *Letters and Papers Illustrative of the Wars of the English in France during the Reign of Henry the Sixth, King of England*, 3 vols (London, 1861–4), II, 575–85; M. G. A. Vale, 'Sir John Fastolf's "Report"

of 1435: A New Interpretation Reconsidered', *Nottingham Medieval Studies*, 17 (1973), 78–84.

6. *Book of Pluscardensis*, cited by Rogers, *War Cruel and Sharp*, 74.
7. C. Given-Wilson and F. Bériac-Lainé, 'Edward III's Prisoners of War: The Battle of Poitiers and its Context', *EHR*, 116 (2001), 803–4.
8. P. Contamine, 'The Growth of State Control, Practices of War, 1300–1800: Ransom and Booty', *War and Competition between States*, ed. P. Contamine (Oxford, 2000), 166. Despite the order to kill the prisoners, significant numbers were taken at Agincourt. French sources put the figure at about 1,500 knights and esquires including two dukes, three counts and a dozen or more great lords. English figures are lower. *Chronique d'Enguerran de Monstrelet*, III, 120–1; *Chronique du Religieux du Saint-Denys, contenant le règne de Charles VI, de 1380 à 1422*, ed. L.-F. Bellaguet, 6 vols (Paris, 1839–52), V, 574; *Gesta Henrici Quinti*, 95–6; Curry, *Agincourt: A New History*, 276–9; R. Ambühl, 'Le sort des prisonniers d'Azincourt (1415)', *Revue du Nord*, 89 (2007), 755–88; R. Ambühl, 'A Fair Share of the Profits? The Ransoms of Agincourt', *Nottingham Medieval Studies*, 50 (2006), 129–50.
9. P. C. Timbal, *La Guerre de Cent Ans vue à travers les registres du parlement (1337–1369)* (Paris, 1961), 305–74.
10. The first general ordinances of war (sometimes called Ordinances of Durham), which stated that a third of spoils were to be paid to one's captain/commander, who in turn paid a third to the Crown, were issued for the 1385 Scottish campaign: BL Stowe 140, ff. 148–51. Prior to 1385 there is evidence of some differences to this practice. Edward III and the Black Prince, for example, demanded a half of the profits from prisoners in some of their indentures and contracts: *BPR*, I, 128–9; III, 251–2, 294–5. For further discussion, see D. Hay, 'The Division of the Spoils of War', *TRHS*, 5th ser. 4 (1954), 91–109. For the distribution of booty in Henry V's reign, see TNA E101/46/4; E101/48/2; 53/7; *The Essential Portions of Nicholas Upton's De Studio Militari, before 1446*, ed. F. P. Barnard (Oxford, 1931), 45–6.
11. R. Ambühl, 'Prisoners of War in the Hundred Years War: The Golden Age of Private Ransoms', unpub. PhD thesis (University of St Andrews, 2009), 30.
12. Walsingham, *Chronica Maiora*, ed. Preest, 69–71.
13. E. Perroy, 'Gras profits et rançons pendant la Guerre de Cent Ans: l'affaire du comte de Denia', *Mélanges d'histoire du Moyen Âge dédiés à la mémoire de Louis Halphen*, ed. F. Lot, M. Roques and C. Brunel (Paris, 1951), 573–80; A. Rogers, 'Hoton versus Shakell', *Nottingham Medieval Studies*, 6 (1962), 74–108; 7 (1963), 53–78.
14. Le Bel, *Chronique*, II, 222. See also Prestwich, 'Why did Englishmen Fight in the Hundred Years War?', 63–4.
15. According to Jonathan Sumption, even before one takes into account the value of Jean II and his son, the ransoms of those captured at Poitiers totalled not less than £300,000, which was almost three times the cost of the English war effort over the past year: *Trial by Fire*, 248; Perroy, 'Les profits et rançons pendant la Guerre de Cent Ans', *Mélanges d'histoire du Moyen Âge*, 574. He calculated that between 1360 and 1370 Edward III received £268,000 from three major ransoms. See also Hay, 'Division of the Spoils of War', 93. However, M. M. Postan argued that little of the ransom money permeated into the national economy: 'The Costs of the Hundred Years War', *Past and Present*, 27 (1964), 34–53. T. F. Tout showed that perhaps as much as a third of King John's ransom was retained in the king's chamber for subsequent use in war disbursements abroad: *Chapters in the Administrative History of Mediaeval England*, 6 vols (Manchester, 1928), III, 243–8. See further: M. Broome, 'The Ransom of John II King of France, 1360–70', *Camden Miscellany*, 14 (1926), xvii–viii.
16. Given-Wilson and Bériac-Lainé, 'Battle of Poitiers', 802–33; K. B. McFarlane, 'The Investment of Sir John Fastolf's Profits of War', *TRHS*, 5th ser. 7 (1957), 91–116.
17. Contamine, 'Ransoms and Booty', 169; Hay, 'Division of the Spoils of War', 100.
18. TNA E30/74: agreement of Charles of Blois to pay 700,000 florins for his own ransom and for that of his wife; his sons Jean and Gui were to remain as hostages while the sum was paid (9 August 1356): C. J. Rogers, 'The Anglo-French Peace Negotiations of 1354–1360 Reconsidered', *Age of Edward III*, ed. Bothwell, 193–214.
19. R. Pernoud, *Joan of Arc by Herself and her Witnesses*, trans. E. Hyams (Harmondsworth, 1964), 182.
20. Pernoud, *Joan of Arc*, 185–6; *Joan of Arc*, ed. and trans. Taylor, 175.
21. TNA SC8/261/13046; Sumption, *Divided Houses*, 182; Jones, *Ducal Brittany*, 74.

22. Randolf had commanded the first schiltron at Halidon Hill, where very few prisoners were taken, and one hundred of those who surrendered were put to death at Edward III's order the next morning: Rogers, *War Cruel and Sharp*, 72, 74.

23. *Scalacronica*, 120; *Rotuli Scotiae in Turri Londiniensi et in Domo Capitulari Westmonasteriensi asservati*, I: *Edward I–Edward III*, ed. D. Macpherson (London, 1814), 371; S. I. Boardman, 'Randolph, John, Third Earl of Moray (d.1346)', *ODNB* (online edn, 2004). See TNA E101/21/22 for John, earl of Moray's expenses in prison; he was ordered to be kept at Windsor and the constable was paid for his maintenance: *CCR, 1339–41*, 568.

24. Rogers, *War Cruel and Sharp*, 187–8. On Edward's 'provincial strategy', see J. Le Patourel, 'Edward III and the Kingdom of France', *History*, 43 (1958), repr. in Rogers, *Wars of Edward III*, 247–64, esp. 254, 258, 260–3. Ufford had served in the Low Countries and France in various diplomatic and military capacities since 1338. He was released after the truce of Esplechin (September 1340) and the payment of a heavy ransom to which Edward III contributed £500: W. M. Ormrod, 'Ufford, Robert, First Earl of Suffolk (1298–1369)', *ODNB* (online edn, 2008).

25. BN Fr.n.a. 9239 f. 269; W. M. Ormrod, 'Montagu, William, First Earl of Salisbury (1301–1344)', *ODNB* (online edn, 2004); Sumption, *Trial by Battle*, 309–12.

26. A. Curry, 'Henry VI, Parliament of 1429: Text and Translation', *PROME*, item 18: The petition was made in recognition of 'the great and notable service given by Lord Talbot both to our present sovereign lord the king and to his father the previous king, whom God absolve, in his realm of France and elsewhere; during which service he was taken prisoner by the king's adversaries of France who imposed an unreasonable and unbearable ransom on him.'

27. Pollard, *John Talbot and the War in France*, 17–18, 113–14.

28. *Lanercost Chronicle*, ed. J. Stevenson (Edinburgh, 1839), 351; A. Grant, 'Disaster at Neville's Cross: The Scottish Point of View', *Battle of Neville's Cross*, ed. Rollason and Prestwich, 33; M. C. Dixon, 'John de Coupland – Hero to Villain', *ibid.*, 36–49.

29. A. A. M. Duncan, 'Douglas, Sir William, Lord of Liddesdale (c.1310–1353)', *ODNB* (online edn, 2006).

30. After 20 years only 76,000 marks of David II's ransom had been paid: TNA E39/36; Rymer, *Foedera*, III, ii, 151–3. Another consequence of the treaty of Berwick was the establishment of a new system of law centring on 'days of march' when judicial tribunals would be held: C. J. Neville, 'Keeping the Peace on the Northern Marches in the Later Middle Ages', *EHR*, 109 (1994), 1–25; A. A. M. Duncan, '*Honi soit qui mal y pense*: David II and Edward III, 1346–52', *Scottish Historical Review*, 67 (1988), 131–41.

31. Rymer, *Foedera*, III, iv, 39–42; MacDougall, *An Antidote to the English*, 46–51.

32. S. I. Boardman, 'Stewart, Robert, First Duke of Albany (c.1340–1420)', *ODNB* (online edn, 2006): Boardman offers a rather more generous interpretation of Albany's actions and motivations.

33. J. Boffey, *Fifteenth-Century English Dream Visions: An Anthology* (Oxford, 2003), 90–157; *The Kingis Quair and Other Prison Poems*, ed. L. R. Mooney and M.-J. Arn (Kalamazoo, MI, 2005), ll. 170–3, 183–4, 191.

34. M. H. Brown, 'James I (1394–1437)', *ODNB* (online edn, 2004). For a discussion of the influence of English court culture on James II, see Stevenson, *Chivalry and Knighthood*, 2, 44–6, 70–2, 170–9.

35. Sumption, *Trial by Fire*, 245; Green, *Battle of Poitiers*, 54.

36. *Froissart: Chronicles*, ed. and trans. Brereton, 144.

37. With regard to the numbers of those made prisoner, sources vary. According to Richard Lescot, 65 barons, 1,500 nobles, townsmen and ecclesiastics were captured at Poitiers, and some 800 *famosi pugnatores* (famous warriors) were killed. Jean Le Bel noted 2,000 prisoners were taken. Knighton and other English chroniclers give a figure of between 2,000 and 2,500 prisoners. The chief sources of English information were the newsletters the Black Prince and his captains sent home. The prince's letter named 42 of the more important captives, added 1,933 further captives and noted the deaths of 19 lords and 2,426 others. The precision of the figures suggests they may have been based on a herald's list. For further discussion, see F. Beriac-Lainé and C. Given-Wilson, *Les prisonniers de la bataille de Poitiers* (Paris 2002), esp. 35–7, 75–6, 86–8, 94–9.

38. Ormrod, *Edward III*, 387–9, quotation at 387.

39. Sumption, *Trial by Fire*, 497–500.

40. *Froissart: Chronicles*, ed. and trans. Brereton, 74–5; Sumption, *Trial by Battle*, 510.
41. Froissart, *Chroniques*, ed. Diller, II, 384.
42. *Froissart: Chronicles*, ed. and trans. Brereton, 179.
43. Ambühl, *Prisoners of War*, 34
44. Ambühl, *Prisoners of War*, 33.
45. Contamine, 'Ransom and Booty', 172.
46. Ambühl, *Prisoners of War*, 141–5.
47. Contamine, *War in the Middle Ages*, 289.
48. *Parisian Journal*, 107; A. King, '"According to the custom used in French and Scottish wars": Prisoners and Casualties on the Scottish Marches in the Fourteenth Century', *Journal of Medieval History*, 28 (2002), 281.
49. Le Bel, *Chroniques*, II, 106; Ayton, 'Crécy Campaign', *Battle of Crécy*, ed. Ayton and Preston, 62–72; E. Porter, 'Chaucer's Knight, the Alliterative *Morte Arthure* and the Medieval Laws of War: A Reconsideration', *Nottingham Medieval Studies*, xxvii (1983), 67.
50. Murimuth, *Continuatio chronicarum*, 247; *Knighton's Chronicle*, ed. Martin, 143.
51. For restrictions regarding the capture of prisoners due to the need for military discipline, see *BPR*, IV, 338: 'to avoid some perils which might perchance have arisen, an ordinance was made by the [Black] Prince and publicly proclaimed in his host before the battle of Poitiers ... that no man should linger over his prisoner on pain of forfeiting him'.
52. Charny, *Book of Chivalry*, 99.
53. Keen, *Chivalry*, 221.
54. *Gesta Henrici Quinti*, 90–3.
55. Vernier, *Flower of Chivalry*, 116–23; quotation at 122. See also Barber, *Knight and Chivalry*, 242.
56. Froissart, *Chroniques*, ed. Luce, VIII, 239; M. G. A. Vale, 'Grailly, Jean (III) de (d.1377)', *ODNB* (online edn, 2008); A. D. Carr, 'Owen of Wales (d.1378)', *ODNB* (online edn, 2004); S. G. Smith, 'What Does a Mercenary Leave Behind? The Archaeological Evidence for the Estates of Owain Lawgoch', *Mercenaries and Paid Men*, ed. France, 317–30. During the same engagement at Soubise in 1372, Sir Thomas Percy, seneschal of Poitou (d.1403), was captured by a Welsh chaplain from Owain's company, Hywel Flint. The captal de Buch had benefited from the ransom system earlier in his career having captured the count of Ponthieu at the battle of Poitiers. He sold him to the Black Prince for 25,000 crowns: TNA E30/1632; Ambühl, 'Prisoners of War' (PhD), 63.
57. A. Bossuat, 'Les prisonniers de guerre au XVe siècle: la rançon de Guillaume, seigneur de Châteauvillain', *Annales de Bourgogne*, 23 (1951), 7–35, esp. 23; Lewis, *Recovery of France*, 418; Ambühl, *Prisoners of War*, 137.
58. See, for example, members of John of Gaunt's retinue captured in his service: TNA DL 28/3/5 f.19; *CPR, 1389–92*, 309; Simon Walker, *The Lancastrian Affinity, 1361–99* (Oxford, 1990), 73.
59. TNA SC8/289/14407.
60. TNA SC8/85/4221.
61. Allmand, *Hundred Years War*, 46; Lewis, *Later Medieval France*, 212.
62. TNA SC 8/85/4217: the money 'the gentlemen of Kent' offered the petitioner was a part of a reward given to them for the capture of Jack Cade. Frogenhale mustered a retinue for service in France on 19 August 1453 and must have been captured very soon afterwards: *CPR, 1452–61*, 124–5.
63. The battle of Bulgnéville (2 July 1431) was fought between René d'Anjou and his cousin, Antoine de Vaudémont, over the partition of the duchy of Lorraine: A. Bossuat, 'Les prisonniers de guerre au XVe siècle: la rançon de Jean, seigneur de Rodemack', *Annales de l'Est*, 5th ser. 3 (1951), 145–62.
64. Given-Wilson, 'Parliament of Jan. 1390: Text and Translation', *PROME*, item 53.
65. TNA SC8/163/8133.
66. Charny, *Book of Chivalry*, 133.
67. *Chronique des quatre premiers Valois*, ed. Luce, 235.
68. *St Albans Chronicle*, I, 659; R. I. Jack, 'Hastings, John, Thirteenth Earl of Pembroke (1347–1375)', *ODNB* (online edn, 2008).
69. Ambühl, 'Prisoners of War' (PhD), 70.
70. Keen, *Laws of Law*, 181; Ambühl, *Prisoners of War*, 25.

71. AN, K 57, no. 28; 59, nos 3–4; BL Add. Ch. 1399; G. Dupont-Ferrier, 'La captivité de Jean d'Orléans, comte d'Angoulême (1412–45)', *Revue Historique*, 62 (1896), 42–74.
72. Ambühl, 'Prisoners of War' (PhD), 50–1, 54–5; Ambühl, *Prisoners of War*, 87–97.
73. *Scalacronica*, xix–xx, xlvi, and n. 123.
74. Such men were far too important to be released to fight against the English once more. Only Artur of Brittany, count of Richemont, was freed before Henry V's death (1422) and thereafter he fought for a period on the English side. Boucicaut died, still a prisoner, in June 1421. In 1438, Charles d'Artois was exchanged for John Beaufort, earl of Somerset, who had been captured by the French at Baugé. See also *Gesta Henrici Quinti*, 96–7.
75. Windsor Castle was used regularly to hold valuable prisoners including the kings of France (Jean II) and Scotland (James I), as well as those whose political status was less certain such as Queen Isabella soon after Edward III claimed his majority through the Nottingham coup in 1330: *CCR, 1330–3*, 434; Bond, 'Constables of Windsor', 223–4; M. Bennett, 'Isabelle of France, Anglo-French Diplomacy and Cultural Exchange in the Late 1350s', *Age of Edward III*, ed. Bothwell, 215–25.
76. McLeod, *Charles of Orleans*, 134.
77. BL MS Harley 682 contains English versions of practically all the poems Charles wrote during his captivity.
78. After paying a ruinous ransom Alençon's wife was very reluctant to let him fight again – Joan of Arc reassured her in person in 1429 that he would be returned safely: Lewis, *Later Medieval France*, 48.
79. Charles was regularly displayed at public occasions such as during the imperial state visit of 1416, which led to the alliance concluded in Canterbury on 15 August, when he was seated next to Emperor Sigismund at a banquet with other French prisoners also in attendance: McLeod, *Charles of Orleans*, 139.
80. BN MS Fr. 12765 f. 3; *Les poésies du duc Charles d'Orléans*, ed. A. L. Champollion-Figeac (Paris, 1842), 416–19; McLeod, *Charles of Orleans*, 138, 144–5, 150–1.
81. Artur had been making arrangements for his own ransom for some time: as early as 30 April 1419 he received permission to travel to France to raise funds: TNA E30/403.
82. Curry, 'Parliament of 1423: Text and Translation', *PROME*, item 34; 'Parliament of 1425', *ibid.*, item 24; R. A. Griffiths, 'Holland, John, First Duke of Exeter (1395–1447)', *ODNB* (online edn, 2008).
83. McLeod, *Charles of Orleans*, 161–2.
84. TNA E30/452: undertaking by Charles d'Orléans, dated 16 October 1440, to pay within six months of his return to France the sum of 6,000 crowns, part of the 120,000 crowns due to Henry VI for his ransom.

Chapter 10 National Identities: St George and *La Mère France* (1449)

1. Thompson, *Contemporary Chronicles of the Hundred Years War*, 337–8.
2. E. Cosneau, *Le connétable de Richemont* (Paris, 1886), 620, cited by Vale, *Charles VII*, 117.
3. Gilles of Brittany became a member of the Order of the Garter and in December 1443 he received various gifts from England including a pension of 1,000 marks: TNA E404/48/333; 60/105; Griffiths, *Henry VI*, 207, 270 n. 110, 511–13.
4. M. Keen and M. J. Daniel, 'English Diplomacy and the Sack of Fougères in 1449', *History*, 59 (1974), 375–91; Vale, *Charles VII*, 115–19.
5. *CPR, 1452–60*, 55; J. Chartier, *Chronique de Charles VII*, ed. A. Vallet de Viriville, 3 vols (Paris, 1858), III, 7; Basin, *Histoire de Charles VII*, II, 195–6; Contamine, *Guerre, état et société*, 313–14; Pollard, *John Talbot and the War in France*, 137–8; M. G. A. Vale, 'The Last Years of English Gascony', *TRHS*, 5th ser. 19 (1969), 119–38.
6. R. Harris, *Valois Guyenne: A Study of Politics, Government and Society in Late Medieval France* (Woodbridge, 1994), 8–14, 180–7.
7. For this concept of nation-building, see B. Anderson, *Imagined Communities: Reflections on the Origin and Spread of Nationalism* (London and New York, rev. edn, 2006).
8. Chartier, *Le quadrilogue invectif*, esp. 12–19. See also *Fifteenth-Century English Translations of Alain Chartier's 'Le traité de l'esperance' and 'Le quadrilogue invectif'*, ed. M. S. Blayney, 2 vols (Oxford, 1974–80); S. Riches, *St George: Hero, Martyr and Myth* (Stroud, 2002), esp. 101–13, quotation at 21; J. Good, *The Cult of St George in Medieval England* (Woodbridge, 2009), 62–86, 95–121.

9. Fortescue, *De laudibus legum Anglie*, ed. and trans. Chrimes, 85; R. W. K. Hinton, 'English Constitutional Doctrines from the Fifteenth Century to the Seventeenth, I, English Constitutional Theories from Sir John Fortescue to Sir John Eliot', *EHR*, 75 (1960), 412; J. H. Burns, 'Fortescue and the Political Theory of Dominium', *Historical Journal*, 28 (1985), 777–97; C. Taylor, 'Sir John Fortescue and the French Polemical Treatises of the Hundred Years War', *EHR*, 114 (1999), 115.

10. J. de Montreuil, *A toute la chevalerie de France*, cited by P. S. Lewis, 'War Propaganda and Historiography in Fifteenth-Century France and England', *TRHS*, 5th ser. 15 (1965), 2–3.

11. See for example: A. G. Rigg, 'Propaganda of the Hundred Years War: Poems on the Battles of Crécy and Durham (1346): A Critical Edition', *Traditio*, 54 (1999), 177; J. Doig, 'Political Propaganda and Royal Proclamations in Late Medieval England', *Historical Research*, 71 (1998), 253–80; A. K. McHardy, 'Some Reflections on Edward III's Use of Propaganda', *Age of Edward III*, ed. Bothwell, 171–89; R. A. Griffiths, 'The Island of England in the Fifteenth Century: Perceptions of the Peoples of the British Isles', *Journal of Medieval History*, 29 (2003), 177–200; Beaune, *Birth of an Ideology*, 20–69, 152–71; J. Bengtson, 'Saint George and the Formation of English Nationalism', *Journal of Medieval and Early Modern Studies*, 27 (1997), 317–40; G. Pépin, 'Les cris de guerre "Guyenne!" et "Saint Georges!", l'expression d'une identité politique du duché d'Aquitaine anglo-gascon', *Moyen Âge*, 112 (2006), 263–82; Curry, 'War, Peace and National Identity', 146; P. Barber, 'The Evesham World Map: A Late Medieval English View of God and the World', *Imago Mundi*, 47 (1995), 13–33; N. Pons, ed., *L'honneur de la couronne de France: quatre libelles contre les Anglais vers 1418–vers 1429* (Paris, 1990); C. Serchuk, '*Cest figure contient tout le royaume de France*: Cartography and National Identity at the End of the Hundred Years War', *Journal of Medieval History*, 33 (2007), 320–38.

12. *Incerti Scriptores Chronicon Angliae de Regnis Henrici IV, Henrici V et Henrici VI*, ed. J. A. Giles (London, 1848), 34–5. See further J. Watts, 'The Pressure of the Public on Later Medieval Politics', *Political Culture in Late Medieval Britain*, ed. L. Clarke and C. Carpenter (Woodbridge, 2004), 159–80, esp. 159–62.

13. Beaune, *Birth of an Ideology*, 17–19, 310–13; Krynen, *L'empire du roi*, 296–338; G. Spiegel, *Romancing the Past: The Rise of Vernacular Prose Historiography in Thirteenth-Century France* (Berkeley, CA, 1993); G. Spiegel, 'Les débuts français de l'historiographie royale', *Saint-Denis et la royauté*, ed. F. Autrand, C. Gauvard and J.-M. Moeglin (Paris, 1999), 395–404.

14. Griffiths, 'English Realm and Dominions', 85; J. Gillingham, *The English in the Twelfth Century: Imperialism, National Identity, and Political Values* (Woodbridge, 2000), 113–60; S. Foot, 'The Making of Angelcynn: English Identity before the Norman Conquest', *TRHS*, 6th ser. 6 (1996), 25–49.

15. W. M. Ormrod, ed., 'Edward III: Parliament of 1344, Text and Translation', *PROME*, item 6; S. Crane, 'Social Aspects of Bilingualism in the Thirteenth Century', *Thirteenth-Century England*, VI, ed. Prestwich, Britnell and Frame, 114 and n. 43; J. H. Fisher, 'Chancery and the Emergence of Standard Written English in the Fifteenth Century', *Speculum*, 52 (1977), 879.

16. Ormrod, ed., 'Edward III: Parliament of 1346, Text and Translation', *PROME*, item 7.

17. R. R. Davies, 'The Peoples of Britain and Ireland, 1100–1400, IV, Language and Historical Mythology', *TRHS*, 6th ser. 7 (1997), 12–14. See also R. Bartlett, *The Making of Europe: Conquest, Colonization, and Cultural Change, 950–1350* (Princeton, NJ, 1993), 198, 201; L. E. Voigts, 'What's the Word? Bilingualism in Late Medieval England', *Speculum*, 71 (1996), 813–26.

18. A. Butterfield, *The Familiar Enemy: Chaucer, Language and Nation in the Hundred Years War* (Oxford, 2009), 11–35; J. Wogan-Browne, 'What's in a Name: The "French of England"', *Language and Culture in Medieval Britain: The French of England, c.1100–c.1500*, ed. J. Wogan-Browne et al. (York, 2009), 1–13.

19. T. Turville-Petre, *England the Nation: Language, Literature and National Identity, 1290–1340* (Oxford, 1996), 10. See also N. Watson, 'The Politics of Middle English Writing', *The Idea of the Vernacular: An Anthology of Middle English Literary Theory, 1280–1520*, ed. J. Wogan-Browne, N. Watson, A. Taylor and R. Evans (Exeter, 1999), 334–5; M. G. A Vale, 'Language, Politics and Society: The Uses of the Vernacular in the Later Middle Ages', *EHR*, 120 (2005), 15, 18.

20. W. M. Ormrod, 'The Use of English: Language, Law and Political Culture in Fourteenth-Century England', *Speculum*, 78 (2003), 750–87, esp. 780 and n. 119. See also J. Catto,

'Written English: The Making of the Language 1370–1400', *Past and Present*, 179 (2003), 38, 44–7, 56; J. H. Fisher, 'A Language Policy for Lancastrian England', *Publications of the Modern Language Association of America*, 107 (1992), 1,168–80.

21. Given-Wilson, *Chronicles*, 142–3.
22. *The Council of Constance*, ed. J. H. Mundy and K. M. Woody, trans. L. R. Loomis (New York, 1961), 344.
23. J.-P. Genet, 'English Nationalism: Thomas Polton at the Council of Constance', *Nottingham Medieval Studies*, 28 (1984), 74; B. Guenée, 'État et nation en France au Moyen Âge', *Revue Historique*, 237 (1967), 17–30.
24. E. Gellner, *Culture, Identity and Politics* (Cambridge, 1987), 18; *idem*, *Nations and Nationalism* (Oxford, 1983), 57. R. R. Davies argued strongly that the nations of the medieval period should be discussed as nations: 'Nations and National Identities in the Medieval World: An Apologia', *Revue belge d'histoire contemporaine*, 34 (2004), 567–79. Anthony Smith has suggested an alternative term, *ethnies*, to describe and categorise medieval 'nations': *The Ethnic Origins of Nations* (Oxford, 1986), esp. 6–18.
25. Le Patourel, 'Edward III and the Kingdom of France', 247–64, esp. 254, 258, 260–3; M. Keen, 'Diplomacy', *Henry V: The Practice of Kingship*, ed. G. L. Harriss (Oxford and New York, 1985), 186–9; Allmand, *Henry V*, 48–9.
26. Henneman, *Royal Taxation, 1322–1356*, esp. 304–29.
27. P. Contamine, 'The Norman "Nation" and the French "Nation" in the Fourteenth and Fifteenth Centuries', *England and Normandy*, ed. Bates and Curry, 216–17, 222; Curry, 'Lancastrian Normandy: The Jewel in the Crown?', *ibid.*, 235–52; Allmand, *Lancastrian Normandy*, 211–40; M. C. E. Jones, '"Bons Bretons et Bons Francoys": The Language and Meaning of Treason in Later Medieval France', *TRHS*, 5th ser. 32 (1982), 91, 97, 101–2; M. P. Holt, 'Burgundians into Frenchmen: Catholic Identity in Sixteenth-Century Burgundy', *Changing Identities in Early Modern France*, ed. M. Wolfe (London, 1997), 345–9; Harris, *Valois Guyenne*, esp. 8–20, 173–90; Labarge, *Gascony*, 117–216; M. G. A. Vale, *English Gascony, 1399–1453: A Study of War, Government and Politics during the Later Stages of the Hundred Years War* (Oxford, 1970), 154–215.
28. *Isidori Hispalensis Episcopi Etymologiarum Sive Originum Libri XX* (Oxford, 1911), XIV, iv, 25; Contamine, *Guerre, état et société*, 277–312.
29. P. S. Lewis, 'France and England: The Growth of the Nation State', *Essays in Later Medieval French History* (London, 1985), 236.
30. G. E. Aylmer, 'The Peculiarities of the English State', *Journal of Historical Sociology*, 3 (1990), 93–4.
31. England in the poem 'The Battle of Bannockburn', dated to the reign of Edward III, was referred to as the matron of many regions (*Regionum Anglia plurium matrona*): Wright, *Political Songs*, I, 262; B. Smith, 'Lordship in the British Isles, *c*.1320–*c*.1360: The Ebb-Tide of the English Empire?', *Power and Identity in the Middle Ages: Essays in Memory of Rees Davies*, ed. H. Pryce and J. Watts (Oxford, 2008), 153–63.
32. R. W. Kaeuper, *War, Justice and Public Order: England and France in the Late Middle Ages* (Oxford, 1988), 22–3, 381–4.
33. Wright, *Political Songs*, I, 273–4.
34. *Acts of the Parliaments of Scotland*, ed. T. Thompson and C. Innes (Edinburgh, 1814–75), I, 474–5; G. W. S. Barrow, ed., *The Declaration of Arbroath: History, Significance, Setting* (Edinburgh, 2003).
35. R. R. Davies has suggested that by the time of the Hundred Years War the tide of Anglicisation had ebbed in the British Isles: *The First English Empire: Power and Identities in the British Isles, 1093–1343* (Oxford, 2000), 172–90. See also A. Ruddick, 'Ethnic Identity and Political Language in the King of England's Dominions: A Fourteenth-Century Perspective', *Identity and Insurgency in the Late Middle Ages*, ed. L. Clarke (Woodbridge, 2006), 17.
36. Frame, 'Overlordship and Reaction', 183.
37. Froissart, *Oeuvres*, ed. Lettenhove, XVIII, 108.
38. Allmand, *Henry V*, 148; Chaplais, *English Medieval Diplomatic Practice*, II, 629–36, esp. clauses 7–11.
39. 'Nothing brought the recognition of a common Englishness nearer home ... than that of being subjects of a single king': R. R. Davies, 'The Peoples of Britain and Ireland,

1100–1400, II, Names and Regnal Solidarities', *TRHS*, 6th ser. 5 (1995), 13; Griffiths, 'English Realm and Dominions', 89, 92–5.

40. Given-Wilson, *Chronicles*, 157; M. A. Norbye, 'A Popular Example of "National Literature" in the Hundred Years War: *A tous nobles qui aiment beaux faits et bonnes histoires*', *Nottingham Medieval Studies*, 51 (2007), 121, 132, 138; *idem*, 'Genealogies and Domestic Awareness in the Hundred Years War: The Evidence of *A tous nobles qui aiment beaux faits et bonnes histoires*', *Journal of Medieval History*, 33 (2007), 307; Curry, 'War, Peace and National Identity', 148.

41. Lewis, 'France in the Fifteenth Century: Society and Sovereignty', *Europe in the Late Middle Ages*, ed. J. Hale, R. Highfield, and B. Smalley (London, 1965), 4–6.

42. Griffiths, *Henry VI*, 533; Lewis, 'France and England: The Growth of the Nation State', 236. On Charlemagne as a royal ancestor and, briefly, as a royal saint, see Beaune, *Birth of an Ideology*, 14, 43, 90–1.

43. T. G. Ashplant, G. Dawson and M. Roper, 'Introduction', *The Politics of War Memory and Commemoration*, ed. T. G. Ashplant, G. Dawson and M. Roper (London, 2000), 7.

44. Beaune, *Birth of an Ideology*, 308.

45. Bonet, *Tree of Battles*, ch. 7.

46. Charny, *Book of Chivalry*, 165.

47. Walsingham, *Chronica Maiora*, ed. and trans. Preest, 210.

48. N. Housley, '*Pro deo et patria mori*: Sanctified Patriotism in Europe 1400–1600', *War and Competition between States*, ed. Contamine, 221–8, esp. 221–2. See also N. Housley, 'France, England, and the "National Crusade", 1302–1386', *France and the British Isles*, ed. Jondorf and Dumville, 183–98; Tyerman, 'Philip VI and the Recovery of the Holy Land', 52; Guard, *Chivalry, Kingship and Crusade*, 194–206.

49. Harvey, 'Ecclesia Anglicana, cui ecclesiastes noster christus vos prefecit: The Power of the Crown in the English Church during the Great Schism', *Religion and National Identity*, ed. Mews, 230; Curry, 'War, Peace and National Identity', 145.

50. Caldwell, 'Hundred Years War and National Identity', 238–41.

51. This was circulated widely and copied into numerous chronicles: *Joan of Arc*, ed. and trans. Taylor, 74–6; Fraoli, *Joan of Arc*, 58, 71, 74, 119.

52. *Parisian Journal*, 191, 240, 337.

53. Beaune, *Birth of an Ideology*, 305; Serchuk, 'Cartography and National Identity', 330.

54. This included the principle of naturalisation: for examples of letters of denizenship in England, see *CPR, 1385–9*, 518; *1388–92*, 361.

55. *Wykeham's Register*, cited by McHardy, 'Edward III's use of Patronage', 184.

56. Rigg, 'Propaganda of the Hundred Years War', 174–5; P. S. Lewis, 'Two Pieces of Fifteenth-Century Political Iconography', *Journal of the Warburg and Courtauld Institutes*, 27 (1964), 319–20; H. S. Offler, 'Thomas Bradwardine's "Victory Sermon" in 1346', *Church and Crown in the Fourteenth Century: Studies in European History and Political Thought*, ed. A. I. Doyle (Aldershot, 2000), 6, 11–12, 16; E. Gellner, *Nationalism* (New York, 1997), 29, 69.

57. Froissart, *Chroniques*, ed. Lettenhove, VII, 341.

58. E. Renan, 'Qu'est-ce qu'une nation?', *Discours et Conferences* (Paris, 1887), 277–310, cited by A. D. Smith, 'The Ernest Gellner Memorial Lecture. Memory and Modernity: Reflections on Ernest Gellner's Theory of Nationalism': http://members.tripod.com/GellnerPage/SmithLec.html; Bossuat, 'The Re-Establishment of Peace', 60–1; Lewis, 'War Propaganda and Historiography in Fifteenth-Century France and England', 21. See also C. Taylor, *Debating the Hundred Years War: Pour ce que plusieurs (La loi salicque) and A declaracion of the trew and dewe title of Henrie VIII* (London, 2007), esp. 8, 29.

Conclusion: 1453 and Beyond

1. Vale, *Ancient Enemy*, 106–7; Lewis, *Later Medieval France: The Polity*, 377.

2. M. M. du Jourdin, *La Guerre de Cent Ans vue par ceux qui l'ont vécue* (Paris, 1992), 153.

3. Allmand, *Society at War*, 189.

4. Small, *Late Medieval France*, 168–70.

5. Ambühl, 'Prisoners of War' (PhD), 188–90; Ambühl, *Prisoners of War*, 262–3.

6. Allmand, *Society at War*, 187–8.

7. Allmand, *Society at War*, 190; Jourdin, *La Guerre de Cent Ans,* 154; Beaune, *Birth of an Ideology,* 283–309.

8. Lewis, *Later Medieval France: The Polity,* 376.

9. D. Potter, 'Conclusion', *France in the Later Middle Ages,* ed. Potter, 210.

10. Ormrod, 'Voicing Complaint and Remedy to the English Crown', 152.

11. Lewis, *Later Medieval France: The Polity,* 377; Harris, *Valois Guyenne,* 8–19.

Bibliography

Manuscript Sources

Archives Nationales de France (Paris)

JJ	Trésor des Chartes (Régistres)
K	Monuments Historiques

Bibliothèque Nationale

Ms Fr.	Manuscrits français

British Library

Cotton Caligula D III	Diplomatic documents
Cotton MS, Nero D VI	Documents relating to the Anglo-French and Anglo-Scottish wars
Cotton MS, Vitellius C XI	Collections relating to royal marriages
MS Harley 682	Poems of Charles d'Orléans
Stowe 140, ff. 50v–56	Treaty of Brétigny (1360)

The National Archives (London)

C 1	Chancery, Early Proceedings
C 64	Chancery, Norman Rolls
DL	Duchy of Lancaster
E 30	Treasury of Receipt, Diplomatic Documents
E 39	Exchequer, Scottish Documents
E 101	Exchequer, King's Remembrancer, Various Accounts
E 403	Exchequer of Receipt, Issue Rolls
E 404	Exchequer of Receipt, Warrants for Issues
SC 7	Special Collections, Papal Bulls
SC 8	Special Collections, Ancient Petitions

Online Sources

The Gascon Rolls Project, 1317–1468: www.gasconrolls.org/index.html/
The Medieval Soldier: www.medievalsoldier.org/
The Online Froissart: www.hrionline.ac.uk/onlinefroissart/
The Oxford Dictionary of National Biography: www.oxforddnb.com/

Printed Primary Sources

Anglo-Norman Political Songs, ed. I. Aspin (Oxford, 1953).
Anonimalle Chronicle, 1333–1381, ed. V. H. Galbraith (Manchester, 1927).
Baker, G. le, *Chronicon Galfridi le Baker de Swynebroke*, ed. E. M. Thompson (Oxford, 1889).
Basin, T., *Histoire de Charles VII*, ed. C. Samaran, 2 vols (Paris, 1933).
Bel, J. le, *Chronique*, ed. J. Viard and E. Déprez, 2 vols (Paris, 1904).
Bel, J. le, *The True Chronicles of Jean le Bel, 1290–1360*, trans. N. Byrant (Woodbridge, 2011).
The Black Book of the Admiralty, ed. T. Twiss, 4 vols (London, 1871).
Bonet, H., *The Tree of Battles of Honoré Bonet*, trans. G. W. Coopland (Liverpool, 1949).
Broome, M., 'The Ransom of John II King of France, 1360–70', *Camden Miscellany*, 14 (1926).
Bueil, J. de, *Le Jouvencel*, ed. C. Favre and L. Lecestre, 2 vols (Paris, 1887, repr. Geneva, 1996).
Calendar of Close Rolls.
Calendar of Patent Rolls.
Capgrave, J., *The Book of the Illustrious Henries*, trans. F. C. Hingeston (London, 1858).
Capgrave, J., *The Chronicle of England*, ed. F. C. Hingeston (London, 1858).
Chandos Herald, *Life of the Black Prince*, ed. and trans. M. K. Pope and E. C. Lodge (Oxford, 1910).
Chaplais, P., 'Some Documents Regarding the Fulfilment and Interpretation of the Treaty of Brétigny', *Camden Society*, 3rd ser. xix (1952).
Charny, G. de, *The Book of Chivalry*, ed. and trans. R. W. Kaeuper and E. Kennedy (Philadelphia, PA, 1996).
Chartier, A., *Le quadrilogue invectif*, ed. E. Droz (Paris, rev. edn, 1950).
Chartier, A., *Fifteenth-Century English Translation of Alain Chartier's 'Le traité de l'esperance' and 'Le quadrilogue invectif'*, ed. M. S. Blayney (London, 1974).
Chartier, J., *Chronique de Charles VII*, ed. A. Vallet de Viriville, 3 vols (Paris, 1858).
Chronique des quatre premiers Valois (1327–1393), ed. S. Luce (Paris, 1862).
Chronique des règnes de Jean II et de Charles V, ed. R. Delachenal, 3 vols (Paris, 1910–14).
Chronique du Mont-St-Michel (1343–1468), ed. S. Luce, 2 vols (Paris, 1879).
'Complainte sur la bataille de Poitiers', ed. Ch. de Beaurepaire, *BEC*, 12 (1851), 257–63.
Contemporary Chronicles of the Hundred Years War from the Works of Jean le Bel, Jean Froissart and Enguerrand de Monstrelet, ed. and trans. P. E. Thompson (London, 1966).
The Coronation Book of Charles V of France: Cottonian MS Tiberius B. VIII, ed. E. S. Dewick (London, 1889).
Cuvelier, G. de, *La chanson de Bertrand du Guesclin de Cuvelier*, ed. J.-C. Faucon, 3 vols (Toulouse, 1990–91).
Debating the Hundred Years War: Pour ce que plusieurs (La loi salicque) & A declaracion of the trew and dewe title of Henrie VIII, ed. C. Taylor (London, 2007).
English Historical Documents, vol. III, *1189–1327*, ed. H. Rothwell (London, 1975).
English Historical Documents, vol. IV, *1327–1485*, ed. A. R. Myers (London, 1969).
Fifteenth-Century English Dream Visions: An Anthology, ed. J. Boffey (Oxford, 2003).
Fortescue, Sir J., *De laudibus legum Anglie*, ed. and trans. S. B. Chrimes (Cambridge, 1942).
Fortescue, Sir J., *The Governance of England*, ed. C. Plummer (Oxford, 1885).
Fribois, N. de, *Abrégé des Croniques de France*, ed. K. Daly (Paris, 2006).
Froissart, J., *Chroniques*, ed. S. Luce, G. Raynaud and L. Mirot, 15 vols (Paris, 1869–1975).
Froissart, J., *Chroniques. Le manuscrit d'Amiens*, ed. G. T. Diller, 5 vols (Geneva, 1991–9).
Froissart, J., *Oeuvres*, ed. Kervyn de Lettenhove, 28 vols (Brussels, 1867–77).
Froissart: Chronicles, ed. and trans. G. Brereton (Harmondsworth, 1978).
Gerson, J., *Oeuvres complètes*, ed. P. Glorieux, 10 vols (Paris, 1960–73).
Gesta Henrici Quinti. The Deeds of Henry the Fifth, ed. and trans. F. Taylor and J. S. Roskell (Oxford, 1975).
The Goodman of Paris: A Treatise on Moral and Domestic Economy by a Citizen of Paris c.1393, trans. E. Power (Woodbridge, new edn, 2006).
Gower, J., *The Complete Works of John Gower*, ed. G. C. Macaulay, 4 vols (Oxford, 1899–1902).
Gower, J., *The Major Latin Works of John Gower*, ed. E. W. Stockton (Seattle, WA, 1962).
Gray, Sir T., *Scalacronica, 1272–1363*, ed. and trans. A. King (Woodbridge, 2005).
Histoire générale de Languedoc avec des notes et les pièces justificatives, ed. C. de Vic and J. Vaisètte, rev. edn A. Molinier, 16 vols (Toulouse, 1872–1904).

The Historical Collections of a Citizen of London in the Fifteenth Century, ed. J. Gairdner (London, 1876).

Hoccleve, T., *The Regiment of Princes*, ed. C. R. Blyth (Kalamazoo, MI, 1999).

Incerti Scriptores Chronicon Angliae de Regnis Henrici IV, Henrici V et Henrici VI, ed. J. A. Giles (London, 1848).

Isidori Hispalensis Episcopi Etymologiarum Sive Originum Libri XX (Oxford, 1911).

Joan of Arc: La Pucelle, ed. and trans. C. Taylor (Manchester, 2006).

Juvénal des Ursins, J., *Les écrits politiques*, ed. P. S. Lewis and A.-M. Hayez, 3 vols (Paris, 1978–92).

The Kingis Quair and Other Prison Poems, ed. L. R. Mooney and M.-J. Arn (Kalamazoo, MI, 2005).

Knighton, H., *Knighton's Chronicle 1337–1396*, ed. G. Martin (Oxford, 1995).

Landry, G. de la Tour, *The Book of the Knight of La Tour-Landry*, ed. T. Wright (London, 1906).

Langland, W., *The Vision of William Concerning Piers the Plowman: In Three Parallel Texts*, ed. W. W. Skeat, 2 vols (Oxford 1886; repr. 1965).

Lescot, R., *The Laws of the Salian Franks*, ed. and trans. K. Fischer Drew (Philadelphia, PA, 1991).

Letters and Papers Illustrative of the Wars of the English in France during the Reign of Henry the Sixth, King of England, ed. J. Stevenson, 3 vols (London, 1861–4).

L'honneur de la couronne de France: quatre libelles contre les Anglais vers 1418–vers 1429, ed. N. Pons (Paris, 1990).

The Libelle of Englyshe Polycye: A Poem on the Use of Sea-power, 1436, ed. G. Warner (Oxford, 1926).

The Life and Campaigns of the Black Prince, ed. and trans. R. Barber (Woodbridge, 1979).

Lydgate, J., *The Minor Poems of John Lydgate*, ed. H. N. MacCracken (London, 1934).

Malory, Sir T., *The Works of Sir Thomas Malory*, ed. E. Vinaver and P. J. C. Field, 3 vols (Oxford, 3rd edn, 1990).

Mézières, P. de, *Letter to Richard II: A Plea made in 1395 for Peace between England and France* (Liverpool, 1975).

Monstrelet, E. de, *La chronique d'Enguerran de Monstrelet: en deux livres, avec pièces justificatives: 1400–1444*, ed. L. Douët-d'Arcq, 6 vols (Paris, 1857).

Murimuth, A., *Continuatio Chronicarum*, ed. E. M. Thompson (London, 1889).

Nesson, P. de, *Pierre de Nesson et ses œuvres*, ed. A. Piaget and E. Droz (Paris, 1925).

Ordonnances des rois de France de la troisième race, ed. D. F. Secours et al., 23 vols (Paris, 1723–1849).

Orléans, Charles d', *Les poésies du duc Charles d'Orléans*, ed. A. L. Champollion-Figeac (Paris, 1842).

A Parisian Journal, 1404–49, ed. and trans. J. Shirley (Oxford, 1968).

The Parliament Rolls of Medieval England (cd-rom), ed. C. Given-Wilson et al. (Woodbridge, 2005).

Paston Letters, ed. J. Gairdner (London, 1872).

Le pastoralet, ed. J. Blanchard (Paris, 1983).

Pernoud, R., *Joan of Arc by Herself and her Witnesses*, trans. E. Hyams (Harmondsworth, 1964).

Petrarca, F., *Le familiari*, ed. V. Rossi, 4 vols (Florence, 1933–42).

Pizan, C. de, *Le livre des fais et bonnes meurs du sage roy Charles V*, ed. S. Solente, 2 vols (Paris, 1936–40).

Pizan, C. de, *Le ditié de Jehanne d'Arc*, ed. A. J. Kennedy and K. Varty (Oxford, 1977).

Pizan, C. de, *The Epistle of the Prison of Human Life; with An Epistle to the Queen of France; and Lament on the Evils of the Civil War*, ed. and trans. J. A. Wisman (New York, 1984).

Pizan, C. de, *The Treasure of the City of Ladies*, trans. S. Lawson (Harmondsworth, 1985).

Pizan, C. de, *The Book of the Body Politic*, ed. and trans. K. L. Forhan (Cambridge, 1994).

Pizan, C. de, *The Book of the City of Ladies*, trans. R. Brown-Grant (Harmondsworth, 1999).

Pizan, C. de, *The Book of Deeds of Arms and of Chivalry*, trans. S. Willard, ed. C. C. Willard (Pennsylvania, PA, 1999).

Pizan, C. de, *The Book of Peace*, ed. K. Green, Con. Mews and J. Pinder (Pennsylvania, PA, 2008).

Political Poems and Songs Relating to English History Composed during the Period from the Accession of Edward III to that of Richard III, ed. T. Wright, 2 vols (London, 1859–61).

Quicherat, J., ed., *Procès de condemnation et de rehabilitation de Jeanne d'Arc dite La Pucelle*, 5 vols (Paris, 1841–9).

Reading, J. of, *Chronica Johannis de Reading et anonymi Cantuariensis, 1346–1367*, ed. J. Tait (Manchester, 1914).

Recueil des Actes de Philippe Augustus, ed. H.-F. Delaborde, 4 vols (Paris, 1916–79).

The Register of Edward the Black Prince Preserved in the Public Record Office, ed. M. C. B. Dawes, 4 vols (London, 1930–3).

The Reign of Richard II: From Minority to Tyranny, 1377–97, ed. A. K. McHardy (Manchester, 2012).

Rotuli Scotiae in Turri Londiniensi et in Domo Capitulari Westmonasteriensi asservati, vol. I, *Edward I–Edward III*, ed. D. Macpherson (London, 1814).

Rotulorum Patentium et Clausorum Cancellarie Hibernie Calendarium, ed. E. Tresham, (Dublin, 1828).

Rymer, T., *Feodera, conventions, litterae etc*, rev. ed. A. Clarke, F. Holbrooke and J. Coley, 4 vols in 7 parts (London, 1816–69).

Salisbury, John of, *Policraticus*, ed. and trans. Cary Nederman (Cambridge, 1990).

Sir Gawain and the Green Knight, trans. B. Stone (Harmondsworth, 2nd edn, 1974).

Statutes and Ordinances, and Acts of the Parliament of Ireland: King John to Henry V, ed. H. F. Berry (Dublin, 1907).

Statutes of the Realm, ed. A. Luders et al., 11 vols (London, 1810–28).

The Statutes of Wales, ed. I. Bowen (London, 1908).

Stevenson, J., 'Sir John Fastolf's Report' (1435), in *Letters and Papers Illustrative of the Wars of the English in France during the Reign of Henry the Sixth, King of England*, ed. J. Stevenson, 3 vols (London, 1861–4), vol. II, 575–85.

Usk, A., *The Chronicle of Adam Usk, 1377–1421*, ed. and trans. C. Given-Wilson (Oxford, 1997).

Venette, J. de, *The Chronicle of Jean de Venette*, ed. and trans. J. Birdsall and R. A. Newhall (New York, 1953).

Wales, Gerald of, *The Journey through Wales*, ed. and trans. L. Thorpe (London, 1978).

Walsingham, T., *Gesta abbatum monasterii Sancti Albani, a Thoma Walsingham*, ed. H. T. Riley, 3 vols (London, 1867–9).

Walsingham, T., *St Albans Chronicle 1406–1420*, ed. V. H. Galbraith (Oxford, 1937).

Walsingham, T., *The Chronica Maiora of Thomas Walsingham (1376–1422)*, ed. and trans. D. Preest and J. G. Clarke (Woodbridge, 2005).

Walsingham, T., *The St Albans Chronicle: The Chronica Maiora of Thomas Walsingham*, vol. I, *1376–1394*; vol. II, *1394–1422*, ed. and trans. J. Taylor, W. R. Childs and L. Watkiss (Oxford, 2003–10).

Westminster Chronicle, 1381–1394, ed. and trans. L. C. Hector and B. F. Harvey (Oxford, 1982).

Wheathamstead, J., *Registrum Abbatiae Johannis Wheathamstede*, ed. H. T. Riley (London, 1872).

Wynnere and Wastoure, ed. S. Trigg (London, 1990).

Printed Secondary Sources

Adams, T., *The Life and Afterlife of Isabeau of Bavaria* (Baltimore, MD, 2010).

Ainsworth, P., 'Froissardian Perspectives on Late Fourteenth-Century Society', *Orders and Hierarchies in Late Medieval and Renaissance Europe*, ed. J. Denton (Toronto, 1999), 56–73.

Aiton, D. J., ' "Shame on him who allows them to live": The Jacquerie of 1358', unpub. PhD thesis (University of Glasgow, 2007).

Allmand, C. T., 'The Lancastrian Land Settlement in Normandy, 1417–50', *Economic History Review*, 2nd ser. 21 (1968), 461–79.

Allmand, C. T., 'La Normandie devant l'opinion anglaise à la fin de la Guerre de Cent Ans', *BEC*, 128 (1970), 345–68.

Allmand, C. T., *Lancastrian Normandy, 1415–1450: The History of a Medieval Occupation* (Oxford, 1983).

Allmand, C. T., *Henry V* (New Haven, CT, and London, 1992).

Allmand, C. T., 'The English and the Church in Lancastrian Normandy', *England and Normandy in the Middle Ages*, ed. D. Bates and A. Curry (London, 1994), 287–97.

Allmand, C. T., 'War and the Non-Combatant in the Middle Ages', *Medieval Warfare: A History*, ed. M. Keen (Oxford, 1999), 253–72.

Allmand, C. T., *The De Re Militari of Vegetius: The Reception, Transmission and Legacy of a Roman Text in the Middle Ages* (Cambridge, 2011).

Allmand, C. T., ed., *Society at War: The Experiences of England and France during the Hundred Years War* (London, 1973).

Almond, R., and Pollard, A. J., 'The Yeomanry of Robin Hood and Social Terminology in Fifteenth-Century England', *Past and Present*, 170 (2001), 52–77.

Ambühl, R., 'A Fair Share of the Profits? The Ransoms of Agincourt', *Nottingham Medieval Studies*, 50 (2006), 129–50.

Ambühl, R., 'Le sort des prisonniers d'Azincourt (1415)', *Revue du Nord*, 89 (2007), 755–88.

Ambühl, R., 'Prisoners of War in the Hundred Years War: The Golden Age of Private Ransoms', unpub. PhD thesis (University of St Andrews, 2009).

Ambühl, R., *Prisoners of War in the Hundred Years War: Ransom Culture in the Late Middle Ages* (Cambridge, 2013).

Anderson, B., *Imagined Communities: Reflections on the Origin and Spread of Nationalism* (London and New York, rev. edn, 2006).

Asch, R. G., 'War and State Building', *European Warfare, 1350–1750*, ed. F. Tallett and D. J. B. Trim (Cambridge, 2010), 322–37.

Ashplant, T. G., Dawson, G., and Roper, M., eds, *The Politics of War Memory and Commemoration* (London, 2000).

Astesano, A., 'Éloge descriptif de la ville de Paris et des principales villes de France en 1451', ed. A. Le Roux de Lincy et L.-M. Tisserand, *Paris et ses historiens aux XIVe–XVe siècles* (Paris, 1867).

Atiya, A. S., 'The Fourteenth Century', *A History of the Crusades*, vol. III, *The Fourteenth and Fifteenth Centuries*, ed. K. M. Setton and H. W. Hazard (Madison, WI, 1975), 3–26.

Autrand, F., 'La déconfiture: La bataille de Poitiers (1356) à travers quelques textes français des XIVe et XVe siècles', *Guerre et société en France, en Angleterre et en Bourgogne, XIVe–XVe siècle*, ed. P. Contamine, C. Giry-Deloison and M. Keen (Villeneuve d'Ascq, 1991), 93–121.

Autrand, F., *Charles V, Le sage* (Paris, 1994).

Autrand, F., 'The Peacemakers and the State: Pontifical Diplomacy and the Anglo-French Conflict in the Fourteenth Century', *War and Competition between States*, ed. P. Contamine (Oxford, 2000), 249–77.

Aylmer, G. E., 'The Peculiarities of the English State', *Journal of Historical Sociology*, 3 (1990), 91–108.

Ayton, A., 'Military Service and the Development of the Robin Hood Legend in the Fourteenth Century', *Nottingham Medieval Studies*, 36 (1992), 126–47.

Ayton, A., 'English Armies in the Fourteenth Century', *Arms, Armies and Fortifications in the Hundred Years War*, ed. A. Curry and M. Hughes (Woodbridge, 1994), 21–38.

Ayton, A., and Preston, P., eds, *The Battle of Crécy, 1346* (Woodbridge, 2005).

Ayton, A., and Price, J. L., eds, *The Medieval Military Revolution: State, Society and Military Change in Medieval and Early Modern Europe* (London, 1995).

Bachrach, D. S., 'The Organisation of Military Religion in the Armies of King Edward I of England (1272–1307)', *Journal of Medieval History*, 29 (2003), 265–86.

Barber, P., 'The Evesham World Map: A Late Medieval English View of God and the World', *Imago Mundi*, 47 (1995), 13–33.

Barber, R., *Edward, Prince of Wales and Aquitaine: A Biography of the Black Prince* (Woodbridge, 1978).

Barber, R., *The Knight and Chivalry* (Woodbridge, rev. edn, 1995).

Barber, R., 'The Military Role of the Order of the Garter', *Journal of Medieval Military History*, vol. VII, *The Age of the Hundred Years War*, ed. C. J. Rogers, K. DeVries and J. France (Woodbridge, 2009), 1–11.

Barbey, J., *La fonction royale. Essence et légitimité d'après les Tractatus de Jean de Terrevermeille* (Paris, 1983).

Bardsley, S., 'Women's Work Reconsidered: Gender and Wage Differentiation in Late Medieval England', *Past and Present*, 165 (1999), 3–16.

Barker, J., *The Tournament in England, 1100–1400* (Woodbridge, 1986).

Barker, J., *Agincourt* (London, 2005).

Barker, J., *Conquest: The English Kingdom of France, 1417–1450* (London, 2009).

Barker, J., 'The Foe Within: Treason in Lancastrian Normandy', *Soldiers, Nobles and Gentlemen: Essays in Honour of Maurice Keen*, ed. P. R. Coss and C. Tyerman (Woodbridge, 2009), 305–20.

Barlow, F., 'The King's Evil', *EHR*, 95 (1980), 3–27.

Barnie, J., *War in Medieval Society: Social Values and the Hundred Years War, 1337–99* (London, 1974).

Barraclough, G., *The Medieval Papacy* (London, 1968).

Barron, C. M., 'The Deposition of Richard II', *Politics and Crisis in Fourteenth-Century England*, ed. J. Taylor and W. Childs (Gloucester, 1990), 132–49.

Barrow, G. W. S., *Robert Bruce and the Community of the Realm of Scotland* (London, 1965).

Barrow, G. W. S., ed., *The Declaration of Arbroath: History, Significance, Setting* (Edinburgh, 2003).

Bartlett, R., *The Making of Europe: Conquest, Colonization, and Cultural Change, 950–1350* (Princeton, NJ, 1993).

Bates, D., and Curry, A., eds, *England and Normandy in the Middle Ages* (London, 1994).

Beaune, C., *The Birth of an Ideology: Myths and Symbols of France in Late Medieval France*, ed. F. L. Cheyette, trans. S. R. Huston (Berkeley, CA, 1991).

Bellamy, J. G., *The Law of Treason in the Late Middle Ages* (Cambridge, 1970).

Benedictow, O. J., *The Black Death, 1346–1353: The Complete History* (Woodbridge, 2004).

Bengtson, J., 'Saint George and the Formation of English Nationalism', *Journal of Medieval and Early Modern Studies*, 27 (1997), 317–40.

Bennett, M., 'The Development of Battle Tactics in the Hundred Years War', *Arms, Armies and Fortifications in the Hundred Years War*, ed. A. Curry and M. Hughes (Woodbridge, 1994), 1–20.

Bennett, M., *Richard II and the Revolution of 1399* (Stroud, 1999).

Bennett, M., 'Isabelle of France, Anglo-French Diplomacy and Cultural Exchange in the Late 1350s', *The Age of Edward III*, ed. J. Bothwell (York, 2001), 215–25.

Bennett, M., 'The Experience of Civilian Populations during the Hundred Years War in France, 1330–1440', *British Commission for Military History Newsletter* (Spring 2009).

Bennett, N., 'Burghersh, Henry (*c.*1290–1340)', *ODNB* (online edn, 2004).

Benz St John, L., *Three Medieval Queens: Queenship and the Crown in Fourteenth-Century England* (New York, 2012).

Beriac-Lainé, F., and Given-Wilson, C., *Les prisonnniers de la bataille de Poitiers* (Paris 2002).

Bernu, P., 'Le rôle politique de Pierre de Brezé au cours des dix dernières années du règne de Charles VII (1451–1461)', *BEC*, 69 (1908), 303–47.

Bessen, D., 'The Jacquerie: Class War or Co-opted Rebellion?', *Journal of Medieval History*, 11 (1985), 43–59.

Binski, P., 'The Liber Regalis: Its Date and European Context', *The Regal Image of Richard II and the Wilton Diptych*, ed. D. Gordon and L. Monnas (London, 1997), 233–46.

Black, A., *Political Thought in Europe 1250–1450* (Cambridge, 1992).

Blanchet, A., *Les souterrains-refuges de la France: Contribution à l'histoire de l'habitation humaine* (Paris, 1923).

Bliese, J. R. E., 'When Knightly Courage May Fail: Battle Orations in Medieval Europe', *Historian*, 53 (1991), 489–504.

Bloch, M., *La société féodale* (Paris, 1939).

Bloch, M., *Feudal Society*, trans. L. A. Manyon, 2 vols (London, 2nd edn, 1971).

Bloch, M., *The Royal Touch*, trans. J. E. Anderson (New York, 1989).

Blumenfeld-Kosinski, R., and Petkov, K., eds, *Philippe de Mézières and His Age: Piety and Politics in the Fourteenth Century* (Leiden, 2011).

Blythe, J. M., 'Women in the Military: Scholastic Arguments and Medieval Images of Female Warriors', *History of Political Thought*, 22 (2001), 242–69.

Boissonnade, P., *Histoire de Poitou* (Paris, 1941).

Boitani, P., 'Petrarch and the "barbari Britanni"', *Petrarch in Britain: Interpreters, Imitators, and Translators over 700 Years*, ed. M. McLaughlin, L. Panizza and P. Hainsworth (Oxford, 2007), 9–25.

Bolton, J., 'The World Upside Down: Plague as an Agent of Economic and Social Change', *The Black Death in England*, ed. W. M. Ormrod and P. Lindley (Stamford, 1996), 17–78.

Bond, S., 'The Medieval Constables of Windsor Castle', *EHR*, 82 (1967), 225–49.

Bossuat, A., 'Les prisonniers de guerre au XVe siècle: la rançon de Guillaume, seigneur de Châteauvillain', *Annales de Bourgogne*, 23 (1951), 7–35.

Bossuat, A., 'Les prisonniers de guerre au XVe siècle: la rançon de Jean, seigneur de Rodemack', *Annales de l'Est*, 5th ser. 3 (1951), 145–62.

Bossuat, A., 'La littérature de propagande au XVe siècle: la mémoire de Jean de Rinel, secrétaire du roi d'Angleterre, contre le duc de Bourgogne (1435)', *Cahiers d'histoire*, 1 (1956), 131–46.

Bossuat, A., 'The Re-Establishment of Peace in Society during the Reign of Charles VII', *The Recovery of France in the Fifteenth Century*, ed. P. S. Lewis, trans. G. F. Martin (London, 1971), 60–81.

Bothwell, J., 'The Management of Position: Alice Perrers, Edward III, and the Creation of a Landed Estate, 1362–1377', *Journal of Medieval History*, 24 (1998), 31–51.

Bothwell, J., *Edward III and the English Peerage: Royal Patronage, Social Mobility and Political Control in Fourteenth-Century England* (York, 2004).

Bothwell, J., *Falling from Grace: Reversal of Fortune and the English Nobility, 1075–1455* (Manchester, 2008).

Bothwell, J., ed., *The Age of Edward III* (York, 2001).

Boulton, D. A. J. D., *The Knights of the Crown: The Monarchical Orders of Knighthood in Later Medieval Europe, 1325–1520* (Woodbridge, 1987).

Boutruche, R., *La crise d'un société: Seigneurs et paysans du Bordelais pendant la Guerre de Cent Ans* (Paris, 1947).

Boutruche, R., 'Anglais et Gascons en Aquitaine du XIIe au XVe siècles. Problèmes d'histoire sociale', *Mélanges d'histoire dédiés à la mémoire de Louis Halphen* (Paris, 1951), 55–60.

Boutruche, R., 'The Devastation of Rural Areas during the Hundred Years War and the Agricultural Recovery of France', *The Recovery of France in the Fifteenth Century*, ed. P. S. Lewis, trans. G. F. Martin (London, 1971), 23–59.

Bradbury, J., *The Medieval Archer* (New York, 1985).

Bradbury, J., *The Medieval Siege* (Woodbridge, 1992).

Bradbury, J., *The Capetians: Kings of France, 987–1328* (London, 2007).

Brown, E. A. R., ' "Franks, Burgundians, and Aquitanians" and the Royal Coronation Ceremony in France', *Transactions of the American Philosophical Society*, n.s. 82 (1992).

Brown, M. H., 'James I (1394–1437)', *ODNB* (online edn, 2004).

Bryant, B. L., 'Talking with the Taxman about Poetry: England's Economy in "Against the King's Taxes" and *Wynnere and Wastoure*', *Studies in Medieval and Renaissance History*, 3rd ser. 5 (2008), 219–48.

Burden, J., 'Re-writing a Rite of Passage: The Peculiar Funeral of Edward II', *Rites of Passage: Cultures of Transition in the Fourteenth Century*, ed. N. F. McDonald and W. M. Ormrod (York, 2004), 13–29.

Burne, A. H., *The Agincourt War: A Military History of the Latter Part of the Hundred Years War from 1369 to 1453* (London, 1956).

Burns, J. H., 'Fortescue and the Political Theory of Dominium', *Historical Journal*, 28 (1985), 777–97.

Burns, J. H., *Lordship, Kingship and Empire: The Idea of Monarchy, 1400–1525* (Oxford, 1992).

Butler, R. R., *Is Paris Lost? The English Occupation, 1422–1436* (Staplehurst, 2003).

Butterfield, A., *The Familiar Enemy: Chaucer, Language and Nation in the Hundred Years War* (Oxford, 2009).

Caldwell, E. C., 'The Hundred Years War and National Identity', *Inscribing the Hundred Years War in French and English Cultures*, ed. D. N. Baker (Albany, NY, 2000), 237–66.

Campbell, J., 'England, Scotland and the Hundred Years War in the Fourteenth Century', *The Wars of Edward III*, ed. C. J. Rogers (Woodbridge, 1999), 207–30.

Capra, P., 'Les bases sociales du pouvoir anglo-gascon au milieu du XIVe siècle', *Le Moyen Âge*, 4ème sér. 81 (1975), 273–99, 447–73.

Capra, P., 'L'évolution de l'administration anglo-gasconne au milieu du XIVe siècle', *Bordeaux et les Îles britanniques du XIIIe au XXe siècle* (Bordeaux, 1975).

Carlin, M., 'Morstede, Thomas (d.1450)', *ODNB* (online edn, 2004).

Carr, A. D., 'Owen of Wales (d.1378)', *ODNB* (online edn, 2004).

Castor, H., *She-Wolves: The Women who Ruled England before Elizabeth* (London, 2010).

Catto, J., 'Written English: The Making of the Language 1370–1400', *Past and Present*, 179 (2003), 24–59.

Cazelles, R., *Société politique, noblesse et couronne sous Jean le Bon et Charles V* (Paris, 1982).

Champion, P., *Guillaume de Flavy, capitaine de Compiègne: contribution à l'histoire de Jeanne d'Arc et à l'étude de la vie militaire et privée au XVe siècle* (Paris, 1906).

Chan Tsin, M., 'Medieval Romances and Military History: Marching Orders in Jean de Bueil's *Le Jouvencel introduit aux armes*', *Journal of Medieval Military History*, vol. VII, *The Age of the Hundred Years War*, ed. C. J. Rogers, K. DeVries and J. France (Woodbridge, 2009), 126–34.

Chaplais, P., 'Réglements des conflits internationaux franco-anglais au XIVe siècle', *Le Moyen Âge*, 57 (1951), 169–302.

Chaplais, P., 'The Making of the Treaty of Paris (1259) and the Royal Style', *EHR*, 67 (1952), 235–53.

Chaplais, P., 'English Diplomatic Documents to the End of Edward III's Reign', *The Study of Medieval Records: Essays in Honour of Kathleen Major*, ed. D. A. Bullough and R. L. Storey (Oxford, 1971), 23–56.

Chaplais, P., *English Medieval Diplomatic Practice, Part One: Documents and Interpretations*, 2 vols (London, 1982).

Chapman, A., 'Welshmen in the Armies of Edward I', *The Impact of the Edwardian Castles in Wales*, ed. D. M. Williams and J. R. Kenyon (Oxford, 2010), 175–82.

Charbonnier, P., 'The Economy and Society of France in the Later Middle Ages: On the Eve of Crisis', *France in the Later Middle Ages*, ed. D. Potter (Oxford, 2003), 47–60.

Cherry, J., and Stratford, N., *Westminster Kings and the Medieval Palace of Westminster* (London, 1995).

Chiffoleau, J., 'La religion flamboyante (v.1320–v.1520)', *Du Christianisme flamboyant à l'aube des Lumières (XIVᵉ–XVIIIᵉ siècles)*, ed. J. Chiffoleau et al. (Paris, 1988).

Childs, W. R., 'Resistance and Treason in the *Vita Edwardi Secundi*', *Thirteenth-Century England*, vol. VI, ed. M. Prestwich, R. Britnell and R. Frame (Woodbridge, 1997), 177–91.

Clark, J. G., *The Benedictines in the Middle Ages* (Woodbridge, 2011).

Clough, C. H., 'Late Fifteenth-Century English Monarchs Subject to Italian Renaissance Influence', *England and the Continent in the Middle Ages: Studies in Memory of Andrew Martindale*, ed. J. Mitchell (Stamford, 2000), 28–34.

Cohen, M., 'An Indulgence for the Visitor: The Public at the Sainte-Chapelle of Paris', *Speculum*, 83 (2008), 840–83.

Cohn, S. K., *Popular Protest in Late Medieval Europe: Italy, France and Flanders* (Manchester, 2004).

Cohn, S. K., *Lust for Liberty: The Politics of Social Revolt in Medieval Europe, 1200–1425* (Cambridge, MA, 2006).

Coleman, J., 'A Culture of Political Counsel: The Case of Fourteenth-Century England's "Virtuous" Monarchy vs Royal Absolutism and Seventeenth-Century Reinterpretation', *Monarchism and Absolutism in Early Modern Europe*, ed. C. Cuttica and G. Burgess (London, 2011), 19–31.

Collins, H., *The Order of the Garter, 1348–1461: Chivalry and Politics in Late Medieval England* (Oxford, 2000).

Contamine, P., *Guerre, état et société à la fin du Moyen Âge. Études sur les armées des rois de France, 1337–1494* (Paris, 1972).

Contamine, P., 'De la puissance aux privilèges: doléances de la noblesse française envers la monarchie aux XIVᵉ et XVᵉ siècles', *La noblesse au Moyen Âge, XIᵉ–XVᵉ siècles. Essais à la mémoire de Robert Boutruche*, ed. P. Contamine (Paris, 1976), 235–57.

Contamine, P., 'Points de vue sur la chevalerie en France à la fin du Moyen Âge', *Francia*, 4 (1976), 255–86.

Contamine, P., 'Crécy (1346) et Azincourt (1415): une comparaison', *Divers aspects du Moyen Âge en Occident* (Calais, 1977), 29–44.

Contamine, P., *War in the Middle Ages*, trans. M. Jones (Oxford, 1984).

Contamine, P., 'La Guerre de Cent Ans: Le XVᵉ siècle. Du "Roi de Bourges" au très victorieux Roi de France', *Histoire militaire de la France*, vol. I, *Des origines à 1715*, ed. A. Corvisier (Paris, 1992), 198–208.

Contamine, P., 'The Norman "Nation" and the French "Nation" in the Fourteenth and Fifteenth Centuries', *England and Normandy in the Middle Ages*, ed. D. Bates and A. Curry (London, 1994), 215–34.

Contamine, P., 'The Growth of State Control, Practices of War, 1300–1800: Ransom and Booty', *War and Competition between States*, ed. P. Contamine (Oxford, 2000), 163–93.

Cooper, H., 'Speaking for the Victim', *Writing War: Medieval Literary Responses to Warfare*, ed. C. Saunders, F. Le Saux and N. Thomas (Woodbridge, 2004), 213–32.

Corvisier, A., *Histoire militaire de la France*, vol. I, *Des origines à 1715* (Paris, 1992).

Cosneau, E., *Le connétable de Richemont* (Paris, 1886).

Cosneau, E., *Les grands traités de la Guerre de Cent Ans* (Paris, 1889).

Coss, P. R., 'Cultural Diffusion and Robin Hood', *Past and Present*, 108 (1985), 35–79.

Coss, P. R., *The Knight in Medieval England, 1000–1400* (Stroud, 1993).

Coss, P. R., *The Lady in Medieval England, 1000–1500* (Stroud, 1998).

Coss, P. R., *The Origins of the English Gentry* (Cambridge, 2003).

Coss, P. R., *The Foundations of Gentry Life: The Multons of Frampton and their World 1270–1370* (Oxford, 2010).

Cox, R., 'Natural Law and the Right of Self-Defence according to John of Legnano and John Wyclif', *Fourteenth-Century England*, vol. VI, ed. C. Given-Wilson (Woodbridge, 2010), 149–69.

Cox, R., 'Wyclif: Medieval Pacifist', *History Today*, 60 (2010), 25–7.

Crane, S., 'Social Aspects of Bilingualism in the Thirteenth Century', *Thirteenth-Century England*, vol. VI, ed. M. Prestwich, R. Britnell and R. Frame (Woodbridge, 1997), 103–15.

Crane, S., *The Performance of Self: Ritual, Clothing and Identity during the Hundred Years War* (Philadelphia, PA, 2002).

Cron, B. M., 'The Duke of Suffolk, the Angevin Marriage, and the Ceding of Maine, 1445', *Journal of Medieval History*, 20 (1994), 77–99.

Crooks, P., 'Factions, Feuds and Noble Power in the Lordship of Ireland, c.1356–1496', *Irish Historical Studies*, 35 (2007), 425–54.

Crouch, D., *The Image of the Aristocracy in Britain, 1100–1300* (London, 1992).

Crouch, D., *The Birth of Nobility: Constructing Aristocracy in England and France, 900–1300* (Harlow, 2005).

Crouch, D., 'Chivalry and Courtliness: Colliding Constructs', *Soldiers, Nobles and Gentlemen: Essays in Honour of Maurice Keen*, ed. P. Coss and C. Tyerman (Woodbridge, 2009), 32–48.

Curry, A., 'Towns at War: Relations between the Towns of Normandy and their English Rulers, 1417–1450', *Towns and Townspeople in the Fifteenth Century*, ed. J. A. F. Thompson (Stroud, 1988), 148–72.

Curry, A., 'The Nationality of Men-at-Arms Serving in English Armies in Normandy and the Pays-de-Conquête, 1415–1450', *Reading Medieval Studies*, 18 (1992), 135–63.

Curry, A., 'Lancastrian Normandy: The Jewel in the Crown', *England and Normandy in the Middle Ages*, ed. D. Bates and A. Curry (London, 1994), 235–52.

Curry, A., 'Bourgeois et soldats dans la ville de Mantes pendant l'occupation anglaise de 1419 à 1449', *Guerre, pouvoir et noblesse au Moyen Âge. Mélanges en l'honneur de Philippe Contamine*, ed. J. Paviot and J. Verger (Paris, 2000), 175–84.

Curry, A., 'Isolated or Integrated? The English Soldier in Lancastrian Normandy', *Courts and Regions in Medieval Europe*, ed. S. Rees Jones, R. Marks and A. J. Minnis (York, 2000), 191–210.

Curry, A., 'Sir Thomas Erpingham: A Career in Arms', *Agincourt, 1415*, ed. A. Curry (Stroud, 2000), 53–110.

Curry, A., ed., *The Battle of Agincourt: Sources and Interpretations* (Woodbridge, 2000).

Curry, A., 'War, Peace and National Identity in the Hundred Years War', *Thinking War, Peace and World Orders in European History*, ed. A. Hartmann and B. Heuser (London, 2001), 141–54.

Curry, A., 'The "Coronation Expedition" and Henry VI's Court in France 1430 to 1432', *The Lancastrian Court*, ed. J. Stratford (Donington, 2003), 29–52.

Curry, A., *The Hundred Years War* (Houndmills, 2nd edn, 2003).

Curry, A., *Agincourt: A New History* (Stroud, 2005).

Curry, A., 'After Agincourt, What Next? Henry V and the Campaign of 1416', *Conflicts, Consequences and the Crown in the Late Middle Ages*, ed. L. Clark (Woodbridge, 2007), 23–51.

Curry, A., 'Montagu, Thomas, Fourth Earl of Salisbury (1388–1428)', *ODNB* (online edn, 2008).

Curry, A., 'The Military Ordinances of Henry V: Texts and Contexts', *War, Government and Aristocracy in the British Isles c.1150–1500*, ed. C. Given-Wilson, A. Kettle, and L. Scales (Woodbridge, 2008), 214–49.

Curry, A., 'Soldiers' Wives in the Hundred Years War', *Soldiers, Nobles and Gentlemen: Essays in Honour of Maurice Keen*, ed. P. Coss and C. Tyerman (Woodbridge, 2009), 198–214.

Curry, A., 'War or Peace? Philippe de Mézières, Richard II and Anglo-French Diplomacy', *Philippe de Mézières and his Age: Piety and Politics in the Fourteenth Century*, ed. R. Blumenfield-Kosinski and K. Petkov (Leiden, 2012), 295–320.

Curry, A., Bell, A., Chapman, A., King, A., and Simpkin, D., 'What Did You Do in the Hundred Years War, Daddy? The Soldier in Later Medieval England', *Historian*, 97 (2007), 6–13.

Curry, A., Bell, A., Chapman, A., King, A., and Simpkin, D., 'Languages in the Military Profession in Later Medieval England', *The Anglo-Norman Language and its Contexts*, ed. Richard Ingham (York, 2010), 74–93.

Curry, A., and Bell, A., with Chapman, A., King, A., and Simpkin, D., eds, *The Soldier Experience in the Fourteenth Century* (Woodbridge, 2011).

Cushway, G. R. ' "The Lord of the Sea": The English Navy in the Reign of Edward III', unpub. PhD thesis (University of Exeter, 2006).

Cuttino, G. P., *English Medieval Diplomacy* (Bloomington, IN, 1985).

Cuttler, S. H., *The Law of Treason and Treason Trials in Later Medieval France* (Cambridge, 1981).

Daly, K., 'The *Vraie cronicque d'Escoce* and Franco-Scottish Diplomacy: An Historical Work by John Ireland?', *Nottingham Medieval Studies*, 35 (1991), 106–33.

Daly, K., and Giesey, R. E., 'Noel de Fribois et la loi salique', *BEC*, 151 (1993), 5–27.

Davies, R. R., 'Colonial Wales', *Past and Present*, 65 (1974), 3–23.

Davies, R. R., *The Age of Conquest: Wales, 1063–1415* (Oxford, 1991).

Davies, R. R., *The Revolt of Owain Glyn Dŵr* (Oxford, 1995).

Davies, R. R., 'The Peoples of Britain and Ireland, 1100–1400, vol. II, Names and Regnal Solidarities', *TRHS*, 6th ser. 5 (1995), 1–20.

Davies, R. R., 'The Peoples of Britain and Ireland, 1100–1400, vol. IV, Language and Historical Mythology', *TRHS*, 6th ser. 7 (1997), 1–24.

Davies, R. R., *The First English Empire: Power and Identities in the British Isles, 1093–1343* (Oxford, 2000).

Davies, R. R., 'Nations and National Identities in the Medieval World: An Apologia', *Revue belge d'histoire contemporaine*, 34 (2004), 567–79.

Delachenal, R., *Charles V*, 5 vols (Paris, 1909–31).

Delogu, D., *Theorizing the Ideal Sovereign: The Rise of the French Vernacular Royal Biography* (Toronto, 2008).

Deluz, C., 'Croisade et paix en Europe au XIVᵉ siècle: Le rôle du cardinal Hélie de Talleyrand', *Cahiers de recherches médiévales*, I (1996), 53–61.

Denifle, H., *La désolation des églises, monastères et hôpitaux en France pendant la Guerre de Cent Ans*, 2 vols (Paris, 1897–99).

Déprez, E., *Les préliminaires de la Guerre de Cent Ans. La Papauté, la France et l'Angleterre, 1328–1342* (Paris, 1902), 127–35.

Déprez, E., 'La conférence d'Avignon (1344): L'arbitrage pontifical entre La France et l'Angleterre', *Essays in Medieval History Presented to T. F. Tout*, ed. A. G. Little and F. M. Powicke (Manchester, 1925), 301–20.

DeVries, K., 'The Impact of Gunpowder Weaponry in the Hundred Years War', *The Medieval City under Siege*, ed. I. A. Corfis and M. Wolfe (Woodbridge, 1995), 228–30.

DeVries, K., *Infantry Warfare in the Early Fourteenth Century: Discipline, Tactics and Technology* (Woodbridge, 1996).

DeVries, K., 'The Use of Gunpowder Weaponry by and against Joan of Arc during the Hundred Years War', *War and Society*, 14 (1996), 9–14.

DeVries, K., 'Teenagers at War During the Middle Ages', *The Premodern Teenager: Youth in Society, 1150–1650*, ed. K. Eisenbichler (Toronto, 2002), 207–23.

DeVries, K., *Joan of Arc: A Military Leader* (Stroud, 2003).

DeVries, K., *Medieval Military Technology* (Ontario, repr. 2003).

DeVries, K., 'The Introduction and Use of the *Pavise* in the Hundred Years War', *Arms and Armour*, 4 (2007), 93–100.

DeVries, K., 'Medieval Mercenaries: Methodology, Definitions and Problems', *Mercenaries and Paid Men: The Mercenary Identity in the Middle Ages*, ed. J. France (Leiden, 2008), 43–60.

Dewald, J., and Vardi, L., 'The Peasantries of France, 1400–1789', *The Peasantries of Europe from the Fourteenth to the Eighteenth Centuries*, ed. T. Scott (Harlow, 1998), 21–47.

Dickinson, J. G., *The Congress of Arras, 1435: A Study in Medieval Diplomacy* (Oxford, 1955).

Dictionnaire de biographie française (Paris, 1967).

Ditcham, B. G. H., 'The Employment of Foreign Mercenary Troops in the French Royal Armies, 1415–1470', unpub. PhD thesis (University of Edinburgh, 1979), 229–60.

Ditcham, B. G. H., 'Mutton Guzzlers and Wine Bags: Foreign Soldiers and Native Reactions in Fifteenth-Century France', *Power, Culture and Religion in France c.1350–c.1550*, ed. C. T. Allmand (Woodbridge, 1989), 1–13.

Dixon, M. C., 'John de Coupland – Hero to Villain', *The Battle of Neville's Cross, 1346*, ed. M. Prestwich and D. Rollason (Stamford, 1998), 36–49.

Dodd, G., *Justice and Grace: Private Petitioning and the English Parliament in the Late Middle Ages* (Oxford, 2007).

Doig, J., 'Political Propaganda and Royal Proclamations in Late Medieval England', *Historical Research*, 71 (1998), 253–80.

Duby, G., *The Chivalrous Society*, trans. C. Postan (Berkeley and Los Angeles, CA, 1977).

Duby, G., *Les trois ordres ou l'imaginaire du féodalisme* (Paris, 1978).

Duby, G., *The Three Orders: Feudal Society Imagined*, trans. A. Goldhammer (Chicago, IL, 1980).

Ducourtieux, P., *Histoire de Limoges* (Limoges, 1925, repr. Marseille, 1975).

Duffy, S., 'The Problem of Degeneracy', *Law and Disorder in Thirteenth-Century Ireland: The Dublin Parliament of 1297*, ed. J. Lydon (Dublin, 1997), 87–106.

Dunbabin, J., 'Government', *The Cambridge History of Medieval Political Thought c.350–c.1450* (Cambridge, 1988), 477–519.

Duncan, A. A. M., '*Honi soit qui mal y pense*: David II and Edward III, 1346–52', *Scottish Historical Review*, 67 (1988), 131–41.

Duncan, A. A. M., 'Douglas, Sir William, Lord of Liddesdale (*c.*1310–1353)', *ODNB* (online edn, 2006).

Dunham, W. H., and Wood, C. T., 'The Right to Rule in England: Depositions and the Kingdom's Authority, 1327–1485', *American Historical Review*, 81 (1976), 738–61.

Dupont-Ferrier, G., 'La captivité de Jean d'Orléans, comte d'Angoulême (1412–45)', *Revue Historique*, 62 (1896), 42–74.

Dupuy, M., *Le Prince Noir: Edouard seigneur d'Aquitaine* (Paris, 1970).

Dyer, C., *Making a Living in the Middle Ages: The People of Britain, 850–1520* (New Haven, CT, and London, 2002).

Dyer, C., 'The Political Life of the Fifteenth-Century English Village', *Political Culture in Late Medieval Britain*, ed. L. Clark and C. Carpenter (Woodbridge, 2004), 135–58.

Edbury, P., 'The Crusading Policy of King Peter I of Cyprus', *The Eastern Mediterranean Lands in the Period of Crusades*, ed. P. M. Holt (Warminster, 1977), 90–105.

Edwards, L. G., 'Joan of Arc: Gender and Authority in the Text of the Trial of Condemnation', *Young Medieval Women*, ed. K. Lewis, N. Menuge and K. Phillips (Stroud, 1999), 133–52.

Estow, C., *Pedro the Cruel of Castile, 1350–1369* (New York, 1995).

Famiglietti, R. C., *Royal Intrigue: Crisis at the Court of Charles VI, 1392–1420* (New York, 1986).

Favier, J., 'Occupation ou connivence? Les Anglais à Paris (1420–1436)', *Guerre, pouvoir et noblesse au Moyen Âge. Mélanges en l'honneur de Philippe Contamine*, ed. J. Paviot and J. Verger (Paris, 2000), 239–60.

Favreau, R., 'Comptes de la sénéchaussée de Saintonge, 1360–2', *BEC*, 117 (1959), 73–88.

Favreau, R., 'La cession de La Rochelle à l'Angleterre en 1360', *La 'France anglaise' au Moyen Âge*, ed. R. H. Bautier (Paris, 1988), 217–31.

Fédou, R., 'A Popular Revolt in Lyon in the Fifteenth Century: The *Rebeyne* of 1436', *The Recovery of France in the Fifteenth Century*, ed. P. S. Lewis, trans. G. F. Martin (London, 1971), 242–64.

Ferster, J., *Fictions of Advice: The Literature and Politics of Counsel in Late Medieval England* (Philadelphia, PA, 1996).

Fiorato, V., Boylston, A., and Knussel, C., eds, *Blood-Red Roses: The Archaeology of a Mass Grave from the Battle of Towton, 1461* (Oxford, 2000).

Fisher, J. H., 'Chancery and the Emergence of Standard Written English in the Fifteenth Century', *Speculum*, 52 (1977), 870–99.

Fisher, J. H., 'A Language Policy for Lancastrian England', *Publications of the Modern Language Association of America*, 107 (1992), 1,168–80.

Fletcher, C. D., 'Manhood and Politics in the Reign of Richard II', *Past and Present*, 189 (2005), 3–39.

Flori, J., *L'essor de la chevalerie: XIᵉ–XIIᵉ siècles* (Geneva, 1986).

Flori, J., *Chevaliers et chevalerie au Moyen Âge* (Paris, 1998).

Foot, S., 'The Making of Angelcynn: English Identity before the Norman Conquest', *TRHS*, 6th ser. 6 (1996), 25–49.

Fowler, K., *The Age of Plantagenet and Valois* (London, 1967).

Fowler, K., *The King's Lieutenant: Henry of Grosmont, First Duke of Lancaster, 1310–1361* (London, 1969).

Fowler, K., *Medieval Mercenaries*, vol. I, *The Great Companies* (Oxford, 2001).

Fowler, K., ed., *The Hundred Years War* (London, 1971).

Frame, R., 'Thomas Rokeby, Sheriff of Yorkshire, Justiciar of Ireland', *Peritia*, 10 (1996), 274–96.

Frame, R., 'Overlordship and Reaction, c.1200–c.1450', *Ireland and Britain, 1170–1450* (London, 1998), 171–90.

Frame, R., 'Rokeby, Sir Thomas (d.1357)', *ODNB* (online edn, 2008).

France, J., ed., *Mercenaries and Paid Men: The Mercenary Identity in the Middle Ages* (Leiden, 2008).

Fraoli, D. A., *Joan of Arc: The Early Debate* (Woodbridge, 2000).

Friel, I., 'Winds of Change', *Arms, Armies and Fortifications in the Hundred Years War*, ed. A. Curry and M. Hughes (Woodbridge, 1994), 183–93.

Gaier, C., 'L'invincibilité anglaise et le grand arc après la Guerre de Cent Ans: un mythe tenace', *Tijdschrift voor gescheidenis*, 91 (1978), 378–85.

Gaude-Ferragu, M., *D'or et de cendres: La mort et les funérailles des princes dans le royaume de France au bas Moyen Âge* (Lille, 2005).

Gellner, E., *Nations and Nationalism* (Oxford, 1983).

Gellner, E., *Culture, Identity and Politics* (Cambridge, 1987).

Gellner, E., *Nationalism* (New York, 1997).

Genet, J.-P., 'English Nationalism: Thomas Polton at the Council of Constance', *Nottingham Medieval Studies*, 28 (1984), 60–78.

Gibbons, R., 'Isabeau of Bavaria, Queen of France (1385–1422): The Creation of an Historical Villainess', *TRHS*, 6th ser. 6 (1996), 51–73.

Giesey, R. E., 'The Royal Funeral in Renaissance France', *Renaissance News*, 7 (1954), 130–1.

Giesey, R. E., *The Royal Funeral Ceremony in Renaissance France* (Geneva, 1960).

Giesey, R. E., 'The Presidents of Parlement at the Royal Funeral', *Sixteenth Century Journal*, 7 (1976), 25–34.

Gilbert, F., 'Sir John Fortescue's *dominium regale et politicum*', *Medievalia et Humanistica*, 2 (1944), 88–97.

Gilbert, J. E., 'A Medieval Rosie the Riveter? Women in France and Southern England during the Hundred Years War', *The Hundred Years War*, vol. I, *A Wider Focus*, ed. D. Kagay and L. J. A. Villalon (Leiden, 2005), 345–6.

Gillingham, J., 'Richard I and the Science of War in the Middle Ages', *War and Government in the Middle Ages: Essays in Honour of J. O. Prestwich*, ed. J. Gillingham and J. C. Holt (Cambridge, 1984), 78–91.

Gillingham, J., *The English in the Twelfth Century: Imperialism, National Identity, and Political Values* (Woodbridge, 2000).

Given, J., *State and Society in Medieval Europe: Gwynedd and Languedoc under Outside Rule* (Ithaca, NY, and London, 1990).

Given-Wilson, C., 'Purveyance for the Royal Household, 1362–1413', *BIHR*, 56 (1983), 145–63.

Given-Wilson, C., *The Royal Household and the King's Affinity, 1360–1413* (New Haven, CT, and London, 1986).

Given-Wilson, C., *Chronicles: The Writing of History in Medieval England* (London, 2004).

Given-Wilson, C., 'Perrers, Alice (d. 1400/01)', *ODNB* (online edn, 2008).

Given-Wilson, C., 'The Exequies of Edward III and the Royal Funeral Ceremony in Late Medieval England', *EHR*, 124 (2009), 257–82.

Given-Wilson, C., and Bériac-Lainé, F., 'Edward III's Prisoners of War: The Battle of Poitiers and its Context', *EHR*, 116 (2001), 802–33.

Given-Wilson, C., and Bériac-Lainé, F., *Les prisonniers de la bataille de Poitiers*, (Paris, 2002).

Given-Wilson, C., Kettle, A., and Scales, L., eds, *War, Government and Aristocracy in the British Isles, c.1150–1500: Essays in Honour of Michael Prestwich* (Woodbridge, 2008).

Glasscock, R. E., 'Land and People c.1300', *A New History of Ireland*, vol. II, *Medieval Ireland 1169–1534*, ed. A. Cosgrove (Oxford, 1987), 212–16.

Good, J., *The Cult of St George in Medieval England* (Woodbridge, 2009).

Goodman, A., 'England and Iberia in the Middle Ages', *England and her Neighbours, 1066–1453: Essays in Honour of Pierre Chaplais*, ed. M. Jones and M. G. A. Vale (London, 1989), 73–96.

Goodman, A., *John of Gaunt: The Exercise of Princely Power in Fourteenth-Century Europe* (Harlow, 1992).

Goodman, A., *The Wars of the Roses: The Soldiers' Experience* (Stroud, 2005).

Grant, A., *Independence and Nationhood: Scotland, 1306–1469* (Edinburgh, 1984), 32–57.

Grant, A., 'Disaster at Neville's Cross: The Scottish Point of View', *The Battle of Neville's Cross, 1346*, ed. D. Rollason and M. Prestwich (Stamford, 1998), 15–35.

Green, D., *Edward the Black Prince: Power in Medieval Europe* (Harlow, 2007).

Green, D., *The Battle of Poitiers, 1356* (Stroud, rev. edn, 2008).

Green, D., *The Black Prince* (Stroud, rev. edn, 2008).

Green, D., 'Lordship and Principality: Colonial Policy in Ireland and Aquitaine in the 1360s', *Journal of British Studies*, 47 (2008), 3–29.

Green, D., 'Jean de Vienne', *The Oxford Encyclopedia of Medieval Warfare and Military Technology*, ed. C. J. Rogers, 3 vols (New York, 2010), vol. II, 440.

Green, D., 'National Identities and the Hundred Years War', *Fourteenth-Century England*, vol. VI, ed. C. Given-Wilson (Woodbridge, 2010), 115–29.

Griffiths, R. A., *The Principality of Wales in the Later Middle Ages: The Structure and Personnel of Government*, vol. I, *South Wales, 1277–1536* (Cardiff, 1972).

Griffiths, R. A., *The Reign of King Henry VI: The Exercise of Royal Authority, 1422–1461* (London, 1981).

Griffiths, R. A., 'The English Realm and Dominions and the King's Subjects in the Later Middle Ages', *Aspects of Late Medieval Government and Society: Essays Presented to J. A. Lander*, ed. J. G. Rowe (Toronto, 1986), 83–105.

Griffiths, R. A., 'The Island of England in the Fifteenth Century: Perceptions of the Peoples of the British Isles', *Journal of Medieval History*, 29 (2003), 177–200.

Griffiths, R. A., 'Holland, John, First Duke of Exeter (1395–1447)', *ODNB* (online edn, 2008).

Grummitt, D., 'Deconstructing Cade's Rebellion: Discourse and Politics in the Mid-Fifteenth Century', *Identity and Insurgency in the Late Middle Ages*, ed. L. Clark (Woodbridge, 2006), 107–22.

Grummitt, D., 'Écorcheurs', *The Oxford Encyclopedia of Medieval Warfare and Military Technology*, ed. C. J. Rogers, 3 vols (Oxford, 2010), vol. II, 13.

Guard, T., *Chivalry, Kingship and Crusade: The English Experience in the Fourteenth Century* (Woodbridge, 2013).

Guenée, B., 'État et nation en France au Moyen Âge', *Revue Historique*, 237 (1967), 17–30.

Guenée, B., *States and Rulers in Later Medieval Europe*, trans. J. Vale (Oxford, 1985).

Guenée, B., *Between Church and State: The Lives of Four French Prelates in the Late Middle Ages*, trans. A. Goldhammer (Chicago, IL, 1991).

Guenée, B., *Un meurtre, une société: l'assassinat du duc d'Orléans, 23 novembre 1407* (Paris, 1992).

Guenée, B., *La folie de Charles VI: roi bien-aimé* (Paris, 2004).

Guillemain, B., 'Les tentatives pontificales de médiation dans le litige franco-anglais de Guyenne au XIVᵉ siècle', *Bulletin philologique et historique du comité des travaux historiques et scientifiques* (1957), 423–32.

Guinan, A., 'The Christian Concept of Kingship as Manifested in the Liturgy of the Western Church: A Fragment in Suggestion', *Harvard Theological Review*, 49 (1956), 219–69.

Gunn, S., 'War and the Emergence of the State: Western Europe, 1350–1600', *European Warfare, 1350–1750*, ed. F. Tallett and D. J. B. Trim (Cambridge, 2010), 50–73.

Hallam, E., and Everard, J., *Capetian France, 987–1328* (Harlow, 2nd edn, 2001).

Hanley, S., *The Lit de Justice and the Kings of France: Constitutional Ideology in Legend, Ritual, and Discourse* (Princeton, NJ, 1983).

Hanly, M., 'Philippe de Mézières and the Peace Movement', *Philippe de Mézières and his Age: Piety and Politics in the Fourteenth Century*, ed. R. Blumenfield-Kosinski and K. Petkov (Leiden, 2012), 61–82.

Harari, Y. N., 'Strategy and Supply in Fourteenth-Century Western European Invasion Campaigns', *Journal of Military History*, 64 (2000), 297–334.

Harari, Y. N., *Special Operations in the Age of Chivalry, 1100–1550* (Woodbridge, 2007).

Harding, A., *Medieval Law and the Foundations of the State* (Oxford, 2002).

Hardy, R., 'The Longbow', *Arms, Armies and Fortifications in the Hundred Years War*, ed. A. Curry and M. Hughes (Woodbridge, 1994), 161–81.

Harris, P. V., 'Archery in the First Half of the Fourteenth Century', *Journal of the Society of Archer-Antiquaries*, 13 (1970), 19–21.

Harris, R., *Valois Guyenne: A Study of Politics, Government and Society in Late Medieval France* (Woodbridge, 1994).

Harriss, G. L., 'Introduction: The Exemplar of Kingship', *Henry V: The Practice of Kingship*, ed. G. L. Harriss (Oxford, 1985), 1–29.

Harriss, G. L., 'Marmaduke Lumley and the Exchequer Crisis of 1446–9', *Aspects of Late Medieval Government and Society: Essays Presented to J. R. Lander*, ed. J. G. Rowe (Toronto, 1986), 143–78.

Harriss, G. L., *Cardinal Beaufort: A Study of Lancastrian Ascendancy and Decline* (Oxford, 1989).

Harriss, G. L., 'Political Society and the Growth of Government in Late Medieval England', *Past and Present*, 138 (1993), 28–57.

Harriss, G. L., *Shaping the Nation: England 1360–1461* (Oxford, 2005).

Harriss, G. L., 'Beaufort, Henry (1375?–1447)', *ODNB* (online edn, 2008).

Harriss, G. L., 'Fastolf, Sir John (1380–1459)', *ODNB* (online edn, 2009).

Harriss, G. L., 'Thomas, Duke of Clarence (1387–1421)', *ODNB* (online edn, 2010).

Harriss, G. L., ed. *Henry V: The Practice of Kingship* (Oxford and New York, 1985).

Harvey, I. M. W., *Jack Cade's Rebellion of 1450* (Oxford, 1991).

Harvey, M., 'Ecclesia Anglicana, cui ecclesiastes noster christus vos prefecit: The Power of the Crown in the English Church during the Great Schism', *Religion and National Identity*, ed. S. Mews (Oxford, 1982), 229–41.

Hay, D., 'The Division of the Spoils of War', *TRHS*, 5th ser. 4 (1954), 91–109.

Hedeman, A. D., *The Royal Image: Illustrations of the Grandes Chroniques de France, 1274–1422* (Berkeley, CA, 1991).

Henneman, J. B., *Royal Taxation in Fourteenth-Century France: The Development of War Financing, 1322–1356* (Princeton, NJ, 1971).

Henneman, J. B., *Royal Taxation in Fourteenth-Century France: The Captivity and Ransom of John II, 1356–1370* (Philadelphia, PA, 1976).

Henneman, J. B., 'The Military Class and the French Monarchy in the Late Middle Ages', *American Historical Review*, 83 (1978), 946–65.

Henneman, J. B., *Olivier de Clisson and Political Society in France under Charles V and Charles VI* (Philadelphia, PA, 1996).

Hewitt, H. J., *The Black Prince's Expedition of 1355–1357* (Manchester, 1958).

Hewitt, H. J., *The Organization of War under Edward III, 1338–62* (New York, 1966).

Hicks, M. A., 'Edward IV's *Brief Treatise* and the Treaty of Picquigny of 1475', *Historical Research*, 83 (2009), 253–65.

Higounet-Nadal, A., *Périgeux au XIV* et XV* siècles* (Bordeaux, 1978).

Hilton, L., *Queens Consort: England's Medieval Queens* (London, 2008).

Hilton, R., *Bond Men Made Free: Medieval Peasant Movements and the English Rising of 1381* (London, 1973).

Hinton, R. W. K., 'English Constitutional Doctrines from the Fifteenth Century to the Seventeenth, vol. I, English Constitutional Theories from Sir John Fortescue to Sir John Eliot', *EHR*, 75 (1960), 410–25.

Holmes, G. A., *The Good Parliament* (Oxford, 1975).

Holt, M. P., 'Burgundians into Frenchmen: Catholic Identity in Sixteenth-Century Burgundy', *Changing Identities in Early Modern France*, ed. M. Wolfe (London, 1997), 345–70.

Hoskins, P., *In the Steps of the Black Prince: The Road to Poitiers, 1355–1356* (Woodbridge, 2011).

Housley, N., 'France, England, and the "National Crusade", 1302–1386', *France and the British Isles in the Middle Ages and Renaissance: Essays by Members of Girton College, Cambridge in Memory of Ruth Morgan*, ed. G. Jondorf and D. N. Dumville (Woodbridge, 1991), 183–98.

Housley, N., '*Pro deo et patria mori*: Sanctified Patriotism in Europe 1400–1600', *War and Competition between States*, ed. P. Contamine (Oxford, 2000), 221–8.

Housley, N., *The Avignon Papacy and the Crusades* (Oxford, 1986).

Hoyt, R. S., 'The Coronation Oath of 1308: The Background of "les leys et les custumes"', *Traditio*, 11 (1955), 235–57.

Hoyt, R. S., 'The Coronation Oath of 1308', *EHR*, 71 (1956), 353–83.

Hughes, M., 'The Fourteenth-Century French Raids on Hampshire and the Isles of Wight', *Arms, Armies and Fortifications in the Hundred Years War*, ed. A. Curry and M. Hughes (Woodbridge, 1994), 121–43.

Huizinga, J., *Homo Ludens: A Study of the Play Element in Culture* (London, 1970).

Huizinga, J., *The Autumn of the Middle Ages*, trans. R. J. Payton and U. Mammitzsch (Chicago, IL, 1996).

Huneycutt, L. L., 'Intercession and the High-Medieval Queen: The Esther Topos,' *Power of the Weak: Studies on Medieval Women*, ed. J. Carpenter and S.-B. MacLean (Chicago, IL, 1995), 126–46.

Ives, E. W., 'Fortescue, Sir John (c.1397–1479)', *ODNB* (online edn, 2005).

Jack, R. I., 'Hastings, John, Thirteenth Earl of Pembroke (1347–1375)', *ODNB* (online edn, 2008).

Jackson, R. A., *Vive le Roi! A History of the French Coronation from Charles V to Charles X* (Chapel Hill, NC, 1984).

Jones, M., *Ducal Brittany, 1364–1399: Relations with England and France during the Reign of Duke John IV* (Oxford, 1970).

Jones, M., 'The Breton Civil War', *Froissart: Historian*, ed. J. J. N. Palmer (Woodbridge, 1981), 64–81.

Jones, M., ' "Bons Bretons et Bons Francoys": The Language and Meaning of Treason in Later Medieval France', *TRHS*, 5th ser. 32 (1982), 91–112.

Jones, M., 'Edward III's Captains in Brittany', *England in the Fourteenth Century*, ed. W. M. Ormrod (Woodbridge, 1986), 99–118.

Jones, M., 'Les capitaines anglo-bretons et les marches entre la Bretagne et le Poitou de 1342 à 1373', *La 'France anglaise' au Moyen Âge*, ed. R. H. Bautier (Paris, 1988), 357–75.

Jones, M., 'War and Fourteenth-Century France', *Arms, Armies and Fortifications in the Hundred Years War*, ed. A. Curry and M. Hughes (Woodbridge, 1994), 103–20.

Jones, M., 'The Last Capetians, 1314–1364', *The New Cambridge Medieval History*, vol. VI, *c.1300–c.1415* (Cambridge, 2000), 388–421.

Jones, M., 'Catherine (1401–1437)', *ODNB* (online edn, 2008).

Jones, M., 'Joan (1368–1437)', *ODNB* (online edn, 2008).

Jones, M., ed., *The New Cambridge Medieval History*, vol. VI, *c.1300–c.1415* (Cambridge, 2000).

Jones, M. K., 'L'imposition illégale de taxes en "Normandie anglaise": une enquête gouvernementale en 1446', *La 'France anglaise' au Moyen Âge*, ed. R. H. Bautier (Paris, 1988), 460–8.

Jones, R. L. C., 'Fortifications and Sieges in Western Europe c. 800–1450', *Medieval Warfare: A History*, ed. M. Keen (Oxford, 1999), 163–85.

Jones, W. R., 'The English Church and Royal Propaganda during the Hundred Years War', *Journal of British Studies*, 19 (1979), 18–30.

Jouet, R., *La résistance à l'occupation anglaise en Basse-Normandie, 1418–1450* (Caen, 1969).

Kaeuper, R., *War, Justice and Public Order: England and France in the Late Middle Ages* (Oxford, 1988).

Kaeuper, R., *Chivalry and Violence in Medieval Europe* (Oxford, 1999).

Kaeuper, R., 'The Societal Role of Chivalry in Romance: Northwestern Europe', *The Cambridge Companion to Medieval Romance*, ed. R. L. Krueger (Cambridge, 2000), 97–114.

Kagay, D., and Villalon, L. J. A., eds, *The Hundred Years War*, vol. I, *A Wider Focus* (Leiden, 2005).

Kagay, Donald, and Villalon, L. J. A., eds, *The Hundred Years War*, vol. II, *Different Vistas* (Leiden, 2008).

Kaminsky, H., 'The Politics of France's Subtraction of Obedience from Pope Benedict XIII, 27 July, 1398', *Proceedings of the American Philosophical Society*, 115 (1971), 367–71.

Kaminsky, H., 'Estate, Nobility and the Exhibition of Estate in the Later Middle Ages', *Speculum*, 68 (1993), 684–709.

Kaminsky, H., 'The Great Schism', *The New Cambridge Medieval History*, vol. VI, *c.1300–c.1415*, ed. Michael Jones (Cambridge, 2000), 674–96.

Kantorowicz, E., *The King's Two Bodies: A Study in Mediaeval Political Theology* (Princeton, NJ, repr. 1997).

Karras, R. M., 'The Regulation of Brothels in Later Medieval England', *Signs*, 14 (1989), 399–433.

Keegan, J., *Face of Battle: A Study of Agincourt, Waterloo and the Somme* (Harmondsworth, 1978).

Keeley, L. N., *War before Civilization: The Myth of the Peaceful Savage* (New York, 1996).

Keen, M., *The Laws of War in the Late Middle Ages* (London, 1965).

Keen, M., 'Chaucer's Knight, the English Aristocracy and the Crusade', *English Court Culture in the Later Middle Ages*, ed. V. J. Scattergood and J. W. Sherborne (London, 1983), 45–61.

Keen, M., *Chivalry* (New Haven, CT, and London, 1984).

Keen, M., 'Diplomacy', *Henry V: The Practice of Kingship*, ed. G. L. Harriss (Oxford, 1985), 181–99.

Keen, M., 'The End of the Hundred Years War: Lancastrian France and Lancastrian England', *England and her Neighbours, 1066–1453: Essays in Honour of Pierre Chaplais* (London, 1989), 297–311.

Keen, M., 'Richard II's Ordinances of War of 1385', *Rulers and Ruled in Late Medieval England: Essays Presented to G. L. Harriss*, ed. R. E. Archer and S. Walker (London, 1995), 33–48.

Keen, M., 'War, Peace and Chivalry', *Nobles, Knights and Men-at-Arms in the Middle Ages* (London, 1996).

Keen, M., 'The Changing Scene: Guns, Gunpowder and Permanent Armies', *Medieval Warfare: A History*, ed. M. Keen (Oxford, 1999), 273–91.

Keen, M., 'Chivalry and English Kingship in the Later Middle Ages', *War, Government and Aristocracy in the British Isles, c. 1150–1500: Essays in Honour of Michael Prestwich*, ed. C. Given-Wilson, A. Kettle and L. Scales (Woodbridge, 2008), 250–66.

Keen, M., ed., *Medieval Warfare: A History* (Oxford, 1999).

Keen, M., and Daniel, M. J., 'English Diplomacy and the Sack of Fougères in 1449', *History*, 59 (1974), 375–91.

Kempshall, M. S., *The Common Good in Late Medieval Political Thought* (Oxford, 1999).

Kilgour, R., *The Decline of Chivalry as Shown in the French Literature of the Late Middle Ages* (Cambridge, MA, 1937).

King, A., 'A Helm with a Crest of Gold: The Order of Chivalry in Thomas Gray's *Scalacronica*', *Fourteenth-Century England*, vol. I, ed. N. Saul (Woodbridge, 2000), 21–35.

King, A., ' "According to the custom used in French and Scottish wars": Prisoners and Casualties on the Scottish Marches in the Fourteenth Century', *Journal of Medieval History*, 28 (2002), 263–90.

King, A., 'The Ethics of War in Sir Thomas Gray's *Scalacronica*', *War, Government and Aristocracy in the British Isles c.1150–1500: Essays in Honour of Michael Prestwich*, ed. C. Given-Wilson, A. Kettle and L. Scales (Woodbridge, 2008), 148–62.

Kingsford, C. L., *English Historical Literature in the Fifteenth Century* (Oxford, 1913).

Knecht, R. J., *The Valois: Kings of France, 1328–1589* (London, 2007).

Krug, I., 'Purveyance and Peasants at the Beginning of the Hundred Years War: Maddicott Reexamined', *The Hundred Years War*, vol. II, *Different Vistas*, ed. D. Kagay and L. J. A. Villalon (Leiden, 2008), 345–65.

Krynen, J., *Idéal du prince et pouvoir royal en France à la fin du Moyen Âge (1380–1440): Étude de la littérature politique du temps* (Paris, 1981).

Krynen, J., *L'empire du roi: Idées et croyances politiques en France XIIIe–XVe siècle* (Paris, 1993).

Labarge, M. W., *Gascony, England's First Colony, 1204–1453* (London, 1980).

Labroue, É., *Bergerac sous les Anglais* (Bordeaux, 1893).

Laidlaw, J., 'Alain Chartier and the Arts of Crisis Management, 1417–1429', *War, Government and Power in Late Medieval France*, ed. C. T. Allmand (Liverpool, 2000), 37–53.

Langdon Forhan, K., *The Political Theory of Christine de Pizan* (Aldershot, 2002).

Le Duc, V., ed., 'Bergerie nouvelle, fort joyeuse et morale, de Mieulx que devant, à quatre personnaiges, c'est assavoir: Mieulx que devant, Plat Pays, Peuple Pensif, et la Bergière', *Ancien théatre françois ou Collection des ouvrages dramatiques les plus remarquables depuis les mystères jusqu'à Corneille*, 10 vols (Paris, 1854–7).

Le Goff, J., 'Le roi dans l'occident médiéval: Caractères originaux', *Kings and Kingship in Medieval Europe*, ed. A. J. Duggan (Exeter, 1993), 1–40.

Le Patourel, J., 'The Plantagenet Dominions', *History*, 50 (1965), 289–308.

Le Patourel, J., 'Edward III and the Kingdom of France', *The Wars of Edward III: Sources and Interpretations*, ed. C. J. Rogers (Woodbridge, 1999), 247–64.

Lewis, P. S., 'The Failure of the French Medieval Estates', *Past and Present*, 23 (1962), 3–24.

Lewis, P. S., 'Two Pieces of Fifteenth-Century Political Iconography: (b) The English Kill their Kings', *Journal of the Warburg and Courtauld Institutes*, 27 (1964), 317–20.

Lewis, P. S., 'France in the Fifteenth Century: Society and Sovereignty', *Europe in the Late Middle Ages*, ed. J. Hale, R. Highfield and B. Smalley (London, 1965), 3–28.

Lewis, P. S., 'Jean Juvenal des Ursins and the Common Literary Attitude to Tyranny in Fifteenth-Century France', *Medium Aevum*, 34 (1965), 103–21.

Lewis, P. S., *Later Medieval France: The Polity* (London, 1968).
Lewis, P. S., 'War Propaganda and Historiography in Fifteenth-Century France and England', *Essays in Later Medieval French History* (London, 1985), 193–214.
Lewis, P. S., ed., *The Recovery of France in the Fifteenth Century*, trans. G. F. Martin (London, 1971).
Lindley, P. G., 'Ritual, Regicide and Representation', *Gothic to Renaissance: Essays on Sculpture in England*, ed. P. G. Lindley (Stamford, 1995), 97–112.
Llewelyn Thompson, G., 'Le régime anglo-bourguignon à Paris: facteurs idéologiques', *La 'France anglaise' au Moyen Âge*, ed. R. H. Bautier (Paris, 1988), 53–60.
Llewelyn Thompson, G., *Paris and its People under English Rule: The Anglo-Burgundian Regime 1420–1436* (Oxford, 1991).
Lombarès, M. de Castillon, 'Dernière victoire de l'artillerie', *Revue historique de l'Armée*, 3 (1976), 7–31.
Lot, F., and Fawtier, R., *Histoire des institutions françaises au Moyen Âge*, vol. III, *Institutions ecclésiastiques* (Paris, 1962).
Lowe, B., *Imagining Peace: A History of Early English Pacifist Ideas, 1340–1560* (Philadelphia, PA, 1997).
Luttrell, A., 'The Crusade in the Fourteenth Century', *Europe in the Late Middle Ages*, ed. J. Hale et al. (London, 1965), 122–54.
Lydon, J., 'The Middle Nation', *The English in Medieval Ireland*, ed. J. Lydon (Dublin, 1984), 12–20.
Lydon, J., 'Nation and Race in Medieval Ireland', *Concepts of National Identity in the Middle Ages*, ed. S. Forde, L. Johnson and A. V. Murray (Leeds, 1995), 103–24.
Lynch, J. H., *The Medieval Church: A Brief History* (Harlow, 1992).
McCulloch, D., and Jones, E. D., 'Lancastrian Politics, the French War, and the Rise of the Popular Element', *Speculum*, 58 (1983), 95–138.
MacDougall, N., *An Antidote to the English: The Auld Alliance, 1295–1560* (East Linton, 2001).
McFarlane, K. B., 'The Investment of Sir John Fastolf's Profits of War', *TRHS*, 5th ser. 7 (1957), 91–116.
McGee Morganstern, A., 'The La Grange Tomb and Choir: A Monument of the Great Schism of the West', *Speculum*, 48 (1973), 52–69.
McGlynn, S., *By Sword and Fire: Cruelty and Atrocity in Medieval Warfare* (London, 2008).
McGrade, A. S., 'Somersaulting Sovereignty: A Note on Reciprocal Lordship in Wyclif', *Church and Sovereignty*, ed. D. Wood (Oxford, 1991), 261–8.
McGuire, B. P., *Jean Gerson and the Last Medieval Reformation* (University Park, PA, 2005).
McHardy, A. K., 'The Alien Priories and the Expulsion of Aliens from England in 1378', *Church, Society and Politics*, ed. D. Baker (Oxford, 1975), 133–41.
McHardy, A. K., 'Liturgy and Propaganda in the Diocese of Lincoln during the Hundred Years War', *Religion and National Identity*, ed. S. Mews (Oxford, 1982), 215–27.
McHardy, A. K., 'The Effects of War on the Church: The Case of the Alien Priories in the Fourteenth Century', *England and her Neighbours, 1066–1453: Essays in Honour of Pierre Chaplais*, ed. M. Jones and M. G. A. Vale (London, 1989), 278–84.
McHardy, A. K., 'Some Reflections on Edward III's Use of Propaganda', *The Age of Edward III*, ed. J. Bothwell (York, 2001), 171–89.
McHardy, A. K., *The Age of War and Wycliffe: Lincoln Diocese and its Bishop in the Later Fourteenth Century* (Lincoln, 2001).
McHardy, A. K., and Orme, N., 'The Defence of an Alien Priory: Modbury (Devon) in the 1450s', *Journal of Ecclesiastical History*, 50 (1999), 303–12.
McLaughlin, M., 'The Woman Warrior: Gender, Warfare and Society in Medieval Europe', *Women's Studies*, 17 (1990), 193–209.
McLeod, E., *Charles of Orleans: Prince and Poet* (London, 1969).
Maddicott, J. R., 'The Birth and Setting of the Robin Hood Ballads', *EHR*, 93 (1978), 276–99.
Maillane, D. de, *Dictionnaire du Droit Canonique et de Pratique Bénéficiale conferé avec les maximes et la jurisprudence de France* (Paris, 1761).
Major, J. R., *From Renaissance Monarchy to Absolute Monarchy: French Kings, Nobles and Estates* (Baltimore, MD, and London, 1994).
Marsden, P., *Sealed by Time: The Loss and Recovery of the Mary Rose* (Portsmouth, 2003).

Martin, F. X., 'John, Lord of Ireland, 1185–1216', *A New History of Ireland*, vol. II, *Medieval Ireland, 1169–1534*, ed. A. Cosgrove (Oxford, 1987), 127–55.

Mast, I., 'Rape in John Gower's *Confessio Amantis* and other Related Works', *Young Medieval Women*, ed. K. J. Lewis, N. Menuge and K. Phillips (Stroud, 1999), 103–32.

Mate, M. E., 'Work and Leisure', *A Social History of England, 1200–1500*, ed. R. Horrox and W. M. Ormrod (Cambridge, 2006), 276–92.

Matthew, D., *Norman Monasteries and their English Possessions* (Oxford, 1962).

Maurer, H., *Margaret of Anjou: Queenship and Power in Late Medieval England* (Woodbridge, 2003).

Menuge, N., ed., *Medieval Women and the Law* (Woodbridge, 2000).

Menut, A. D., 'Maistre Nicole Oresme: Le *Livre de Politiques* d'Aristote. Published from the Text of the Avranches Manuscript 223', *Transactions of the American Philosophical Society*, new ser. 60 (1970), 1–392.

Mercer, M., *Henry V: The Rebirth of Chivalry* (London, 2004).

Meron, T., 'The Authority to Make Treaties in the Late Middle Ages', *American Journal of International Law*, 89 (1995), 1–20.

Michael, M., 'The Iconography of Kingship in the Walter of Milemete Treatise', *Journal of the Warburg and Courtauld Institutes*, 57 (1994), 35–47.

Michael, M., 'The Little Land of England is Preferred before the Great Kingdom of France: The Quartering of the Royal Arms by Edward III', *Studies in Medieval Art and Architecture Presented to Peter Lasko*, ed. D. Buckton and T. A. Heslop (Stroud, 1994), 113–26.

Miller, S. J. T., 'The Position of the King in Bracton and Beaumanoir', *Speculum*, 31 (1956), 263–96.

Mirot, L., 'Raoul d'Anquetonville et le prix de l'assassinat du duc d'Orléans', *BEC*, 72 (1911), 445–58.

Miskimin, H. A., 'The Last Act of Charles V: The Background of the Revolts of 1382', *Speculum*, 38 (1963), 433–42.

Moeglin, J. M., 'Édouard III et les six bourgeois de Calais', *Revue Historique*, 292 (1994), 229–67.

Morgan, P., *War and Society in Medieval Cheshire, 1277–1403* (Manchester, 1987).

Morrow, J., *History of Political Thought: A Thematic Introduction* (Basingstoke, 1998).

Mourier, J., 'Nobilitas quid est? Un procès à Tain-l'Hermitage en 1408', *BEC*, 142 (1984), 255–69.

Munby, J., Barber, R., and Brown, R., *Edward III's Round Table at Windsor* (Woodbridge, 2007).

Mundy, J. H., Woody, K. M., and Loomis, L. R., eds and trans., *The Council of Constance* (New York, 1961).

Musson, A., 'Queenship, Lordship and Petitioning in Late Medieval England', *Medieval Petitions: Grace and Grievance*, ed. W. M. Ormrod, G. Dodd and A. Musson (York, 2009), 158–63.

Neville, C. J., 'Keeping the Peace on the Northern Marches in the Later Middle Ages', *EHR*, 109 (1994), 1–25.

Newton, S. M., *Fashion in the Age of the Black Prince: A Study of the Years 1340–1365* (Woodbridge, 1988).

Nicholson, H., *Medieval Warfare* (Basingstoke, 2004).

Norbye, M. A., 'A Popular Example of "National Literature" in the Hundred Years War: *A tous nobles qui aiment beaux faits et bonnes histoires*', *Nottingham Medieval Studies*, 51 (2007), 121–42.

Norbye, M. A., 'Genealogies and Domestic Awareness in the Hundred Years War: The Evidence of *A tous nobles qui aiment beaux faits et bonnes histoires*', *Journal of Medieval History*, 33 (2007), 297–319.

Offler, H. S., 'Thomas Bradwardine's "Victory Sermon" in 1346', *Church and Crown in the Fourteenth Century: Studies in European History and Political Thought*, ed. A. I. Doyle (Aldershot, 2000), 1–40.

Ormrod, W. M., 'The Peasants' Revolt and the Government of England', *Journal of British Studies*, 29 (1990), 1–30.

Ormrod, W. M., 'In Bed with Joan of Kent: The King's Mother and the Peasants' Revolt', *Medieval Women: Texts and Contexts in Late Medieval Britain: Essays for Felicity Riddy*, ed. J. Wogan-Browne et al. (Turnhout, 2000), 277–92.

Ormrod, W. M., *The Reign of Edward III: Crown and Political Society in England, 1327–1377* (updated edn, Stroud, 2000).

Ormrod, W. M., 'A Problem of Precedence: Edward III, the Double Monarchy and the Royal Style', *The Age of Edward III*, ed. James Bothwell (York, 2001), 133–53.

Ormrod, W. M., 'The Use of English: Language, Law and Political Culture in Fourteenth-Century England', *Speculum*, 78 (2003), 750–87.

Ormrod, W. M., 'Knights of Venus', *Medium Aevum*, 73 (2004), 290–305.

Ormrod, W. M., 'Montagu, William, First Earl of Salisbury (1301–1344)', *ODNB* (online edn, 2004).

Ormrod, W. M., '*For Arthur and St George*: Edward III, Windsor Castle and the Order of the Garter', *St George's Chapel, Windsor, in the Fourteenth Century*, ed. N. Saul (Woodbridge, 2005), 13–34.

Ormrod, W. M., 'Who was Alice Perrers?', *Chaucer Review*, 40 (2006), 219–29.

Ormrod, W. M., 'Alice Perrers and John Salisbury', *EHR*, 123 (2008), 379–96.

Ormrod, W. M., 'Ufford, Robert, First Earl of Suffolk (1298–1369)', *ODNB* (online edn, 2008).

Ormrod, W. M., 'Murmur, Clamour and Noise: Voicing Complaint and Remedy in Petitions to the English Crown, *c.*1300–*c.*1460', *Medieval Petitions: Grace and Grievance*, ed. W. M. Ormrod, G. Dodd and A. Musson (York, 2009), 135–55.

Ormrod, W. M., *Edward III* (New Haven, CT, and London, 2011).

Otway-Ruthven, A. J., 'Ireland in the 1350s: Sir Thomas Rokeby and his Successors', *Journal of the Royal Society of Antiquaries of Ireland*, 97 (1967), 47–59.

Painter, S., *French Chivalry: Chivalric Ideals and Practices in Mediaeval France* (Ithaca, NY, 1957).

Palmer, J. J. N., 'The Anglo-French Peace Negotiations, 1390–1396', *TRHS*, 5th ser. 16 (1966), 81–94.

Palmer, J. J. N., 'The War Aims of the Protagonists and the Negotiations for Peace', *The Hundred Years War*, ed. Kenneth Fowler (London, 1971), 51–74.

Palmer, J. J. N., *England, France and Christendom, 1377–99* (London, 1972).

Palmer, J. J. N., 'England, France, the Papacy and the Flemish Succession, 1361–9', *Journal of Medieval History*, 2 (1976), 339–64.

Parsons, J. C., 'The Queen's Intercession in Thirteenth-Century England', *Power of the Weak: Studies on Medieval Women*, ed. J. Carpenter and S.-B. MacLean (Chicago, IL, 1995), 147–77.

Paz, C. A. González, 'The Role of Mercenary Troops in Spain in the Fourteenth Century: The Civil War', *Mercenaries and Paid Men: The Mercenary Identity in the Middle Ages*, ed. J. France (Leiden, 2008), 331–43.

Pearsall, D., ' "Crowned King": War and Peace in 1415', *The Lancastrian Court*, ed. J. Stratford (Donington, 2003), 163–72.

Penman, M., *David II* (Edinburgh, 2004).

Pépin, G., 'Les cris de guerre "Guyenne!" et "Saint Georges!", l'expression d'une identité politique du duché d'Aquitaine anglo-gascon', *Moyen Âge*, 112 (2006), 263–82.

Pépin, G., 'Towards a New Assessment of the Black Prince's Principality of Aquitaine: A Study of the Last Years (1369–72)', *Nottingham Medieval Studies*, 50 (2006), 59–114.

Pépin, G., 'The Parlement of Anglo-Gascon Aquitaine: The Three Estates of Aquitaine (Guyenne)', *Nottingham Medieval Studies*, 52 (2008), 133–45.

Pépin, G., 'Towards a Rehabilitation of Froissart's Credibility: The Non-Fictious Bascot de Mauléon', *The Soldier Experience in the Fourteenth Century*, ed. A. R. Bell and A. Curry (Woodbridge, 2011), 175–90.

Pépin, G., 'Does a Common Language Mean a Shared Allegiance? Language, Identity, Geography and their Links with Polities: The Cases of Gascony and Britanny', *Contacts and Exchange in Later Medieval Europe: Essays in Honour of Malcolm Vale*, ed. H. Skoda, P. Lantschner and R. L. J. Shaw (Woodbridge, 2012), 79–101.

Perkins, N., *Hoccleve's 'Regiment of Princes': Counsel and Constraint* (Cambridge, 2001).

Perroy, E., 'Gras profits et rançons pendant la Guerre de Cent Ans: l'affaire du comte de Denia', *Mélanges d'histoire du Moyen Âge dédiés à la mémoire de Louis Halphen*, ed. F. Lot, M. Roques and C. Brunel (Paris, 1951), 573–80.

Phillips, K., 'Written on the Body: Reading Rape from the Twelfth to Fifteenth Centuries', *Medieval Women and the Law*, ed. N. Menuge (Woodbridge, 2000), 125–44.

Phillips, S., *Edward II* (New Haven, CT, and London, 2010).

Phillpotts, C. J., 'The French Plan of Battle during the Agincourt Campaign', *EHR*, 99 (1984), 59–66.

Phillpotts, C. J., 'John of Gaunt and English Policy towards France, 1389–1395', *Journal of Medieval History*, 16 (1990), 363–86.
Phillpotts, C. J., 'The Fate of the Truce of Paris, 1396–1415', *Journal of Medieval History*, 24 (1998), 61–80.
Pitt-Rivers, J., 'Honour and Social Status', *Honour and Shame: The Values of Mediterranean Society*, ed. J. G. Peristiany (London, 1965), 18–77.
Plöger, K., *England and the Avignon Popes: The Practice of Diplomacy in Late Medieval Europe* (London, 2005).
Pollard, A. J., 'Idealising Criminality: Robin Hood in the Fifteenth Century', *Pragmatic Utopias: Ideas and Communities, 1200–1630*, ed. R. Horrox and S. Rees Jones (Cambridge, 2001), 156–73.
Pollard, A. J., *John Talbot and the War in France, 1427–1453* (Barnsley, 2nd edn, 2005).
Pollard, A. J., 'Talbot, John, First Earl of Shrewsbury and First Earl of Waterford (*c.*1387–1453)', *ODNB* (online edn, 2008).
Pons, N., 'Latin et français au XVᵉ siècle: le témoignage des traits de propagande', *Le Moyen français* (Milan, 1986), 67–81.
Pons, N., 'La Guerre de Cent Ans vue par quelques polémistes français du XVᵉ siècle', *Guerre et société en France, en Angleterre et en Bourgogne, XIVᵉ–XVᵉ siècle*, ed. P. Contamine, C. Giry-Deloison and M. H. Keen (Lille, 1991), 143–69.
Porter, E., 'Chaucer's Knight, the Alliterative *Morte Arthure* and the Medieval Laws of War: A Reconsideration', *Nottingham Medieval Studies*, 27 (1983), 56–78.
Postan, M. M., 'The Costs of the Hundred Years' War', *Past and Present*, 27 (1964), 34–53.
Potter, D., 'Chivalry and Professionalism in the French Armies of the Renaissance', *The Chivalric Ethos and the Development of Military Professionalism*, ed. D. J. B. Trim (Leiden, 2003).
Potter, D., ed., *France in the Later Middle Ages* (Oxford, 2003).
Powell, E., *Kingship, Law and Society: Criminal Justice in the Reign of Henry V* (Oxford, 1989).
Prestwich, M., 'Why did Englishmen Fight in the Hundred Years War?', *Medieval History*, 2 (1992), 58–65.
Prestwich, M., *Armies and Warfare in the Middle Ages: The English Experience* (New Haven, CT, and London, 1996).
Prestwich, M., 'Was there a Military Revolution in Medieval England?', *Recognition Essays Presented to E. B. Fryde*, ed. C. Richmond and I. Harvey (Aberystwyth, 1996), 19–38.
Prestwich, M., *Edward I* (New Haven, CT, and London, 1997).
Prestwich, M., *Plantagenet England, 1225–1360* (Oxford, 2005).
Prétou, P., 'Les poisons de Jacques Cœur', *Cahiers de recherches médiévales*, 17 (2009), 121–40.
Prosser, G., ' "Decayed Feudalism" and "Royal Clienteles": Royal Office and Magnate Service in the Fifteenth Century', *War, Government and Power in Late Medieval France*, ed. C. T. Allmand (Liverpool, 2000), 175–89.
Prosser, G., 'The Later Medieval French *noblesse*', *France in the Later Middle Ages*, ed. D. Potter (Oxford, 2003), 182–209.
Pugh, T. B., 'Richard Plantagenet (1411–60), Duke of York, as the King's Lieutenant in France and Ireland', *Aspects of Late Medieval Government and Society: Essays Presented to J. R. Lander*, ed. J. G. Rowe (Toronto, 1986), 107–41.
Puisseux, L., *L'émigration normande et la colonisation anglaise en Normandie au XVᵉ siècle* (Paris, 1866).
Ramsay, A., 'On the Link between Rape, Abduction and War in C. de Pizan's *Cité des dames*', *Contexts and Continuities: Proceedings of the Fourth International Colloquium on Christine de Pizan* (Glasgow, 2002), 693–703.
Rawcliffe, C., *Medicine and Society in Later Medieval England* (Stroud, 1995).
Rawcliffe, C., 'The Insanity of Henry VI', *Historian*, 50 (1996), 8–12.
Renan, E., 'Qu'est-ce qu'une nation?', *Discours et Conférences* (Paris, 1887), 277–310.
Richardson, H. G., 'The English Coronation Oath', *Speculum*, 24 (1949), 44–75.
Riches, S., *St George: Hero, Martyr and Myth* (Stroud, 2002).
Richmond, C., 'The War at Sea', *The Hundred Years War*, ed. K. Fowler (London, 1971), 96–121.
Richmond, C., 'An Outlaw and Some Peasants: The Possible Significance of Robin Hood', *Nottingham Medieval Studies*, 37 (1993), 90–101.
Rigby, S. H., 'Introduction: Social Structure and Economic Change in Late Medieval England', *A Social History of England, 1200–1500*, ed. R. Horrox and W. M. Ormrod (Cambridge, 2006), 1–30.

Rigg, A. G., 'Propaganda of the Hundred Years War: Poems on the Battles of Crécy and Durham (1346): A Critical Edition', *Traditio*, 54 (1999), 169–211.

Rodger, N. A. M., *Safeguard of the Sea: A Naval History of Britain*, vol. I, *660–1649* (London, 2004).

Rogers, A., 'Hoton versus Shakell', *Nottingham Medieval Studies*, 6 (1962), 74–108; 7 (1963), 53–78.

Rogers, C. J., 'The Military Revolutions of the Hundred Years' War', *Journal of Military History*, 57 (1993), 241–78.

Rogers, C. J., 'The Efficacy of the English Longbow: A Reply to Kelly DeVries', *War in History*, 5 (1998), 233–42.

Rogers, C. J., 'The Age of the Hundred Years War', *Medieval Warfare: A History*, ed. M. Keen (Oxford, 1999), 136–60.

Rogers, C. J., 'The Anglo-French Peace Negotiations of 1354–1360 Reconsidered', *The Age of Edward III*, ed. J. Bothwell (York, 2000), 193–214.

Rogers, C. J., *War Cruel and Sharp: English Strategy under Edward III, 1327–1360* (Woodbridge, 2000).

Rogers, C. J., 'By Fire and Sword: *Bellum Hostile* and "Civilians" in the Hundred Years War', *Civilians in the Path of War*, ed. M. Grimsley and C. J. Rogers (Lincoln, NB, 2002), 33–78.

Rogers, C. J., *Soldiers' Lives through History: The Middle Ages* (Westport, CT, 2007).

Rogers, C. J., 'The Battle of Agincourt', *The Hundred Years War*, vol. II, *Different Vistas*, ed. L. J. A. Villalon and D. J. Kagay (Leiden, 2008), 57–63.

Rogers, C. J., 'Tactics and the Face of Battle', *European Warfare, 1350–1750*, ed. F. Tallett and D. J. B. Trim (Cambridge, 2010), 203–35.

Rogers, C. J., ed., *The Military Revolution Debate: Readings on the Military Transformation of Early Modern Europe* (Boulder, CO, 1995).

Rogers, C. J., ed., *The Oxford Encyclopedia of Medieval Warfare and Military Technology*, 3 vols (New York, 2010).

Rose, S., *Medieval Naval Warfare, 1000–1500* (New York, 2002).

Rose, S., *The Medieval Sea* (London, 2007).

Rose, S., *Calais: An English Town in France, 1347–1558* (Woodbridge, 2008).

Rosenthal, J. T., 'The King's Wicked Advisors and the Medieval Baronial Rebellions', *Political Science Quarterly*, 82 (1967), 595–618.

Ross, C. D., 'Forfeiture for Treason in the Reign of Richard II', *EHR*, 71 (1956), 560–75.

Roux, S., *Paris in the Middle Ages*, trans. J. A. McNamara (Philadelphia, PA, 2009).

Ruddick, A., 'Ethnic Identity and Political Language in the King of England's Dominions: A Fourteenth-Century Perspective', *Identity and Insurgency in the Late Middle Ages*, ed. L. Clarke (Woodbridge, 2006), 15–32.

Runyan, T. J., 'Ships and Mariners in Later Medieval England', *Journal of British Studies*, 16 (1977), 1–17.

Russell, R., 'The Longbow–Crossbow Shootout at Crécy (1346): Has the "Rate of Fire Commonplace" been Overrated?', *The Hundred Years War*, vol. II, *Different Vistas*, ed. L. J. A. Villalon and D. J. Kagay (Leiden, 2008), 233–57.

Russell, P. E., *The English Intervention in Spain and Portugal in the Time of Edward III and Richard II* (Oxford, 1955).

St John, G., 'Dying beyond the Seas: Testamentary Preparation for Campaigning during the Hundred Years War', *Fourteenth-Century England*, vol. VII, ed. W. M. Ormrod (Woodbridge, 2012), 177–96.

Sandquist, T. A., 'The Holy Oil of St Thomas of Canterbury', *Essays in Medieval History Presented to Bertie Wilkinson*, ed. T. A. Sandquist and M. R. Powicke (Toronto, 1969), 330–44.

Saul, N., 'Chaucer and Gentility', *Chaucer's England: Literature in Historical Context*, ed. B. A. Hanawalt (Minneapolis, MN, 1992), 41–55.

Saul, N., *Richard II* (New Haven, CT, and London, 1997).

Saul, N., 'The Kingship of Richard II', *Richard II: The Art of Kingship*, ed. A. Goodman and J. Gillespie (Oxford, 1999), 37–58.

Saul, N., 'A Farewell to Arms? Criticism of Warfare in Late Fourteenth-Century England', *Fourteenth-Century England*, vol. II, ed. C. Given-Wilson (Woodbridge, 2002), 131–45.

Saul, N., 'Anne (1366–1394)', *ODNB* (online edn, 2004).

Saul, N., 'Introduction', *St George's Chapel, Windsor in the Fourteenth Century*, ed. N. Saul (Woodbridge, 2005), 1–12.

Saul, N., *The Three Richards* (London, 2005).

Saul, N., *For Honour and Fame: Chivalry in England, 1066–1500* (London, 2011).

Saunders, C., 'A Matter of Consent: Middle English Romance and the Law of *Raptus*', *Medieval Women and the Law*, ed. N. Menuge (Woodbridge, 2000), 105–24.

Scattergood, J., 'The Libelle of Englyshe Polycye: The Nation and its Place', *Nation, Court and Culture: New Essays on Fifteenth-Century English Poetry*, ed. H. Cooney (Dublin, 2001), 28–49.

Schaefer, C., 'L'art et l'histoire. Étienne Chevalier commande au peintre Jean Fouquet le diptyque de Melun', *Art et architecture à Melun au Moyen Âge, Actes du colloque d'histoire de l'art et d'archéologie* (Paris, 2000), 293–300.

Schnerb, B., 'Vassals, Allies and Mercenaries: The French Army Before and After 1346', *The Battle of Crécy, 1346*, ed. A. Ayton and P. Preston (Woodbridge, 2005), 265–72.

Sekules, V., 'Dynasty and Patrimony in the Self-Construction of an English Queen: Philippa of Hainault and her Images', *England and the Continent in the Middle Ages: Studies in Memory of Andrew Martindale*, ed. J. Mitchell (Stamford, 2000), 157–74.

Serchuk, C., '*Cest figure contient tout le royaume de France*: Cartography and National Identity at the End of the Hundred Years War', *Journal of Medieval History*, 33 (2007), 320–38.

Shahar, S., *The Fourth Estate: A History of Women in the Middle Ages* (New York, 1983).

Sherborne, J. W., 'The Hundred Years' War. The English Navy: Shipping and Manpower 1369–1389', *Past and Present*, 37 (1967), 163–75.

Small, G., *George Chastellain and the Shaping of Valois Burgundy: Political and Historical Culture at Court in the Fifteenth Century* (Woodbridge, 1997).

Small, G., *Late Medieval France* (Basingstoke, 2009).

Smith, A., *The Ethnic Origins of Nations* (Oxford, 1986).

Smith, A., 'The Ernest Gellner Memorial Lecture. Memory and Modernity: Reflections on Ernest Gellner's Theory of Nationalism': http://gellnerpage.tripod.com/SmithLec.html

Smith, B., 'Lordship in the British Isles, *c*.1320–*c*.1360: The Ebb-Tide of the English Empire?', *Power and Identity in the Middle Ages: Essays in Memory of Rees Davies*, ed. H. Pryce and J. Watts (Oxford, 2008), 153–63.

Smith, R. D., 'Artillery and the Hundred Years War: Myth and Interpretation', *Arms, Armies and Fortifications in the Hundred Years War*, ed. A. Curry and M. Hughes (Woodbridge, 1994), 151–60.

Smith, R. D., and DeVries, K., *The Artillery of the Dukes of Burgundy, 1363–1477* (Woodbridge, 2005).

Smith, R. M., 'The English Peasantry, 1250–1650', *The Peasantries of Europe from the Fourteenth to the Eighteenth Centuries*, ed. T. Scott (London, 1998), 338–71.

Smith Spencer, G., 'What Does a Mercenary Leave Behind? The Archaeological Evidence for the Estates of Owain Lawgoch', *Mercenaries and Paid Men: The Mercenary Identity in the Middle Ages*, ed. J. France (Leiden, 2008), 317–30.

Solon, P. D., 'Popular Response to Standing Military Forces in Fifteenth-Century France', *Studies in the Renaissance*, 19 (1972), 78–111.

Solterer, H., 'Making Names, Breaking Lives: Women and Injurious Language at the Court of Isabeau of Bavaria and Charles VI', *Cultural Performances in Medieval France*, ed. E. Doss-Quinby, R. L. Krueger and E. J. Burns (Cambridge, 2007), 203–18.

Spencer, M., *Thomas Basin (1412–1490): The History of Charles VII and Louis XI* (Nieuwkoop, 1997).

Spiegel, G., *The Chronicle Tradition of Saint-Denis: A Survey* (Brookline, MA, and Leiden, 1978).

Spiegel, G., *Romancing the Past: The Rise of Vernacular Prose Historiography in Thirteenth-Century France* (Berkeley, CA, 1993).

Spiegel, G., 'Les débuts français de l'historiographie royale', *Saint-Denis et la royauté*, ed. F. Autrand, C. Gauvard and J.-M. Moeglin (Paris, 1999), 395–404.

Stafford, P., *Queens, Concubines and Dowagers: The King's Wife in the Early Middle Ages* (Leicester, 1998).

Steane, J. M., *The Archaeology of Power: England and Northern Europe AD 800–1600* (Stroud, 2001).

Stevenson, K., *Chivalry and Knighthood in Scotland, 1424–1513* (Woodbridge, 2006).

Stirland, A. J., *The Men of the Mary Rose* (Stroud, 2005).

Storey-Challenger, S., *L'administration anglaise du Ponthieu après le traité de Brétigny, 1361–1369* (Abbeville, 1975).
Strickland, M., and Hardy, R., *The Great Warbow: From Hastings to the Mary Rose* (Stroud, 2005).
Strohm, P., *Hochon's Arrow: The Social Imagination of Fourteenth-Century Texts* (Princeton, NJ, 1992).
Sumption, J., *The Hundred Years War*, vol. I, *Trial by Battle* (London, 1990).
Sumption, J., *The Hundred Years War*, vol. II, *Trial by Fire* (London, 1999).
Sumption, J., 'Angle, Guichard (IV) d', Earl of Huntingdon (c.1308/15–1380)', *ODNB* (online edn, 2006).
Sumption, J., *The Hundred Years War*, vol. III, *Divided Houses* (London, 2009).
Sutton, A. F., and Visser-Fuchs, L., with Griffiths, R. A., *The Royal Funerals of the House of York at Wind*sor (London, 2005).
Swanson, H., 'The Illusion of Economic Structure: Craft Guilds in Late Medieval English Towns', *Past and Present*, 121 (1988), 29–48.
Swanson, R. N., 'Problems of the Priesthood in Pre-Reformation England', *EHR*, 105 (1990), 845–69.
Taylor, C., 'Sir John Fortescue and the French Polemical Treatises of the Hundred Years War', *EHR*, 114 (1999), 112–29.
Taylor, C., 'War, Propaganda and Diplomacy in Fifteenth-Century France and England', *War, Government and Power in Late Medieval France*, ed. C. Allmand (Liverpool, 2000), 70–91.
Taylor, C., 'Edward III and the Plantagenet Claim to the French Throne', *The Age of Edward III*, ed. J. Bothwell (York, 2001), 155–69.
Taylor, C., 'The Salic Law, French Queenship, and the Defence of Women in the Late Middle Ages', *French Historical Studies*, 29 (2006), 543–64.
Taylor, C., 'English Writings on Chivalry and Warfare during the Hundred Years War', *Soldiers, Nobles and Gentlemen: Essays in Honour of Maurice Keen*, ed. P. Coss and C. Tyerman (Woodbridge, 2009), 64–84.
Taylor, J., 'Richard II in the Chronicles', *Richard II: The Art of Kingship*, ed. A. Goodman and J. Gillespie (Oxford, 1999), 15–36.
Taylor, L. J., *The Virgin Warrior: The Life and Death of Joan of Arc* (New Haven, CT, and London, 2009).
TeBrake, W. H., *A Plague of Insurrection: Popular Politics and Peasant Revolt in Flanders, 1323–1328* (Philadelphia, PA, 1993).
Templeman, G., 'Edward III and the Beginnings of the Hundred Years War', *The Wars of Edward III*, ed. Clifford J. Rogers (Woodbridge, 1999), 231–46.
Thompson, G. L., *Paris and its People under English Rule: The Anglo-Burgundian Regime, 1420–1436* (Oxford, 1991).
Timbal, P. C., *La Guerre de Cent Ans vue à travers les registres du parlement (1337–1369)* (Paris, 1961).
Tourneur-Aumont, J. M., *La bataille de Poitiers (1356) et la construction de la France* (Poitiers, 1943).
Tout, T. F., 'Firearms in England in the Fourteenth Century', *EHR*, 26 (1911), 666–702.
Tout, T. F., *Chapters in the Administrative History of Mediaeval England*, 6 vols (Manchester, 1920–33).
Tuck, Anthony, 'Edmund, First Duke of York (1341–1402)', *ODNB* (online edn, 2008).
Turner, R. V., 'The Meaning of Magna Carta since 1215', *History Today*, 53 (2003), 29–35.
Turner, W., 'Mental Incapacity and the Financing of War in Medieval England', *The Hundred Years War*, vol. II, *Different Vistas*, ed. D. Kagay and A. L. J. Villalon (Leiden, 2008), 387–402.
Turville-Petre, T., *England the Nation: Language, Literature and National Identity, 1290–1340* (Oxford, 1996).
Tyerman, C. J., 'Philip VI and the Recovery of the Holy Land', *EHR*, 100 (1985), 25–52.
Ullmann, W., *Medieval Political Thought* (Harmondsworth, 1975).
Vale, M. G. A., 'The Last Years of English Gascony', *TRHS*, 5th ser. 19 (1969), 119–38.
Vale, M. G. A., *English Gascony, 1399–1453: A Study of War, Government and Politics during the Later Stages of the Hundred Years War* (Oxford, 1970).
Vale, M. G. A., 'Sir John Fastolf's "Report" of 1435: A New Interpretation Reconsidered', *Nottingham Mediaeval Studies*, 17 (1973), 78–84.
Vale, M. G. A., *Charles VII* (London, 1974).

Vale, M. G. A., *War and Chivalry: Warfare and Aristocratic Culture in England, France, and Burgundy at the End of the Middle Ages* (Athens, GA, 1981).

Vale, M. G. A., *The Origins of the Hundred Years War: The Angevin Legacy, 1250–1340* (Oxford, 1996).

Vale, M. G. A., *The Princely Court: Medieval Courts and Culture in North-West Europe* (Oxford, 2001).

Vale, M. G. A., 'Language, Politics and Society: The Uses of the Vernacular in the Later Middle Ages', *EHR*, 120 (2005), 15–34.

Vale, M. G. A., *The Ancient Enemy: England, France and Europe from the Angevins to the Tudors* (London, 2007).

Valente, C., 'The Deposition and Abdication of Edward II', *EHR*, 113 (1998), 852–81.

Vauchez, A., *Sainthood in the Later Middle Ages*, trans. J. Birrell (Cambridge, 1997).

Vaughan, R., *John the Fearless: The Growth of Burgundian Power* (Woodbridge, new edn, 2002).

Vaughan, R., *Philip the Bold: The Formation of the Burgundian State* (Woodbridge, new edn, 2002).

Vaughan, R., *Philip the Good: The Apogee of Burgundy* (Woodbridge, new edn, 2002).

Verbruggen, J. F., *The Art of Warfare in Western Europe during the Middle Ages*, trans. S. Willard and Mrs R. W. Southern (Woodbridge, 2nd edn, 1997).

Verbruggen, J. F., 'Women in Medieval Armies', trans. K. DeVries, *Journal of Medieval Military History*, 4 (2006), 119–36.

Vernier, R., *The Flower of Chivalry: Bertrand du Guesclin and the Hundred Years War* (Woodbridge, 2003).

Viard, J., 'La campagne de juillet-août et la bataille de Crécy', *Le Moyen Âge*, 2nd ser. 27 (1926), 1–85.

Villalon, L. J. A., 'Spanish Involvement in the Hundred Years War and the Battle of Nájera', *The Hundred Years War*, vol. I, *A Wider Focus*, ed. D. Kagay and L. J. A. Villalon (Leiden, 2005), 3–74.

Voigts, Linda E., 'What's the Word? Bilingualism in Late Medieval England', *Speculum*, 71 (1996), 813–26.

Wadge, R., *Arrowstorm: The World of the Archer in the Hundred Years War* (Stroud, 2007).

Ward, J., *Women of the English Nobility and Gentry, 1066–1500* (Manchester, 1995).

Watson, F., 'Settling the Stalemate: Edward I's Peace in Scotland, 1303–1305', *Thirteenth-Century England*, vol. VI, ed. M. Prestwich, R. H. Britnell and R. Frame (Woodbridge, 1997), 127–43.

Watson, F., 'Dunbar, Patrick, Eighth Earl of Dunbar or of March, and Earl of Moray (1285–1369)', *ODNB* (online edn, 2008).

Watson, N., 'The Politics of Middle English Writing', *The Idea of the Vernacular: An Anthology of Middle English Literary Theory, 1280–1520*, ed. J. Wogan-Browne, N. Watson, A. Taylor and R. Evans (Exeter, 1999), 331–52.

Watts, J., 'Pole, William de la, First Duke of Suffolk (1396–1450)', *ODNB* (online edn, 2004).

Watts, J., 'The Pressure of the Public on Later Medieval Politics', *Political Culture in Late Medieval Britain*, ed. L. Clarke and C. Carpenter (Woodbridge, 2004), 159–80.

Watts, J., 'Usurpation in England: A Paradox of State-Growth', *Coups d'état à la fin du Moyen Âge? Aux fondements du pouvoir politique en Europe occidentale*, ed. F. Foronda, J.-P. Genet and J. M. Nieto Soria (Madrid, 2005), 51–72.

Watts, J., 'Richard of York, Third Duke of York (1411–1460)', *ODNB* (online edn, 2009).

Whitely, M., 'The Courts of Edward III of England and Charles V of France: A Comparison of their Architectural Setting and Ceremonial Functions', *Fourteenth-Century England*, vol. III, ed. W. M. Ormrod (Woodbridge, 2004), 153–66.

Wilks, M., *The Problem of Sovereignty in the Later Middle Ages* (Cambridge, 1963).

Wilks, M., 'Royal Patronage and Anti-Papalism from Ockham to Wyclif', *Wyclif: Political Ideas and Practice* (Oxford, 2000), 135–63.

Wilson, C., 'The Tomb of Henry IV and the Holy Oil of St Thomas of Canterbury', *Medieval Architecture and its Intellectual Context: Studies in Honour of Peter Kidson*, ed. E. Fernie and P. Crossley (London, 1990), 181–90.

Windeatt, B., ed., *English Mystics of the Later Middle Ages* (Cambridge, 1994).

Wogan-Browne, J., 'What's in a Name: The "French of England"', *Language and Culture in Medieval Britain: The French of England, c.1100–c.1500*, ed. J. Wogan-Browne et al. (York, 2009), 1–13.

Wolfe, B., *Henry VI* (New Haven, CT, and London, 2001).

Wolfthal, D., *Images of Rape: The 'Heroic' Tradition and its Alternatives* (Cambridge, 1999).

Wood, C. T., '*Regnum Francie*: A Problem in Capetian Administrative Usage', *Traditio*, 23 (1967), 117–47.

Wood, C. T., 'The Mise of Amiens and Saint Louis' Theory of Kingship', *French Historical Studies*, 6 (1970), 300–10.

Wood, D., '*Omnino Partialitate Cessante*: Clement VI and the Hundred Years War', *The Church and War*, ed. W. J. Shiels (Oxford, 1983), 179–89.

Wood, D., *Clement VI: The Pontificate and Ideas of an Avignon Pope* (Cambridge, 1989).

Woolgar, C. M., *The Great Household in Late Medieval England* (New Haven, CT, and London, 1999).

Wright, N., *Knights and Peasants: The Hundred Years War in the French Countryside* (Woodbridge, 1998).

Wylie, J. H., and Waugh, W. T., *The Reign of Henry the Fifth*, 3 vols (Cambridge, 1914–29).

Zmora, H., *Monarchy, Aristocracy and State in Europe, 1300–1800* (London, 2000).

Zutshi, P. N. R., 'The Avignon Papacy', *The New Cambridge Medieval History*, vol. VI, *c.1300–c.1415*, ed. M. Jones (Cambridge, 2000), 651–73.

Acknowledgements

I'm very grateful to all those who have helped in the preparation of this book. Heather McCallum, Rachael Lonsdale and Richard Mason at Yale University Press have seen it through to publication with remarkable patience and diligence. Caroline Hamilton was a great help with the index.

Many people offered help and guidance at various stages of research and writing. In addition to the anonymous readers of the initial proposal and an early draft, I should like to thank April Harper, Katherine Lewis, Jan Marquardt, Caroline Palmer, Lewis Ward and friends and colleagues at Harlaxton College.

Aspects of the research underpinning a number of chapters have been presented at various conferences and seminars. My thanks to the organisers for the opportunity to speak and to all those who have helped with clarifications and references and by asking questions. In particular I am grateful to those involved with meetings convened at the Royal Armouries (Tower of London), the Medieval Research Seminar at Trinity College, Dublin, the very splendid and only partially fictitious Society for the White Hart, and the Society for Fourteenth-Century Studies. Funding to attend those meetings has generously been provided by Harlaxton College.

As I was writing this, I gained another godson. Up until now I haven't been terribly diligent in my duties. I hope Oliver will accept this book (one day) as a token of my affection.

Index